ELEANOR
APRIL QUEEN OF AQUITAINE

DOUGLAS BOYD

SUTTON PUBLISHING

To all our tomorrows:
Chloe, Edward, Eleanor, Eve,
Gwyneth, Hannah, Jessie and Lily

Vivant in pace!

This book was first published in 2004 by
Sutton Publishing Limited · Phoenix Mill
Thrupp · Stroud · Gloucestershire · GL5 2BU

This paperback edition first published in 2005

British Library Cataloguing in Publication Data
A catalogue record for this book is available from the British Library.

ISBN 0 7509 3290 2

Typeset in 10/11.5 pt Goudy.
Typesetting and origination by
Sutton Publishing Limited.
Printed and bound in Great Britain by
J.H. Haynes & Co. Ltd, Sparkford.

Contents

CONTENTS

Acknowledgements

My thanks are due to Friedrich Heer, who shone Burckhardt's light into many dark places of history; to my Gascon friends Nathalie and Eric Roulet, at whose home in Les Landes I first heard Occitan as a living language; to Eric Chaplain, managing editor of the Occitan publishing house Princi Neguer in Pau, for lending precious source material that saved both travel and much sitting in libraries; to Alain Pierre for keeping Occitan alive and making me probably the only author ever interviewed live on radio in that language; to fellow-author and horsewoman Ann Hyland for equestrian advice; to Dr Harold Yauner for his medical knowledge and many jokes; to Jennifer Weller for maps, seals and photographic help; to portraitist Norman Douglas Hutchinson for bringing his demon's eye to bear on Eleanor's likenesses; to Valérie de Reignac of the Musée des Arts Décoratifs de Bordeaux; to Caroline Currie for photo-reconnaissance; to Gabor Mester de Parajd of Les Monuments Historiques; to Les Amis du Vieux Chinon for permission to photograph the fresco in the Chapelle Ste Radegonde; to the staffs of La Bibliothèque Nationale, the British Library, the Public Record Office and the Bibliothèque Municipale de Bordeaux for their anonymous work, so vital to writers and scholars; to my partner Atarah Ben-Tovim for unflagging companionship in Eleanor's footsteps in Europe, Turkey and the Levant; to 'Biggles' Turner for piloting my airborne camera platform G-AYYI; and to Elizabeth Stone and Sarah Flight at Sutton Publishing for their skill in making a readable book from so many pages of text and images.

To my agent Mandy Little I owe thanks especially for placing this book with Jaqueline Mitchell at Sutton, who treated the author as a long-distance swimmer tugged repeatedly off-course by fascinating currents of research, and repeatedly showed him the way to landfall. In this time of corporate publishing, that is rare. To Jaqueline, my deepest thanks.

List of Illustrations and Maps

Black and white plates

Introduction

When the occasional lists of the all-time rich and powerful are compiled by the media the name of Eleanor of Aquitaine is almost always present. The London *Sunday Times* in its list of the '50 Richest Ever' labelled her the richest woman of all time. In its survey of the 100 most important people of the second millennium *Time* magazine dubbed her 'the most powerful woman' and 'the insider' of her century.

Charismatic, beautiful, highly intelligent and literate, but also impulsive and proud, Eleanor inherited just after her fifteenth birthday the immense wealth and power that went with the titles of countess of Poitou and duchess of Aquitaine. From that moment she played for the highest stakes, often with the dice stacked against her, until her spirit was finally broken by the death at the siege of Châlus of her favourite son, Richard the Lionheart. Neither before nor since has one woman's lifetime been more crowded with excess of wealth and poverty, power and humiliation.

Although she was born in 1122 and died in 1204, this mysterious figure who was uniquely both queen of France and of England did not conform to preconceptions of medieval European womanhood. Raised in the Mediterranean troubadour society that esteemed amorous adventures, verse and music on a par with prowess at arms, she scandalised the tonsured schoolmen who wielded much political power in the north of France by her liberated behaviour and thinking. Even after two of her great-grandsons were canonised as St Louis of France and St Ferdinand of Spain, nothing could persuade the Church to reappraise its first judgement of her as a young whore who became an old witch. Borrowing plot and characters from the chronicles, four centuries after her death Shakespeare unkindly labelled her in his play *King John* a 'cankered grandame'.

The first European poet since the fall of the Roman Empire was her crusading troubadour grandfather, Duke William IX, whose verse was philosophical but also amorous and full of humour – as befitted a man whose mistress was called La Dangerosa! The troubadours, male and female, depicted women as sensual, empowered beings and not sinful chattels whose only proper function was childbearing, and the ideal of courtly love associated with Eleanor and her daughters was in that tradition.

At a time when even monarchs rarely set foot outside their own kingdoms in peace and few women except noble and royal brides ever left the country of their birth, she travelled extensively on both sides of the English Channel and much farther afield, seeing for herself the squalor of medieval Rome whose citizens had recently killed a pope, the decadent glory of Constantinople and the ugly truth behind the romance of the Latin Kingdom of Jerusalem. Returning from the Second Crusade after a year as prisoner of her estranged husband Louis VII of France, she was hijacked by Byzantine pirates and forced by Pope Eugenius III to share Louis' bed against her will.

Like materials, people reveal their qualities when tested nearly to destruction; the courage of this extraordinary woman is best exemplified at the time her fortunes hit an all-time low. In 1173 the armed rebellion of her three adult sons by the marriage to Henry of Anjou was defeated by his swift and ruthless counter-offensive. Her one chance of escape lay in throwing herself on the mercy of his greatest enemy – Louis, the first husband whom she had tormented and divorced.

Betrayed to Henry by men she trusted in her own household when within a few leagues of safety on Frankish territory, she knew that he would pardon his sons but deal with her more harshly. Her death would permit him to remarry and sire more legitimate sons, playing them off against the first brood in his usual fashion with the threat of a punishment or the promise of a bribe that was never honoured. Yet, unless in one of the berserker rages that betrayed his part-Viking ancestry, he would not kill her for fear of losing her dowry of Poitou and Aquitaine. In addition, another murder would not go down too well in Rome so soon after being flogged in his underwear by monks at Canterbury Cathedral and Avranches as penance for his part in Becket's death.

On the other hand, the pope would grant him an annulment if asked, for the degree of consanguinity was even closer than that which provided the spurious grounds for her divorce from Louis. However, that solution would also involve handing back her dowry of Poitou and

Aquitaine – and Henry never gave anything back, not even a son's rejected fiancée whom he kept as his own mistress.

Eleanor knew exactly what lay ahead. Henry was eleven years her junior, a man in his prime who would never forgive her. He would allow her the illusion of freedom from time to time – an appearance at an Easter or a Christmas court, some cloth for a new dress or the privilege to go riding each morning, or to have books. But each carrot would be withdrawn when she refused to bite, and the stick would be used again harder than before.

Accustomed as she had been from birth to the luxury of good food and fine wine, fashionable clothes, amusing company, literature, poetry, music and dancing, how long could a queen live, deprived of all this and her liberty and dignity too? She was already fifty-two, in a time when most women died young in childbirth or from overwork or disease. To Louis of France she had borne two daughters. To Henry she had given five sons and three daughters to use as pawns in marriages arranged to seal the knots of alliances.

Judged by any standards, Eleanor had already lived a remarkable life. Born under the Roman laws of Aquitaine, which did not disqualify the female line from succession, she was raised to inherit the duchy after her only legitimate brother's early death. This made her a teenage multi-millionairess, who married a crown prince and became queen of France two weeks later. Was that not enough glamour for one lifetime?

Not for Eleanor. Her years with Louis included rumours of scandalous love affairs in Paris and in the Holy Land on the Second Crusade. Divorcing him, she twice escaped kidnap and rape on the flight to safety in her own domains. There followed her years as duchess–queen of the Angevin Empire, on the move with Henry's court as he crossed and recrossed the Channel to bring his restless magnates to heel as only William the Bastard had done before. How many women, or men for that matter, have lived such adventures and come home to tell the tale?

When Henry discarded her at the menopause, she revived the civilised lifestyle of her own court at Poitiers, where art glorified love and praised womanhood – and where she was effectively queen in her own right, not a mere consort. Yet she risked everything in an intrigue worthy of the Roman Empress Julia to unite in rebellion three sons who detested each other as much as they hated their manipulative and brutal father. Why? And why, on being taken prisoner by him, did she not accept the honourable alternative he offered, and which most women of her class and age would have preferred: to renounce her titles and retire to a convent? Frustratingly for the historian, during her fifteen years as Henry's captive she had all the time in the world to dictate her memoirs but was deprived of secretary, quill, parchment – and at times of everything else except food.

On Henry's death, she returned to the world stage aged sixty-seven as vigorous physically and mentally as any man or woman of half her age, demanding her jailer's obedience by declaring herself still the crowned queen of England and thereby regent for her son Richard the Lionheart. Armed initially only with her own willpower, she governed England until he arrived and for much of his reign.

Her great moment of glory came at his coronation in Westminster Abbey, where the new monarch, who had no place in his life for women and certainly not for a wife, installed her as his dowager queen. This adored son of hers was among the worst rulers the realm would know, twice milking it dry of taxes in a ten-year reign, of which only a few months were spent in England – a country he despised, and whose language he never learned. Yet of all its kings, he alone has his statue in Westminster Square at the seat of government.

The crusades are no longer seen as a glorious episode in European history, yet for cinema and television audiences he remains King Richard of the Last Reel, heroically returning in the last minutes of the film from a mysterious Outremer to vindicate loyal Robin and his merry men and put the villainous supporters of his usurping brother John in their proper place. That web of myth, obscuring the terrible reality of what was called 'knightly warfare', has stood the test of eight centuries because it was spun by his mother as PR to drag out of an exhausted and over-taxed empire the enormous ransom demanded for his return from captivity, against the opposition of Prince John in league with King Philip of France, and the many Anglo-Norman barons who preferred to keep Richard locked up in Germany.

Rightly trusting no one else to conclude the deal, Eleanor then risked piracy on the high seas to convoy in person the thirty tons of ransom silver to Germany, bringing her son home after out-bluffing the Emperor, who had been offered bribes to renege on the bargain. To do all this in her mid-seventies tells us what strength of purpose she had, even then.

Why then have historians treated her so meanly?

The misogynistic Pauline clerks who penned the chronicles that are our primary sources polarised women as Eve or the Virgin Mary. For them, a woman as powerful and impious as Eleanor *was* Eve incarnate, and thus the cause of all man's sin and suffering. The influential clerics with whom she fearlessly crossed swords while queen of France – from the ascetic St Bernard of Clairvaux and the great statesman Abbé Suger to the Templar eunuch Thierry Galeran – did their best to thwart her in life; the chroniclers merely continued the character assassination after her death.

But surely historians take such bias of primary sources into account?

Friedrich Heer, Professor of the History of Ideas at the University of Vienna, was trained as a historian in the Swiss tradition of Burkhardt. He observed that his colleagues educated in the Rankean nineteenth-century German system of cause-and-effect, were so intent on fitting events into 'logical' sequences and making each one appear to have been inevitable that they snipped the pieces of the jigsaw to make them fit into what seemed evidence of a Divine Plan, with the steady hand of God ultimately in control of man's actions.

So it was for Ranke's British followers, including Bishop William Stubbs (1825–1901), whose influence on the teaching of medieval history at British universities lasted into the second half of the twentieth century. If history were made logically, then every human event would be predictable. But it isn't. Making it appear so requires distortion of inconvenient happenings and sidelining history's losers, of whom Eleanor was one of the most magnificent. It is significant that the first modern biography of her – Amy Kelly's *Eleanor of Aquitaine and the Four Kings* (Harvard, 1950) – appeared as Stubbs' influence was at last waning.

Heer offered a second reason why his academic colleagues had devoted scant space to this queen of France and England in their writings. Although her lifetime, spanning four-fifths of the twelfth century, fell within the academic province of European medievalists, he considered them ill equipped by their training to understand this transitional period when feudalism had many forms, monarchy was experimental, the concept of nations had not crystallised and frontiers were permeable by pilgrimage and trade, even between Christian and Moor. In the throes of an economic and cultural transition, Europe was then awash with revolutionary ideas and the new music, poetry and technology brought back by pilgrims, merchants and crusaders who had travelled to the East. Nowhere was this truer than in Aquitaine, so near in spirit and geographically to the light of Moorish Spain and so far from the gloom of Capetian Paris.

Herodotus' original concept of *historia* was not the recital of dates and battles, but the gaining of knowledge by enquiry. Happily, in recent years medieval history has evolved, thanks to cross-fertilisation with other academic disciplines and the expansion of women's studies, which throw a different light on Eleanor's lifetime. Yet her biographers since Amy Kelly have produced little new information about Eleanor, her husbands and children – and failed to explain why she chose repeatedly to pursue her own path at such great cost to herself.

In part, this is because documentation of the early twelfth century is sparse, compared with the later Middle Ages, so that the chronicles touch on Eleanor largely through hearsay tainted by scandal. In part, it is because women's lives – even queens' lives – were ill documented, compared with those of male contemporaries. In addition, there has been a tendency by Anglo-Saxon writers to treat her as a 'French' duchess, when she was effectively the queen by birth of a people who differed from the Germanic Franks in the north of what is now France by racial origin, language, culture, lifestyle and a whole system of values. Some English-speaking biographers have also betrayed an ignorance of even modern French, let alone Old French, Latin and Eleanor's first language, Occitan – all of which are necessary to demystify this important historical figure.

Work on this biography began a quarter-century ago when I bought a partly medieval stone farmhouse in south-west France, where the local post office is in a castle built by Eleanor's son John, of Magna Carta fame. Being bilingual in English and French, my ear was caught by the different usage and *accent chantant* of the locals, so different from the northern *accent pointu* which I and most foreigners learned in school. It was like being in the Highlands or Wales or Ireland, where Celtic people speak English with the cadence of their own language and using figures of speech that sound merely picturesque to outsiders but are the echo of its emotionally richer and more expressive idiom.

At that time the grandparental generation in the villages here still spoke what northerners despise as *patois*, meaning 'the speech of those little better than animals'. Properly called Occitan or *la lenga d'oc* by those who speak it, it had been stubbornly giving ground during a century of prohibition in schools, where children were beaten for using the tongue they spoke at home. Since then, the media have achieved what the whip and the rod could not, killing a living language in less than two generations.

As a Scot, I sympathised with a people whose culture was being strangled by a more powerful neighbour. As a linguist I became fascinated by the language of the troubadours, which evolved from Latin so rich in shades of emotion and rhyming possibilities as to be the ideal tool of a civilisation to which the whole of Europe owes an inestimable debt for producing the first flowering of the Renaissance and influencing all European lyric poetry since.

Banned from public use in France by François I early in the sixteenth century, Occitan changed so little that studying the everyday speech of my elderly neighbours was the vital first step to understanding Eleanor's own language as she knew it and reading first hand the thoughts and feelings of her contemporaries and intimates. This in turn has opened windows into her values and her world that were closed to previous biographers.

Douglas Boyd
Gironde, south-west France, 2004

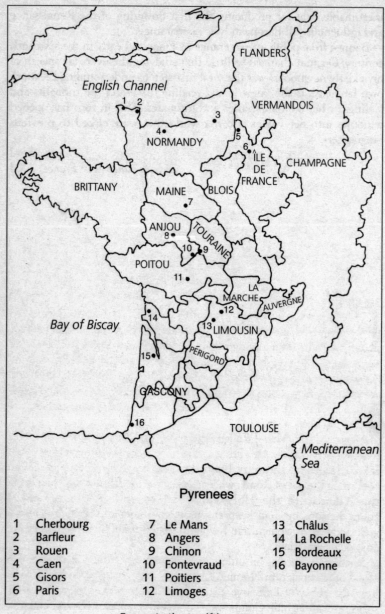

France in the twelfth century.

1	Cherbourg	7	Le Mans	13	Châlus
2	Barfleur	8	Angers	14	La Rochelle
3	Rouen	9	Chinon	15	Bordeaux
4	Caen	10	Fontevraud	16	Bayonne
5	Gisors	11	Poitiers		
6	Paris	12	Limoges		

ONE

The Aquitaine Succession

Eleanor was just fifteen years old in May 1137. At an age that was considered adult for either sex she had the poise and confidence that came from having ridden with her father Duke William X[1] of Aquitaine for hundreds of miles in the same direction without meeting a soul who did not owe him allegiance. She was beautiful, she loved music and dancing, poetry and song. In a time when few men and fewer women could read, she was also literate in three languages and mature beyond her years.

Eleanor's grandfather had used force of arms to weld the dissident barons of south-west France into a restive aristocracy that acknowledged his authority, but he had also been the greatest European poet since the fall of Rome, whose verses were declaimed and sung from the Atlantic to the Holy Land and beyond. A man of many contradictions, he had been the most courteous of suitors but also a great seducer of women. He had both defied the Church and been on crusade to Jerusalem.

But her father was an unlettered warlord, who had spilled so much blood on campaign in Normandy the previous year that he had set out from the abbey of La Sauve Majeure on Easter pilgrimage to the holy shrine of Santiago de Compostela[2] in Spain to purge his soul. This was in preparation for marrying the widowed daughter of his vassal

9

Viscount Aymar of Limoges in response to his counsellors' urging that it was time to ensure a male heir for the rich county of Poitou and the vast duchy of Aquitaine.

Eleanor had passed the weeks since his departure with her younger sister Aelith in the ducal palace of L'Ombreyra at the south-east corner of the city of Bordeaux, two teenagers amusing themselves in the huge warren of apartments, audience chambers and tiled courtyards shaded by fig and olive trees. Aelith was two years younger, but both sisters were aware this would be Eleanor's last springtime of freedom before an arranged marriage to some rich and powerful prince. With their mother and brother dead and their father absent, the girls were flattered and courted by the young unattached knights of the ducal court, while minstrels sang with lute and lyre their grandfather's praises of women and love.

In the north, such behaviour would have been considered scandalous intimacy. Here it was one of the normal pleasures of life. And the scandal was that the duke's betrothed had been carried off by a neighbouring baron and forcibly married in his absence – a deed that would cost him dearly when William X returned.[3]

Then, at the beginning of May, everything changed. Maidservants came running through the palace with news that the knights who had accompanied Duke William X on his pilgrimage to Santiago de Compostela had posted in haste past the monastery at Cayac and the great abbey of La Sainte Croix south of the city without stopping to give alms to the monks at the wayside. Once within the gates of Bordeaux they had ridden straight to the archiepiscopal palace in the south-west corner of the city, where they were closeted with the most powerful man in Bordeaux, the newly appointed Archbishop Geoffroi de Lauroux. But of Duke William there was no sign.

Within an hour Eleanor learned he was dead. A vigorous and healthy warrior of thirty-eight, he had succumbed to food poisoning or drinking contaminated water on Good Friday. His companions had borne him to the cathedral of Santiago and had him buried close to the high altar in clouds of incense and to the chanting of Latin plainsong. Their prayer, 'Sant Jacme, membre us del baro que denant vos jai pelegris . . .'[4] – pray for him, Saint James, this pilgrim baron lying here – was echoed in all the languages of Europe by the thousands of pilgrims present.

In front of trusted witnesses shortly before dying, William X had orally bequeathed everything to Eleanor. Although Aquitaine's Roman laws permitted succession by the female line, there was in Poitou a custom of *viage ou retour*, by which a feudal domain might pass to the nearest collateral male relative in the absence of a direct male heir. Similarly, north of the Channel two years previously Matilda, the only surviving child of Henry I, had been deprived of the succession to the English throne by a majority of the Anglo-Norman barons preferring her cousin, Stephen of Blois, with the result that civil war divided the country. Eleanor's father had therefore orally requested his overlord the king of France to take Poitou and Aquitaine under his personal protection, to confirm his elder daughter's inheritance and to arrange both girls' marriages to suitable husbands.

Since such wealth, power and beauty made Eleanor a highly desirable prey for any baron with the nerve by rape and a forced wedding to make himself the new duke of Aquitaine, William's companions hurried back to Bordeaux, keeping the news of his death to themselves. The lack of a written testament being not unusual in those times of sudden death, Archbishop Geoffroi decided that his duty to the Church lay in executing William X's instructions[5] and dispatched an embassy of discreet bishops and barons to the court of King Louis VI.

To Eleanor's question as to what he looked like, the answer was that all princes were handsome and brave, great lovers of women.

In those days a royal court was not a building, but wherever the monarch and his chancery staff happened to be. King Louis was at his hunting lodge near Béthisy in the forest of Compiègne where he had gone to escape the noise, the stench and the fevers of Paris in midsummer – and to die. In his prime, when taking the field in a war that lasted twenty-five years against his vassal Henry Beauclerc, duke of Normandy,[6] or when fighting off external enemies like the German Emperor, he had been known as Battling Louis and 'the king who never sleeps'. But his subjects changed this to Fat Louis as he fought increasingly bad health, rumoured to be the result of his mother attempting to poison him in childhood.

By the summer of 1137 his body was so swollen by fluid retention that he could no longer bend down to put on a shoe, never mind wield a sword or mount a horse. The doctors and apothecaries of Paris had tried every remedy they could think of. 'He drank so many kinds of potions and powders . . . it was a miracle, the way he endured it', as a contemporary wryly remarked.[7]

The king of France was fifty-six, a ripe old age for the time. For twenty-nine years he had excelled at the balancing act which was the lot of a Capetian monarch, several of whose vassals controlled far more territory directly than the royal domains, which lay mostly in the area around Paris later known as Ile de France.

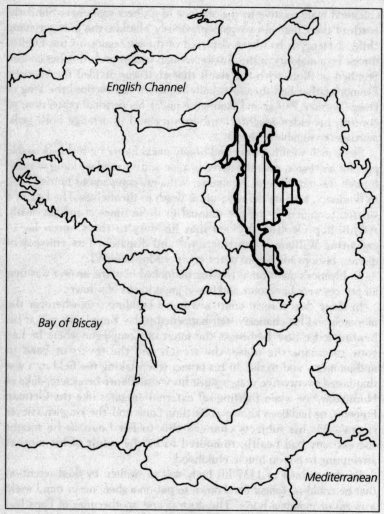

The Capetian royal domains.

Astute and far-sighted, Fat Louis had made his court a model of feudal justice and his capital a seat of learning, with Paris the only university in Europe until the expulsion of the English students in 1167 led to the foundation of a university at Oxford. Had his eldest son Philip been alive to succeed him, he would have accepted death as a blessed release, for Philip had been an accomplished warrior. But he had been killed in a banal traffic accident when a startled sow, foraging in the garbage that littered the unpaved streets of Paris, ran between the legs of his stallion, leaving him paralysed with a broken neck in the filth.

Subsequently anointed heir to the Capetian throne on the advice of the chancellor, Abbot Suger of St Denis, Fat Louis' second son was a very different person. Never was De Loyola's dictum *Give me a boy until he is six . . .* more true. Young Louis, as he was called, had been raised in the cloister of Notre Dame for high office in the Church until catapulted by a sow's panic to a place in history he would not have chosen. For the rest of his life, he oscillated between trying to be a strong king and behaving like the credulous, mystical monk he would have preferred to remain. Usually the monk won. When his father lay dying in the torrid summer of 1137, he was a deeply religious youth of seventeen, in whom Fat Louis saw none of the attributes of monarchy in that turbulent time of transition.

It must therefore have seemed an answer to his prayers when he learned from his old school friend Abbot Suger that the messengers from Bordeaux had arrived. After hearing their news, one name that cropped up in his private discussion with Suger was that of the handsome Count of Anjou, Geoffrey the Fair, whose lands bordered Poitou on the north and extended all the way from there to the English Channel.

A great champion of the tournament circuit, he and William X had the previous year laid waste territory which Fat Louis claimed in the Vexin – a disputed border strip that divided the royal domains from Normandy. Should Count Geoffrey learn too soon about the death of Eleanor's father, there was every chance of him swooping southwards and adding Eleanor's possessions to his own by marrying her under duress to his four-year-old son Henry. Once master of all western France, his territorial ambitions would be unstoppable.

The archbishop of Bordeaux wanted rewarding for the part he was playing; it was not too late for him to change sides. On his behalf the archbishop of Chartres demanded complete freedom for the Church in Aquitaine from all feudal and fiscal obligations, with the election of future bishops and archbishops to be according to canon law and free of influence by any temporal overlord.

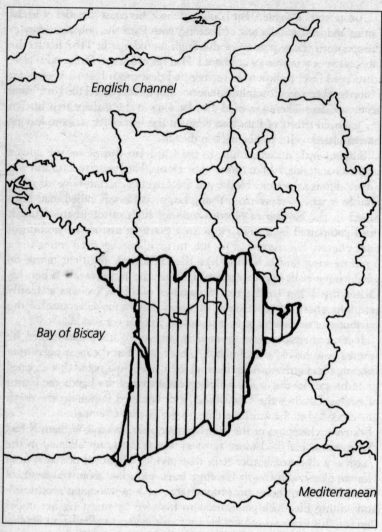

English Channel

Bay of Biscay

Mediterranean

Eleanor's inheritance of Poitou and Aquitaine

The right to appoint bishops was a contentious issue that was splitting Church from state all over Europe. Known as the investiture contest, it had been at the root of William IX's excommunication, for to his mind and that of continental nobility, a bishop was a vassal like any other, to be chosen by his temporal overlord so that in return he owed advice in council and support in the field with his own armed forces when called upon to give it.

That Fat Louis immediately acceded to Geoffroi de Lauroux's demands shows how crucial for the precarious Frankish monarchy was Eleanor's vast inheritance – the south-western third of France, extending from the Atlantic coast inland to the extinct volcanoes of the Auvergne in the Massif Central. Any magnate who added this to his own possessions would destabilise the kingdom;[8] on the other hand, if anything could give so inadequate a prince as Young Louis a chance of governing the kingdom, it was a wife whose dowry made him the richest man in France.

Eleanor and Young Louis being fourth cousins and therefore within the prohibited degrees of consanguinity, a prelate willing to marry them without first seeking a papal dispensation deserved reward. A charter granting all Archbishop Geoffroi's demands was therefore prepared and witnessed by 'Louis, our son already made king'[9] and by Geoffrey of Chartres as papal legate, Bishop Stephen of Paris and Abbot Suger.[10] And so the marriage between Eleanor and Louis was arranged as an affair of state without either of them being consulted.

To avoid the risk of Eleanor being abducted on the 400-mile journey to Paris, Fat Louis gave instructions for a royal cortège to travel to Bordeaux, making a show of force that would warn off the barons of Aquitaine. That Bordeaux was chosen for the wedding and coronation, rather than Limoges where the dukes of Aquitaine were traditionally crowned, suggests that it would have been dangerous for Eleanor to travel even that far unprotected. Or maybe Geoffroi de Lauroux was too shrewd to allow her to leave the city his knights and men-at-arms controlled until everything was doubly confirmed in writing.

Too ill to travel himself, Fat Louis decided not to billet the cortège by feudal right in the lands through which they travelled, but to pay for food, accommodation and forage for the animals. Although speed was important, the treasury was bare and such an expedition required financing by an especially promulgated *auxilium* or aid-tax on his vassals, which took time to raise.[11] So it was mid-June when the prince set out with 500 Frankish barons and knights under Count Thibault of Champagne and Raoul de Vermandois, Young Louis' cousin who served as steward of the princely household.[12] Travelling with them to sort out any canonical problems were three of the best legal brains in France: Abbot Suger, Archbishop Hugh of Tours and the abbot of Cluny.

Behind the bishops, barons and knights rode the squires, leading the highly bred and trained *destriers* or warhorses. With the wagons of the sumpter train and the packhorses and mules laden with armour, weapons, food and tents, they constituted a small army of several hundred men and animals on the move. In addition there was a corps of foot-soldiers, but what limited the speed at which they proceeded across the drought-parched centre of France was the pace of the draught oxen. Each day billeting officers were sent ahead to find grazing or fodder and water for man and beast. Frequent rests were necessary, for neither horse nor ox could be driven hard in such hot weather and during the full moon the cortège travelled at night.

They crossed from Frankish territory onto Eleanor's lands near Bourges in central France, where their numbers were swollen by the retinue of Archbishop Pierre of Bourges and the counts of Perche and Nevers with their personal entourages. Three weeks elapsed before they encamped outside Limoges on 30 June, in time to celebrate the feast-day of Aquitaine's patron St Martial. Present for the occasion was Count Alphonse Jourdan of Toulouse – another neighbour with every incentive to kidnap Eleanor, had he known in time of Duke William's death. But with Louis' little army encamped beside the River Vienne within a few days' ride of Bordeaux, neither he nor Geoffrey of Anjou would have dared kidnap the young duchess at that stage.[13]

From Limoges, the army continued past Périgueux. Emerging from the virgin oak forests above Lormont on Friday or Saturday, 9 or 10 July,[14] Young Louis led his cortège through land cleared by slash-and-burn where cattle and sheep grazed. The first cut of hay was drying for the winter. In the sheltered side valleys leading down to the plain of the River Garonne, small fields of millet ripened in the sun. Male peasants worked stripped to their *brais* – a cross between loincloth and underpants. Their womenfolk laboured alongside them, ankle-length skirts hitched up for convenience. Few horses were in use; although the padded shoulder collar had been invented towards the end of the previous century, making it possible for horses to pull ploughs, oxen were cheaper and more resistant to disease. The poorest peasants had to drag harrow and plough themselves.

The windmill, that landmark of the later Middle Ages, had not yet reached south-western France, so corn was ground by water-mills and at home by women using hand-mills or by blindfolded mules walking round and round a hollowed stone two metres wide, harnessed to a beam that dragged a wheel crushing the grain, afterwards scooped out by hand. If the peasant was obliged to use his lord's mill, a tax was deducted for the service, as well as a tenth or tithe for the Church. The surplus was stored in raised wooden silos, out of reach of field rodents, or carted off to safer storage behind castle or city walls.

This bucolic scene belied the back-breaking labour of the peasants gaping at the long train of squires and servants with the baggage-laden ox-carts lumbering after them. Of greater interest than the rich apparel of the Frankish knights and nobles were their caparisoned palfreys and mettlesome warhorses, for people then judged wealth and social standing by the quality of one's mount.[15] Yet if the illiterate peasants, whose memories went back no more than three generations, were marvelling that their teenage duchess Eleanor was to marry a king's son and go off to live in such splendour herself, the lettered monks on Church lands who watched the cortège ride past had only to consult their chronicles to recall how often a band of armed men from the north had signalled slaughter of man and beast and widespread devastation of lay and Church property.

The Frankish camp set up on the right bank of the Garonne was as large as many towns, with its own temporary market where food and other necessaries could be bought from the local peasantry, horses reshod by farriers and wagon-wheels damaged by the dry heat repaired by wheelwrights. Between it and the city lay the crescent of water busy with shipping that had given Bordeaux its title 'Port of the Moon'. Reflected in it was the silhouette of the Roman city walls, marked at regular intervals by round towers. Above them projected the domed roof of the cathedral, the bell walls[16] of the churches and the towers and pointed gables of the ducal palace.

On the left or southern side of the city, but divided from it by the harbour in the mouth of the Peugue tributary, was the unwalled suburb called Borc St Elegi where the market was held and the new class of merchants and free artisans was rapidly establishing itself. On the right, in open ground to the north of the walls, stood the imposing columns of a Roman temple built to honour the tutelary gods of the city then known as Burdigala. Beyond that was the immense bulk of the amphitheatre capable of holding 15,000 spectators.

The nearest ford being a two-day ride upriver, Suger, Thibault and other important members of Louis' court crossed by boats sent over to collect them, to begin the formalities which included Geoffroi de Lauroux presenting the keys of Bordeaux to the prince.

The walls of Bordeaux followed the rectangular Roman town plan, but enclosed far less ground than the imperial city had covered. Not every street was lined with houses. There were vineyards and gardens within the walls and grazing – necessary during a time of siege – with wasteland where animals brought in for slaughter could be penned overnight. The south-west corner of the city was Church property, surrounding the cathedral of St André and the archbishop's palace where Geoffroi de Lauroux held his own court. Eleven other churches within the walls and a dozen or more outside the city also owned property in Bordeaux. Dominating the town, the market and the port, whose customs dues were an important source of revenue for the ducal family, was Eleanor's palace.

From the vantage point of a window in her apartments that evening and with the sun in her favour, she could see the whole of the Frankish encampment on the opposite bank. The tents of the knights and men-at-arms were grouped around the pavilions of their barons with pennants floating in the evening breeze blowing in off the Atlantic. In the centre was the pavilion decorated with the lilies of France, where the monkish prince she had never met was giving thanks to God for his safe arrival. His compliant nature, which had accepted the translation from cloister to court, now accepted the obligation to marry a girl he had never met and provide the kingdom that would soon be his with an heir by her.

Girls' births not always being recorded, Eleanor is thought to have been born in April 1122, either in the palace of L'Ombreyra or at the family castle in Belin, a small village lying about thirty miles south of Bordeaux on the pilgrim trail to Compostela. Her name, originally spelled Alianor, was composed from *alia Anor*, Latin for 'the other Anor', her mother being Anor or Ænor of Châtellerault.[17] She was described as friendly, gracious, strong and courtly,[18] but also of precocious intelligence.

Spring arrives in Aquitaine three or four weeks earlier than north of the English Channel. April showers are the *giboulées* of March and the old saying, 'Never cast a clout till May is out' translates there as 'Don't take off a stitch until the end of April'.[19] A song composed by an anonymous twelfth-century troubadour and probably sung to Eleanor by her favourite minstrels translates as 'At the beginning of spring'.[20] In it, *la reina aurilhosa* or the April Queen corresponds to the northern Queen of the May, whose fertility ritual of lads and lasses entwining their ribbons around the maypole until their bodies touch is her dance also. Eleanor epitomised the April Queen.

Qui donc la vesés dançar
e son gent còrs deportar
ben pogrà dir' de vertat
qu'el mond non aja sa par,
la reina joiosa!

[He who sees her lead the dance, / sees her body twist and twirl, / can see that in all the world / for beauty there's no equal / of the queen of joy!]

But the words of the last verse sound as though they were added on that day in the summer of 1137 when Young Louis, crown prince of the Franks, arrived with an army to claim as his bride the rich and beautiful young duchess of Aquitaine.

Lo reis i ven d'autre part
per la dança destorbar
que el es en cremetar
que om no lo volh emblar
la reina aurilhosa.

[From afar the king has come / come to interrupt the dance / for he fears another man / may boldly seize the chance / to wed the April Queen.]

What were Eleanor's thoughts on going to bed, the night before the wedding? She had known even before her brother's death that her body was a tool of policy, to be used in the best interest of the duchy – for which it was far better she should meet the future king of the Franks in the bedchamber than on the battlefield. Girls of her class knew that they, their mothers and sisters, were human brood-mares, whose function was to merge the bloodlines of great ancestors – which is why the sexual integrity of a queen was so carefully checked on marriage and guarded thereafter to prevent any alien seed fertilising her, while for a king to spread his genes far and wide was seen as an ennoblement of the recipients and an enrichment of the race.

Almost as soon as she could speak, Eleanor had known that her high calling was to be the vessel through which the blood of her grandfather William the Troubadour and the nine other Williams who had been dukes of Aquitaine would be transmitted to posterity. Her model, if she needed one, was her ancestress Azalais, the widowed countess of

Toulouse who in 979 had saved her county from war and destruction by marrying another Louis, also a crown prince of the Franks.

It must have been difficult for the two teenage daughters of William X to stop talking and get some sleep that hot summer night with the Franks encamped just across the Garonne. Yet although she could aspire no higher than to be married to the future king of France, Eleanor knew that her independence would end at the moment of the wedding. From that moment, authority over her lands would be vested in her husband.

Expecting a warrior prince like her father and grandfather, her heart must have sunk when she set eyes on flabby, blond-haired Young Louis, his cheeks pale from vigil, his blue eyes unable to look a girl in the face. Against that, an entirely justifiable self-confidence must have inclined her to believe that she would soon wean him away from the priests surrounding him. Having been raised in a society with a frank attitude to carnal love – of which he, having been raised in the all-male world of the cloister, knew nothing – she was well aware of the power a woman can wield over the man who lusts for her. And even a few minutes' formal conversation sufficed to tell her that her intellect far outstripped his.

Yet there was romance of a kind in the air. With all the knights, barons and bishops from the north paying attention to Aelith as sister of their future queen, she was – like any girl of her age in such a position – looking her attractive best. At thirteen she was older than many noble brides, with a fresh young beauty that caught the eye of Louis' knightly cousin, Raoul de Vermandois. It was a *coup de coeur* that was to cost a thousand lives and more.

Normal feudal practice after the wedding would have been for the new duke and duchess to go on a tour of Aquitaine, meeting their subjects, confirming gifts and grants of the previous ruler, settling disputes and receiving oaths of loyalty. There were debts to claim and Young Louis' administrators to be installed for the taxation and governing of the duchy. However, Fat Louis' ill-health dictated a swift return north, so the vassals of Aquitaine were summoned to witness the marriage and to swear fealty to the new duke in Bordeaux.

To give them time to assemble, it was not until two weeks later – on Sunday 25 July – that the wedding was celebrated in the cathedral of St André.[21] Archbishop Geoffroi, flanked by two other archbishops and with Suger in attendance, united Eleanor and Young Louis in holy matrimony, after which the prince put on the coronet of the dukes of Aquitaine – an ornament that was to bring him in the long term little pleasure and great grief.

The dimly lit interior of the multi-domed cathedral was garishly painted and gilded floor to ceiling in the fashion of a Roman temple. Emerging into the daylight to the acclamation of the common people and the burgesses, the young couple walked back to the palace in procession through streets strewn with flower petals and bay leaves which filled the air with perfume when trodden on. Yet there were many who whispered that the groom, with the humble demeanour of a novice,[22] looked more dove than hawk, and some who said outright as he passed that he was *colhon* – as stupid as a testicle.

At the wedding feast in the thirteenth-century romance *Flamenca* the guests ate bustards, swans, cranes, partridges, ducks, capons, geese, chicken and peacocks, bread and pastry, root vegetables and fruit, wafers and fritters, with iced and spiced wines to drink.[23] Banquets in Aquitaine often included eighteen dishes of venison, wild boar, game birds, river and sea fishes washed down with spiced wine and ending with fritters and wafers.

One delicacy Eleanor's guests would have been offered was oysters from the coast of Médoc, praised in verse by Ausonius, the fourth-century Prefect of Aquitania, who judged them fit for the tables of the Caesars. But the atmosphere on her wedding feast was uneasy. The independent barons of Gascony deeply resented their new duke being a foreigner. To them, Young Louis was *lo princi del nord* – a prince who spoke an alien language, dressed like a monk and was neither warrior nor poet, either of which would have earned him some respect in their eyes. To them, Eleanor's wedding was a betrayal; she ought to have married one of their kind, a valiant troubadour like her grandfather or at least a man who spoke their own language.

For their part, Louis' Frankish retinue must have suspected even the food they were offered, seasoned with spices strange to their palates. With bay leaves, mustard, mint, ginger and vinegar they were familiar, and with the use of olive oil and honey to preserve fruit and savoury delicacies, but coriander, saffron, mace, cinnamon and cloves from nearby Spain were new tastes that might conceal more dangerous flavours. How could they trust the cooks when they certainly mistrusted Eleanor's vassals who had obeyed the summons to attend?

The Pilgrim's Guide, written in Latin between 1139 and 1173 for pilgrims to Compostela, summed up the northern view of Eleanor's Gascon subjects as talkative, boastful, lustful, greedy drunkards, who dressed in rags, ate without tables, all drinking from the same cup – and shamelessly slept together, with servants, master and mistress all lying on the same thin and rotten mattress.

The southern image of northerners was even worse. According to the troubadour Bernart Sicart de Maruejols:

> Lo frances n'a merces sonque s'en pot
> aver d'argent, sens autre drech.
> A eles l'abondança e la granda bombança.
> Engana e traïson, aqui lor confession.

[Your Frank shows mercy just to those who can pay him. / There's no other argument ever can sway him. / He lives in abundance; his table's a feast, / but mark my words, he's a treacherous beast.]

Weddings are a favourite device of dramatists to provoke outbursts on both sides. Whether the mutual mistrust of north and south erupted into blows and bloodshed on this occasion is unknown. Suger keeps a diplomatic silence, but had there been good news to report, he would have included it in his account. What particularly worried both him and Thibault of Champagne was the absence from the wedding of the rebel count of Angoulême.

Was there some fracas in the streets of Bordeaux, or had rumours reached Suger and Thibault of an ambush in force being planned by him on the journey north? It is hard to account otherwise for the precipitate and furtive departure from Bordeaux of the new duke and his duchess after Archbishop Geoffroi had obtained Louis' charter confirming his father's grant of freedoms to the Church, now sealed by him as duke of Aquitaine by marriage to Eleanor.[24] Bride and groom spent little time at the table, and must have left before their subjects had finished feasting, for they slipped out of the palace and across the Garonne by boat to where Young Louis' tented camp had already been struck.

The short route back to Paris via Bourges would have enabled Louis to be installed as count of Poitou in Limoges on the way. But either Suger thought it important to win over the citizens of Poitiers, who could turn out to be useful allies of Louis and Eleanor in the struggles with their vassals that he foresaw, or else the count of Champagne had reason to fear an ambush on the road to Limoges. So they rode north along the old Roman road to Poitiers, crossing the Dordogne and pressing on past Bourg to Blaye.

The image of a gracious duchess elegantly mounted aside is misleading. The three-pommelled side saddle was invented for nineteenth-century ladies who wished to go hunting. Although there were earlier women's saddles facing sideways, these were rigid boxes on which the lady perched with her feet on a board or *planchette* while the horse was led at walking pace by a groom. This would have been impractical and dangerous for the sort of mileage that Eleanor frequently covered in a day, so she rode astride.

And this was no pleasant day's ride in the country. Leaving Bordeaux at midday, they covered eighty miles at breakneck speed, changing horses at each river crossing[25] or more often, to reach at dusk the safety of the castle of Taillebourg on the north bank of the Charente a few miles past Saintes. There, the young couple could relax and consummate the marriage,[26] installed in the private quarters of Taillebourg's master, Geoffroi de Rancon. It was ironically he, the most loyal of all Eleanor's Poitevin vassals, who would be the cause of her great disgrace in Turkey on the Second Crusade.

Safety did not mean privacy. 'Dining in hall' as at some universities today meant that the nobles were seated at a table on a raised dais with everyone else in the body of the hall. All could see the newly-weds leave the table and enter the adjoining bedchamber, which was certain to be shared on such an important occasion so that no sleight of hand could counterfeit the bride's virginity. Servants regularly slept in the same room as their masters and mistresses. In the retelling of the legend of Tristan and Isolde by Béroul, a Norman *trouvère* contemporary with Eleanor, the king and queen sleep in the bed, while Tristan, a dwarf and another person slumber on the floor of the chamber.

After another gruelling eighty-mile ride to Poitiers, Eleanor and her groom were lodged in the Maubergeonne Tower of the comital palace, now part of the law courts. Suger's report that the inhabitants of the city received their new count and countess with a great show of joy may well be true, for the town-dwelling traders and artisans wanted the peace and stability in which business could prosper and the common people spoke a dialect of *la langue d'oïl* comprehensible to the Franks. However, before the year was out, the same townsfolk would have good reason to hate their new count. In any case, the proud Poitevin nobility, whose language of choice was Eleanor's own *lenga d'oc*, were almost as hostile to Young Louis as the barons of Gascony had been.[27]

On 8 August, Eleanor's husband was crowned with the coronet of Poitou in the cathedral of St Pierre during a ceremony staged by Suger in imitation of the coronation of the kings of France at Reims to show the world that a new dynasty ruled the county of Poitou and therefore by tradition the duchy of Aquitaine. Within hours of the ceremony came the announcement of Fat Louis' death in Paris on the first day of the month. Clad in a monk's shift and with arms outstretched in symbolic crucifixion on a bed of ashes placed on the floor, the sick king had felt able to give up the ghost in the knowledge that his kingdom was as safe as it was ever going to be with his monkish son on the throne. Young Louis already having been anointed successor, the news automatically made him king of France.

In the space of a few days during her sixteenth summer, Eleanor had risen from being the vulnerable unmarried daughter of a dead duke to be queen of all France.

TWO

Mistress of Paris, Aged Fifteen

Within hours of the news from Paris of his father's death, Louis was confronted by the first crisis of his reign. Profiting from the brief window of opportunity in what they thought would be an interregnum, the citizens of Orleans had formed a commune to take over the government of their city. Splitting his forces, the young king departed with the cavalry and Suger at his side to restore order, leaving Eleanor and her sister to follow more slowly with the infantry under the archbishop of Chartres.

The medieval convention was to call noblewomen beautiful in the same way that courage was automatically ascribed to knights, wisdom to kings and piety to clerics, whether or not merited. However, although there are many descriptions of the appearance and clothing of kings, princes and lesser men in the twelfth century, women were of little interest to the celibate chroniclers.

The quest for Eleanor's likeness is not easy because the later medieval passion for portraiture had not begun in her time. Luckily, in Aquitaine it was customary to have commemorative heads carved after a change of overlord and placed in churches where the people could see what their new masters looked like. Three heads commemorating the July wedding are now set into the rebuilt wall of the nave of Bordeaux Cathedral. Hidden in the gloom high above an enormous wooden pulpit, Eleanor's shows her filled with life and spirit on the threshold of a new life; Archbishop Geoffroi looks quietly pleased with his political coup; Louis looks worried already with his down-turned mouth – as well he might, given his hostile reception by the Gascons (plates 2, 8 and 9).

The young duchess wears the coronet of Poitou; the archbishop, his mitre; Prince Louis wears no crown, but what looks like a monk's cowl. Unfortunately, the nose of the crowned female head has been broken in the distant past, it is badly lit and can only been seen at an angle and with difficulty. Yet this is the face of a strong, intelligent, well-nourished and confident young woman, excited at the great destiny ahead of her.

There are several other carved heads said to be of Eleanor. One is in the reconstructed medieval cloister of the Metropolitan Museum in New York, but this is Romanesque sculpture, more symbol than portrait. A carved head at Oakham Hall in Rutland reputed to be of her tells us even less.

The Plantagenet effigies at Fontevraud Abbey, where she was buried sixty-seven years after the August wedding, are among the earliest known. Eleanor's features there are smooth, with not a wrinkle in sight, because the noble dead were represented in their prime; it was reasoned that on the Day of Resurrection they would revert to the age of thirty-three – Christ's supposed age at the Crucifixion.[1] So how much this proud, intelligent face resembles hers at the age of eighty-two is impossible to guess; it may have been carved several years after her death from drawings or memory. But there is a clue in the open book she holds. This is not a closed missal piously clasped to the breast of an illiterate believer, but a book in the process of being read when she fell asleep for the last time (plate 29).

More informative is a statue at Chartres Cathedral, consecrated in 1260. The Royal or Western Portal[2] is older, having been built and carved for the Romanesque church that stood on the same spot until destroyed by fire in 1194. While no one can prove that the life-size queen in her mid-twenties carved here in fine detail is indeed a true likeness of Louis' consort, the work is dated to 1142–50, when Eleanor was of that age and the only queen in France. The statue's clothing belongs to the period and, despite a certain impassivity in the features, the high skill of the sculptor is beyond question (plate 3).

The expression on the face is regal, challenging and untroubled, exuding self-confidence and intelligence. Seeing this statue in profile, the damage to the head in Bordeaux Cathedral is doubly regrettable, for the strong nose at Chartres is very distinctive. The hair is elegantly coiffed, but constrained by no modest veil or wimple, as one might expect of a married woman. Its luxuriant femininity must have disturbed the clerics by whom Young Louis was surrounded. The saintly Bernard of Clairvaux refused to look even at his own sister Humbeline, the prioress of Jully, so deep was his horror of sex that caused mankind to be 'begotten in filth, gestated in darkness and born in pain'.[3]

Beside this proud queen standing in the Royal Portal as though she owns it and holding an open book to symbolise the literacy of which she was proud, the anguished king is dressed like a monk, his cheeks gaunt from fasting. It is a face racked by guilt, as Louis' was after the massacre of Vitry – an outrage during his first major campaign after the marriage, to expiate the guilt for which was his main reason for going on crusade. And – it is only a detail, but details count in a search for which records are few – his mouth is definitely down-turned, as in the head at Bordeaux.

In her second marriage, Eleanor was depicted in a stained-glass window she and Henry of Anjou donated to the cathedral being built at Poitiers, but in a very stylised fashion which tells us little; the hair is covered and repairs to the glass obscure much of the facial detail.

Discovered in 1964 in a ruined chapel at Chinon, a short walk from Henry's treasure castle, is a contemporary mural depicting her on horseback (plate 4). The artist has painted her thirty years older than at Chartres, which would make sense, for the setting is just after the rebellion of 1173–4. While the painting is crude in comparison with the finesse of the carving at Chartres, the face is boldly intelligent, the hair free-flowing and auburn. The colour could be the most important detail, for Eleanor's granddaughter Blanca of Castile resembled her grandmother and was described as having long brown hair and cool classical looks.

A carved head on the wall of the nuns' kitchen at the abbey of Fontevraud, whose construction was partly paid for by Eleanor, shows her as an old woman of eighty gazing at another carving either of herself as the girl who married Louis or of Blanca going off to marry another Prince Louis two generations later, which amounts to the same thing (see plates 1 and 5).

So, the nearest description of the bride on her wedding day in 1137 is that she was as tall as Prince Louis and quite broad-shouldered, as befits an accomplished horsewoman. Her face was humorous and alert, framed by long auburn hair flowing freely from beneath the coronet. Her eyes, according to legend, were green and fearless. Indeed, Eleanor's courage was never in dispute. Nor was her willingness to confront the Church.

After his return from the disastrous First Crusade, her troubadour grandfather William IX had taken for his mistress the countess of Châtellerault, well named La Dangerosa, causing his second wife Philippa to retire to the nunnery in which his first wife Ermengarde already lived! Undeterred by excommunication and the reprimands for this and other outrageous behaviour from the papal legate Giraud, he commented that hairs would grow on the prelate's bald pate before he would give up the woman he loved, and made his point by bearing La Dangerosa's portrait on his shield in tournaments – in return, he said, for her bearing him in bed.

In what he called *An Embarrassing Poem*, he explained the problem of choosing between wife and mistress in terms any knight would understand:

> *Dos cavalhs ai a me selha ben e gen*
> *Bon son e adreg per armas e valen*
> *Mas no'ls puesc amdos tener*
> *que l'us l'autre non cossen.*

[I have two purebred horses for my saddle, / fine-spirited and both well trained for battle / but I can't stable them together / for neither tolerates the other.]

In that horse-obsessed age, the selective breeding that worked well for the most noble of animals was thought to produce the best results in humankind too. William IX therefore ordered his legitimate son to marry his mistress' daughter by her estranged husband. In this case the breeder's expectations were fulfilled, with the first-born daughter of that union being of the same independent character and physical toughness as her grandfather. Eleanor's brother William, who should have inherited the ducal title, was born a year or two later. The second sister, Aelith or Petronilla, was born a year after that.

Eleanor was five when William IX's death placed her one heartbeat away from wearing the coronet of Aquitaine that she watched her father put on for the first time in Limoges Cathedral. When she was seven, her mother and young brother died. As their father's feudal duties and military campaigns took him away from home for long periods, a strong bond grew up between the two sisters, with Eleanor becoming very protective towards Aelith. One of her less glorious distinctions is to be the only woman recorded as having unleashed a war in support of a sister's right to marry the man she loved.

Ruling Aquitaine called for a warrior chieftain perpetually on the move, using diplomacy, bluff and armed force to keep refractory vassals in their place. The southern culture treated women as men's equals, but this was *paratge* – an equality of dignity, not power. In practice, a duchess ruling a province so vast and unruly would require a very powerful husband to keep her vassals in order. From the age of seven Eleanor had known that she would one day be the virtual queen of what had once been an independent kingdom, and that while a warrior-duke might have redeemed its former greatness by force of arms, her duty lay in sacrificing her personal freedom in marriage to the most powerful suitor available.

The education she received following her brother's death was wide-ranging. From her father and his vassals in council she learned statecraft and how to tell a good horse, dog, hawk or man from the bad ones. From her clerical tutors she also acquired literacy in Latin, which was the language of diplomacy and the Church, and in the official language of the duchy, *la lenga d'oc*.

It says much that the Romans had no word for 'yes'. The affirmative could be indicated in Latin by 'thus'; *sic* has become *si* in Spanish, Portuguese and Italian. The slightly pedantic *mihi placet* – literally, 'it pleases me' – survives at high tables in a few universities. But commonly the phrase *hoc ille*, meaning 'that's it', was used. In the language spoken in the north of France, this was corrupted to *oïl* and later to *oui*. Hence the correct name of the northern language: *la langue d'oïl*. In the south of France, *hoc ille* became simply *oc* and the language is therefore known as *la lenga d'oc*. Sister to Catalan and first cousin to Spanish and Italian, it is not a dialect of the northern tongue, but a separate language.

Among Eleanor's relaxations was the fashionable game of chess recently imported from the East, where the crucial piece that changed the fate of kings on the chequered board was called *firz* or vizier. First transliterated to *vierge* – the French for 'virgin' – it became in the European game the 'queen'. Nothing symbolises better than the chess queen, who changes the fate of kings, this daughter of a duke who became queen of France and queen of England and had three sons anointed kings of England.

Although it is convenient to call her queen of 'France', Louis' title was not *rex franciae* but *rex francorum*, meaning that he was king of the Frankish people, not the land itself. The idea of nationhood did not yet exist, frontiers were still flexible and the eastern fifth of modern France lay within the German Empire.

Modern genetic research has proven what Strabo and Caesar both knew: the Celts of the north were of a different ethnic stock from the shorter, darker, more relaxed, outgoing and sensuous people of the south. By the twelfth century the differences were greater, due to the entailing Salic law and grim guilt-ridden religion of the Germanic Franks who ruled the north and the more liberal attitude to religion of the Gothic aristocracy ruling the south under Roman law.

Little physical evidence remains of the *limes* or fortified frontier that separated the two peoples before Rome unified by force what it called the province of Gaul. However, the great north–south divide that split the country in the twelfth century still shows up in the differing patterns of blood groups in the modern population, which coincide closely with the isoglosses or lines on the map of France separating areas where two different languages were in everyday use until recently. Before the introduction of modern farming methods there was a tradition of rotating crops triennially north of the old *limes* and biennially to the south. Roofs to the south are of canal tiles laid with a shallow pitch; to the north they are steeper, with tiles or slates pinned on.

In Julius Caesar's description of the province of Gaul, Aquitaine was that third which lay between the Pyrenees and the River Garonne; Augustus extended its borders northwards to the Loire and eastwards to the Massif Central, but the ethnic and linguistic boundary ran from the Atlantic to the Alps.

South of the line there had been no necessity during the *pax romana* to concentrate power in fortified cities. Far from the unconquered barbarians menacing the vulnerable north-east of the empire, life in the south-west had been lived in a few unwalled cities and many villas, where each local chieftain ruled several thousand dependants in the area surrounding his palace, within which he lived in Roman style with hot and cold bathing facilities and central heating. Although by Eleanor's time this golden age was only a memory, the independence of each local chieftain continued.

Like the Nile, both major rivers of Aquitaine enjoy a prevailing wind blowing upstream. Drifting down with the current and sailing up with a favourable wind, traders penetrated deep inland since prehistoric times. But where traders could go, so could raiders. With

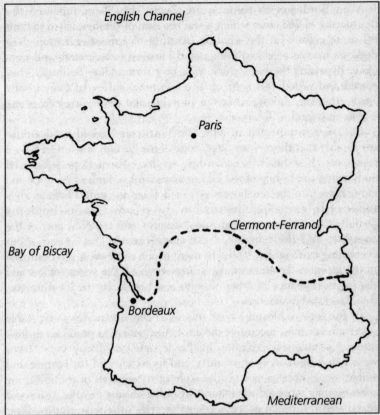

Map of Isogloss. To the north of the dotted line *la langue d'oïl* was spoken; to the south, Occitan.

the collapse of the Roman Empire, the rich and fertile province that had been the posting of choice outside Italy for administrators and soldiers became an irresistible target for every invader. Its perimeter reduced, walled and turreted towards the end of the third century, Bordeaux was nevertheless sacked by the Vandals twice and by the Visigoths and Franks.

Devastation continued with the Muslims carving their way north with fire and sword in 732 at such cost to life and property that the Occitan place name *Sarrazins* still means a ruined house. Charles Martel stopped the Moors at Poitiers and pursued them southwards, leaving Bordeaux in ruins again. Pepin the Short repeated the destruction in 768, after which it was the turn of Vikings, based in their off-shore colony on the whaling island of Noirmoutier, to sail their *drakkars* up the rivers to pillage and burn city, monastery and farm alike. Bypassing the high, thick walls now surrounding Bordeaux, they rowed and sailed and rode up the Garonne Valley halfway to the Mediterranean, looting what was movable and destroying everything else as far inland as Toulouse.

On their return visit in 848, the Northmen sacked Bordeaux so thoroughly that thirty years later 'none of the faithful any longer have a roof over their head'[4] – according to the bull of Pope John VIII authorising the bishop of the city to abandon his diminished flock and move his see to the much safer city of Bourges in central France. As a result of this repeated destruction and reconstruction, Bordeaux dwindled to little more than ruins of baths and temples, part of the aqueduct and the remains of the amphitheatre. Yet, if just about everything material left by the Romans in the south-west was destroyed in the repeated devastation, two things survived: the system of law and the pagan tolerance of other customs and beliefs. In the local tongue, this was called *convivença*.

By the time of Eleanor's birth improved climate and relatively stable government under successive dukes of Aquitaine had produced a slow-burning population explosion in the depopulated duchy. New towns were being built in open country and forest cleared for pasture and arable use. Although not on the scale of the *bastides* of the following century, they attracted inhabitants by enfranchising anyone who could reach them, a precious inducement to serfs otherwise tied to their owner's land until death. An astonishing 25 per cent of place names of the south-west date from this period,[5] as do the thousands of large and small Romanesque churches that dot the landscape.

Gradually the old Roman vineyards[6] were being replanted and new ones brought into production. The cartularies recording gifts to religious foundations bear witness to a resurgence of viticulture around Bordeaux, on the eastern side of the Gironde and in the triangle of Entre Deux Mers[7] between the lower reaches of the Dordogne and Garonne.

Yet although Eleanor's lifetime fell within what is called 'the medieval warm period', when temperatures were several degrees milder than today and the vineyards of southern Britain were more extensive than they would ever be again, reaching further north than Ely in Cambridgeshire, this warmer weather did not necessarily bring good harvests: the lack of winter cold to kill off pests and disease meant that famine was an ever-present possibility. Medieval varieties of cereal produced extremely low yields by modern standards. Deducting taxes and/or a tithe to the Church, plus the seed for sowing, left little of the meagre harvest for food.

A dry spring and summer meant a poor harvest; a damp autumn saw grain crops rotting on the stalk. Two bad years in succession meant a choice between watching children and old people starve and having insufficient seed to plant the following spring. In time of conflict, the age-old defence tactic of scorched earth combined with Vegetius' maxim 'First destroy his land, then attack the enemy', meant not only hunger for the combatants but also a spiralling death-rate among the peasantry after hostilities ceased.

However, Louis' first demonstration of kingly power at Orleans was more a show of force than a campaign. The dissidents punished, he continued to Paris, where Eleanor joined him, installing herself and her personal servants in the palace of the Capetian kings. It was a comfortless Merovingian fortress at the western end of the Ile de la Cité where her lavish lifestyle and exuberant personality disturbed the sober household headed by her pious mother-in-law, Adelaide de Maurienne. The once-powerful dowager queen had little reason to welcome a daughter-in-law whose arrival deprived her of her dower lands. After a short battle of wills, she retired to one of her own castles in Champagne and married a minor noble by name of Mathieu de Montmorency, leaving Eleanor the only queen on the Ile de la Cité.[8]

There she scandalised the establishment by her sheer exuberance, her unbridled curiosity, her *gai saber* and the introduction of southern culture in the shape of poets and musicians playing on the traditional instruments such as flutes and tabors and bagpipes, and also the plucked and bowed stringed instruments introduced from the East – rebec and viol, cithara and fiedel – that concerted together for the pleasure of the ear and the delight of idle minds with no thought of praising God.

The young queen made it easy for her enemies to criticise her use of cosmetics and jewellery, ignoring the jibes from Clairvaux against 'the beauty that is put on in the morning and taken off at night'.[9] A born leader of fashion, her own extravagant dress incited the ladies of her court to wear garments of fur-lined silk, a material that had reached the west only in the previous century, transforming the cut of fashionable clothes in the process. Over linen shifts that were the only female undergarments, their ankle-length underdresses had close-fitting embroidered sleeves that peeped through the floor-length sleeves of their overgarments, buttoned back at the cuff to reveal the richness beneath. On their wrists were bracelets of gold to match the settings of the gemstones in their earrings. Their overdresses not only reached to the floor, but trailed on it behind them, with sleeves worn so long they were often knotted up out of the way. The origin of Cinderella's mislaid slipper was the footwear worn by Eleanor and maids- and ladies-in-waiting, fashioned not from *verre*, meaning glass, but the homophone *vair*, which is the soft fur from a squirrel's belly that kept their elegant feet insulated from the chill of stone-flagged floors in the palace on the Ile de la Cité.

Good Christian men then required women to disguise their curves and hide their hair. Yet instead of modest, all-obscuring wimples suitable for married women, Eleanor and her ladies wore fashionably draped veils of fine linen held in place by bejewelled circlets, revealing as much as they hid. We owe the description that fits so well the statue at Chartres to a description by saintly Bernard of Clairvaux of the behaviour and dress at court, when warning nuns how they should *not* behave and dress. Of the ladies likened to snakes for dragging the trains of their dresses behind them, he upbraided those 'not so much adorned as burdened with gold, silver and precious stones in regal splendour'.[10]

Much of the time, Eleanor ruled the palace because Louis kept to his old habits, returning to the cloister of Notre Dame whenever his kingly duties permitted, observing the offices, fasting and making vigil like any monk. If his regal status brought him to the forefront occasionally to read the canticles – *Benedictus* at Lauds, *Magnificat*, the canticle of the Virgin Mary, at Vespers and *Nunc Dimittis* at Compline – he eschewed any distinction of dress and maintained an attitude so humble and self-effacing[11] that no stranger attending the services would have guessed he was the ruler of the Franks, those bellicose Germanic warriors who had swept out of the Rhine Valley and subdued the former Roman province of Gaul in the fifth and sixth centuries.

Sharing the monks' privations did not mean that he forewent much in the way of creature comforts. With no table linen or individual plates in the royal palace until Eleanor introduced such luxuries for herself and her ladies, a place setting at table consisted of a drinking vessel and a knife to hack off portions of meat or skewer vegetables, which were then placed on flat breads used as plates[12] and afterwards eaten by the servants. The windows of the palace were narrow and few for defensive reasons but still a source of draughts in winter, being closed with wooden shutters until the queen introduced glazing in her apartments.

Beneath the palace foundations were vestiges of hypocausts dating from the Roman city, but the only heating above ground level before Eleanor arrived was by charcoal braziers, whose carbon monoxide fumes could be lethal in enclosed spaces, and open wood fires in the centre of large and high-ceilinged public rooms with a hole above through which the smoke could escape, but which also let in wind and rain. There was virtually no privacy on the Ile de la Cité until the advent of the masonry fireplace, seemingly introduced by her, or at any rate shortly after her arrival. Built against a wall with a mantelpiece supporting a chimney through which smoke could escape without letting in too much weather, this new architectural device altered for ever the communal lifestyle of early medieval times by enabling small private rooms to be heated, so that a lord or his lady could at last keep to their private apartments without freezing.

West of the palace buildings and extending to the tip of the island was a triangular area of gardens planted with herbs, fig trees, olives, cypresses, vines and shrubbery, beyond which the divided waters of the Seine rejoined to flow seawards. Though a pleasant enough place, opened on occasion to commoners, it was hardly compensation for an energetic and vivacious teenage queen, accustomed to range throughout the length and breadth of Aquitaine.

Among the few escapes from this claustrophobic existence was an occasional day trip to the abbey of St Denis, a dozen miles north of Paris, where Suger had just started construction of a great basilica with no expenses spared, in the belief that everything excellent and beautiful should be used to glorify God. For this, he received regular admonitions for his excessive love of luxury and magnificence from the ascetic and saintly Cistercian abbot of Clairvaux.[13] Occasionally too there was a pilgrimage to Sens, where William the Mason's masterly use of the ogive or broken arch in the new cathedral of St Etienne[14] had been Suger's inspiration to build in the new style that would later be dubbed Gothic.[15]

The shops in Paris had not changed since Roman times. Open-fronted, they resembled lock-ups in an Arab *souk*, with their wares spilling out into the street, in the middle of which ran the open drain. Cows and small flocks of goats were driven into the city to be milked directly into customers' receptacles – the only way to be certain the milk was fresh. Traffic in Paris was as chaotic as it had been in Rome when Augustus banned wheeled vehicles, not only because they caused frequent accidents and obstructed the narrow streets but also because the daily accumulation of dung from draught animals was such that stepping stones were needed for pedestrians to cross busy thoroughfares dry-shod.

On the Ile de la Cité knights, barons, abbots and rich merchants on horseback forced a passage through streets no wider than two spans of a man's arms between wagons bringing merchandise into the city and others carrying away the daily quota of waste and excrement; often the same cart would be used for both purposes and the river downstream was an open sewer. The side streets were even narrower, the timber-framed houses of lath and plaster leaning over them from both sides to gain maximum space on the upper floors at the cost of perpetual gloom for passers-by.

Pedestrians pushed between the mounts of the mighty with priest, pilgrim, poor student, potboy and ash-covered penitent treading the same filth underfoot as the most learned and famous teachers in the world. Here and there scavengers with rakes and brooms shifted the rubbish ineffectually from place to place until it was eventually tipped into the Seine, on whose surface floated the aloof and immaculate swan, the royal bird of the Capetians so unlike its Aquitain counterpart, the proud and colourful peacock.

The most congested areas were where traffic converged to cross the two offset stone bridges that linked the island to the north and south banks of the Seine, each protected by a *chatelet* or small castle at the landward end. The Grand Pont led from the royal palace to the hustle and bustle of the business quarter on the right bank; the Petit Pont led from near the *parvis*[16] of Notre Dame to the left bank whither the schools had moved to escape the physical and metaphysical lack of space on the island.

Beneath the bridges, floating water-mills whose design had not changed in a thousand years were moored to grind grain for palace and city, an activity forbidden on Sundays because its noise disturbed the faithful at prayer. Washerwomen knelt on the wet flagstones of the sloping quays summer and winter, beating clothes on flat stones as they washed them without soap in the river water. Above their heads, cramped apothecaries' shops were stocked with the repertoire of Hippocrates and Galen: therapeutic herbs, but also narcotics like opium, henbane to cure contractions, toothache and hysteria – and squill, an extract of lilies used as an expectorant, cardiac stimulant and diuretic. They also sold viper toxin, the dried and crushed excrement and organs of various animals, and worse. Moneychangers in booths on the bridges bought and sold all the coinage of Europe and farther afield, weight and purity of the metal deciding the rate of exchange.

Paris had around 50,000 inhabitants when Eleanor arrived there. Before the end of the century it would number half as many again, with the constantly expanding commercial area on the Right Bank pushing outwards into the vineyards and orchards and fields. There the butchers had their slaughter-houses, the odiferous fellmongers cleaned and prepared the hides and skins which the tanners converted into leather for the shoemakers, saddlers, clothiers, armourers, the makers of furniture and mugs and buckets and a host of other objects in daily use. Their stinking effluent of offal, oak bark and dog's excrement mingled in the streams running down to the Seine with the fermented urine from the fulling mills, which is why these activities were usually grouped together.

Tailors, ironmongers, carpenters, bakers and candle-makers, the smiths and metalworkers, the potters and rope-makers all plied their skills and carried on the myriad specialised activities that kept the city alive. Ironbound wheels and shod hooves added to the din. Crying their wares were peddlers and sellers of cakes and sweetmeats balancing trays on their heads in the hope of keeping the delicacies out of the reach of urchins on the loose night and day because the single room they shared with the rest of their family had no space for play.

Water-sellers promised clean drinking water from their leather and wooden buckets to people who had no access to a well and no fountain nearby. Flat-bottomed barges brought food and wood for cooking and heating from up and downriver, and salt and wax and wine and millet for the flour that filled most of the stomachs in the city. Local fishermen delivered their catch fresh from the water while fast, light wherries brought food of all descriptions from further afield. Live animals and fowl arrived by land and water for slaughter.

To facilitate landing merchandise actually on the island, breaches had been made in the Roman wall that girdled it and crude wharves built that suffered in each winter flood, increasing the general effect of dilapidation. And through the thronging thousands, living and dying, tax collectors threaded their way, for like death, tax was already unavoidable. Tavern-keepers, goldsmiths, fish- and fowl-mongers, oil-sellers and pastry-cooks were among those taxed at the highest rate, with cobblers, potters, forgers of fish-hooks and dressmakers treated more favourably. Only the water-sellers and the poorest peddlers with a few trinkets on a tray were exempt.

Because of cheap and simple construction methods, fire was an ever-present menace in cities; in the first quarter of the thirteenth century the Norman capital Rouen burned six times. Lack of adequate sanitation and ignorance of hygiene encouraged vermin, in whom the plague bacillus lurked. In the same year that Eleanor arrived to live on the Ile de la Cité, Dijon was ravaged by plague; three years before it had been the turn of Chartres. No one knew when it would strike Paris. Because disease and death were never far away and pain ubiquitous, even the poorest gave to the Church in the hope of a better world to come.

However, vocation played little part among the oblates dominant in many monasteries, who had been literally offered in infancy or childhood by their parents. Other monks were younger sons with no property to fight for, or an aversion to the violent life of males in the equestrian classes. Thousands of women took the veil each year to escape a repugnant arranged marriage, usually buying their way into a convent with a dowry from their families.

Yet many people were devout, their fervour ignited by the wonderment aroused in those whose lives were spent in hard labour, pain, grief and hunger at the idea of a Godhead *choosing* to suffer even worse than they had to. So deeply did it touch them that countless thousands left the little they had every year, to set out penniless for Rome, Compostela or the Holy Land – only to die on the way. There were also Christian groups living in towns to serve the sick and the poor and to educate children: women known as Beguines and men called Beghards did not take vows but lived in poverty, humility and service to others – some for life, others until they entered a monastery or convent, or returned to normal life.

Balancing the temporal power at the western end of the Ile de la Cité was the archbishop's palace at the eastern end. Lately repaired by Fat Louis, the twin basilicas built on the remains of a Roman temple dedicated to Jupiter or Zeus Pateras – God the Father in His Greco-Roman incarnation – would shortly be demolished to make way for Notre Dame Cathedral. Around the basilicas were crowded the lodgings of the prelates and the canons. Bells tolled night and day on a dozen lesser churches clustered there. To the sound of plainsong, monks processed through narrow streets that had not been repaved since the Romans left, chanting and swinging their censers to briefly perfume the foetid air with lingering traces of incense, the sweetest of all perfumes to Louis' nostrils.

THREE

The Scandalous Pagan Queen

I f the clamour of street life in Paris was similar to that of Eleanor's own cities of Bordeaux, Poitiers and Limoges, the intellectual pace of the Frankish capital was very different. Latin, spiced by all the accents of Europe, was the common language of academics and their pupils from all over Christendom. The area still called 'the Latin quarter' was a cauldron of learning, bubbling with a naïve hunger for all knowledge. Like restaurants of the mind, each of the schools on the Left Bank displayed its menu to attract a body of students so hungry for instruction in the theoretical and practical sciences and the trivium[1] and quadrivium[2] that they accepted poor food and cramped attic dormitories, often paid for from the king's purse. And if some slavishly repeated their lessons parrot-fashion, others endorsed Peter Abelard's assertion that students' criticism of teachers was a healthy way of testing the truth of instruction, for no one should teach what he did not fully understand.

Occasionally Louis threw open the palace gardens to the doctors and their boisterous followers to pursue the debate ongoing since Plato and Aristotle as to whether universals – the properties that each member of a class of things must possess if the same general word were to apply to them all – were 'real' as the Realists argued or merely words, as the Nominalists asserted.

The theology expounded in Eleanor's Paris also had wide variations between the orthodox teachings of Bernard of Clairvaux and those of Peter de Bruys, a vigorously campaigning apostate monk who maintained that baptism did not save infants from original sin, that all churches should be destroyed as unnecessary, that the representation of a crucified man was not fit for veneration, that prayers and alms offered for the salvation of the dead were a useless waste of time and money and that the new doctrine of transubstantiation was nonsense because anyone could see that the bread and wine did *not* become the body and blood of Christ when offered upon the altar.[3]

Peter Abelard's application of rational methods to questions of faith repeatedly offended believers. Yet Bernard, who opposed Eleanor and engineered Abelard's final downfall, was not a mad visionary monk. His voluminous correspondence reveals a humane and widely read man, as liable to quote Terence or Ovid as the Fathers of the Church.

And although Abelard had a mindset more logical in the modern sense, inventing etymology to clarify doctrinal contradictions due to changes in usage and stressing that language by itself cannot demonstrate the truth of things which lie in the domain of physics, his downfall was due not so much to the views he propounded as the arrogance that made him boast of being able to prove by citing accepted authorities that God was one or that He was three, that He was able or unable to prevent evil, that He had free will or that He had not.

Somewhere in the centre of the spectrum was Abbot Suger, the churchman–politician who served both king and God for the good of Church and society both. Ruling the most opulent monastery in France, he was accused by Bernard of turning it into an office for the affairs of state under Fat Louis, where voices were raised in argument and soldiers *and even women* came and went.[4] But Suger was also attacked by Abelard, who used the methods of his banned book *Yes and No*[5] to prove that the abbey's patron saint was not an Athenian convert of St Paul called Dionysius the Areopagite, but a less prestigious local martyr of similar name. The resultant clamour at St Denis that Abelard be tried for heresy forced Héloïse's castrated ex-lover to flee the capital yet again and seek asylum in Champagne.

It was this intellectual vigour and diversity of thinking that made Paris unique.

Into the all-male world of doctors and students, the ladies of Eleanor's court occasionally intruded. Her sister Aelith was a constant companion; others of her inner circle were Mamille de Roucy, Florine de Bourgogne, Torqueri de Bouillon, Faydide de Toulouse and Countess Sybille of Flanders. They shared the queen's outdoor amusements of riding and hawking in the countryside around Paris. Indoors, they embroidered, played board games like chess and backgammon or amused themselves with simple games like blind man's buff. They watched court productions of stage plays in Latin and were regaled in risqué Occitan by troubadours brought by the young queen from Aquitaine and the sober *trouvères* of the north retelling *chansons de geste* and the Arthurian legends called *la matière de Bretagne*.

But they also attended the lectures of fashionable doctors – Abelard for one – where they rubbed shoulders with students both penniless and rich, the latter including the ambitious son of a successful Norman merchant in London. Tall, gangling, with a mop of unruly hair and a tendency to flush with passion in argument, Thomas Becket was only four years the queen's senior, but it is unlikely that the colourfully dressed ladies of the queen's court distracted a man so little interested in women. John of Salisbury, later secretary to Canterbury's most famous archbishop, reminded his former fellow-student in a letter long afterwards of the euphoria they had shared at that time in Paris. He likened having their youthful minds stretched by the learned discourse of the greatest teachers in Christendom to gazing in wonderment at a Jacob's ladder of knowledge, up which the angels of enquiry ascended to the heaven of learning.[6]

Albeit less ecstatic than John of Salisbury about days spent in philosophical debate, Eleanor nevertheless mastered the dialectic and the art of clinching her arguments with neat syllogisms in which both premises and conclusion are statements constructed using only three simple terms, each term appearing twice. For example, all men are mortal; no gods are mortal; therefore no men are gods. It is impossible to assert the premises and deny the conclusion without contradicting oneself.

Abelard's teaching influenced the subsequent evolution of European education, in which the liberal arts and the emphasis on grammar and the reading of classical authors was replaced by new methods stressing logic, dialectic and the new sciences. In philosophy, there was a decline in Platonism and a growing interest in the methods of Aristotle, translated into Latin because few scholars could read Greek. Latin translations of many philosophical and scientific works of Greek and Arabic origin were illuminating a Europe still emerging from the Dark Ages.

Living in this cultural revolution was exhilarating for an enquiring mind like Eleanor's. It may seem strange that a fun-loving queen of sixteen summers should attend day-long debates as to whether the Blessed Virgin had mastered the trivium and quadrivium, and whether she would have been free from original sin if she had died before Christ was born. Yet, on the days when the royal gardens were opened to the schoolmen and their students, these and other riddles served Eleanor and the ladies of her court as exercises in lateral thinking. Then as now, an intelligent mind sought food for thought and Paris had the best diet available, but where in the spectrum of *belief* did Eleanor fit?

Louis' views influenced her not at all, in religion or anything else. In the course of her first marriage, she confronted Suger, Bernard and many other powerful churchmen. Yet she had no especial sympathy for Peter de Bruys or Abelard either, even if the thought of so powerful a man castrated for love of a girl who had been approximately her own age at the time was exciting.

Throughout her life, Eleanor gave generously to religious foundations and solicited their prayers for herself and family, but this was no more than conventional prudence. Warriors like her father dropped dead in their prime, healthy young women like herself died in child-birth, children died for no known reason; the bite of a flea could lead to agonising death. In such uncertain times, it was foolish not to pay one's respects to the deity one might meet so soon. Of all her children, only the devout Richard Coeur de Lion – the child she most influenced – paid more than lip-service to religion, and John was an atheist. She herself narrowly escaped excommunication on at least one occasion, treating papal legates as lackeys and once calling a pope to heel.

The key to understanding Eleanor is to see her as the true granddaughter of William IX – a pagan, happy to give donations and outwardly respect the Church but lacking the instinct for monotheism. The Romans had not persecuted Christians because of their faith, but because they refused to observe the cult of the emperor. Augustus even exempted the monotheistic Jews from sacrificing to him, but his successors could hardly exempt all Christians from whatever race, since to do so was tantamount to abolishing the imperial cult. What other deities the subject races worshipped in addition was their own business. Intolerance came in only after Constantine made Christianity the state religion in the fourth century, but pagan, tolerant Aquitaine did not change. Bordeaux had no equivalent of the martyrology of Paris and Lyon, for the early Christians had been tolerated there, not persecuted.

Throughout the fifteen years of their marriage, Louis' queen fell foul of the Church time and again because she saw it as not deserving any more respect than other religions and its bishops as vassals whose duty was to support their overlord with counsel when asked and military support when required – nothing more. While William IX and his son had been able to get away with such an attitude as dukes of faraway Aquitaine, it was to the Frankish establishment deeply offensive in the queen of France, who was supposed to be a model of piety and modesty.

Eleanor had to wait until Christmas 1137 for her first real escape from the claustrophobic life on the Ile de la Cité. Although Louis had been crowned king in Reims Cathedral by Pope Innocent II in 1131 when his brother died, Suger thought it politically a good move to have him formally recrowned and Eleanor officially installed as queen. The place chosen was Bourges in central France, once capital of Charlemagne's kingdom of Aquitaine and whose archbishop still holds the title 'Primate of the Aquitains'.

In the Romanesque cathedral[7] surmounting the town girdled by its Roman walls with fifty towers and four great gates leading north, south, east and west, the barons of France came to pay homage. There was little space to accommodate their entourages within the walls, so, despite the season, tents and pavilions spread out into the countryside from the Bourg St Sulpice where the market and fair were held. With the lack of quality grazing at that time of year, even to cater for the two or three horses of each of the several thousand knights was a logistical achievement.

Eleanor and her ladies visited the shrine of St Solange, patron of the county of Berry, and offered prayers to the saint who had chosen martyrdom rather than renounce her virginity, after which the queen watched Louis recrowned in the incense-scented gloom of the gilded, painted cathedral, lit by hundreds of flickering candles. After accepting vows of fealty from the battle-hardened barons of his realm, the young king gave each one the kiss of peace upon the lips. Eleanor's feelings were mixed. Thus far, the novelty of her position was exciting: continually testing her power over her husband, she had won the battle with his formidable mother and distanced him from his father's advisers and his own teachers. Yet he fell far short of the men she had learned to admire in childhood; though besotted with her, when he was not making all-night vigil on his knees in the palace chapel, he usually slept alone or like a sister beside the queen of France, reputed as far away as Germany for being the paragon of beauty.[8]

Less than a month after the coronation, in January 1138, her influence over Louis caused him to show blatant disregard for the Church he had so loved. The see of Reims being vacant after the death of Archbishop Reynald, the citizens set up a self-governing commune. Fat Louis would have put down the rebellion to strengthen the position of the future archbishop, their immediate overlord. Instead, Young Louis accepted payment to grant them a charter of rights, thereby weakening the authority of the incoming prelate and indirectly of his own most important vassal, Thibault of Champagne, who had been his father's palatine count.[9]

Soon afterwards came news of similar unrest at Poitiers, where the comital palace had been occupied by the townsfolk, who were fortifying city walls fallen into disrepair with hurriedly thrown-up earth ramparts surmounted by palisades. A fuse of civil unrest had been lit and was travelling throughout Poitou.

At Orleans, Louis had been firm but fair. At Reims, he had been prepared to negotiate for money and political advantage. At Poitiers, Eleanor's influence on him is clear, for his reaction had more in keeping with her father and grandfather than an ex-novice of Notre Dame. Instead of sounding out the threat to his comital power, he ordered Thibault of Champagne to join him in suppressing the rebellion by force of arms.

To put this inexperienced monarch and his dominant young wife in their places, Thibault replied that custom demanded he first consult his vassals, who included Louis' mother. Angrily, Louis departed precipitately for Poitou with a small force of 200 knights, plus archers and some siege engines. Once there, their numbers were swollen by the nobles of the county, who had good reason to strangle at birth this new social development.

Seeing the forces arrayed against them, the rebels surrendered, but Louis showed a side of his character that would increasingly alarm Suger and his other ecclesiastical mentors. Forcing priests to release the ringleaders from their oath of conspiracy, he announced that their children of both sexes would be taken hostage and dispersed throughout the kingdom as a guarantee of future good behaviour.[10]

Suger had been celebrating the feast-day of St Denis at the abbey. When the offices ended, he took horse for Poitiers in the hope of calming the situation. Before he even came in sight of the city, distraught citizens were throwing themselves prostrate in his path, begging him to use his influence with the king. In a private meeting between abbot and monarch, Suger counselled clemency as a way of earning future loyalty. Preparations for the exile were then allowed to go ahead until the square in front of the palace was crowded with weeping parents and children, and the horses, mules and wagons which were to take them away. Only then did Louis announce amid great rejoicing that he had rescinded the order on condition that there was no more talk of rebellion.

Confirming as seneschal William X's man Guillaume de Mauzé, he then rode with him the length and breadth of the county, appointing new administrators or confirming the existing ones in office, a step that would normally have been taken immediately after the marriage. It was in the course of this feudal exercise that Louis was guilty of his first atrocity. North of La Rochelle, a vassal named Guillaume de Lezay had taken advantage of the civil unrest to occupy the town of Talmond, with its comital hunting establishment of servants, dogs, horses and the rare white gyrfalcons.

Persuaded with difficulty to return the town to the king's representatives, Lezay retreated into the castle, refusing to surrender except to Louis, with whom he was co-seigneur. Scenting an ambush, Suger and the bishop of Soissons kept the king in the rear of the cortège while the advance guard entered the castle. Wrong-footed by this precedence, Lezay allowed through the gate only ransomable knights. Forcibly disarmed, they shouted a warning to their fellows still outside, whereupon he ordered his knights and men-at-arms to make a sortie and attack.

Driven off by Louis' escort, they were pursued back to the castle. Before the gate could be closed or portcullis lowered, the king's men were inside. Giving no quarter, they drove the handful of survivors into the donjon. What happened to Lezay is unknown, but there is no mention of him after that day. Suger, however, records that Louis punished two of the rebel knights by personally cutting off their feet. It was not an unusual sentence, but was rendered the more horrific because the slightly built young king had not the strength to do the job cleanly, and had to hack his way through bone and sinew with repeated blows of his sword.[11]

Eleanor had remained in Paris, possibly because she was pregnant. Occasionally she did manage to get Louis to do his kingly duty, for at some unrecorded point in the first two years of the marriage she lost a child she was carrying, whether by a fall, an incident on horseback or a simple miscarriage. It was a sad reminder for a vigorous and confident young woman still in her teens that queens too have their sorrows.

Nor was all games and poetry for her and the ladies of her court. The maids-in-waiting were the king's property, to bestow as a way of controlling marriage alliances that might otherwise build dangerous power blocks in the kingdom. However, evidence is accumulating that medieval queens played a large part in arranging the marriages of their own daughters and the unattached women of their court. Eleanor's position of power meant that she could persuade Louis to arrange marriages which ensured knights owing her gratitude for their wives' dowries when they were consulted in council by their overlords. Her mother-in-law Adelaide de Maurienne had exercised considerable power during Fat Louis' reign, partly in this way. Given the unrelenting hostility of the Frankish nobility towards Eleanor, however, it would seem that she failed to exploit this powerful weapon, displaying an unwarranted assumption of her own political invulnerability.

It was a similar failing that caused Abelard's fall. Popular as he was with the ladies of Paris – Héloïse mentioned in a letter[12] how they clustered at windows of their houses to watch him pass by – and with the students, high on the rarified intellectual air of Paris and avid for controversy, he continued to provoke the religious establishment. No one felt able to risk putting the great master of rhetoric in his place until Abbot Guillaume de St Thierry begged the most influential figure in western Christendom to leave the peace of Clairvaux Abbey and return briefly to the world whose pleasures and temptations he despised. The conflict of emotions inspired by Abelard's intellect and teachings is evident in Guillaume's letter to Bernard: 'God knows I love this man, but in a case like this no one is my relative, no one my friend.'[13]

Abbé Bernard was living in what was considered the image of Christ: poverty and near-constant fasting in his cell at the abbey. Yet his otherworldliness did not prevent him from lobbying in the service of God. Condemning the employment of learning and secular philosophy in matters of faith, he wrote to cardinals, bishops and the pope, likening Abelard to the Philistine giant Goliath.[14]

Born like Abelard into an equestrian family, Bernard was twenty-one when he decided upon the religious vocation in 1111, and saw in the practice of parents presenting oblates to the Church the main cause of lack of commitment in many religious. His own choice of order was the little-known foundation of Cîteaux, set up by Robert de Molesme some years before in order to return to the original teachings of St Benedict. So harsh was the Cistercian Rule under the ascetic English abbot and future saint Stephen Harding that the community was dying out for lack of recruits until Bernard arrived with thirty friends and such a fire of true belief burning in his soul that within three years he was charged with establishing a daughter house at Clairvaux.

His popular image in an age when great preachers had followings like those of modern media stars was of a man so withdrawn from the world as to be already on the threshold of heaven. Yet he never hesitated to criticise wrongdoers, both religious and lay, and lobbied tirelessly for causes in which he believed, from the disputed election of the bishop of York or the German Emperor's support of the anti-pope Anacletus II against Innocent II.

There is in Bernard's letters a wealth of good sense and a richness of poetry, playful punning and a pleasure in the precision and conciseness of Latin that challenge the translator.[15] The energy he put into them is best expressed in his own words:

> How can the mind be quiet when composing a letter and a turmoil of expressions is clamouring and all sort of phrases and diversity of senses are jostling each other, when words spring into the mind but just the one word one wants escapes the mind, when literary effect, sense and how to convey a meaning clearly, and what should be said and in what order it should be said, has to be carefully considered?[16]

Every writer knows the feeling.

Regretting his time spent otherwise than in contemplation and governing his monastery and its daughter houses, Bernard deprecated himself for being 'a sort of modern chimera, neither cleric nor layman. I have kept the habit of a monk but have long ago abandoned the life.'[17] Emerging from Clairvaux at St Thierry's behest and racked by the ill-health that dogged him – not helped by a punishingly poor diet, repeated all-night vigils and a workload that exhausted two secretaries – Bernard spent Lent of 1140 in the schools of Paris, by sheer revivalist charisma weaning many young minds away from Abelard's teaching.[18]

Although maintaining that he prepared nothing for these public appearances, but relied on the inspiration of the Holy Spirit, the future saint of Clairvaux was a far shrewder person than his popular image suggested. His tactics worked brilliantly to drive Abelard into a corner, where he appealed for an examination of his alleged heresies by a competent consistory.

Paris being in the see of Sens, it was there that he must be judged. The throng of pilgrims, curious to see the relics and the latest progress of William of Sens' cathedral, would anyway have been dense even without Bernard's announcement that he would sit with the doctors judging the case. After Mass in the cathedral on the feast of Pentecost, he offered prayers for an unnamed unbeliever – which Abelard never professed to be. That evening there was a meeting between the two adversaries before witnesses.

On the following day, the cathedral was crowded. It is safe to assume that neither Eleanor nor Becket would have missed such a contest of giants. In the presence of the bishop of Chartres as papal legate, no fewer than ten bishops in their regalia sat on one side of the choir, supported by uncounted abbots in all their pomp and finery. In their midst, dressed his simple monk's robe, sat the misleadingly frail figure of Abbé Bernard.

Bernard was extremely emaciated. The mass of the population who were hungry most of their lives were impressed by the idea of voluntary starvation by someone to whom food was available. Also, fasting helped depress sexual urges and increased the frequency of visions in those disposed to them. In addition, many religious believed, like the early Church Father Tertullian, that an emaciated body would more easily pass through the portals of paradise.[19]

Representing the temporal power in the opposite stalls, Louis sat with his barons led by Thibault of Champagne and the count of Nevers. Between them, facing the altar and with his back to the crowded nave, stood the solitary figure of Abelard, marshalling his powers of rhetoric for the performance of his life.

However, Bernard would not give the devil an even break. Instead of allowing himself to be drawn into a verbal slugging match, he read out one offending passage after another from Abelard's books without giving their author a moment to defend himself. The congregation, come to witness the debate of the century, began to whisper that the case must have been already judged by the bishops in camera – which is exactly what Bernard had arranged the previous evening in the chapter house.

Seeing from the faces of the prelates and the nobility that he was condemned, Abelard anticipated his judges' decision by announcing that he refused to be reprimanded like a disobedient clerk and would appeal to Rome. Mustering his supporters – those in holy orders would later be punished – he strode out of the cathedral to the astonishment of all except Bernard. As far as he was concerned, the Holy Spirit had driven the instrument of the devil from the sanctuary.

The findings of the Council of Sens were confirmed by Pope Innocent II, primed in advance by Bernard. Broken in spirit and physically ailing, Abelard retired to the Benedictine abbey of Cluny founded two centuries before in southern Burgundy by Duke William the Pious of Aquitaine. There he spent his last months, dying in the habit of a Cluniac monk at the priory of St Marcel on 21 April 1142. He was survived for twenty-two years by the passionate lover who had once written to him, 'I should rather be your whore than the wife of the Emperor Augustus', but was later reduced to asking his advice for her nuns following the Rule intended by St Benedict for monks, which laid down the wearing of woollen drawers. These, she complained, were unsuitable for women by virtue of the 'monthly purging of their superfluous humours'.[20] Abelard's remains, first buried at her convent of the Paraclete, now lie side by side with hers in the Parisian celebrity cemetery of Père Lachaise.

It was at Sens that Eleanor and Bernard first crossed paths for, unlike Suger, the abbot of Clairvaux eschewed the company of temporal rulers. Yet neither abbot would have approved the next move she was planning. In December of the same year, she and Louis travelled to Orleans, where they met a delegation from Poitou including Geoffroi de Rancon and his namesake, the self-exiled archbishop of Bordeaux,[21] together with the seneschal Guillaume de Mauzé.

In the customary mixture of feudal administration, while Louis was discussing the choice of a new bishop for Poitiers, Eleanor's aunt the abbess of Saintes was seeking confirmation of the abbey's exclusive franchise for currency exchange in the diocese. Although Louis signed the charter as duke, Eleanor placed her signature cross on the document to make the point that she was still very much the duchess. Many of his charters issued during the marriage bear a formula such as 'with the consent of Queen Eleanor, duchess of the Aquitains'.[22] Her position was not as secondary as might appear from charters.

The main business at Orleans was the advance planning of a campaign in support of her claim to the breakaway duchy of Toulouse through her grandmother Philippa, the discarded second wife of William IX. At Easter 1141, with the rest of the realm temporarily at peace, a Frankish army led by Louis marched south against Toulouse, its numbers smaller than he had hoped because the influential Thibault of Champagne again refused his support. Correctly, he argued that the king had no business taking arms against a vassal who had given him no offence, whatever the queen's interests.

Instead of awaiting the arrival of his Aquitain allies, Louis attempted to take the city by surprise – and failed. Attempting a siege, for which he was poorly equipped, he failed a second time. What arrangement he reached with Count Alphonse Jourdan is unknown, but must have included reparations. Perhaps as salve for Louis' wounded ego, Eleanor came to meet him in Poitiers. Whatever her political failings, perseverance was not a quality she lacked. The question of Toulouse, which remained an obsession with her throughout both marriages and long afterwards, was eventually to cost her the life of a daughter more than half a century later.

FOUR

'I married a monk'

Eleanor's whole worldview differed from that of Louis and his Frankish court. In the north, suspicion was the normal reaction to new ideas or strange people; in Aquitaine there was a love of novelty and that pagan *convivença* which she never lost, having been brought up in a society enriched by foreigners including Moors and Jews – who came not only to trade fine glassware, jewels, damascene metalwork, exotic textiles and spices from the East but also stayed to settle on the western flank of a vine-covered hill just outside the walls of Bordeaux, still known as *le mont judaïque*.

Merchants from the Port of the Moon are recorded living not only in Christian Spain but also in Toledo, while in Montpellier at the eastern end of the Pyrenees rabbis and imams taught alongside the doctors of the Christian law, to the horror of Simon de Montfort's Frankish bishops just after Eleanor's death. Traders from Bordeaux and Bayonne adventuring into Moorish Spain in time of peace and knights who departed on impromptu crusade all contributed to the melting pot of Aquitaine. So too did the tens of thousands of pilgrims traversing the duchy each year, called in Occitan *romieus* because the original pilgrimage had been a visit to the tombs in Rome of Peter, Paul and other martyrs, although the most popular destination now was Santiago de Compostela, where William X lay buried.

The artefacts these travellers brought back with them ranged from whittled pieces of cork bark for stopping their water gourds to musical instruments like the Arabic *al-yud*, which became 'lute'. Innovative ideas they brought back included the concept of harmony that enabled European music to develop, medicine, astronomy, algebra,[1] and architectural concepts made possible by Hindu–Arabic numerals. The most enduring evidence of the Moorish influence in Eleanor's Aquitaine can be seen in the architecture of the many Romanesque churches and other twelfth-century buildings.

European society had until recently been divided into the three estates of those who fought, those who prayed and those who laboured. The peasants were considered by the Church to be just above the level of the beasts they tended, since God had created Man between himself and the animals, with the potential to resemble whichever he was closer to. Between fifteen and thirty peasant families were required to provide the means for one unpretentious knightly household to be freed from the need to work and equipped to provide military service to the overlord who had enfeoffed it.

The fourth element in the social equation was the centralised monarchy, constantly being challenged by vassals in the continental feudal structure. Increasingly important in Eleanor's lifetime was the fifth element, composed of free craftsmen and merchants in the towns and cities carving out a social niche for themselves and demanding increasing political independence for providing services without which urban civilisation could not develop.

The eventual triumph of monarchy over the Church and magnate government, and the successful interpolation of the bourgeoisie in the social structure, can be said to mark the end of the medieval period. Yet in the twelfth century the Church played a stabilising role in evolving European society through two episcopal initiatives that limited the senseless strife which had inhibited progress for centuries.

The Peace of God[2] was a measure to protect ecclesiastical property and the persons of clerics, pilgrims, merchants, women and peasants. Cattle and domestic animals excepting warhorses were also protected, together with agricultural machinery,[3] because its destruction led to misery and starvation among the peasantry. In Eleanor's Gascony, fishermen too were protected.[4]

The Truce of God[5] prohibited warfare theoretically from Wednesday evening to Monday morning in every week and also during the great vigils and feasts of the Blessed Virgin, the Apostles and a few other saints, plus the seasons of Advent and Lent. March, named for the god of war, thus became a time of truce, although this may have had more to do with the poor nutritional quality of early grass for armies dependent on large numbers of horses than with respect for the Truce.[6]

Infringements against Peace or Truce were sanctioned by penances, interdict and excommunication. The crushing strength of the English monarchy after the Norman Conquest made these measures largely unnecessary north of the English Channel, but in Eleanor's France the Church had the power to make government easier for an overlord who established a *modus vivendi* with his bishops. It can be argued that the attitude of her family to the bishops of Aquitaine was a major reason why the irreligious duchy was virtually ungovernable, outside the major towns like Bordeaux and Bayonne, where the Church did have authority.

Louis' kingdom was not just divided between north and south. There was no common system of law. Loyalties were local or regional at best. The Bretons in the north-west continued to use their Celtic language and the Flemings in the north-east spoke a Low German dialect, both of which survive to this day. Elsewhere in the northern half of Louis' realm his subjects spoke various dialects of the *langue d'oïl*.

This Babel was the source of much ecclesiastical power. The lowest clergy, living in villages with their concubines or 'hearth-women' and broods of children, were forever being criticised for mumbling a few prayers and biblical quotations learned by heart. However, those in holy orders conversed and corresponded fluently in Latin with each other. Diplomacy and the civil service therefore became 'clerical' business, a dual meaning that still survives.

It was thus a very serious matter when Eleanor's dominance caused Louis to fall out with the Church a second time. If the incident at Reims could have been passed off by a little episcopal diplomacy as an error on the part of a young and inexperienced monarch, there was no such excuse for him deliberately refusing to endorse the election of the new archbishop of Bourges in 1141 in order to install his own candidate – exactly as William IX had done.

The chapter had elected Pierre de la Châtre, a Cluniac who was in Rome on Church business. Invested by the pope, he found himself on return to France locked out of his own cathedral on the king's orders. Seeking asylum in the territory of Thibault of Champagne, he was ordered by Innocent II to return to Bourges and take up his duties. At the same time, Innocent admonished Louis for behaving like a foolish schoolboy who should cease meddling in church affairs.

It was hardly a tactful way of reprimanding Eleanor's twenty-year-old husband. With her backing, he escalated the dispute by swearing on holy relics a solemn oath not to recant,[7] to which the pope replied by excommunicating him. Appalled that this should happen to a pupil who had been so promising in his youth, Louis' former teachers pointed the finger of blame at Eleanor.

Yet on their next visit to Poitou in the summer of 1142 he and she as count and countess confirmed all the gifts and privileges that their predecessors had granted to the churches and monasteries of Saintonge and Poitou and ordered some Limousin nobles to repair damage they had done to the abbey of Solignac. They arbitrated a dispute over the succession to the viscounty of Limoges, the most important of the four into which the county was divided and ordered a certain Gausbert de Nobiliaco to release one of their functionaries he had imprisoned.

Some petitioners never knew when to stop. Having succeeded in her first request, Eleanor's aunt the abbess of Saintes had a hundred others to make. The queen's charter granting them was approved not only by Louis but also by ever-present Aelith, which implies that she had some rights in the matter. The presence of Eleanor's chaplain Pierre, acting as her chancellor, shows that she had acquired a seal of her own.

This was the longest sojourn in Poitou of the entire marriage. After a few days in the royal palace at St Jean d'Angély, they travelled onwards to Niort, Louis' cousin Raoul de Vermandois acting as his steward as usual. From Niort, the household wended its way west for a holiday in the pacified Talmond hunting forest, where a less bellicose son-in-law of Guillaume de Lezay was now Louis' co-seigneur of the castle. Progress was interrupted repeatedly by petitioners waiting en route for a hearing. Abbots and abbesses requesting largesse alternated with a troupe of lepers playing flutes as a way of earning a living without actually begging or the distressed widow of a knight who had mortgaged all his property to go on crusade and never returned. For those with no chance of going or sending a petition to Paris, or even to Poitiers, it was a rare chance to seek justice or charity.

An incident during this idyllic interlude marks the beginning of the end of Eleanor's marriage to Louis. Aelith, who had caught the eye of Raoul de Vermandois at the wedding in Bordeaux, was now seventeen and in the full bloom of womanhood. Wealthy in her own right and with the poise and polish that came from four years of being treated as the queen's sister, and travelling everywhere with her, she was a very desirable catch.

At some point on the trip through Poitou during the late summer of 1142, which the two spent in close proximity, Vermandois asked Louis' permission to marry Aelith[8] and thus unite her dower properties in Burgundy to his spread of fiefs between Flanders and the Vexin. That the king's cousin was more than twice the age of Aelith and already married cannot have seemed a great impediment to either granddaughter of William IX, but Louis should have taken pause for thought since his cousin's wife Eleanor of Champagne was a niece of Count Thibault. Instead, to please Eleanor, he consented, providing the canonical requirements for a divorce could be satisfied.

Eleanor was still trying to make a warrior out of Louis. While the royal household mixed business and pleasure in the Talmond, his army had been marching north from Toulouse. The feudal obligation of knight service for forty days a year was already going out of fashion. Louis, like so many other overlords, preferred *scutage* or shield-money in lieu of service, which enabled him to hire reliable professional mercenaries – the word 'soldier' meaning originally anyone who serves for pay.

Joining the army at Tours, whose citizens had dug defensive ditches and fortified the walls without permission, he set up camp outside the city. From this position of strength he made a deal very different from his reaction to the uprising in Poitiers. In return for payment of a fine of 500 marks, which enabled him to pay off his mercenaries, Tours was permitted to keep its walls and ditches. After the return to Paris, three compliant bishops were found outside the see of Sens to dissolve Raoul de Vermandois' marriage on the usual ground of consanguinity, after which the bishop of Noyon – who was his brother – joined with the prelates of Laon and Senlis to unite the disparate couple in holy matrimony.

Count Thibault, as befitted a grandson of William the Conqueror, was not a man to take lightly the humiliation of a niece who, deprived of her dower lands, placed herself and her children under his protection. He enlisted Bernard of Clairvaux in her cause, the land on which Clairvaux stood having been given to the Order by Thibault's father, Hugh of Champagne. No sooner had Bernard's letter reached the pope than the three offending bishops were excommunicated at the council of Lagny-sur-Marne in Champagne, Aelith's marriage was declared invalid and Vermandois was ordered to take back his lawful wedded wife. He refused and was also excommunicated.

With the Vermandois domains placed under interdict, Eleanor persuaded Louis that Thibault needed to be taught a lesson. The month of January 1143 saw the royal army laying Champagne waste in a campaign that culminated in the torching of the lath-and-plaster houses with thatched roofs in the town of Vitry on the River Marne. The only military target was the wooden motte-and-bailey castle, which was attacked with fire arrows and set alight. From his vantage point on a nearby hill, Louis watched as the mercenaries also set fire, whether by accident or design, to the houses around the castle. The terrified civilians fled to the sanctuary of the church, whose roof too caught fire from wind-borne embers. When this fell in on the mass of people beneath, 1,300 unarmed men, women and children died.

While it was inevitable that the masses suffered in every campaign, such a blatant transgression of the Peace of God earned excommunication for Louis. Denied the consolation of confession, absolution and the Blessed Sacrament, torn between his fear of the Last Judgement and his puppyish devotion to Eleanor, he fell into a deep depression, which she could neither understand nor cure.

To repair the royal finances, diminished by the campaign in Champagne, was an immediate priority. The expanding economy of the cities all over Europe required venture capital, which was hard to obtain because lending money at interest was forbidden to Christians. Informed that the progressive citizens of Tours were nevertheless making a very lucrative business out of usury, Louis returned there in August 1143 – not to put a stop to it, but to name his price. In return for a payment of 30,000 *sous*, the banking activities were legalised and repayment of loans made legally binding.

After Pope Innocent died on 24 September, his successor Celestine II lifted the interdict on the royal household at the instigation of Bernard of Clairvaux.[9] His guilt still unassuaged, Louis fell ill. On his recovery, he became even less kingly and more monkish, wearing a gown and sandals and having his head shaved into a tonsure.

The still-exiled archbishop of Bordeaux was one of many prelates present at the council at Corbeil, called early in 1144 to settle the dispute with the count of Champagne. The bishop of Laon had changed sides and drawn up a genealogical table proving what everyone knew: that Aelith and her husband were within the prohibited degrees. Bernard of Clairvaux was tirelessly active behind the scenes, corresponding with Louis and Pope Innocent, among many others.[10] To Bishop Stephen of Palestrina, he wrote of Louis, 'What right has this man to break up the marriage (between

Vermandois and his first wife) on the grounds of consanguinity when, as all the world knows, he himself married a woman to whom he is related in the fourth degree?'[11]

The council ended in stalemate, with the matter transferred to the abbey of St Denis as a court of appeal. Eleanor went there herself to plead the cause of her sister, but without success. No longer was the abbey of St Denis a combined chancery and war office, as it had been during Fat Louis' reign. In response to Bernard's nagging, Suger had reduced the pomp and circumstance of his personal life and was devoting himself to the construction of his new basilica.

Abbé Bernard had no doubt about the true cause of Suger's exclusion from the councils of state, and warned the king by letter not to listen to the counsel of the devil.

> For from whom can I say this comes that adds fire to fire and slaughter to slaughter, which raises the laments of the poor and the groans of the captives to the ears of the father of orphans and the judge of widows? Do not, O king, lift your hand against the terrible Lord who takes away the breath of kings. If I speak sharply, it is because I fear sharp things for you.[12]

It was saintly Bernard's way to admonish Louis while praying for his soul; Suger the statesman, dismissed by his king, devised a more practical solution to the problem of bringing Louis back into the bosom of the Church by inviting him to play an important part in the imminent inauguration of the partly built basilica, in the hope that this would stimulate his hunger for the religious life in which he had been so active before Eleanor came on the scene.

Not since the dedication of Cluny by Pope Innocent twelve years before had there been a consecration on this scale in France. On 10 June 1144 Louis arrived at St Denis in time to share the all-night vigil of the monks. Reconciled for the occasion with her son and Eleanor, Adelaide de Maurienne was in the royal party. Next morning the magnificent gleaming bronze doors of the basilica depicting the Passion and Resurrection opened wide for the greatest in the land. Above them, as a *memento mori*, the carved tympanum showed Christ enthroned in judgement over the elders of Israel. Inside, eyes used to the thick columns and round arches of the Romanesque style were literally opened wide by the new perpendicular style, with soaring columns topped by broken arches and the ribbing of the roof floating far above the worshippers' heads.

On every side, precious metals gleamed in the light shafting down from the slim and elegant windows that retold biblical stories in rainbow-hued stained glass for the edification of the illiterate majority gaping at the riches on display. The floor could have been strewn with gold dust or ashes, for all anyone could see. There was not an inch of unoccupied space. Louis, accorded no regal respect in his anonymous penitent's gown, had to beat a passage through the throng with a staff.[13] In contrast, Eleanor was dressed in a costly gown of damask and wearing a queenly diadem.

A total of nineteen prelates, including the archbishops of Paris, Rouen, Canterbury and Bordeaux asperged the still incomplete building with holy water and consecrated the many altars. Hymns were chanted, blessings pronounced, prayers offered up like the clouds of incense writhing higher and higher through the beams of light. In Suger's scenario, the king and a dozen knights played the parts of Christ and the Apostles.[14] To proclaim his rehabilitation, Louis was entrusted with carrying in the procession the holiest reliquary of all, a bejewelled chest containing – *pace* Abelard – bones reputedly of Dionysius the Areopagite.

To the chanting of the choirs and the obeisance of the congregation, he bore it to the shrine of porphyry and marble with its retable of gold encrusted with gemstones. In front of that towered the huge golden cross of the transept, studded with cabochon-cut gems. Standing there, only a few paces from the tombs of his brother and the preceding Capetian monarchs, Louis could not fail to reflect on the mortality of kings, of which Bernard had reminded him.

'No one,' said Gervase the chronicler, 'would have taken the king for that scourge of war who had recently destroyed so many towns, burned so many churches and shed so much blood. The spirit of penitence shone in his face.'[15]

For the occasion, Eleanor's gift was an antique vase of rock crystal set with gold from the family treasury in Poitou, for use at the high altar of St Denis. One of the few objects extant that are known to have been handled by her, it is today in the Louvre Museum, the subject of a twofold mystery. First, Suger diplomatically distanced himself and the Church from the donor by having it engraved, 'This vase Mitadolus gave to an ancestor of Aanor [Eleanor]; she, his bride, gave it to King Louis; the king gave it to me; and I, Suger, gave it to the saints.'[16] Second, old things then had no especial value and a more appropriate present from Eleanor would have been an altarpiece in the intricate enamelwork for which Limoges was famous.

The donations were organised in the manner of an *auxilium* tax, for the basilica was the daughter of the Church and every grandee of France had contributed something precious. Thibault of Champagne had given a present of cabochon rubies and zircons for the altar. Euphoric with the spirit of the proceedings, Louis found himself face to face with the count he had done much to injure in the seven years since coming to the throne. Abbé Bernard had come from Clairvaux for the occasion. Louis' evident contrition confirmed the future saint's belief that the king was not to blame for the evil advice which had led to Vitry. Instead of haranguing him on the sinfulness of his ways, Bernard spoke of redemption and forgiveness, warning Eleanor to use her great influence over Louis to save his soul from eternal damnation.

She showed none of the king's anguish and soul-seeking, but instead tried to manoeuvre Bernard into getting the pope to reverse his decision and bless the marriage of Aelith and Vermandois. Despite her use of dialectic to prove the rightness of her cause and the offer of what amounted to a bribe for his monastery, Bernard refused. How could this daughter of Eve be so insensible to her husband's agony of soul, for which she was responsible? Rebuking her for meddling in the affairs of state, he turned his back on her and strode away.

It was the first time he had met her since the Council of Sens, but not even an anchorite could have failed to hear about her scandalous life of music and poetry, cosmetics and jewellery, in which modesty and piety were absent. Even in his cell, reputedly the least comfortable of any in the abbey of Clairvaux – more of a broom cupboard under the stairs than a proper room – her reputation had reached him.

Like father, like daughter, he must have thought. For Bernard knew Eleanor's family well, being distantly related to them. After refusing to rubber-stamp the election of bishops, William X had, like his father, been excommunicated and refused to give in to pressure from his subjects in those sees deprived by interdict of the sacrament on his account. To resolve the deadlock, the bishops of Poitou appealed to Bernard, who relentlessly pursued the duke, seeking a confrontation on their behalf.

Determined to sort out the meddlesome cleric, William rode to Parthenay where Bernard was preaching. Since not even he dared defy excommunication by entering the church, he dismounted and waited in the narthex.[17] Hearing his arrival, Bernard interrupted the service, grabbed the pyx – the ornamented box in which consecrated bread was kept – and ran down the aisle, to emerge brandishing it in William's face like an exorcist defying the foul fiend.

The disparity in their physical appearance verged on the ridiculous: Bernard tall and gaunt from illness and fasting; William a broad-shouldered warrior with all the confidence of one born to rule. But it was he who quailed and Bernard who prevailed, adjuring the duke to restore his dispossessed bishops, confess his sins and do penance. Recoiling from this verbal assault, William stumbled and fell, speechless and foaming at the mouth, whether from rage or because he was stunned. Eyewitness accounts of the brief fracas became part of the legend of Bernard of Clairvaux, for shortly thereafter the Host was restored in Aquitaine and bells summoned the faithful to Mass once more after William's acceptance of his elected bishops.

Suger's success was less miraculous, but by bringing together Louis and Thibault at the consecration ceremony, he had laid the foundation for a treaty. Louis agreed to recant his impetuous oath preventing Pierre de la Châtre from taking up his duties as bishop of Bourges and to restore to the count his war-ravaged territory in return for some concessions on the other side. However, despite Eleanor's intervention, there was no mention of lifting the interdict on the house of Vermandois. Nor could anyone think of a suitable penance to atone for the king's sin at Vitry.

Eleanor's public rebuttal by Bernard at St Denis did not stop her consulting him over a more intimate problem. This time, she approached him not as a queen but as a humble supplicant, knowing that he turned away no one in need. Widows, orphans, the dispossessed and those seeking guidance on matters spiritual – they wrote to Bernard in their hundreds. To judge by the extant copies of his correspondence, he was never too busy to use his influence in their favour in prayer or by threatening with hellfire or seducing with sweet talk their temporal oppressors.

Louis' queen was twenty-two and had yet to produce a living child. Given the frequent pregnancies of her second marriage, her fertility is in no doubt. Louis also fathered children without problems after their separation. The seven childless years since the wedding in Bordeaux Cathedral were due to the rarity of their coupling. Possibly he was unmanned from the beginning by her physical beauty and sexual appetite. Certainly, weighed down by his burden of guilt, he spent more nights after Vitry on his knees in the royal chapel than in her bed. Eleanor's frequent complaint, 'I thought I had wed a king and found I had married a monk',[18] says everything about the frustration of her marriage.

Bernard assured her that he would support her prayers to the Virgin Mary for a child. Since many monks worked as doctors until this was forbidden by canon law, it is possible that the assistance he gave went further than prayer. Or perhaps a letter of Bernard's urging the king to do his conjugal duty has gone astray? At any rate, shortly afterwards Eleanor was pregnant.

Midwifery as then practised was non-interventionist; although the French *sage-femme* implies some learning, the corresponding Anglo-Saxon term 'midwife' means merely an attendant who is 'with the woman'. The probably Salernitan[19] midwife attending Eleanor was no different from any other specialist servant with herbal lotions, fumigation and pepper, used to speed up a birth by making the mother sneeze repeatedly. The only intervention permitted was a Caesarean section such as Eleanor's daughter Matilda would undergo in Rouen, but this was sanctioned by the Church uniquely when the mother was already dead and it was the only way to save the soul of the infant by baptism, even if it died immediately afterwards.

The birth went well. Eleanor's first live child was born in the palace on the Ile de la Cité without complications but in front of witnesses, so that there could be no substitution. This was not the son Louis needed, but a daughter named Marie in honour of the Virgin hearing the queen's and Bernard's prayers. The fashion of the times required noble ladies to have small, high bosoms and offered little in the way of underpinnings to counterfeit this. Partly for that reason and also because breast-feeding was thought to prevent production of 'female sperm' necessary for conception and the state still urgently needed a prince, the infant princess was put out to a carefully selected wet-nurse and therefore took up little of her mother's time.

FIVE

Crusading Fever Sweeps Europe

Boredom – or *accidia*, the condition of spiritual aridity – was a mortal sin. But Eleanor, raised in the intellectual freedom of Aquitaine, could not be satisfied for ever by debates about Universals and the unfathomable nature of the Holy Trinity. Her reaction was mingled relief and excitement when messengers from the Latin Kingdom of Jerusalem brought to Paris early in 1145 an appeal that was to trigger the Second Crusade.[1]

The Latin Kingdom – referred to as Outremer, or 'Overseas' – corresponded roughly to modern Israel plus parts of southern and coastal Lebanon and a section of Jordan. It included four baronies – the lordship of Krak or Montréal in the south, the county of Jaffa and Ascalon on the coast, and the principalities of Galilee and Sidon in the north – with Jerusalem and Judea plus the cities of Tyre and Acre comprising the royal domain. To the north of the kingdom lay the crusader buffer states of Tripoli, Antioch and Edessa, whose strategic function was to keep at bay the warring Seljuk Turks, followers of Mahomet although ethnically unrelated to the Arab races.

It was already rumoured in Europe that their wily *atabeg* Zengi had made an unprovoked sneak attack during the festivities of Christmas on the Christian city of Edessa, known as Rohais in the West, and desecrated its altars, murdering 16,000 of its inhabitants and driving the rest off into slavery.

The truth was that Count Joscelin of Edessa, who preferred living in sybaritic luxury at his estate of Tel Bashir on the upper reaches of the Euphrates to governing his city-state, had been buying off the Turks with presents of European horses, arms and specialists in the making of horse armour. Zengi, as a good strategist, had simply awaited the right moment to besiege Edessa, inhabited by peaceful Armenian and Syrian traders, at a time when it was defended only by a small corps of discontented mercenaries to whom Joscelin owed a year's back-pay. The Syrian Bishop Abu el-Farraj, who was in the city, declared that Joscelin had left few men to man the walls apart from 'shoemakers, weavers, silk merchants, tailors and priests'.[2] He also maintained that Zengi gave the citizens several chances of surrendering and saving their lives.

The nearest crusader city from which help could have been dispatched was Antioch, just north of the modern Syrian/Turkish border. But Antioch was ruled by Eleanor's uncle Raymond, who detested Joscelin to the point of refusing help in the hour of need. Given the rules of the game, Zengi would have been a poor player not to strike when he did.

As reported by Archbishop William of Tyre in his generally trustworthy *History of Deeds Done Overseas*,[3] the Turkish attack had been a textbook military operation. While Joscelin kept out of the way at Tel Bashir, waiting for help from Jerusalem or Antioch, an efficient blockade of Edessa, stocked neither with food nor weapons thanks to his parsimony and indolence, was followed by a brief siege. Barrages of arrows from the ground and the platforms of siege-towers higher than the walls kept them virtually unmanned as catapults and rams battered away at their bases and sappers tunnelled beneath them. When the props were fired and a section of wall collapsed, the Turks rushed through the breach into the city.

The terrified inhabitants made for the safety of the citadel, in whose entrance there was such a crush of people that, long before the Turks reached them, men and women were climbing over the bodies of those crushed to death in the effort to get in.[4] Casualties included Archbishop Hugh of Edessa, clutching a chest full of the taxes he had levied to pay the mercenaries, but kept for himself.

Zengi personally intervened to halt the massacre of civilians, sending his second-in-command to negotiate with Abu el-Farraj, in return for whose oath of loyalty sworn on the New Testament safe conducts were given to the Syrians and Armenians. From the Franks, however, everything was taken: gold, silver, holy objects and jewellery. Their priests and notables were led off in chains to the slave market of Aleppo, while skilled artisans were put to work at their trades. About 100 Frankish knights and men-at-arms were executed.[5]

During the entire disaster, in which 6,000 people died, Prince Raymond did nothing, despite the fact that the fall of Edessa put his principality next in line for Turkish attack. By the time distant and disorganised Jerusalem had concerted help, it was too late.

Founded after the First Crusade, the Latin Kingdom was carpet-bagger territory, up for grabs from start to finish by French lords audacious enough to carve out a fief for themselves and strong and ruthless enough to hold it. Many died prematurely from disease or in combat with each other or the common enemy, leaving sons too young to govern or daughters who were forcibly taken in marriage to give a cloak of legitimacy to their successors. Between the conflicts with Muslim neighbours, the princes and barons of Outremer squabbled and skirmished, conspiring with Greeks against Turks and with Turks against their fellow Christians and welcoming traders of any race or religion.

Among the emissaries sent to beg for military support from Europe after the fall of Edessa was Prince Raymond's friend and vassal, the bishop of Djebail. To the first rumours of disaster in the East, he added political and military argument. The recent death of King Fulk of Jerusalem had left the Latin Kingdom in the hands of his widow Queen Melisende as regent for their thirteen-year-old son, Baldwin II. With Joscelin's city firmly in the hands of the infidel and the ruling houses of the kingdom enfeebled by deaths and disputes over succession, the Holy Land might soon be lost again to the infidel.

> Pris est Rohais, ben le savetz.
> Dunt crestiens sunt esmaietz.
> Les mustiers ars e desertez.
> Deus n'i est mais sacrifietz.

[Edessa has fallen, as well you know. / For Christians this is great woe. / Her altars are desecrated / and Mass no more celebrated.]

If Louis listened in pious horror, Eleanor's concern was personal. Prince Raymond was her father's younger brother, only ten years older than herself. Casting about for his place in the sun, he had rejected the clerical career of a landless younger son of the nobility because he preferred a sword in his hand, food in his belly and the rousing music of a *chanson de geste* in his ears to the bishop's crosier, fasting and the sound of the litany.

The first time fortune smiled on him was after the calamity of the sinking of the White Ship at Barfleur in 1120, when Henry I of England lost his bastard sons and his heir. Taking Raymond into his household, he dubbed him knight – at the time *adouber* meant giving arms, a destrier and armour to the candidate, and ceremonially buckling on his sword belt.

As a landless knight errant Raymond still had to marry a rich heiress or show prowess in the field that might be rewarded by a fief of his own. His second break came in 1135 with the news that Bohemund, Prince of Antioch, had died leaving no son to succeed him. His vassals, unwilling to lose their privileges by being absorbed directly into the fief of Jerusalem, were seeking urgently to replace Bohemund by an unattached knight of noble lineage who was not too closely related to any royal family.

Politely described as *sage et apercevanz*, Raymond was both shrewd and ruthless. He was also courageous and skilled at arms, all of which made him an ideal choice. Knowing that he was not the only contender, and to make sure of arriving first in the field, he divided his entourage into small groups that travelled separately through France and along the Mediterranean littoral mingling with the stream of pilgrims, traders and fortune-hunters flowing from Europe to the East and back.

Arriving in Antioch disguised as a humble pilgrim or peddler, and with his rivals far behind, he quickly summed up the situation. The original offer had been for him to marry Bohemund's pragmatic widow, who had been putting out feelers to the Turks in Edessa for an accommodation that would permit her to keep the reins of power in her hands. While initially accepting the widow's lavish hospitality and letting her suppose he intended marriage, Raymond decided to espouse Bohemund's more pliant nine-year-old daughter Constance, who was also a cousin of the king of Jerusalem.

What deal he cut with the patriarch of Antioch is unknown, but prelates in the Latin Kingdom closed their eyes to the moral shortcomings of those strong enough to protect the holy places. The marriage between Raymond and Constance was hastily celebrated in secret, after which the furious discarded widow was banished from the principality, leaving Eleanor's uncle to rule Antioch for ten years of intermittent strife, during which he spared little thought for the land of his birth.

With the fall of Edessa, however, it was to Aquitaine he turned – or more precisely to its reservoir of footloose younger sons of the nobility, of whom he had been one. Later to be immortalised in fiction as the *cadets de Gascogne* in Edmond Rostand's *Cyrano de Bergerac* and Alexandre Dumas' character d'Artagnan, these hotheads with nothing to lose were a permanent source of unrest and brigandage at home, but ideal material for the all-or-nothing adventure of coming to the rescue of the Latin Kingdom established by their own grandfathers. And who better to organise their raising and equipping than Raymond's niece, the queen of the Franks,[6] who, as countess of Poitou and duchess of Aquitaine was also the overlord to whom many of their families owed allegiance?

William of Tyre relates that the prince of Antioch sent to the Capetian royal couple costly presents from all over the Levant. Eleanor certainly needed no such inducement; she would have grasped at any excuse to escape the stifling routine of court life in Paris. Whether they influenced Louis is doubtful, for material greed was not one of his failings, but at last he saw a penance big enough to atone for his sins. What better way to redeem his immortal soul than by answering the call to crusade launched by the new Pope Eugenius III, and at the same time executing his dead elder brother's promise to carry the oriflamme – the golden banner of St Denis, patron saint of the Franks – to Jerusalem and there to deal such a blow to the Saracen hordes as to secure the holy city for ever from the infidel?[7]

> *Chevaliers, cher vus purpensetz*
> *Vus qui d'armes estes preisetz*
> *A celui vos cors presentetz*
> *Qui pur vos fut en cruiz dressetz.*

[O Knights, when you bethink you / what your prowess at arms can do, / offer your bodies to Him who / was nailed to the cross for you.]

While Christian France was deploring the tragedy and whipping up crusading fever, Zengi had been forced to return to Edessa when a plot was discovered for Armenian supporters of Count Joscelin to massacre the Turkish garrison. After they had been killed, he moved into the city 300 Jewish families, on whose loyalty he could rely.[8]

To his credit, Abbot Suger was both sceptical of the crusade's chance of military success[9] and aware that the credulous and mystical nature which would have been so appropriate for Louis' intended career in the priesthood made his monarch, so ill equipped for statecraft, even worse fitted for warfare. Against the perspicacious advice of Suger and his other counsellors that the problems of government required his presence in France, but encouraged by Eleanor for her own personal reasons, Louis wrote to the pope of his burning desire to lead an army to Jerusalem. To his great joy, the reply promised in return remission of the sin of Vitry.

Exiled to the papal estate of Viterbo in Tuscany by the presence of an anti-pope in Rome and fighting heresy and schism on both sides of the Alps, Eugenius III was a former pupil of Bernard of Clairvaux. He saw in the kindling of a pan-European ardour for another crusade the possibility of uniting his divided Church with himself as undisputed patriarch. Naturally he enlisted the support of Abbé Bernard, to whom Louis had confided his ambition. Lacking Suger's political sense, Bernard – until then the advocate of universal peace – endorsed the papal blessing on this martial enterprise and the die was cast.

The long delay before decision was translated into action was partly due to the need to raise finance by taxes and tithes, but there were also diplomatic démarches to be accomplished. So appalling had been the vandalism and looting on the people's crusade led by Peter the Hermit and Walter the Penniless just before the First Crusade that the king of Hungary had afterwards demanded hostages from Godefroi de Bouillon – including his own brother, wife and children – before allowing the French army to transit his country in 1097. Louis therefore wrote to his fellow monarchs in Germany and Hungary requesting safe conducts for the French army to cross their territory on its holy mission.

Further east, Constantinople was the vital jumping-off point where the gap between Europe and Asia narrows to 800 yards in the strait of the Bosporus.[10] From there came a reply from the Byzantine Emperor Manuel Comnenus, promising his Christian brother the king of the Franks all necessary support and encouragement.

The Capetian Christmas court was held that year in Bourges, where Louis was innocently counting on the precedent of the First Crusade, for which the main support had come from a France on the crest of an economic revival after three generations' population growth. Its forest lands were being cleared for cultivation, frontiers pushed forward, markets organised and trading routes from its Mediterranean ports developing as Muslim dominance of the Mediterranean was challenged by armed Italian merchantmen. At the time, England was still adjusting itself to the Norman occupation, Christian Spain was preoccupied with pushing the Moors back into North Africa and Germany had been divided by internal strife, which had enabled Pope Urban II to assume a more active role than his predecessors.

Exactly why European prosperity should have been channelled into a series of holy wars against distant Muslims is something about which historians differ. Part of the answer lay in the eternal greed for land and loot, which the insecure monarchs of continental Europe preferred to deflect towards the lands of the infidel. Partly, the answer lay in the strength of religious feeling among illiterate and ignorant men. To peasants who could never otherwise leave the fields in which they had laboured since birth, the idea of travel to the Holy Land was like a ray of sunlight in the fog-bound claustrophobia of serfdom. For most knights and barons who could rarely afford to be away from their fiefs for long, the two- or three-year expedition, during which their property and families were protected by the Peace of God, was a once-in-a-lifetime adventure. To warriors whose consciences were burdened with guilt for the lives they had taken, remission of sins was another reward. Nor did debts need to be repaid until after the crusade, no interest on borrowed money accruing throughout its duration.

When Urban II preached both the Peace and Truce of God and simultaneously war in the shape of what was to be the First Crusade, his words at the Council of Clermont in 1095 did not seem paradoxical: the holy places were at risk from the Turks; it was therefore the duty of all Christian knights to protect them. His argument was more rhetoric than logic, ignoring the fact that many of the sites were sacred also to Muslims and Jews, and that successive Islamic dynasties controlling the Holy Land had taxed but tolerated Christian and Jewish pilgrimage through the centuries.

However, when Louis argued at the Christmas court of 1145 in Bourges for what would become known as the Second Crusade, the ignorant optimism of the first crusaders had been tempered by hard experience. His barons, assembled to renew their oaths of fealty, were not enthusiastic about sharing his penance by accompanying him to the Holy Land at their own expense.

There were many among them whose grandfathers had set out like Eleanor's, dreaming of gold and glory. If the lucky few had reached the Holy Land and grabbed a personal fief on what had been Muslim soil, many had earned only enough ground to cover their corpses and 70,000 lay still unburied in Cappadocian wadis a long way short of Jerusalem's walls. Of the survivors, most returned to France ruined by an enterprise they had expected to enrich them. Small wonder, then, that Louis' exhortations fell largely on deaf ears.

Eleanor, however, did not present the idea of a new crusade as a penance. In the rousing idiom of their own language, she sold it to her vassals as high adventure, for which it was well worth liquidating assets equal to four or five times their annual income.[11] Among the first to rally to her was the loyal Geoffroi de Rancon, together with two notoriously violent brothers, Hugues VII de Lusignan and Guy de Thouars. Though Louis was cheered by their more enthusiastic response, he was surprised when Eleanor announced the price tag attached to the revenues and reserves of manpower in her domains vital for financing and manning the expedition.

Nothing could shake her firm intention of coming along on the crusade with him and bringing with her a company of adventurous ladies, self-styled Amazons whose participation she justified by saying that their determination to reach Jerusalem would shame the laggards, should the men's enthusiasm flag on the long and arduous journey. As precedents, she cited the tradition of married couples going on pilgrimage together – many thousands of couples traversed Aquitaine every year en route to Compostela. Some women had also accompanied the First Crusade, among them the extraordinary Margravine Ida of Austria who was captured by the Turks and reputedly ended her days in a harem.

In an inspired flight of poetic fantasy, Eleanor likened herself to Penthesilea, the legendary queen who led her fellow Amazons into battle at the siege of Troy. Since Louis intended taking a vow of chastity for the duration of the crusade, it seemed to the chronicler William of Newburgh, writing the *History of English Affairs*[12] in the peace of his Augustinian priory fifty years later, that the king's personal reason for giving in to Eleanor's plan of accompanying him was a gnawing fear of what she might get up to sexually and politically at home during his absence.

Then, as now, business found its niches; by the middle of the twelfth century the constant flow of travellers on the routes to the Holy Land had caused facilities to spring up that had not existed for the First Crusade. These included money-changers at the frontiers, wayside hostels and markets where horses and draught animals could be replaced and provisions purchased for man and beast. There were route maps of the type used by the Romans, useless for giving an idea of the geography of a whole country but adequate for finding one's way from point to point along a set route.

The Brothers of the Militia of the Temple, originally charged by the patriarch of Jerusalem with protecting all Christian pilgrims, had been placed by Pope Innocent II in direct obedience to the papacy. Thus freed from allegiance to local magnates and princes of the Church, the Templars were setting up a chain of castles, estates and treasure houses along the principal pilgrimage routes in fulfilment of their brief. This enabled them to transport valuables safely and issue letters of credit encashable by travellers both en route and in the Holy Land itself. It was the shrewd business acumen of the masters of the Order – whose severe Rule was paradoxically drawn up by unworldly Abbé Bernard after the Council of Troyes in 1128[13] – that would bring about the Templars' ruin. But that lay long in the future.

With all these recent developments to make the journey easier in twelfth-century terms, Eleanor's adventurous ladies regarded joining a crusade as a sort of Grand Tour and a welcome break from their duties of châtelaine and the routine of childbearing, thanks to their husbands' vows of celibacy.

From Viterbo in March 1146 came the letter which was the signal everyone was awaiting. At the end of Lent the great pilgrim church of St Mary Magdalene in Burgundian Vézelay was found too small by far to shelter the crowds who had come to hear Abbé Bernard preach the Christian equivalent of *jihad*. On Easter Day, 31 March, he harangued the common people and assembled lords in the presence of their king and queen, still bound by their Easter vows. In a pulpit erected on the open hillside outside the town, holding aloft the bull bearing Eugenius' seal, the frail old monk, worn out by years of fasting and self-denial, read out in his quavering voice the call, to answer which conferred automatic remission of sins.

Bernard's voice cannot have been heard far from the pulpit, but so many volunteers pressed forward that the supply of crosses ran out and the white woollen cassocks of Bernard and his brother Cistercians had to be cut up to make the signs that would keep a crusader safe from harm on earth or be his passport to paradise.

If legend can be believed, Eleanor and her Amazons showed their usefulness for the first time that very day, galloping around the fringes of the crowd on white stallions and tossing distaffs to faint-hearted or prudent knights, as women were to hand white feathers to men in civilian clothes during the First World War – but with the difference that the Amazons were going to share many of the men's risks.

The bishops of Lisieux and Langres pledged their hosts and the fervour of a gospel congregation erupted when Louis, wearing the

Pope's cross on his shoulder, prostrated himself, weeping at the feet of his poorest subject, the monk from Clairvaux.

> *Qui ore irat od Lovis*
> *Ja mar d'enfern avrat paur*
> *Car s'arma en iert en pareïs*
> *Od les angles de nostre Segnor.*

[For he who goes now with Louis / will never need to fear hell. / His soul will go to paradise / and with our Lord's angels dwell.]

The Frankish barons followed their king's example, most noble families offering a male adult. Families that had been locked in armed struggle for generations forgot their private causes for the sake of the greater overriding one. Even Thibault of Champagne enlisted his eldest son under the banner of France. With him were the counts of Flanders, Angoulême and Toulouse and Louis' jealous brother Robert, count of Dreux.

Contagious religious fervour drove many to take the cross that day; others sought fortunes denied them in France. Perhaps the most romantic crusader of all was Eleanor's vassal from Blaye, the noble troubadour Jaufre Rudel, the object of whose poetic *amor de lonh*, or yearning for an unattainable lady, was the countess of Tripoli. Agonised by longing to be near her, he wrote, *Luenh es lo castels e la tors / o elha jay e sos maritz . . .* Far distant is the castle tower, wherein she lies with her husband . . .

For love of this woman he had never seen, he was prepared to risk death in battle or capture by the Saracen, yet never reached the end of his journey. At some point in the long and arduous voyage the lord of Blaye died of dysentery, but was afterwards depicted by fellow poets as expiring more romantically in his mistress' arms on arrival in Tripoli.

After Louis had 'taken the cross', the 24-year-old queen knelt before Bernard and offered herself and her vassals. After her came the countess of Flanders, a half-sister of the king of Jerusalem, and many other noble ladies of Eleanor's court, plus 300 low-born women volunteers to care for the wounded. From the beginning of this crusade, women were in the forefront and it took the courage of Suger to query openly what a martial expedition destined to end in slaughter could possibly gain from the presence of so many ladies of Eleanor's court, plus their attendant maidservants, cooks and washerwomen.

Not regarding themselves bound by Bernard's proscription of luxury for the duration, they intended travelling with servants, furniture and wardrobes. Thierry or Dietrich Galeran, the Templar eunuch appointed Louis' treasurer for the crusade because of his connections along the route, warned the king that the enormous additional baggage train this required would be an encumbrance and source of danger in hostile territory. But no one listened to him either.

After Vézelay came anticlimax while the necessary funds were raised. In any case, Eugenius did not wish the French to depart before the German Emperor Conrad III Hohenstaufen had also taken the cross and Conrad was not a man to come running at the call of a pope, certainly not one in exile. Nor had he, a seasoned campaigner, any intention of subordinating himself and his vassals on the field of battle to a tyro like the young king of the Franks.

Eugenius therefore summoned his former master Bernard to leave his retreat and travel to Germany as apostolic envoy. Many who had seen the emaciated future saint preaching at Vézelay thought him already in death's grasp, yet he mustered all the resources of the daughter houses of Clairvaux to spread the call to arms and himself carried the message to the Low Countries and the cities of the Rhine as far south as the Alps. Odo of Deuil, a monk from the abbey of St Denis, was appointed by Suger as Louis' chaplain[14] and charged with compiling the official record of the expedition, according to which Bernard's inspired preaching was so charismatic that the deaf were made to hear, and the blind to see and the lame to walk again. It was said that so many men responded to his call that only one uncommitted adult male remained for every seven women in the territory he had personally covered. [15]

The German Emperor, however, was neither an ignorant peasant, nor a credulous believer like Louis. Each time the pope's persistent Cistercian envoy waylaid him, Conrad III used a different excuse for not taking the cross until, a full year after Louis' Christmas court at Bourges, Bernard celebrated Mass in Speyer on 27 December 1146. Exemplifying the true meaning of *charisma*, when the Holy Spirit is said to enter into a person chosen as the instrument of God's will, Bernard was once again seized with preacher's fervour. In the congregation was Conrad, who heard himself summoned to stand and account before the altar for the state of his soul and his stewardship of his lands and possessions.

As at Vézelay, the words and the fire with which they were delivered provoked an outbreak of crusading fever in which the emperor pledged himself and his vassals to the cause. So great was the press of volunteers that Conrad, fearing the frail monk would be crushed to death, wrapped Bernard in his own cloak and carried him from the church.

Preparations political, financial and logistical took several more months on both sides of the Rhine. Barons mortgaged their lands and the common people found in the heavy taxes a topic for complaint to replace the five-year famine they had just endured. While for the equestrian classes departure on crusade was either a penance or an adventure, for the peasants and urban poor accompanying them it was the equivalent of death: they kissed their wives and children goodbye in the expectation of meeting again only in heaven.

The differences of personality between Louis and Eleanor were typified in their preparations. While he visited monasteries and hospitals, begging the prayers of his humblest and therefore most Christ-like subjects for the success of the crusade, she travelled the length and breadth of Aquitaine and Poitou, bullying and cajoling her richest and most powerful vassals to raise more money and men.

One of Suger's many worries was the possibility that Louis would be killed or die from disease, leaving only Princess Marie to succeed him. To prevent the king's brother Robert from usurping the crown, Eleanor and Louis considered marrying her to Henry, the fourteen-year-old son of the Count Geoffrey of Anjou, whom Louis had lately confirmed as duke of Normandy. The meeting between Eleanor and Geoffrey to discuss this would afterwards lead to scandal, but Bernard's voice was heard loud and clear protesting that the mothers of the queen and Henry of Anjou were related in the third degree: Louis was to have nothing to do with the idea. And as for Count Geoffrey, how could so valiant a warrior not take the cross when his half-brother Baldwin was the king of Jerusalem, whose call for help they were answering?

Meantime, the widespread impatience to fight the perceived Muslim menace to Jerusalem found a much easier infidel target nearer home. At the time of the First Crusade, Jews had been victimised in France and killed in cities all over Germany, culminating in the great massacre of Mainz, where on the third day of Sivan according to the Hebrew calendar the entire community of 1,100 men, women and children was massacred in a bloody dress rehearsal for what would happen to the Jews in Jerusalem when the crusaders took the city.

While Eleanor and Louis were making their preparations, an itinerant monk by name of Randulf sanctioned the pillage of Jewish property in Germany and Alsace, using terms that were an incitement to fresh massacres. In condemning him,[16] pacific Bernard preached against harming the Children of Israel, whether in the Diaspora or the Holy Land. This was not because he loved Jews but taught – echoing St Augustine and Pope Gregory – that they were collectively guilty of deicide and must be punished but not killed, so that they could continue to exist as witnesses of Christ's Passion.

Because Easter and therefore Pentecost were late in 1147, Louis decided to postpone departure until the feast of St Denis on 11 June, so that the endeavour might be properly begun under the auspices of the patron saint of France. In Aquitaine, the bees were busy in the olive blossom and the water pastures were green in Poitou when Eleanor ended her recruiting drive and set out on the road north at the same time as the pope was crossing the Alps. Their paths converged inside Suger's glorious new basilica, where Eugenius blessed the assembled banners that would serve as rallying points for desperate men in the press of battle. He handed a pilgrim's staff and scrip to Louis, who was clad in a simple tunic devoid of decoration. Then the pope lifted from the altar the oriflamme symbolising the saint's protection and consecrated it to the holy purpose.

Although Eugenius' bull proscribed luxuries like fine clothes and cosmetics – along with swearing, gambling, camp followers, concubines, falcons and hounds – so long was the ladies' baggage train that they and their retainers were sent ahead after the ceremony to ensure that the numerous ox-wagons would not impede the marching foot-soldiers and mounted knights. Abbot Suger's thoughts on seeing France's glamorous queen and so many other ladies thus fortuitously leading the crusade against which he had fought in vain are not recorded.

In his hands he held Louis' crown, entrusted to him as regent for the duration of the crusade or until the king's death – whichever came first. Despite the continual enormous drain on the finances of state, the abbot of St Denis governed well, showing himself an enlightened, far-sighted and humane ruler, enacting new and fairer systems of taxation and even passing conservation laws to protect the forests under threat. Prefiguring the attempt of that other younger brother – John Lackland – to usurp Richard Coeur de Lion's throne during his absence on the Third Crusade, a group of nobles did conspire to set on the throne of France Louis' younger brother, Count Robert of Dreux, when he returned from the Holy Land several months before the king. Invoking the threat of excommunication for this defiance of the protection afforded to every crusader, Suger put down the rebellion before it got started. Undermining his influence on Louis was the greatest disservice Eleanor did to her first husband during their marriage.

The polyglot Frankish host, including Bretons, Poitevins, Gascons, Normans and Burgundians, all speaking their own languages, rendezvoused in the Moselle Valley at Metz, the capital of Lorraine. If the knights and barons were motivated by a mixture of religious fervour and desire for adventure, many of the poorer crusaders were there simply for food. Dependent on Eleanor for daily handouts, thousands of her subjects had been starving at home and would have signed on for any enterprise that guaranteed food in the belly. Others were robbers, rapists and murderers for whom Abbé Bernard had procured pardon conditional on their taking the cross. To Suger's objection, he had replied that it was a wondrous demonstration of the love of God that France should be thus rid of its scum and paupers while they in turn would be rewarded with paradise, from which they would otherwise be excluded.[17]

By this time Conrad's smaller army was far ahead in the Danube Valley. After securing the election of his son Henry as his successor under the guardianship of the archbishop of Mainz, the emperor had not waited for the French to arrive. For one thing, it would have been logistically impossible to feed the combined armies off the land in the same areas at the same time. Even travelling separately, the sanitary problems caused by 100,000 men and women on the move in conditions of zero hygiene defies the modern imagination. In addition there was the excrement of their animals; each knight had at least one destrier or warhorse and two palfreys for general riding – plus the thousands of draught and pack mules and oxen.

Except for the outbreaks of plague, disease was to some extent contained during the feudal period by the immobility of the mass of population, but an army on the move for thousands of miles was a mobile reservoir of infection from which the locals had no immunity, and vice versa. More people died on crusade from diarrhoea than cold steel, and wastage from disease on campaign was a factor taken into account by every successful military leader from Nebuchadnezzar to Napoleon.

Nor were humans the only ones at risk. Daily checking of the horses' hooves and legs for injury by stone, thorn or a loose nail was routine. Yet several thousand horses kept together for months, however healthy they were at the outset, provided ideal conditions for epidemics. In one campaign Charlemagne lost to disease nine-tenths of the thousands of horses on which his army depended for mobility and combat.[18] In addition to the diseases to which they were prone at home, there were others, fly-borne, tick-borne and contagious, to which they would be exposed while crossing Europe and in the East – even a form of equine venereal disease, dangerous for mares and almost always fatal for stallions.[19] None of the many thousand horses that survived to reach the Holy Land ever returned to Europe.

Logistical considerations were not the only reasons for Conrad III's early departure. Whether he had indeed been outmanoeuvred by Bernard and tricked into volunteering, or whether he had had his own agenda all along is unclear, but the main reason for his relatively speedy departure was a firm determination to arrive first in Byzantium and make his own terms with its emperor, the equally wily Manuel Comnenus, before pressing on to the Holy Land.

Conrad rightly suspected the barons and ruler of the Latin Kingdom of Jerusalem of blatant self-interest and wanted to see for himself what the situation was before the arrival of innocent and emotional Louis could cloud the issues. At this stage there was no agreement on the specific aim of the crusade, let alone how the French and Germans might operate under joint command. With Jerusalem in Christian hands and not immediately menaced, to secure the Latin Kingdom long term required a far-reaching campaign directed by a leader more gifted in strategy than Louis, who trusted God to govern his actions and surrounded himself with clerical advisers like Odo. Conrad III might have proved himself such a leader of men, but disaster en route would deprive him of four-fifths of his army before he could show his mettle.

Its progress limited to the speed of an ox-cart, Louis' contingent wound its way eastward across central Europe, making twelve or fifteen miles on a good day with regular rests for man and beast. For the wagons of the supply train, the roads were horrendous, having been laid by the Romans and plundered for building materials during eight centuries or more.

On the First Crusade, Godefroi de Bouillon had sent ahead of the main column a regiment of pioneers whose duty was to widen roads through forested areas and strengthen bridges where fords were lacking. Even so, the First Crusade had taken eighty-nine days to reach Constantinople, of which only fifty-nine were spent on the march. If half of the rest days were Sundays, the others were necessary to reorganise and regroup a column so long that the rear-guard passed three days after the leaders.

By now what had seemed in advance to the ladies an exciting taste of freedom had turned into discomfort and sickness for many. The few luxuries they had enjoyed at home were unavailable and increasingly they took to dressing as men, as being more convenient for long days in the saddle. For feminine hygiene there was little privacy.

Even to call the contingent an army is misleading, for it lacked any integrated command structure, was fraught with rivalry and composed for the major part of peasants without any formal military training.

Louis left his squabbling barons to take turns in leading the way, with himself bringing up the rear. Beginning each day with Mass celebrated by Odo, he saw himself as the Good Shepherd, bringing compassion and generosity to the needy while dealing harshly with pillage – and rape, inevitable among the rabble with camp followers forbidden by the papal bull.

The punishments by mutilation and death he personally meted out were not only for the sake of keeping order and from the sensible desire not to alienate too far the people through whose lands they travelled, but also because he believed the failure of the First Crusade had been divine punishment for the misbehaviour of the rabble led by Eleanor's godless grandfather. It was an argument that Abbé Bernard was to dust off for reuse when the Second Crusade failed so dismally.

Odo had commenced his preparations by consulting an account of the First Crusade in the library at St Denis.[20] For the benefit of future pilgrims following the same route, his own diary anticipates Baedeker in describing scenery but also giving useful directions:

> Three-day stages separate the prosperous cities of Metz, Worms, Würzburg, Ratisbon and Passau from one another. From the last-named city it takes five days to Wiener-Neustadt and thence one more day to the Hungarian border. . . .

> The cities of Nish, Sofia, Philippopolis and Adrianople are four days' apart. From Adrianople is five days to Constantinople. Close on right and left, mountains hem in the fertile and pleasant plain.[21]

Apart from a few hints,[22] the diary maintains a diplomatic silence about the activities of Eleanor, barred from Louis' celibate tent by Thierry Galeran, the eunuch who considered it his duty to keep away from the impressionable young monarch all time-wasters and opportunists, including his strong-willed queen.

This left her free to make a virtue out of the necessity that dictated travelling in linguistic groupings to avoid friction and conflict. Revelling in the company of her fellow countrymen after eight years cooped up in the stifling court on the Ile de la Cité, she spent the warm summer days on the plains of Hungary and the banks of the Danube flirting and being flattered in her own language by her young gallants in what passed for normal behaviour in Aquitaine but was considered scandalously intimate by the Franks. Her enemies of both sexes in the royal entourage watched and bided their time as she passed the balmy evenings entertaining the other finely dressed noble ladies with the music and wit of her favourite troubadours, brought along regardless of the papal interdiction.

While the mass of the army slept under canvas or the stars and devout Louis offered prayers in his spartan quarters policed by Odo and Thierry Galeran, the ladies retired to comfortable, if chaste, beds in elegant pavilions and tents. On waking each morning encamped among her own vassals and the spirited, emotionally and territorially unattached younger sons of her nobility out for adventure and romance, Eleanor must have felt that she had come back to life in the glorious southern sun after a long sleep beneath gloomy northern skies.

Disapproval or discretion stopped Odo from commenting on how she and the other Amazons dressed and behaved in daytime while on the march but Nicetas Acominatus, the Byzantine statesmen and historian, reported that there were indeed in the Frankish train some women dressed as men, armed with lances and riding astride, of whom the most richly apparelled was known as the lady of the golden boot.[23] Even in the context of a huge crusading army, the April Queen stood out a mile.

But the idyll of summer days and nights on the road in convivial company was not to last.

SIX

Luxury in Constantinople, Massacre on Mount Cadmos

Once on Byzantine territory the reality was harsher. To buy provisions for themselves and fodder for the animals, Eleanor's household servants were obliged to exchange their silver and gold coins for copper ones bearing Comnenus' likeness. Odo describes their reaction:

> After entering Greek territory [Bulgaria], we loaded up with supplies in the poverty-stricken town of Branicevo because the territory ahead was uninhabited. There were so many boats there, which the Germans had brought, that our men crossed the river and bought supplies from a Hungarian fortress not far away.
>
> We had to exchange five *denarii* for one *stamina* and a mark for twelve *solidi*. Thus did the Greeks perjure themselves at the very entrance to their country for the Emperor's representatives had sworn on his behalf that they would allow us to trade in their markets at a fair rate of exchange.[1]

Manuel Comnenus' reply to Louis' first letter of intention had been, in Odo's words 'sweeter than honeycomb'. At Bavarian Regensburg, then known as Ratisbon, the French court had been given eloquent promises by emissaries of the imperial court in Constantinople. Eleanor had received friendly letters from Comnenus' wife, the Empress Irene, a Bavarian noblewoman whose sister was married to Conrad. What was a Greek promise worth? the Franks now asked.

> We crossed this deserted region and entered the most beautiful and fertile country that stretches all the way to Constantinople. Elsewhere they had sold supplies correctly and found us peaceful. The Greeks, however, shut themselves in their cities and castles, letting merchandise down to us by ropes. The supplies thus received being insufficient for our needs, the pilgrims therefore satisfied their needs by plundering and looting, since they could not bear to go short in the midst of plenty. It seemed to some that the Germans were to blame for the situation, because they had looted everything and burned several unwalled suburbs.[2]

So who was to blame? The 'wily Greeks' or the excesses of Conrad's contingent? The duke of Philippopolis – modern Plovdiv, Bulgaria – had had to intervene after a drunken brawl between armed Germans and local people resulted in slaughter of the unarmed Greeks and the burning of everything outside the city walls. On another occasion an advance party of French knights, charged with arranging supplies for the main body, collided with Conrad's rearguard in a market. The Germans carried off at sword-point everything for sale. The outnumbered Franks took up their weapons and bloodshed ensued.

So the hostility of the locals was the fault of the Germans. Or was it? At Adrianople – modern Edirne, Turkey – even Louis' innocence was dented on learning that Comnenus had just signed a twelve-year truce with the Turks, during which they could do anything not directly in conflict with Byzantium's interests. Comnenus' army was thus freed to play a watching role while the two European contingents were on Byzantine soil. In addition, the great Zengi had been murdered by a palace eunuch caught stealing his wine. His son and successor, Nur ed-Din was so pious that the rules for his troops resembled those of Pope Eugenius III for the crusaders: no luxury garments, no alcohol and no 'tambourine, flute or other objects displeasing to God'.[3] Nur ed-Din was also a warrior out to prove himself before he was usurped.

In council, Louis was reminded that Eleanor's grandfather had considered destroying Constantinople as more of an obstacle than an ally to the First Crusade. It was a project that the rulers of the Latin Kingdom had also considered many times. The devout bishop of Langres, an appointee of Louis who was the Franks' best strategist, drew up a plan to lay siege to the Christian capital on the Bosporus after poisoning the water supply. To sustain such a siege would have necessitated the cooperation of the German contingent, who were supposed to be waiting for their French allies to catch up on the European banks of the Bosporus. But Comnenus was one jump ahead: the third piece of bad news for Louis was that Conrad III had already crossed into Asia with his whole army and was heading towards Cappadocia and distant Jerusalem. Recalling Abbé Bernard's advice to let nothing distract him from reaching the holy city, Louis decided to press on regardless.

To French and German alike, suspicion of the Greeks came easily. Seen from Constantinople, the situation was very different. Straddling the crossroads between Europe and Asia, it was beset by enemies on all sides, including the Normans pressing in from Sicily and Albania. The son of a Hungarian princess, Comnenus understood very well European territorial ambitions in the Levant. As a Christian owing no allegiance to Rome, he regarded more pragmatically than Louis the possible loss of Jerusalem to Turkish or Arab Muslims. He also had no love for crusader princes like Raymond of Antioch, whose city should have been handed over to Constantinople as part-payment for Byzantine support during the First Crusade after its recapture from the Turks.

Since the Seljuk nomads from central Asia who controlled the formerly Greek territory of what is now Asiatic Turkey would break the fragile truce the moment it was to their advantage to do so, the last thing Comnenus needed was to have on the loose within his frontiers two very large European armies whose leaders might combine forces to plunder his capital as a way of financing the most difficult and costly part of the crusade, which lay ahead.[4] He had therefore separated the French and German forces neatly by exploiting Conrad's desire to arrive first in the Holy Land and providing every facility for the Germans to leave Constantinople early while at the same time delaying the French with the problems of apparently inadequate supplies.

By the time Eleanor reached Constantinople on 4 October 1147, she had been on the road for three months since leaving Metz. The sophisticated Byzantines looking down from the city walls saw the French army as an exhausted and travel-stained rabble that took several days to assemble. To the mass of the travellers, the golden domes of the legendary city behind its double wall of fortifications, some dating back to Septimus Severus' rebuilding of the city in AD 196, was cause for thanksgiving. Was this not the city of Constantine the Great, who had imposed Christianity on the whole Roman Empire?

Known simply as 'the city',[5] Byzantium had twice outgrown its extensive fortifications like a snake sloughing off old skin. Those fortifications and the favourable site had enabled it to resist sieges by the Persians and Avars, the Arabs more than once, by the Bulgars and Russians – and more recently by the nomadic Pechenegs. The setting was beautiful, with the Golden Horn dividing the main city from Galata, where the Italian traders from Venice, Pisa and Amalfi lived in their own fortified quarters with the other foreign residents. With a population estimated at 400,000 – nearly ten times that of Paris – the sheer size of Constantinople made it a source of wonder even to the commonest crusader, who would never be allowed to set foot within the gates.

Nor was the emperor of Byzantium a mere western monarch, prepared to sally out and welcome the pilgrim king of the Franks as a brother. Remaining prudently in the Boukoleon palace overlooking the Bosporus, he sent minions to order the foreigners to make camp at the tips of the Golden Horn. If such a welcome was less warm than the promises at Ratisbon, Louis was reassured when a delegation of nobles bearing gifts arrived with an invitation for him and a few companions to enter the gates and wait upon the imperial pleasure within.

Odo's chronicle was essentially hagiographic, to show his king as a great leader. He skates over the welcome to describe Constantinople as 'the glory of the Greeks'.

Rich in fame, richer yet in wealth, the city is shaped like a triangular sail and hemmed in on two sides by the sea. Approaching the city, we had the Arm of St George on our right; on our left, an estuary four miles long.

The [landward] side of the city is fortified by towers and a double wall that extends for nearly two miles from the sea to the Blachernae palace. Within the walls are cultivated fields and market gardens that provide vegetables for the citizens. Subterranean conduits flow into the city under the walls, bringing abundant fresh water.

The city is rather squalid and foetid [and] the rich build their houses overhanging the streets, making these dark and dirty places for travellers and the poor, where murders and robberies occur as well as other sordid crimes which love the dark. Constantinople excels in everything, surpassing other cities in wealth, but also in vice. It has many churches which, although not comparable with Santa Sophia for size, are beautified with numerous venerable relics of the saints.[6]

Odo's account is relatively unprejudiced. If he holds the Greeks' generous hospitality to be proof that their intentions were less than honest, he understands them keeping city gates closed against the drunken French rabble who had burned many houses and cut down olive trees for firewood. The punishments frequently witnessed by Eleanor and her ladies – executions and amputations of ears, hands and feet ordered by Louis – did little to reduce these excesses.

The opulent emperor and the king in unadorned pilgrim's tunic met accompanied by bodyguards and interpreters outside the Boukoulion imperial palace. After exchanging the kiss of peace, they moved inside for the long-drawn-out diplomatic courtesies of the East, Comnenus offering the Blachernae Palace within the outer walls for the accommodation of Louis and his nobles so that not too many of them would ever be within the inner city at any one time. The rest of the French were to sleep under canvas or in the open for the duration of their stay.

Of the Blachernae, Odo writes:

The palace affords its residents the pleasure of gazing on sea, countryside and town. The exterior of the palace is extremely beautiful and the interior excels all I can say. The walls are of gold and various colours and the floor is paved with mosaics. I do not know whether the subtlety of the craftsmanship or the preciousness of the materials gives it the greater beauty or value.[7]

The sumptuousness of Comnenus' guest accommodation was an eye-opener to Eleanor after her quarters in the dilapidated palace on the Ile de la Cité. For the first time in their lives the Amazons enjoyed running water, brought into the city by the aqueduct of Valens and distributed through a system of cisterns. Another luxury for them were the flushing toilets. Thanks to Roman sewerage, both surface run-off and 'brown' water were effortlessly and comparatively hygienically disposed of into the sea.

The Blachernae was a warren of several hundred audience rooms, bedrooms, cloistered harems, ornate chapels and busy kitchens. Between the outer wall of Theodosius and Constantine's inner wall, it was on the scale of, and in the same haphazard layout as, the Topkapi

Palace. But whereas Topkapi is now bare of figurative art offensive to the Muslim eye, the Blachernae was then a treasure house of gilt and mosaic, tapestry and fresco, crystal and marble, filled with beauty from the days of the city's ancient glory and trophies from all over the Roman Empire, from Baghdad and Mosul and India and far-off Cathay.

Within the palace precincts was a deer park stocked with game for the hunt – a pleasure forbidden by their oath to the crusaders – as well as landscaped gardens from whose shady pavilions Eleanor's ladies could enjoy the view across the Golden Horn. From the Blachernae, they looked down on the Philopation, another palace in a park outside the walls, which had been equally luxurious before being vandalised by the German contingent recently accommodated there.

On arrival, Louis dictated to Odo a letter to Suger, praising God for bringing them safely through the dangers and hardships of the journey so far. Like so many commanders-in-chief, he seemed surprised that expenditure was way over budget. The letter ended, as they all did, with an urgent plea for more money.[8]

Once she had explored the marvels of the palace the 25-year-old queen and her ladies could explore the city itself. The back streets may have been narrow, dark and gloomy, as Odo said, but so were most of the streets in Paris, whereas Constantinople's main thoroughfare had a grandeur unknown in Europe's capitals. From the emperor's palace a long arcaded street ran west, linking forums and marketplaces adorned with monuments and fountains and bordered by the domes and minarets of a hundred churches. Sumptuously decorated, they enshrined relics, many brought back by Constantine's mother Saint Helena from her visit to the Holy Land in the third century. These included alleged bones of several disciples, the True Cross from Golgotha and a thorn from the Crown of Thorns.

But the greatest marvel was the glorious Hagia Sophia or Church of the Holy Wisdom. Built six centuries earlier to replace Constantine's basilica, which had been destroyed in a riot, and completed in less than six years, Constantinople's architectural masterpiece was at the time of Eleanor's visit more than an object of beauty, with its columns of finest marble to delight the senses of sight and touch and its walls and roof decorated entirely in rich mosaics that have now disappeared.

It was also a technical triumph by Antithemius of Tralles and Isidorus of Miletus. By brilliant use of the Persian squinch and the innovative Syrian pendentive – among the first devices that deflected vertical thrust and avoided unsightly masses of load-bearing masonry – the two architects of genius had solved the apparently impossible challenge of translating a square ground plan into a load-bearing circle flanked by two semicircles on which the immense and perfectly circular dome and its two flanking semi-domes rested in lofty eastern grandeur, so different from the vertical Gothic lines of Suger's basilica at St Denis and more breathtaking by far than any Romanesque church. To Louis, all was symbolic: the square represented man's creation, the circle above the perfection of Heaven.

When he was invited to Mass in Hagia Sophia, eyes and ears were equally pleasured. The polyphony and counterpoint of the Greek litany sung by disciplined choirs of *castrati* echoing from the glittering dome outdid anything in contemporary western music. With the emperor and his guests surrounded by ranks of functionaries and accorded obsequious oriental respect, there was no need for Louis to beat a passage for himself through the common mob with a staff, as he had been obliged to do at the consecration of St Denis. The servility of the imperial eunuchs and slaves contrasted with the casual attitude of Eleanor's servants. Even the satraps of Byzantium humbled themselves before the emperor and spoke in his presence only when he told them to. It was all most unlike the physical jostling and constant challenges to her authority which were the norm among her own insubordinate vassals.

On the Greek Orthodox feast of Louis' patron saint Dionysius the Areopagite, Manuel sent to the Blachernae a chorus of priests chosen for their superb voices. Bearing crosses and lit candles, they performed for Eleanor and Louis an exquisitely choreographed sung Mass in the saint's own language. It was a most thoughtful gift for a king who dressed like a pilgrim and spent in venerating the relics of the saints and in fasting the time he should have devoted to preparing for departure before the approach of autumn.

For Eleanor's ladies with money to enjoy the pleasure of shopping, the souks of the city and the warehouses of the Italian merchants across the water in Galata provided the more sensuous pleasures of perfumes, jewellery and works of art in silver and gold, glass from Hebron and Antioch, carved ivory from India and Africa. There was fine metalwork of a quality unobtainable in the West, carpets from Persia and Afghanistan, and sumptuous materials including the finest silk from China, linen from Egypt, brocades from Tripoli, Baghdad and even the Turkish capital of Mosul, which had been fabled Nineveh in the time of Assyrian greatness. As entertainments, there were horse races, tournaments and public games in Constantine's hippodrome adjacent to the imperial palace, which she attended with Comnenus' European wife. The empress and the queen had much in common: they were young and beautiful, each had been married for political reasons to a husband who spoke another language and sent to live in what was, to her, a foreign and friendless court.

But an enormous gulf of culture separated the Byzantines from most of their unwanted French guests. Eleanor had many times ridden past the imposing ruins of the Roman baths at Chassenon on the main road from Saintes to Lyon, but in Constantinople the public baths were still functioning and well patronised, as were the scores of *hammams*.[9] In Europe *alousia* or not washing was considered a sign of holiness. The Byzantines abhorred the stink of the unwashed French and the smell of their breath, due to their habit of chewing raw garlic as a prophylactic.

Although the Roman amphitheatre with over thirty rows of banked seating held no more spectators than had in their heyday those at Bordeaux and Saintes with which Eleanor was familiar, those were ruins used as quarries for their marble and dressed limestone. In what had been the capital of Rome's eastern empire, the public still gazed up at life-size and gigantic statues of men and animals atop the walls, some of them automata that moved or roared or appeared to sing for the crowd's amusement. Like Caesar's entourage at the games in Rome, Comnenus and his guests were not hustled by the crowd in the *vomitoria* – the claustrophobic corridors by which the common people gained their seats – but moved sedately through a separate network of private passages to the royal lodge, in which they presided over and were part of the spectacle.[10]

Invited to dine with the emperor in the Boukoleon, a palace even more luxurious than their own lodgings in the Blachernae, the French royal party did not sit, but reclined on couches in the old Roman fashion to be regaled with delicacies of which their palates could not distinguish the subtly combined ingredients. In late summer there was still snow a-plenty from the Caucasus to chill the sherbets and cool the wine, served in precious glasses. Spices unknown in Europe teased the palate, as new and exciting harmonies teased the ear, vying with the plashing of scented fountains and the singing of golden birds in a mechanical tree. Musicians, dancing girls and acrobats entertained them during the banquet.

The purpose of all this oriental hospitality was to delay the French until they could not possibly join up with Conrad's army to defeat the Turks and turn back to Constantinople in force. If Eleanor and the ladies were happy to continue enjoying the delights of the most civilised city of the day, Thierry Galeran and Louis' other military advisers were chafing at the inactivity because they knew how important it would be to cross the high mountain passes of what is now southern Turkey before the first snows of winter.

After Louis' uncle the Count of Maurienne arrived with a smaller contingent that had travelled via Italy, the king's last letter to Suger before departure echoed the first: *send more money*. The expedition was already way over budget, but the army could not move through a hostile semi-desert country without adequate supplies. They crossed the Bosporus into Asia Minor about 16 October 1147 and followed the line taken by the modern motorway along the Izmit inlet to Nicomedia.

From there, three possible routes diverged, the shortest being the age-old caravan trail from Constantinople to Tarsus – where St Paul was born – and onward to Aleppo and Edessa. Odo spells out the advantages and disadvantages of each route:

> The left-hand road is the shortest. However, after twelve days it reaches Konya, the Sultan's capital, which is a very noble city. Five days beyond, this road reaches the land of the Franks. An army strong in faith and numbers could fight its way through, except in winter when the mountains are snow-covered. The right-hand road is less dangerous and better-supplied, but three times as long, running along

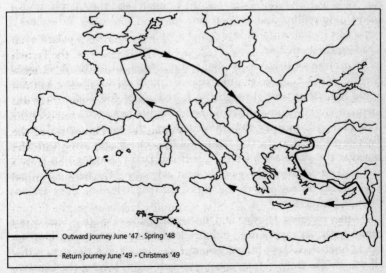

Eleanor and Louis on the Second Crusade

the indented littoral with rivers and torrents in winter as dangerous as the Turks and the snow on the other road. The middle road is a compromise between the other two, longer but safer than the left route, and shorter than the right route, but ill-provided with food.

Therefore the Germans split into two parties. Many risked setting out with the Emperor via Konya, the others turning right under his brother. The middle road was chosen by us.[11]

On 26 October an eclipse – taken as a bad omen – obscured the sun as Louis was travelling from Chalcedon, now a suburb of Istanbul on the Asiatic side of the Bosporus by name of Kadiköy, to Nicea. The pagan ruins of Nicomedia – now Izmit – held no interest for him, but Nicaea on the eastern shore of Lake Iznik was where in AD 451 the fourth ecumenical council of the Christian Church had adopted the Nicene Creed and where the seventh ecumenical council had ruled that icons deserved veneration but not adoration.

While he was pursuing this pilgrimage from the scene of one religious event to another, Conrad and his knights were being harassed daily by the Turks. Lightly armed with slings and short bent-back composite bows designed for use on horseback, the Seljuks were mounted on Asiatic ponies slightly smaller than the German knights' mounts. Their traditional hit-and-run tactics concentrated on the weaker elements of the columns by harassing the rear, the wounded and the baggage train – relentlessly raiding and disappearing into the landscape. Whenever a posse of German knights attempted a riposte, they found themselves lured into ambush.

In dividing his forces to make sure of reaching the Holy Land first, Conrad took a gamble that he and his armoured knights could fight their way through the heartland of the Turks while the German engineers and other non-combatants required for siege work travelled with most of the infantry along the slower coastal route. This decision led to the first disaster of the crusade. His alibi afterwards was that the guides supplied by Comnenus kept promising that grazing and water were available over the next ridge or in the next valley, but were in fact in league with the Turks and simply leading the Germans to their destruction.

As they progressed further and further along the network of semi-desert camel trails, an experienced military leader like the German Emperor would surely have kept his guides under close guard. But the story is that all the Greeks escaped from camp one dark night, leaving the Germans stranded. Dawn on the day of the eclipse brought the Turks swarming in force out of the hills, raining slingstones and arrows on the huddled masses of the German contingent. The confused foot-soldiers, stumbling along blind with hunger and thirst, died as William IX's men had, not far away. Only the mounted knights had a chance against so mobile and determined an enemy that used the landscape as a weapon – not a chance to give battle against this elusive foe, but merely to escape with their lives. By nightfall Conrad's treasury had been captured and he himself was, like the troubadour duke of Aquitaine fifty years earlier, lucky to escape alive with approximately one in five of his knights.[12]

The official story continued with the Greek guides finding their way to Louis' camp and reporting Conrad's army safely arrived at Inconium or Konya after destroying large numbers of Turks on the way. Hardly had the Franks rejoiced at this news when the best mounted of the German knights, intent on saving their skins by putting the maximum distance between themselves and the pursuing Turks, rode into camp to give the lie to the Greek story. Among them was Conrad's nephew Frederik Barbarossa, who begged Louis to send help to his uncle, attempting to rally the remnants of his army. There was an element of they-got-what-was-coming-to-them in the Frankish council of war but Louis, always at his best in adversity, forgave the slights he had suffered from Conrad and dispatched a heavily armed party to the scene of the ambush to guarantee a Christian burial for the tens of thousands of corpses while he pressed on to rendezvous with the German survivors and offer them some safety in numbers.

Railing at what he called 'the Greek betrayal', the wounded German Emperor announced his intention of abandoning the crusade and stopping in Constantinople on the way home to tell his brother-in-law Comnenus what he thought of him. Louis tried to talk him out of this plan, for even the much-reduced force of German knights who had survived the massacre would be of crucial importance in the Holy Land. He reminded Conrad that abandoning the crusade automatically invoked the papal interdicts which applied to any crusader returning before his mission had been accomplished.

Whether because of this or for his own reasons, the German Emperor agreed to continue with the French, despite permitting many of his nobles to renounce their vows and go home. It was after the return of these men, who preferred excommunication to continuing the crusade, that rumours of the great disaster crossed the Rhine to disturb Suger at the abbey of St Denis soon after Christmas 1147.

Taking to heart the lessons learned, the French decided to avoid inland areas where the Turks were strongest, which meant heading westwards to the coast and then following the littoral in what was theoretically still Greek territory, where they would never be at a great distance from the nearest port for communications and provisions. At the beginning of November, they reached the sea and turned south.

Lulled into a false sense of security by the unseasonably mild weather, the army headed south along the coast, where the Greek islands rise like hump-backed whales out of the heat haze over the Aegean Sea. The barons took it in turn to have the honour of leading. As in Europe, Louis brought up the rear. Eleanor and the Amazons could ride on the wagons when they tired of horseback, but the majority of the army was on foot as Louis lengthened the journey. In a state of sustained religious ecstasy, he visited shrines in Pergamon and Smyrna – modern Bergama and Izmir – before continuing south to Ephesus.

To Eleanor the ruined cities were the glory of the past, but Louis had no eye for pagan splendour. He saw Ephesus as the place where the apostles who had known the Saviour personally during His brief ministry had come in person to preach the Gospel to the first Christians. For him the once-mighty city dedicated to many-breasted Diana of the Ephesians had interest only because the ancient flagstones had been trodden by St Paul's feet when he came there to abominate the goddess' cult. There, too, Paul's letters written in captivity at Rome had been read out to his Ephesian converts, to whom St John the Evangelist had also preached. And in the hills not far away was the house where the Virgin Mary was reputed to have ended her days, and which continues to attract tourists by the coachload.

It was ironically the totally opposed natures of the two leaders – Conrad's arrogance in taking an ill-considered gamble and Louis' piety that insisted on washing his soul at every font of Christianity along the route – that led inevitably to the failure of the crusade.

Whatever was in the minds of Odo and Thierry Galeran as Louis led them from one religious site to the next, the French barons were increasingly aware that they were two months behind schedule. Many of the knights had been on crusade before, and knew what it meant to be caught by winter on the wrong side of the mountains lying between them and Antioch. However, no one could persuade the king to keep on the move during the Feast of the Nativity. Three whole years after the fall of Edessa, the French army was encamped at an unknown location near the sea in a river valley wide enough to set up a tented township, with wagons unloaded and horses and draught animals sent away to pasture, where they could regain strength for the mountains ahead.

The weather changed abruptly: winter came in with a bang. On Christmas Eve, torrential rain began before Midnight Mass. Next morning while the bishops for the nobles and the priests for the commoners were celebrating the office of Lauds there was a cloudburst with a gale of wind that blew away many tents. Fuelled by heavy rains in the nearby mountains, a flash flood swept away men, animals, tents, wagons, weapons and equipment, washing them in one tangled mess far out to sea.

How many men and women drowned is unknown, but this natural disaster, which could so easily have been avoided by a better choice of camp site, so demoralised the surviving Germans that they decided to return to Constantinople despite all Louis' pleas. With Conrad hardly able to mount his horse – in addition to his head wound, he was suffering from a severe attack of malaria – the Germans rode away gaunt from the meagre provisions the Franks had been able to spare, leaving Louis' army to tighten its belts, turn their backs to the winter gales blowing in off the sea and head eastwards, inland along the valley of the Meander – rightly a metaphor for twists and turns – in the direction of the city of Laodicea, a few kilometres from the modern industrial town of Denizli.

If Louis was sustained on the march by the prospect of visiting the church in Laodicea, which was one of the seven to which St John's Revelation had been addressed, the mass of the army was more interested in the food to be found there. But the cupboard was bare when they arrived, possibly because of a local famine, although the Franks held the Greek governor of the city guilty of collusion with the Turks in virtually denuding the region of all supplies. Wearily they changed direction, turning south-east to the coast, a route that lay across several ranges of uncharted mountains, up and down which they struggled with only intermittent glimpses of the pale winter sun for direction.

On foot or horseback, following the steep and winding mountain trails was hard enough, without the decomposing bodies of massacred Germans they were constantly coming across. If the ladies could take shelter behind the leather curtains of the horse-borne litters, for the wagon-drivers and their beasts and the pack mules, it was hellish. When, despite goads and whips, the exhausted animals could not move their loads up the steep gradients, the only recourse was for every available man literally to 'put his shoulder to the wheel'. Feet slipping and sliding in the mud, they heaved in unison until the gradient eased. For the unwary or simply exhausted, it was easy to slip right off the trail and hurtle to their deaths far below. The only incentive to keep going was the certain fate of laggards, for Nur ed-Din's Turks were watching like vultures. But this slow agony was nothing to what lay in wait.

On an evening when Eleanor's vassal Geoffroi de Rancon was sharing the leadership of the vanguard with the count of Maurienne, orders were given for camp to be pitched on a flat-topped hill near Mount Cadmos that looked from the distance large enough to accommodate the whole army. Arriving there to find it both inhospitable and exposed, Rancon saw, some way ahead and below him, a green and sheltered valley with pasture and water. Defying his orders, he headed downhill towards it, behind him the royal standard that the army was following.

To what extent Eleanor is personally to blame cannot be ascertained, but since she was not harmed in the débâcle, she must have been riding at the head of the army with the other Poitevins. Odo is frustratingly silent as to whether Geoffroi de Rancon asked her permission for his action and was told by her to ignore his orders.

The certain facts are that, with the vanguard accelerating downhill towards comfort for the night and the main body of the army still struggling slowly upwards along the winding trails in the deep gorges, unable to see either the plateau ahead of them or the valley beyond, the army became so spread out that it was effectively cut in two. This classic military error presented the opportunity that the lurking Seljuks had been so patiently awaiting.

They erupted from the ravines on all sides, screaming and beating drums and tambourines in the manner that had panicked Conrad's army. The French knights, sweating from the hard climb, had discarded their helmets and body armour. Fleeing the slingshot and arrows raining down from the sky, they rode right into the main ambush. Boulders, bodies, wagons and animals fell or were thrown from the winding trail, landing on the struggling mass below and carrying more victims to their deaths. If nightfall had not put an end to the slaughter, there might have been no survivors.

The resourceful Odo caught the bridle of a runaway horse and eventually rode into the camp in the valley, where news of the disaster had already sown panic. Scouts sent back to discover what had happened reported mountain trails impassable in the darkness, blocked by piles of bodies. As the hours passed there was no news of the king from the shocked survivors straggling into camp. It was after daybreak when a monk led Louis on a stray mount into the camp where Eleanor and the others waited.[13] His life had been saved in the darkness by his modest pilgrim's clothing, which did not single him out as a rich target. On foot with only a small bodyguard, he had spent the night shivering among some stunted trees.

Geoffroi de Rancon's guilt was Eleanor's to share. There was talk of hanging from the nearest tree her vassal who had caused the disaster. Instead, he was sent back to France in disgrace. That he escaped with his life had less to do with clemency than the embarrassing presence of the king's equally guilty uncle at his side throughout. The surviving Amazons who had signed up for Eleanor's great adventure now blamed her for the fate of their less fortunate kinswomen, killed or taken hostage by the Turks. How Louis and Eleanor sorted the matter out between themselves will never be known because, once again, Odo preserves a diplomatic silence.

Having lost most of the baggage train to Turkish looters, what remained of the French army now faced another enemy: starvation that was staved off only by eating what flesh remained on the bones of mules and horses which had themselves perished of starvation.[14] Late in January 1148 the sorry band straggled out of the mountains north of the Greek seaport of Satalia – the modern Atalya. The ladies had lost most of their clothes and furniture; bishops and knights had lost their mounts and were walking barefoot, gaunt and famished, with their clothes in tatters.

The onward route presented them with another dilemma. The land route along the coast to Antioch – now called Antakya – involved a two-month journey over range after range of arid mountains with neither forage for animals nor supplies for humans. In February weather they would have been a challenge even to fit, well-fed men on fresh mounts. The alternative was to embark the army in small coast-hugging merchant ships. However, there were far too few available to accommodate everyone.

Even if there had been sufficient shipping, the Byzantine captains demanded a fare of four silver marks per passenger for the 400-mile sea passage during the period of winter storms and with the constant risk of piracy. While the bishops and barons and most knights had such funds remaining, there was no money – nor were there enough ships – to transport the common soldiery. Yet staying put was also prohibitively expensive, for at the end of winter there was little surplus food or fodder. In obedience to the age-old law of supply and demand, the inhabitants of Satalia inflated the price of all foodstuffs to their unbidden guests sky-high.

Indecisive and unwarlike, Louis was not without courage. Instead of saving himself, he determined to continue on foot with his common soldiers, sharing their hardships all the way to still distant Jerusalem. His advisers would have none of this Christian humility from a monarch without heir whose brother, returned prematurely to France, had just made a bid to usurp him in his absence. So they forced him to embark in one of the more seaworthy ships. The small convoy set sail for the haven of Antioch, bearing the king and Eleanor with those ladies who had survived the nightmare in the mountains. Left ashore were the count of Flanders and Archimbaud de Bourbon, whose job it was to rally the demoralised infantry and the wounded in a desperate endeavour to break through by the land route.

When this inevitably failed, they returned to Satalia and, in the belief that they would accomplish nothing in that godforsaken place, abandoned their troops and took ship for Antioch themselves. Approximately 7,000 rank-and-file – less than 10 per cent of those who had set out from Metz eight months before – remained trapped in the narrow space between the inner and outer walls of Satalia. Desperate and starving, they were understandably forbidden entrance to the city, yet stayed there for fear of the Turks in the hills and surrounding countryside. In the stench and hunger of their unsheltered encampment where they lived in their own filth, dysentery was rife.

Their nightmare was resolved by an outbreak of plague that drove the able-bodied to leave Satalia and negotiate an armistice with the Turks, who offered the choice between a painful death and embracing Islam to benefit from the hospitality that the Prophet enjoined for believers in need. Who could blame those starving peasants from Aquitaine, Brittany and Champagne for abandoning the faith that had brought them nothing but suffering, hardship and misery?

SEVEN

Accusation in Antioch, Joy in Jerusalem, Defeat at Damascus

Shipwreck was such a common occurrence as to prompt many questions for Greek and Roman students of ethics. Eleanor would have been familiar with them from her time in the schools: 'In a tempest, the captain says the ship must be lightened to give a chance of survival. Which do you throw overboard, an old slave who has served you well but no longer has any monetary value or your expensive new horse?' It was a dilemma that would have made any twelfth-century knight think twice before doing the right thing.

With a fair wind in summer, it might have been a pleasant week's voyage to Antioch's crusader port of St Simeon – now Simangad – but Eleanor and her ladies embarked on that small convoy of frail Byzantine merchantmen knew the risks they ran by putting to sea before the end of winter. Before the advent of the magnetic compass,[1] it was necessary to hug the coastline and navigate by sight and soundings from one landmark to the next, which increased the risk of being driven onto a lee shore where no headland was available for shelter from a storm.

The 'round ships' in which they were embarked were uncomfortable in any conditions above a light breeze. With dual lateen sails, short-keeled and wide-beamed to give the maximum cargo space for their length, they rolled abominably when tacking against the wind. In storm conditions cooking fires had to be doused, leaving only stale bread and cold food until the next calm. With adverse winds repeatedly blowing Louis' small convoy off course and separating the vessels, and the individual captains being obliged to head seaward to ride out the tempests, the voyage lasted for three uncomfortable and frightening weeks, during which Prince Raymond waited for news in Antioch.

Since the demise of the Roman imperial postal system – by which a letter from Britain carried by relays of riders changing horses at twenty-kilometre intervals could reach Rome in less than a week – news travelled unreliably. Yet, despite the hardships and dangers of travel, there were always merchants avid to make their fortune providing 'their ship came home' and pilgrims both civil and military who undertook the long and arduous journey from Europe to the Holy Land. In return for hospitality en route, they carried letters and verbal messages and told travellers' tales to entertain their hosts.

Through such intrepid travellers Raymond of Antioch had been able to track Eleanor's progress. Although in the intervening three years since taking Edessa the Turks had made no move except to refortify the city, he knew that they were only biding their time. His spirits must have lifted when Louis was making good progress across Europe, only to plunge with the news of Conrad's disastrous defeat and plummet still further on hearing of the Christmas flood and the massacre at Mount Cadmos. The loss of all the rank-and-file soldiery would not have concerned him, for what he wanted was a corps of trained and well-mounted knights to help him retake Edessa, using local labour to do all the heavy siege-work, digging saps and constructing siege- towers and catapults under the instructions of the engineers.

After ten years in the shifting sands of the Levant, Eleanor's uncle cannot have been surprised to hear that Conrad III had spent the winter in Constantinople. The story of the treacherous Greek guides who had delivered him into a Turkish trap would be used for home consumption to explain the German defeat. However, he and his brother-in-law Comnenus were on such good terms now there was no German army on Byzantine territory that he was nursed back to health by the staff of the Pantokrator monastery, which was both the mausoleum of the imperial family and a hospital staffed by trained doctors on a scale undreamed of in the West.[2]

When at last the first sails of the separated ships were sighted on the horizon, Raymond rode the ten miles from his palace in Antioch down to the port of St Simeon. Eleanor was still in disgrace, but her greatest strength lay in being able to put aside past failure as firmly as her spirit overcame present adversity. Stepping ashore at St Simeon on 19 March 1148, her morale must have soared at the warmth of Raymond's welcome. Not since crossing the Rhine had the French been truly welcome anywhere, yet here it was not Louis and his Frankish nobles who counted, but Eleanor the queen.

She had every justification for thinking her nightmare over as musicians and choirs led the way to the church by the harbour where thanks were given for their safe arrival, after which the royal pilgrims rode up the Orontes Valley to spend the night on dry land safe behind the walls of Raymond's city, where their host allotted accommodation in palaces and villas according to rank.

The conscientious Odo wrote that night to Suger, ascribing Louis' safe arrival in the Holy Land to divine providence:

King Louis has reached Antioch after shipwreck carried off three other vessels of the convoy. He is in good health and has never faced the enemy without first receiving the Sacrament. On returning, he recites Vespers and Compline, God being the alpha and omega of his labours.[3]

Crusaders motivated like Louis by genuine belief were careful to keep to the letter of religious observance in order to die in a state of grace that would guarantee an immediate place in heaven.

On the morning after their arrival, clad in clean clothes and with their hunger sated for the first time in months, the survivors looked southward to the valley between Mount Lebanon and the Anti-Lebanon used by the camel trains from Alexandria. To the north, the same trail led onwards to fabled Trebizond across the fertile Amik plain, whose fields were green between the olive and lemon groves, where the trees were heavy with fruit ripening for local consumption and trade. Westward shimmered the sea they had crossed. Inland, the flanks of Mount Silpius were ablaze with wild flowers brought to life by the winter rains.[4]

Raymond's decaying city and restored palace were not Constantinople, but this was comfort and plenty after the dangers and semi-starvation of the overland journey and the weeks of mainly uncooked food at sea. Founded by one of Alexander the Great's generals in 300 BC, Antioch was the richest port serving the Latin Kingdom by virtue of being the most logical Mediterranean terminus for caravan routes from Persia and further east. Because it also commanded the north-to-south land route across what is now north-west Syria, and customs dues were payable on every camel-load of costly spices, dyes, silk and porcelain passing through or terminating there for shipment to Europe, the geographical position alone made Raymond extremely wealthy. Lebanese cedar was shipped to Egypt in return for fine cotton, subsequently shipped with spices and silk on Italian vessels back to Europe. It was to facilitate this trade that the *lingua franca* – a bastard pidgin of Frankish, Italian and Arabic – had become the common tongue of the Levant.

Graced with villas and shady colonnaded gardens, temples, theatres, aqueducts and public baths on the terraces above the Orontes, and surrounded by a high wall that climbed the slopes of Mont Silpius, Antioch had been the capital of the province of Syria and third largest city of the empire, after Rome and Alexandria. More importantly to Louis, St Paul had made it his base for several years between AD 47 and 55, and it was there that the term 'Christian' had first been used to describe the followers of Christ. Because its original church had been founded by the apostles Peter and Paul, Antioch's bishop ranked just below the patriarchs of Jerusalem, Rome and Alexandria in the international hierarchy of the Church.

The city Eleanor saw was rich in mosaics and frescoes and vestiges of classical Greek architecture still standing or reused in the crusader buildings. To stand on the ramparts above the Orontes was to breathe the same air as those heroes Godefroi de Bouillon, Tancred and Bohemund, the first crusader overlord of Antioch. Borne on the wind were echoes of *chansons de geste* celebrating their fearless leaping from the scaling ladders onto the battlements to wrest the city from the infidel.

Who can blame Louis' neglected queen if her spirit was moved on finding herself not just in safety and comfort, but regal luxury, after the nightmare of climbing endlessly up and down bleak mountains, enduring rain, hail and snow? She would not have been human if, after all those weeks and months of disgrace and rejection, she had failed to react to her new standing as niece of an oriental despot who literally owned everything the eye could see. Tall, handsome, courtly and of proven courage in the hunt and at war, Raymond embodied all she found wanting in Louis. In listing all the moral shortcomings of Antioch's prince – his deviousness, inconsistency and lack of principles – William of Tyre adds that he was no glutton or drunkard or womaniser.[5] But he was a charmer, and only ten years older than his niece.

Eleanor's pleasure in her reception did not pass unobserved by her enemies. She was not alone in blossoming under the blandishments of her host: many of her vassals were lodged in villas and palaces belonging to their own kin, who were Raymond's vassals. Whether or not the Frankish and Flemish barons and knights really were treated as second-class visitors, they felt that this was the case and became increasingly paranoid about the closeness between Eleanor's followers and the natives of Antioch with whom they conversed in Occitan.

In putting his case to Louis' council, Raymond faced an uphill fight because Count Joscelin's relationship with the house of Capet made Louis reluctant to believe his indolence and corruption had caused the loss of Edessa. Raymond's plan to retake Edessa and conquer Aleppo and Caesarea[6] with an army of Frankish knights, plus the barons of Antioch and some Knights Templar and freelances recruited in Tripoli and Jerusalem, fell on deaf ears. Thierry of Flanders was one who might have responded – but only to install as the new overlord of Edessa one of his sons, Henry or Theodoric who, with their mother, had accompanied him on the crusade in the hope of securing fiefs for themselves.

Louis' Franks and Flemings had not mortgaged their possessions to enrich still further a Toulousain relative of their disgraced queen. To their hostile counsel was added the clerics' argument that Louis was on crusade to redeem his endangered soul, while Raymond's plan was not holy crusade but a secular military adventure, in which the king should take no part, for had not Bernard of Clairvaux said to let nothing distract him from going to Jerusalem?

Wrongly, it was decided to leave things in Edessa as they were for the moment and move on to Jerusalem, there to take counsel among the leaders of the Latin Kingdom who might be expected to give a less biased oversight. Since the decision was not immediately conveyed to Raymond because they intended to carry on enjoying his hospitality until the remainder of the contingent caught up with them from Satalia, he continued bestowing costly presents on all his guests in eastern fashion.[7] He took them hunting beyond the lake of Antioch and generously let them loose his falcons upon the game birds in the marshes along the Orontes.

Eleanor's followers recovered from the privations of winter in the Antiochene spring, which was so like that of Aquitaine. Peire Vidal, a Toulousain troubadour who wrote and sang his way through Spain, Provence, Italy and Hungary, captured the mood:

Be m'agrada la covinens sazos
e m'agrada lo cortes tems d'estiu
e m'agradon l'auzel quan chanton piu
e m'agradon floretas per boissos.

[Oh, how I love the gentle season / foretelling the dalliance of summer / when the birds sing again to one another / and every bush is bright with blossom.]

But while the joys of Antioch were expunging the nightmare of Turkey, the rift between Eleanor and Louis widened even further. Entertained and lodged in luxury with their own blood-relations, her followers naturally sided with the Prince of Antioch, who had in mind that even if the rest of the French contingent continued to Jerusalem, they alone would be enough to serve his immediate ends. The Franks and Normans, resentful that they had suffered so much worse than the southerners at Mount Cadmos, despised the rich and decadent lifestyle of these first representatives of the Latin Kingdom with whom they came in contact. They had a word for the expat type, softened in some cases by two generations of oriental living. *Poulain* meant literally a foal, protected by the mare, but was used disparagingly in the sense of 'degenerate'.

The culture gap worked both ways. Fulcher of Chartres, who went to the Holy Land with Baldwin of Flanders on the First Crusade in 1099 and died there in 1127, wrote in his *History of Jerusalem*, 'We used to be Westerners. Now we are Easterners. You may once have been a Roman or a Frenchman; here and now, you are a Galilean or a Palestinian. For we have forgotten the lands of our birth; to most of us they are strange, forgotten countries.'[8]

Eleanor was accustomed to the sight of Moorish, Sicilian and Jewish traders stepping ashore from their vessels moored below the walls of Bayonne and Bordeaux. She saw in Antioch again all the excitement of a vivid and colourful Mediterranean lifestyle that suited her far better than the claustrophobic court on the Ile de la Cité. However, Louis viewed with horror the locals who had intermarried not only with Greeks and Syrians but also with Saracens, whose costume they wore in public and whose language they spoke fluently.[9]

On ground that had been trodden by holy Luke and Peter, Barnabas and Paul, they ate and gamed and did business with turbaned pagans and Muslims in the shadow of statues of Apollo and Diana. The coinage of Baghdad and Damascus circulated alongside that of Paris,

Venice or Constantinople in this city that resembled a vast caravanserai.[10] For every church there was a mosque, from whose minaret the muezzin's call to prayer competed with church bells calling Christians to worship.

Learning that the Franks intended continuing to Jerusalem as soon as the rest of the army caught up with them, Raymond realised that his only hope lay in enlisting Eleanor's support. His flattery and courting of her was, despite all the malicious slanders that pursued her afterwards, motivated by the desire to use her influence. Vulnerable to Raymond's southern charm and his love of music and draughts and chess, she allowed to grow up between them a close relationship that marked the end of the marriage to Louis, with which she had long grown bored.

Reluctant as ever to believe ill of anyone, he could not but be aware of her pleasure in her uncle's company, while to Raymond's mind a king who had to be protected from his own beautiful, strong-willed wife by a monk and a eunuch was a figure of mockery, unworthy of respect. Louis' advisers, unable to understand exactly what was going on between the queen and her uncle, perhaps read more than necessary into the jokes and jibes in Occitan. The flirting, natural enough for a healthy young woman after all the long months without any sex, thanks to Louis' vow of celibacy, was to them the outward sign of a clandestine carnal relationship.

Throughout her life, Eleanor seems to have been unaware when others set out to damage her. She was at this time twenty-five years old, clothed and bejewelled by Raymond, lodged by him and flattered by his gifts and personal attentions. To Raymond she could confide the boredom of her life in Paris and the frustration of her marriage. *I found I had married a monk . . .*

In addition, there was her resentment at being refused a seat at Louis' council on the march, to which she should have been entitled as overlord of a sizeable portion of the contingent, yet which had been denied her all along by the hostility of his Frankish advisers. As to who concerted this, the clue may be in her open mockery of Thierry Galeran,[11] a eunuch being an obvious butt for humour in Antiochene society.

Although openly blamed by the Franks for the massacre in the mountains, she had been denied the right to defend herself in council and put her view that Louis was at least as much at fault, for had he done as Abbé Bernard counselled and proceeded to Jerusalem without diversion instead of dawdling from one holy site to another, they would never have been at Mount Cadmos in the middle of winter.

When the count of Flanders and Archimbaud de Bourbon arrived with a mere handful of foot-soldiers and the news that the rest of the infantry was lost to disease and death at Satalia or had converted to the religion of the enemy, Raymond presented his plan with all the right military arguments at a plenary council of war, from which Eleanor was again excluded. Louis replied, 'It was to go to the Holy Sepulchre that I made my crusader's vow. I will not make war until after fulfilling my pilgrimage. Afterward I shall listen to the Prince of Antioch and the other barons of Syria in council and will, according to my power, offer myself to God's will.'[12]

At this denial of what was the original purpose of the crusade, William of Tyre records that the tap of generosity was abruptly turned off. The prince of Antioch now informed Louis' Frankish and Flemish nobles and knights on whom he had lavished so much hospitality that they were no longer welcome on his territory. In the midst of marshalling his troops for the road to Jerusalem, Louis received notice from Eleanor that she insisted on speaking with him face to face. As his wife, she announced that she no longer wanted anything to do with him or the house of Capet.[13] As countess of Poitou and duchess of Aquitaine, she informed him that she and her vassals intended to continue the crusade by remaining in Antioch and assisting Raymond in retaking Edessa, as had been planned from the beginning.

Those seeking scandal can find it anywhere, but it was natural for her political sympathies to lie with Raymond's cause. Not only was he her father's brother, but in taking his side she was favouring her own cause in the breakaway duchy of Toulouse. In purely military terms, what remained of the French army could not possibly clear all the Turks and other Muslims from Outremer, but they could recapture Edessa which, under a stronger overlord than Joscelin, would again be the north-eastern bulwark of the Latin Kingdom. What better result could they hope to achieve?

For the details of the conversation between Eleanor and Louis, the record is sparse. Having studied in Paris under Peter Abelard, John of Salisbury certainly knew both Eleanor and Louis by reputation and probably in person. Later Becket's secretary and thus present in Canterbury Cathedral at the time of the murder before going on to become bishop of Chartres, he was a reliable chronicler. He reports that Louis was deeply upset at Eleanor's outpouring of her grievances, ending with a reminder that no less a person than Abbé Bernard had written, after Louis had refused consent for two of his vassals to marry heirs of Thibault of Champagne to whom they were related, 'How is it that the king is so scrupulous about con-sanguinity in [this] case when it is common knowledge that he has married his own cousin in the fourth degree?'[14]

Eleanor's attendance at the contests of dialectic between Abelard and his rivals enabled her to put her case well, arguing that by holding her to a marriage which was sinful Louis was placing his immortal soul in jeopardy. A crusader's past sins were to be remitted on arrival at Jerusalem but this would be future sin, for which he would pay with his soul.

The argument was perhaps too good. Louis was stunned as the commander who needed every knight under Eleanor's command, stunned as a husband whose wife wanted no more of him, and stunned as a sovereign whose most important vassal was renouncing her feudal obligations.

The Frankish barons united with the Normans and Flemings in blaming Raymond for putting Eleanor up to this, for what woman could have made such a case for herself? To their way of thinking a queen, once married, was her husband's chattel until death did them part or he sent her away. The only exception was the wife who had the decency to retire to a nunnery. The council was in uproar. If Raymond was allowed to get away with this, what would he think up next? Marry Eleanor off to one of his vassals? Get rid of Constance and marry her himself? In their righteous indignation, it seemed to them that anything was possible in this sink of corruption that had once been the holy city of Antioch.

Whatever Raymond's plans, it was unthinkable for Louis to depart and leave Eleanor behind with some or all of her vassals. How could he explain to the young king of the Latin Kingdom and his mother Queen Melisende, to the master of the Templars and the patriarch of Jerusalem that, in addition to all the losses caused by disease, drowning and the enemy, he had now lost also that part of his army which came from Aquitaine?

It was the cold military logic of Galeran the eunuch that provided the short-term answer to Louis' dilemma – and at the same time came near to ruining the king in the long run. In the middle of the night, Eleanor was seized in her apartments and taken at sword-point by Galeran's men to St Paul's Gate. Long before the first muezzin called the faithful to dawn prayer from the minarets of Antioch, she was riding under guard through the mountains that led to Jerusalem.

In the cool light of day, Louis became aware that, whatever the outcome of the crusade, he had a choice between alternatives, each of which held significant disadvantages. He could divorce Eleanor on their return to France, which would leave him free to marry again and obtain the son needed for the succession. Against that, releasing her would mean returning her dowry, which would – as proved to be the case – dangerously strengthen the power of any other vassal of his whom she chose to marry.

Alternatively, he could imprison the queen and confiscate her territories as the price of treason. But where was the treason? There never was any proof of an illicit relationship between her and Raymond. Were unsupported hearsay and conjecture enough to convince her barons that she had no right to renounce her feudal obligations to Louis and that theirs towards him continued, no matter what she decided? It was an unclear area.

There was another drawback to this course in that he would still be married in the eyes of the Church and thus unable to sire the heir that France demanded. Even if he could talk Eleanor round on the journey home, what about the sin of consanguinity? As ever, it was to Suger that he turned for advice when all else failed. The letter has been lost, or was destroyed by the canny regent of France. But the reply remains: 'If the queen has given you offence, conceal your resentment until you both have returned to your estates, when this matter may be dealt with.'[15]

The immediate problem was to justify to the slimmed-down French army and particularly the vassals who owed allegiance to the duchess of Aquitaine why she was travelling under guard and incommunicado. And thus was born one of the great slanders against Eleanor. William of Tyre refers soberly to her 'indiscretions in Antioch and afterwards', when he finds her 'disregardful of her marriage bond',[16] but that could mean no more than a wife's disobedience to her husband. John of Salisbury repeats the accusation that she had been guilty of too great familiarity with the prince of Antioch.[17] Gervase of Canterbury recommends silence about Eleanor's conduct in the Orient.[18]

Had the king of the Franks been a lustier man than Louis and caught in adultery with some princess in Antioch, every knight in the army would have approved this proof of manhood, never mind what penance was imposed for breaking the vow of celibacy. The Ten Commandments, including the prohibition of adultery, were not Christian, but Mosaic. Only in the following century would they be incorporated into a manual of instruction for those coming to confess their sins and eventually into the catechism used as religious training of the young.

So a king might beget his bastards freely – one of Henry II's ended up as archbishop of York – but a queen's body was state property. For her to use it in pleasure or fulfilment of her own emotions was effectively treason. While there was never a shred of proof that Eleanor and

Raymond had done more than flirt together, the slur against her good name was to follow her to the grave and beyond. Even if they had conspired together, it was not against Louis personally, but to concert their efforts in order to accomplish the original aim of the crusade by retaking Edessa.

The patriarch of Jerusalem had ridden most of the way to Antioch with a bodyguard of Templars not just to welcome Louis but to make sure he did not patch up his quarrel with Raymond or get embroiled with the count of Tripoli on the way. He had been wise to do so; Louis found it difficult to resist the stream of pleas for assistance from all corners of the Latin Kingdom that reached him daily.[19]

Prayers were offered as the party reached Nebi Samwil, the traditional site of the tomb of the Prophet Samuel, dubbed by the Franks Montjoie or *Mons Gaudi* in Latin because it afforded the first view of Jerusalem. The Judean capital was to them not so much a city as the gateway to heaven, of which Bernard of Cluny had written, 'I seek you, I live in you, I burn for you, I desire you, I sing you, I salute you.'[20]

As the French approached the holy city, the entire population came out to welcome them. This was not an exaggeration by the chroniclers, for when the city was taken in the First Crusade, all its Jewish and Muslim inhabitants had been murdered with the oriental Christians living there, whom the crusaders found difficult to distinguish. In 1148 it was peopled exclusively by Christians of European, mostly Frankish, origin. The Sephardi pilgrim Benjamin of Tudela arrived there in 1170 to find only four Jewish inhabitants, earning a living as dyers near the Tower of David.[21]

Among the welcoming party waiting to greet Louis with the half-Armenian Queen Melisende and her son the boy-king Baldwin, was Conrad III, now restored to health by Comnenus' physicians. He had achieved his ambition of being first in Jerusalem, but with only the rump of an army under his command.

Louis refused to be treated as other than a humble pilgrim. On foot and fasting, transported in pious ecstasy, he entered Jerusalem by David's gate, next to the Citadel, which had been David's tower, where the biblical king was said to have composed his psalms. From there he was conducted in procession past the Pool of the Patriarchs and along the Street of the Patriarchs to the church of the Holy Sepulchre built over one of many rock-cut tombs, which Constantine's mother had decided in AD 326 was where the body of Christ had been taken after the Crucifixion two centuries earlier. She had also claimed the discovery of the True Cross during the construction of her church on one of the possible sites of Golgotha. That True Cross had been taken entire to Constantinople, although Queen Melisende had also enclosed a fragment of wood said to be from it in her first plea for help addressed to Abbé Bernard.

As the Protestant John Calvin remarked four centuries later, if all the extant fragments were reassembled they would fill a very large ship. His logic was countered by contemporary Catholic theologians, who argued that contact with the blood of Christ had given the wood the quality of being infinitely divisible. For the devout such as Louis, everything was true – as it is for twenty-first-century pilgrims marching in transports of ecstasy along the Via Dolorosa bearing polystyrene crosses on their shoulders.

Within the church, Louis was dazzled by the mixture of Norman and eastern architecture, by the cistern in which the True Cross had been found, by the chapels of the Crown of Thorns, of the Flagellation, of the Division of the Garments. At last, in placing the oriflamme on the altar directly above the Tomb of Christ, he fulfilled his penance and felt his soul lightened of the guilt that had burdened it since Vitry.

Yet the dispute with Eleanor soured his long-anticipated bliss. The royal household was lodged in the Tower of David as guests of the patriarch, but no mention is made of her in these arrangements. Whether she was present and kept out of sight, so that she could not influence her vassals, is unknown. To all intents and purposes, she had become an unperson for the duration of the crusade. It is perhaps coincidental that Suger's man, the chaplain Odo, seems to have been distanced from Louis at this point.[22] Had he lost out to Galeran in pressing the more subtle temporising arguments of the abbot of St Denis against shortsighted Templar high-handedness? The eunuch's star was in the ascendant in the city where his Order had been founded, and he was to be one of those dispatched ahead of the royal party to prepare for Louis' return to France, putting his side of the story to the pope en route so that Eleanor never got a fair hearing in Rome.

The late king of the Latin Kingdom, Fulk of Anjou, had formerly been a vassal of Louis' father. Also the countess of Flanders was a daughter of Fulk, which made her half-sister to young King Baldwin. And many of Louis' northerners found kin among those who spoke the *langue d'oïl* in Jerusalem. Here the Franks were fêted by the populace in a reversal of the situation at Antioch. The day after his arrival, Louis attended a meeting of Jerusalem's clerical and lay rulers, at which Conrad III managed to muster an impressive presence of German barons and bishops. Unable to decide what, if anything, could be accomplished by the small number of crusaders who had actually made it to the Holy Land, that meeting agreed to call a plenary council at the port of Acre, which would take stock of the fortunes of the Latin Kingdom and decide what should be done.

At the council in Acre, noble ladies including Melisende and the countess of Flanders were present, but Eleanor was not among them.[23] It is inconceivable that she would have refused to attend and put her case in public for the first time. The sole credible explanation for her absence is that she was under arrest.

After much debate, the Acre council could only manage to agree on one objective: to attack Damascus. There was no dispute with Mu'in al-Din Unar, its emir. On the contrary, he and his people traded peacefully with the Latins and since he was the only Arab leader to have signed a treaty with the Franks, by attacking his city they did themselves a great disservice and stiffened the Muslim resistance to all Christians.[24]

As the troubadour Guiraut Riquier wrote later:

> Per erguelh e per malvestat
> dels Christias ditz, luenh d'amor
> e dels mans de Nostre Senhor
> em del sieu Sant Loc discipat.

[It was by arrogance and by pride / that these Christians so-called / lacking love and respect for Our Lord / from His holy place did turn aside.]

The Great Mosque of Damascus – built by the Umayyads on the same site as the Byzantine Church of St John, a previous Roman Temple of Jupiter and the original Aramaean sanctuary of Hadad – was only one of many houses of worship to different cults. At the eastern end of the 'street called straight' stood the Ananias Chapel, commemorating the blinding and conversion of St Paul. Jews, Christians, Muslims and pagans lived in mutual toleration, not side by side but in their autonomous quarters. The misfortune of the Damascenes was that there was no apparently softer target and the Europeans could not simply go home without doing anything; Nur ed-Din was to capture the city six years later and make it an all-Muslim capital, thanks to the weakening effect of the crusader attack.

On the tenuous argument that Damascus might one day be the link to unite the caliphates of Egypt to the south and Baghdad to the north-east, it was decided to set 25 May as the day for all Christian knights to assemble at the city of Tiberias, founded by Herod's son Antipas on the shores of Lake Galilee. From there the long column of the French army, strengthened by indigenous knights and men-at-arms, estimated by the contemporary historian Ibn Al-Qalanisi at 50,000 men plus their horses and draught camels and oxen, marched north via Magdala, birthplace of Mary Magdalene. Past Heptapegon – scene of the miracle of the loaves and fishes – they continued to Capernaum, where Christ had made his base in the house of the fishermen brothers Simon Peter and Andrew, and St Matthew had been a toll-collector.

Still heading north along the lake shore to the silted-up mouth of the Jordan, they passed the site of Bethsaida, where Peter and Andrew had lived before going into partnership with James and John for the better fishing off Capernaum. Up the Jordan Valley they rode to the ruins of Caesarea Philippi, founded by another son of Herod. From its shrine they took another True Cross which was to guarantee victory and continued over the Anti-Lebanon in the pleasant early summer weather, following the oriflamme of France and the *gonfanon bausent*[25] of the Templars towards Damascus itself, which they reached on Saturday 24 July 1148.

The chroniclers' description of their heroic valour is an attempt to gloss over dissension between the various contingents from the very beginning of the siege. The first Christian camp was sited at Manazil al-Askar, a defensible position but with the enormous disadvantage that the Damascenes had destroyed their entire irrigation system on that side of the city and blocked or poisoned the wells when laying waste their orchards, vineyards and fields to deny any sustenance to the invaders.[26]

If one believes William of Tyre, the decision to relocate to the other side of the city on the following day was the result of certain crusader leaders accepting bribes from the Damascenes to urge this course at the very moment when victory was in their grasp.[27] In fact, the move was simply to be nearer a source of water sufficient for over 100,000 men and animals, whose supplies of food were inadequate. The water was defended, but not too strongly, and the crusaders gave thanks to God after driving off the Damascene forces and making their new camp in the devastated orchards just outside the city walls, unaware that they had moved into a carefully laid trap.

Inside Damascus the citizens were erecting barricades in the streets, but on the second day Muslim reinforcements began arriving from the Beka'a Valley. Cowering under a hail of arrows behind hastily erected barricades of tree trunks, the Frankish army waited for their cavalry to be given the order to attack each sortie from the city, but there was no room for men on horseback to manoeuvre in the broken ground of orchards and gardens near the walls. Each group of mounted Franks bold enough to get close to the city was ambushed, their heads being cut off and carried back inside the walls to earn a reward. To avoid being taken alive, many knights carried a misericord, which was a thin-bladed dagger that could be slipped between the joins of body armour by themselves or a comrade to deliver a *coup de grâce* – literally a 'stroke of mercy' to a badly injured knight.

The Damascenes had at least a rudimentary medical service. On campaign, Saladin had a camel-mounted ambulance service, with a camp for the wounded kept separate from his main encampment for sanitary reasons. He had doctors and one specially trained surgeon in Aleppo, who was skilled in setting broken limbs. But on the Christian side, although the Hospitallers had built a 2,000-bed hospital for sick pilgrims in Jerusalem, caring for the wounded in battle meant little more than the consolation of the last rites; deep slash or stab wounds often meant death from infection.

On the Monday, Turkish, Kurdish and Arab cavalry began to arrive from the north. When messengers were intercepted bearing news that Nur ed-Din was arriving on the Tuesday with the army of Aleppo and his brother Safadin with the army of Mosul, the crusaders abandoned their tents and retreated to safe territory in disarray, having achieved absolutely nothing for which they had come. Ibn Al-Qalanisi records that this was thought to be a feint, but it was a retreat. As he piously remarked, 'may God be praised'.[28]

So ended the Second Crusade, after four inglorious days of ineffectual strife against neutrals who had done no wrong. No one seems to have given another thought to the unchanged situation of Edessa far to the north when Louis discharged his vassals of further crusading obligation. Those who had not succeeded in finding a niche in the Latin Kingdom set off for France, the needy being provided with money for the journey home out of the king's pocket. However, he resisted the urging from St Denis that his duty lay with his people in Paris: 'Why do you persist', Suger wrote, 'in enduring so many desperate ills after your barons and nobles have returned? For what fault of ours, or plan of your own, do you delay your return?'[29]

It is not as if all was peace and quiet on the home front. One of the lesser problems confronting the abbot of St Denis was unrest in Aquitaine. Guillaume de Mauzé, the seneschal of Poitou, was complaining that Ebles de Mauléon and others were refusing to settle their tax bills, inflated by the crusade, and that lawlessness in Bordeaux had resulted in 'enemies of the king and citizens killing each other'.[30] Mauzé was fretting at the leash to get out to the Holy Land before all the action was over, and begged Suger to replace him with someone 'honest and subtle'.

His replacement turned out to be none other than Geoffroi de Rancon, freshly returned from his disgrace in Turkey. His new appointment, which was a mark of the king's favour, and the fact that he had been charged with using the revenues of the duchy to pay off the enormous debt Louis had run up with the Order of the Templars, provokes the question whether he really had caused the massacre on Mount Cadmos, or had been merely the alibi for Louis' bad generalship.

Whatever the reasons for his new appointment, Rancon had no more success in restoring order in the duchy, writing to Suger at St Denis that what Aquitaine needed was a lord who could 'rebuild damaged homes and restore the walls of fortresses'.[31] The most obvious person to do that was in the Holy Land, apparently a prisoner if for no other reason than that Louis' advisers would not allow her to return to France before him and take refuge on her own lands.[32] In the end it was Archbishop Geoffroi who took command of the city and did his best to restore order, begging from the regent–abbot at St Denis the money necessary to repair the breached ramparts.

There is no record of Louis' reply to Suger's urging him to return. Months passed. While there is no explicit evidence that Eleanor was under lock and key, what other explanation is there for her staying so long in Outremer after the abduction from Antioch? Whatever the precise form of the ladies' vows at Vézelay, no one expected them to go into combat; therefore simply by coming to Jerusalem she had gained the right to return home with the blessing of the Church.

Had she been at liberty, it is inconceivable that she would have chosen to stay on in the Holy Land, disgraced and sidelined. The richest woman in Christendom, after a decade and a half learning palace politics on the Ile de France and among the squabbling barons during the crusade and its preparations, would have been perfectly able to charter for herself a ship, had she been at liberty. So one has to conclude that she was under some form of constraint or confinement as Louis' prisoner.

Christmas came, and spring. More than a year had passed since they landed at St Simeon. Only after celebrating Easter of 1149 in Jerusalem did Louis at last ride down through the Judean mountains and head north along the coast, embarking at Acre in one small high-pooped pilgrim transport while Eleanor and her small household travelled separately in another ship. Thus ended the first of sixteen years she was to spend as a prisoner at the whim of her two husbands.

On the visit to Rome during the journey home, her hatred of Galeran was vehemently expressed to the pope, which poses the question: had the lost year of her life been the Templar eunuch's idea? Were the first months of her confinement to hide a pregnancy resulting from the relationship with Raymond? Because the adultery would have debarred Louis from remarrying, it is conceivable that this would have been kept secret at the time. If there was a child, what happened to it?

There were reports of Thierry Galeran being seen in Belin after his return to France, despite Aquitaine being a region where he was not welcome. One of the accusations against Eleanor after the divorce from Louis was that she had buried her bastards in the churchyard there. So, did Galeran kill a child by Raymond, whose birth had to be hidden, and afterwards in accordance with a Templar's oath fulfil an undertaking to bury the small corpse in the discreet churchyard, where Eleanor could visit the grave in secrecy? It would account for the rumour. Yet, even if this had been hushed up at the time, it is unlikely that her detractors would have failed after Louis' death to write up so great a slur on her name.

But there is a second possible explanation of what happened during the missing year.

EIGHT

Eleanor's Greatest Gamble

The homeward voyage was uneventful until some Sicilian galleys were sighted off the southern tip of mainland Greece in worsening weather. Coming alongside one of them for the latest news from Europe, Louis learned that King Roger of Sicily was at war with Comnenus because the homebound German Emperor had concluded a deal in Constantinople for joint military action with Byzantine forces against Sicilian expansion into Byzantine territory along the Adriatic seaboard. So much for the story of the 'treacherous Greek guides' who had caused Conrad's defeat by the Turks. . . .

Hardly had the vessels separated to continue on their way when a squadron of Byzantine galleys captured Eleanor's ship together with Louis' escort and baggage and drove them away as a prize of war in the direction of the nearest harbour. The captain of Louis' ship avoided the same fate by running up a false flag – a common device in those pirate-infested waters. So why had the queen's ship not done the same? Any hopes Eleanor had of escaping in the confusion were dashed when the

112

Sicilians' galleys returned and forced the Byzantines to release their slower-moving prize in order to save themselves.

High seas and poor visibility then separated Louis' small convoy, after which he and Eleanor were not to see each other again for two whole months. Unsubstantiated legend says that she spent part of this time in what is now Tunisia, but it seems to have been adverse weather and possibly health problems that caused the delay. Two days before the end of July Louis reached the Italian mainland somewhere in Calabria with a few companions, having been so ill from seasickness that he swore never again to set foot in a boat.

Local Normans loyal to Roger of Sicily provided the royal pilgrim with food and clothing, and also gave him news of Eleanor, who had landed at the Sicilian port of Palermo shortly before. Having suffered prolonged seasickness while tossed for days on end in gales off what was called the coast of Barbary, it is not surprising that she did not feel up to making even the short crossing over the straits of Messina to the mainland. But three weeks later she did so and caught up with Louis at the Sicilian court in Potenza, where they were well received and gave thanks for their deliverance in the cathedral whose twelfth-century apse and rose windows still survive after much rebuilding made necessary by earth tremors.

On the journey north, Louis and Eleanor visited St Benedict's monastery of Monte Cassino, where Pope Innocent II had been captured by Roger of Sicily ten years before. There, some monk avid for gossip gleaned that Louis had travelled back to Antioch after the siege of Damascus.[1] As to why he had done this and whether alone or with Eleanor, the annals of the monastery are mute, which only adds to the mystery of the missing year.

Immediately after his return from crusade, emboldened by his alliance with Byzantium, Conrad III had reopened hostilities against the papal territories in central Italy. With the southern third of the peninsula already within the Kingdom of the Two Sicilies, the pope was exiled from Rome and staying at his castle of Tusculum[2] on the northern slopes of the Alban hills, fifteen miles south-east of Rome.

In the halls whose ruins stand above the town he received Eleanor and Louis as returning pilgrims who had suffered much for their faith during the two years since he had blessed the oriflamme at St Denis. Louis confided his ambition of raising finance for another expedition to the Holy Land to carry out all the Second Crusade had so signally failed to achieve, but Eleanor had more personal issues on her mind. As papal secretary, John of Salisbury recorded the queen's skilful presentation of her case for an annulment of the marriage to Louis on the grounds of consanguinity, in which she cited the authority of Bernard of Clairvaux, whom the pope himself consulted on points of canon law.

Smiling but firm, Eugenius would hear none of this. Ignoring Eleanor's arguments and Bernard's judgement, he confirmed to her horror that the marriage was legitimate and threatened with anathema anyone rash enough to refer to the matter of this consanguinity in future. Eleanor was furious that Galeran and the king's other clerical advisers had turned Eugenius' ear against her before she had had a chance to put her case. Abandoning dialectic, she poured out to him the long list of her legitimate grievances, including her abduction from Antioch by the Templar eunuch and the continual constraint under which she lived in Louis' household.

In best diplomatic style, the pope listened but, far from taking any notice of a woman desperate to escape from a hated and frustrating marriage, gave instructions that a double bed be prepared for the royal spouses and spread with his own bedcovers. The following day he acted the part of marriage guidance counsellor until he at least was convinced that he had reconciled the royal couple after all their past differences, then gave them presents before watching them leave with tears in his eyes. It was an unusual display of emotion for this reserved and celibate priest.[3]

Ahead of them lay Rome. Squalid, reduced to less than a quarter of its imperial size and with vast tracts of wasteland within the walls, ruined by repeated invasion and damaged anew during the recent fighting, the once eternal city was a sad mockery of vibrant Byzantium. What Eleanor did to contain her fury at being treated by Eugenius like a wayward child is not recorded. Louis the pilgrim was welcomed at the gate of the city by a deputation of senators representing the commune that had killed a pope trying to assert his pontifical rights only six years before. Accepting the freedom of the city and guided by the senators, the pilgrim king toured the most important holy sites followed by a claque chanting in Latin, 'Blessed is he that comes in the name of the Lord.'

Just as important to pilgrims as the apostles' tombs was the multitude of relics in Rome credited with the ability to re-transmit some of the virtue absorbed from contact with the saints and martyrs. Chief of these was the 'Veronica', a handkerchief-sized piece of cloth on which Christ was said to have wiped His face and imprinted his features on the way to His crucifixion. Nor would Louis have missed the grisly relics of the circumcision and the birth in the manger, nor the phial of the Virgin's milk.

But it was unwise to linger in Rome at this time of year, when *la mal'aria* – literally 'bad air', from the swamps around the city – was blamed for killing off many visitors, although most Romans seemed to have developed some tolerance for it. So the royal couple travelled on by the Via Aurelia, crossed the Alps and arrived in Auxerre, Burgundy, where Abbot Suger met them to give an account of his exemplary stewardship of the kingdom and mediate between Louis and Eleanor in comparative privacy before they were exposed to the courtiers in that gossip factory which was the Ile de la Cité. It was all to no avail; Eleanor's mind was made up.

Together with Suger, they journeyed on to Paris, arriving at Martinmas in November 1149. The abbot of St Denis, who would be given Augustus' ultimate accolade of *pater patriae* on his death by Louis for all he had done for the country and the monarchs he served, had somehow found time to have Eleanor's apartments refurbished in the hope that this would make her homecoming at least more comfortable. It was a gesture she spurned; as far as she was concerned, he had merely gilded the bars of her cage. Two and a half years after setting out on her great adventure, Eleanor was back in Louis' palace more deeply ensnared in her unwanted marriage than ever.

Medals were struck commemorating the great achievements of the crusade, with Louis seated in a triumphal chariot and Victory above him bearing palm and crown. Others depicted heaps of Turks slain by the faithful. The legends around the outside read, 'The citizens of Paris joyfully welcome their king returning victorious from the Orient, 1149' and 'Fleeing Turks slain on the banks of the Meander'.[4] The spin doctors had a field day proving that the Second Crusade had been a success, while churchmen, including the pope, tied themselves in knots seeking signs of God's will in the obvious failure of the great enterprise that had cost so many lives. Abbé Bernard's rationalisation was that mankind was as yet unworthy to be rewarded with success, while Bishop Otto of Freising, Odo's counterpart as official German chronicler, described the crusade as a boon to those it had enabled to gain a martyr's crown.[5]

The winter of 1149/50 was unusually severe across the whole of northern Europe. Rivers and sea froze in many places, but Louis' immediate problem was the political chill between him and his barons. If they continued to blame the Poitevins – and therefore the now-pregnant queen on the Ile de la Cité – for the disaster in the mountains and her alleged treason in Antioch, they also blamed his criminal vacillation in leadership for consuming their personal fortunes to no effect. Suger had foreseen this when urging Louis to hurry home.[6] So the king had only himself to blame for allowing the political balance to turn against him for a whole year after his enemies returned to spread their side of the story. He must have had a powerful reason to ignore Suger's pleas.

At some unknown date in 1150 Eleanor gave birth to another daughter, christened Aelith after her aunt. Most historians have assumed that this occurred at least nine months after the pope's marriage guidance counselling at Tusculum, but Professor Friedrich Heer calculated the birth as having taken place in the winter of 1149/50.[7] If he was right, the alternative explanation of Eleanor's missing year is that she was kept a prisoner in the Holy Land for several months until she finally consented to pay the price of the journey home, which was allowing Louis to get her with child.

That would never have been his own idea, but it would account for her hatred of Galeran, for only he would have dreamed up such a scenario. Had she been suffering prolonged seasickness in addition to the inconvenience of pregnancy during the mystery weeks when she was missing at sea, that might also account for her needing to convalesce for three weeks before crossing from Sicily to the main-land and the slow rate of subsequent progress northward.

After the birth of his second daughter Louis' political enemies added the inability to beget a son to the list of their monarch's shortcomings. For Eleanor, Aelith's birth was a mixed blessing. Had the newborn been male, it is possible that she would have recouped some respect among the Franks as the mother of their future king and resigned herself to her position, which would have changed the course of European history for 300 years. As it was, Louis was under increasing pressure to find himself another wife who would perform the most important duty of a queen.

Just when he most needed them, Suger's wise and temperate counsels ceased with the abbot's death on 11 January 1151 at the age of seventy. One of the problems of a feudal king whose political credit was low was keeping even a semblance of loyalty among his vassals. Among many who had failed to pay homage to Louis were Count Geoffrey of Anjou, which adjoined Eleanor's Poitou on the north, and his son Duke Henry of Normandy, which spread from Anjou to the English Channel. After Louis sent the bishop of Lisieux to remind father and son of their obligations, they duly came to Paris.[8]

The counts of Anjou were said to be descended from an ancestress named Mélusine, whose satanic origins were proven by the fact that she never remained in church to take communion. Being a son of the late

King Fulk of Jerusalem and thus well aware of the realities of the Latin Kingdom, Count Geoffrey had remained aloof from the crusading fever (plate 10). More important to him was keeping a firm control over his own domains.[9]

Geoffrey the Fair was still in his forties, handsome, brave, courtly and exceptionally literate. His equally literate son was known as Henry fitz Empress. The *fitz* prefix of noble Norman names being a corruption of the Latin *filius*, meaning 'son of', he owed the grand surname to his mother Matilda, the daughter of England's Henry I who had previously been married to the German Emperor Henry V. After his death she had at the age of twenty-six married Count Geoffrey, then aged fifteen. For a decade and a half afterwards, she had been one of the two principal belligerents in the civil war that ravaged England after the death of her father. Although courageous and militarily competent, the Empress Matilda was a hard and bitter woman who had raised her eldest son to be as scheming and devious as herself. Her philosophy modelled on the sport of venery, the main lesson she imparted to him was to show the reward to the hawk but always take it away at the last moment to keep the bird hungry. It was a policy that Henry used throughout his life.

When Eleanor met him for the first time, the young duke of Normandy was no courtly fop, but a swaggering, barrel-chested young man with freckles, grey eyes and short reddish hair, so toughened by continual exercise that he disdained wearing a glove when out hawking, but accepted the bird's sharp talons on his bare wrist. Recently knighted by his cousin the king of Scotland,[10] he had already proved himself in battle although only nineteen years old. Through his mother's bloodline he had Normandy and claims on the English throne; through his father he was heir to Anjou, Maine and Touraine. Thanks to his mother, he was also remarkably well educated for a layman, having been tutored in boyhood by Matthieu of Loudun and William of Conches, who dedicated to him a treatise on moral philosophy. During his years in England the great scientist Adelard of Bath had also dedicated a book to him.

All this made him quite a catch, politically speaking – which is why the idea had been mooted before the crusade of marrying him to Princess Marie to guarantee a strong new dynasty on the throne of France, should Louis die in Outremer without an heir. Abbé Bernard had vetoed the idea on the grounds of consanguinity,[11] but Louis had rejected it because he favoured the claim to the English throne of Henry's rival, Eustace of Blois.

Later it would be said that the saint of Clairvaux had predicted a bad end for Henry when seeing him for the first time as an infant,[12] but this sort of retroactive prophecy was often invented in hagiographic biographies. Certainly, when Henry of Anjou rode across the Petit Pont onto the Ile de la Cité with his father to pay belated homage for the duchy of Normandy, no one in Paris would have prophesied other than a brilliant future for Count Geoffrey's son.

The two Plantagenets – the family nickname derived from Count Geoffrey's use of a sprig of bright yellow broom, or *planta genista*, stuck in his helmet as an identification in the mêlée of battle – had not come all the way from their domains in the heat of midsummer just to do homage on bended knee. Henry needed the king's formal assent to his installation as duke of Normandy. In addition, Geoffrey had brought with him a prisoner, for laying hands on whom Bernard of Clairvaux had excommunicated him on the grounds that the man was a servant of Louis and therefore protected at the time by the crusader's immunity of his master.

In this tangled story, the seneschal for Poitou, through whom Louis governed Eleanor's Poitevin domains, had been allegedly caught red-handed laying waste some of Henry's territory. Only the Peace of God, swore the count of Anjou, had stopped him taking his own vengeance on the ruffian. Refusing Abbé Bernard's offer to lift the excommunication in return for the seneschal's release, Count Geoffrey hauled him before the king and demanded justice, declaring to all who cared to listen that if holding such a captive were indeed a sin, then God would pardon him for it.[13] The blasphemy must have amused Eleanor as much as it amazed the Franks because this sort of behaviour was so like that of her father and grandfather. These neighbours were her kind of people. She could talk to them.

Geoffrey was looking for a well-endowed wife for his son. After the divorce she had so long been denied, but which was now being actively promoted by all her enemies at the Capetian court, Eleanor would be obliged immediately to marry a new husband powerful enough to defend her birthright, or risk seeing it snatched away by force the moment she was no longer protected by being Louis' wife. It is true she was eleven years older than Henry, but the same age-gap had not stopped his father marrying the Empress Matilda[14] and Eleanor still had her beauty and a decade or so of childbearing years ahead of her.

The clincher for Henry was that, the stronger he was in France, the greater was his chance of succeeding his mother's cousin Stephen of Blois to become the next king of England. As to an heir, it was common knowledge how rarely Louis had slept with his wife, so the lusty young duke of Normandy had no fears that he would be able to get Eleanor pregnant again and again until she bore him a son. And if she didn't? To the Plantagenet way of thinking, should she have failed to do so by the time of her menopause, Henry would still be in his early thirties and able to find a way of dumping her and keeping his hands on her dowry. Or so he thought.

Normally, sounding out the ground in a situation like this would have been done through clerical intermediaries. However, Suger was dead and Bernard no friend of the queen. Surrounded by enemies, Eleanor had no alternative but to conduct negotiations with the Plantagenets herself. A lesser man than Geoffrey might have found it impossible to talk with her in secret among the ears and eyes in the corridors and courtyards of the Ile de la Cité, but the count who had defied Bernard of Clairvaux's anathema had no qualms about frightening away anyone trying to eavesdrop on his private talks with the queen of France in the palace gardens. It was these conversations without witnesses that provided 'the proof' for a second set of slanders after her remarriage – in this case that the Whore of Aquitaine had slept with the father before marrying the son.

Abruptly, Count Geoffrey released the captive seneschal and abandoned any claim for damages in respect of his misconduct. He also ceded to the king his claims to the disputed border territory of the Vexin, standing witness as his son swore fealty for the duchy of Normandy *sans* Vexin. The vassalage ceremony had three elements by this time: the enclosing of the vassal's hands within those of his overlord, the kiss of peace given on the lips and the swearing of the oath. After kneeling before Louis and pledging himself to defend his liege lord against all his enemies, the young duke of Normandy received the kiss of peace.[15]

There is no record of what had calmed Geoffrey's anger, but for two arrogant and ambitious vassals like the Plantagenets to knuckle down so swiftly and quietly go away implies a clandestine plan.

The city of Angers, with its original twelfth-century stained-glass windows in the cathedral of St Maurice, lies almost two hundred miles from Paris. It was a long, hot ride home for father and son in the first days of September. Pleased with the outcome of their trip, they halted at the River Loir near their own city of Le Mans and stripped off to cool down in the water. Spending the night at the nearby castle of Le Lude, Geoffrey went down with a high fever – probably from swallowing contaminated river water. Three days later, he was dead, the devout believing it his due for defying Bernard of Clairvaux.

His last thoughts were to advise Henry to govern each of his possessions appropriately and not impose a single code of law throughout. He also instructed his followers not to bury him until his stubborn son had taken an oath that, if and when he became king of England, he would yield Anjou, Maine and Touraine to a younger brother also called Geoffrey. This Henry refused to do until his companions persuaded him that it would be a scandal to keep his father's corpse above ground any longer in the midsummer heat. Weeping with rage and frustration, he complied despite knowing that he would never honour the oath.

With his twentieth birthday still ahead of him, Henry buried his father in Le Mans and hurried to Angers, where his vassals recognised him as their new count.[16] A few days later, Eleanor set out for Aquitaine to make a comprehensive survey of her domains. Louis' large retinue in the cavalcade included her arch-enemy Galeran and Suger's successor, Hugues de Champfleury. Escorting the queen were many of her bishops and other vassals, with Archbishop Geoffroi of Bordeaux as her chief spokesman. The entire period of the vintage was spent in negotiation in the privacy of her personal estates, after which a tour of inspection of the duchy lasted until Christmas.

This was no routine progress from castle to castle and city to city checking accounts and hearing grievances. Although no public announcement had yet been made about divorce, the long tour was nothing less than a handover audit, with the bishops on both sides keeping tally so that each party received what was due. To avoid a power vacuum, the withdrawal of Louis' garrisons and administrators from her dower lands had to be synchronised with the installation of Eleanor's machinery of government prior to the public announcement of the dissolution of the royal marriage.[17]

The Christmas court was held at Limoges and a plenary council at St Jean d'Angély while celebrating Candlemas in the first week of February. Behind the scenes the midnight candles burned as the men of God busied themselves undoing the knots of Eugenius' validation in perpetuity of the marriage, given at Tusculum. Eleanor's unlikely ally in this was Bernard of Clairvaux who, unlike Suger and Hugues de Champfleury, cared nothing for political considerations. In his view the value of Eleanor's dowry to the Capetian kingdom was but dross, compared with the need to dissolve Louis' incestuous marriage to a woman in whose veins flowed the blood of William IX, the adulterous troubadour, and his son who had corrupted bishops and defied excommunication. Was it not she who had led Louis to the massacre of

Vitry, and her fault that God had not blessed the Second Crusade with success? Christ had said in the Sermon on the Mount that an eye which sinned should be plucked out and thrown away, for it was better to lose a hand or an eye than for the whole body to be cast into hellfire.

On the Friday before Palm Sunday, which would have been 21 March 1152, the Archbishop of Sens – who had presided over the condemnation of Abelard – convened a synod in Louis' castle at Beaugency, midway between Orleans and Blois. Present were his fellow archbishops of Reims, Rouen and Bordeaux, other senior churchmen and numerous barons and other nobles. Louis, with a genuine nobility and charity rare among royalty of any period, still refused to accuse Eleanor of anything that might be prejudicial to her. It was therefore agreed for the dignity of the monarchy that his representatives should present the case for consanguinity. All Eleanor had to do was to sit and listen. Acting as her chief spokesman Geoffroi de Lauroux, who had arranged the marriage fifteen years before, received the other side's assurance that all her lands would be restored to her as they were at the time of the marriage on condition that she remained a loyal vassal of the king.

The decree was read out[18] and that, for Eleanor, was that. The prize of release from the marriage to Louis, which she had sought for so long, had been obtained at the cost of a year of her life, plus a pregnancy she had not wanted. But she was free, at a price. Her daughters were the property of the house of Capet; it was extremely unlikely she would ever see them again and if she did, they would be strangers.

Having conveniently forgotten Eleanor's outburst in Tusculum, John of Salisbury later described this annulment as her 'repudiation'. Later writers would fictionalise the event, casting her as the wife discarded because she had produced no heir, and describing her departure from Beaugency, tearful and distraught.

The cheapest way to tarnish the reputation of the queen who had outwitted the house of Capet to regain her own freedom was to allege that she was an adulteress. Which is exactly what happened. The slanders to prove that Louis had repudiated an unfaithful wife had a long life. In the mid-1990s the audio-commentary at Chinon castle still averred that she had been 'unfaithful to the king in front of the whole court'.[19] It would have taken a lot of arranging on the Ile de la Cité, where she had been spied upon since the day of her arrival by hostile courtiers, priests and servants. As to what she had done with the inevitable results of her illicit liaisons, it was after the separation at Beaugency that the rumours about Belin churchyard began to circulate.

Generations of historians have repeated the calumnies against her, but Henry Plantagenet certainly knew the situation better than they. He was paranoid and had been raised by his mother, the former German Empress, for the highest of royal destinies. Yet he was eager to marry Eleanor at the risk of a war with Louis. One has to ask, would such a man have taken as wife to provide his heirs a woman who had – in the forensic view of the time – soiled her 'female semen'? And the only sane answer to that question is 'no'.

Eleanor rode away from Beaugency with a small escort of her own vassals, once again, at the age of thirty, fair game for any noble with the nerve to kidnap her and marry her by force. Near Blois, she came near to being ambushed by men commanded by Henry of Anjou's younger brother Geoffrey, an upstart of sixteen who had all the Plantagenet nerve, but little else in his favour.[20] Another ambush by Thibault of Blois, second son of Louis' vassal the count of Champagne, had been prepared where she was to cross the River Loire near Tours, as the shortest way to safety on her own territory.[21] A last-minute change of route left him empty-handed, and saw Eleanor at long last mistress of her own possessions.

In the Tour Maubergeonne of the ducal palace at Poitiers she could draw breath and plan her next move. She was fairly certain that the arrangement secretly arrived at with the late count of Anjou would be honoured by his son for his own selfish reasons, but Henry Plantagenet was a man who made promises and broke them all his life, so one could never be sure where one stood with him – as she was to find out.

On 6 April he called a meeting of his vassals in Normandy. In acquainting them with his intention of marrying the ex-queen of France without the king's permission in accordance with feudal custom, he was warning them to be ready for incursions from Frankish territory. As one of his assembled bishops must have pointed out to him, there was a significant impediment to his plan to marry Eleanor in that she was even more closely related to him than she had been to Louis. Leaving that detail to his clerics, Henry prepared to make his move.

In Aquitaine, Eleanor was busy with administrative chores, repudiating all the charters she had signed jointly with Louis on the grounds that they had been granted under constraint. It was with great relief that she welcomed the arrival in Poitiers during the second week of May of the nineteen-year-old duke of Normandy. Married life with him was certain to be more exciting than with Louis. So much so that even the sober Alfred Richard, nineteenth-century archivist of the *département* of Vienne, who devoted several hundred pages to Eleanor in his comprehensive study of the counts of Poitou, stated that she was bored with Louis' platonic love and deliberately sought a brutal new lover in Henry because she was 'one of those women who like to be knocked around'.[22]

Like all the other slanders, the accusation is baseless. The facts are that though she had been denied a proper hearing in Louis' councils for the past few years, all Eleanor's life had been spent in the corridors of power. This was no love match. In marrying Henry, she was wedding the thirteen counties of Aquitaine and the county of Poitou to the duchy of Normandy, plus Anjou, Maine and Touraine. This master stroke created a power bloc that stretched all the way from the snows of the Pyrenees to the waters of the English Channel and eventually united nearly half of Louis' kingdom. On 18 May a ceremony in due form in Poitiers Cathedral[23] made her wife to the man who not only solved her pressing need for a spouse strong enough to protect her domains from present enemies, but owed her a lifelong debt of gratitude for making him the most powerful man in France. Ironically, he would become in the course of time her most implacable enemy of all.

NINE

A Son at Last

The immediate consequence of the May wedding was a war. Although of brief duration, it was the first round in a protracted series of hostilities caused by Eleanor's divorce and remarriage that would last for three centuries and cost uncounted lives.

The first move was taken in Paris, when Louis was advised that Henry should be summoned to court on a charge of treason for failing to ask permission to marry from the suzerain to whom he had so lately sworn fealty. Technically, Eleanor was equally guilty, but no such accusation was levelled against her; nor was Louis ever overtly hostile to her in the future.

Curiously, neither Abbé Bernard nor Pope Eugenius could be persuaded to support the charge of treason. The Church was playing another game behind the scenes: in obedience to Eugenius' instructions, Archbishop Theobald of Canterbury had refused to crown Stephen of Blois' son Eustace of Boulogne as his successor to the crown of England.

No one at the Capetian court expected Henry of Anjou to put in an appearance; the summons was a way of clearing the ground for the next step. Just over a month later that step was taken in concert with Stephen of Blois, who saw it as a way of weakening his son's chief competitor for the throne of the island realm after his death. Attack being the best defence, he concerted with Louis a pre-emptive invasion of Henry's territory, in which his contingent was to be led by Eustace. Robert of Dreux, forgiven for the attempted *coup d'état* while the king was in Outremer, joined the coalition, as did Thibault of Blois and Geoffrey Plantagenet, Henry's younger brother, both of whom had failed to kidnap Eleanor on the flight from Paris. Having lost the mother, Thibault had gained the daughter, having just been betrothed to Eleanor's second daughter, two-year-old Aelith. Henry of Champagne, another of Louis' party, had just married Eleanor's elder daughter Marie, which gave him a tentative claim to the duchy of Aquitaine that he would lose if she gave birth to a son by Henry of Anjou.

Deprived of his most trusted advisers by the recent deaths of Raoul de Vermandois and Thibault of Champagne, Louis belatedly realised that he was commander-in-chief in name only. Each member of the coalition was intent on carving up Henry's and Eleanor's domains from the Channel to the Pyrenees and grabbing the largest possible slice for himself.[1]

Henry of Anjou had been anticipating this move ever since his council of war on 6 April. As events would prove repeatedly, he was adept at making his enemies think he was doing one thing when in fact he was doing another. In this case, when the coalition invaded just after Midsummer Day, they thought him preoccupied with his preparations to invade England from Barfleur, the little port in the lee of the Cotentin peninsula.

That was just a feint. If his true qualities had in the past been hidden by those of his father, now for the first time he showed his true mettle, riding horses into the ground and laying waste Robert of Dreux's lands. Courage is better than numbers in war, said Vegetius, and speed better than courage. The speed and fury of Henry's counter-attack appalled Louis, who fell ill with some kind of fever and retreated as soon as the Church called for a truce.

His blood up, Henry rode back to Anjou, which his brother had attempted to rise against him, and broke the rebellion there by capturing the castle at Montsoreau, garrisoned by Geoffrey's supporters. Far from weakening Henry's position, the abortive invasion had actually done him a double favour in forcing him to show his strength as a warning to his neighbours not to try to profit from his absence

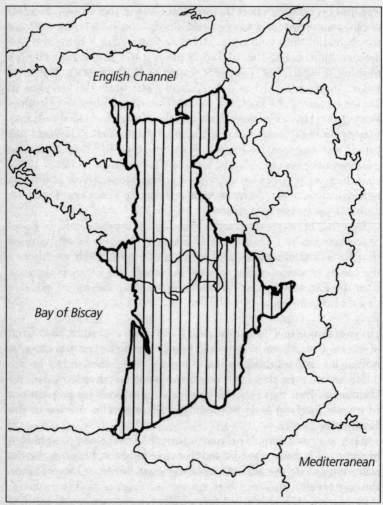

Eleanor's and Henry's combined possessions on 19 May 1152.

when he did eventually invade England, and also obliging him to delay that invasion until the following year, when he was better prepared.

After seeing off the coalition, Henry spent the autumn with Eleanor. Their feudal progress through Aquitaine was hardly a honeymoon. After enjoying the grape harvest on her estates in Poitou – although 'enjoying' is perhaps the wrong word, for Henry never relaxed – they continued southward with the new duke of Aquitaine assessing the castles and fortified towns of Gascony both militarily and fiscally, and assuring himself that the new administrators who had replaced Louis' men knew exactly who was now in charge.

He had already developed the style of travel that would anguish all but the hardiest of his courtiers on both sides of the Channel. That first journey Eleanor shared with him in the summer and autumn of 1152 fits the description by her sometime secretary Peter of Blois of his travels with Henry's court a few years later:

> If the King has announced that he will depart early next morning, the decision is sure to be changed . . . and he will sleep to midday. You will see pack animals waiting under their loads, teams of horses standing, heralds sleeping, court traders fretting, and everyone . . . grumbling. One runs to the whores . . . to ask them where the King is going, for this breed of courtier often knows the palace secrets.[2]

That was a euphemism for saying how Henry spent his nights.

Peter also commented on those members of the court who had undergone bloodletting or taken laxatives but followed Henry's precipitate departures, forfeiting their dignity and sometimes their lives, 'risking to lose themselves rather than lose what they haven't got and are not going to get'. Court life, he said, was death for the soul.[3]

His fellow courtier Walter Map conveyed this hectic lifestyle in his *Courtiers' Gossip*,[4] quoting St Augustine's observation that he was in time and spoke of time, yet knew not what time was. 'With a similar sense of amazement,' wrote Map, 'I could say that I am in the court and I speak of the court, but God knows what the court is. [It] is a pleasant place only for those who obtain its favour [which] comes regardless of reason, establishes itself regardless of merit, arrives obscurely from unknown causes.'[5]

According to him, the entire retinue wore out their clothes, their mounts, their bodies and their souls, such was the relentless pace Henry expected of everyone in his service. Yet no courtier could risk not being present when summoned at any hour of the day or night, for those Henry had raised to greatness, he could cast down. And when they fell, they pulled others with them. 'Friendship among those who are summoned to give the King counsel and undertake his business is one of the rarest things. Anxious ambition dominates their minds; each of them fears to be outstripped by the endeavours of the others. So is born envy, which necessarily turns immediately into hatred.'[6] Thus Arnulf of Lisieux, a Norman vassal of Henry's, wrote from his own bitter experience.

Yet Henry could be affable when hearing out petitioners. He could be generous to a captain who had lost his ship or a vassal who had lost a limb in the royal service or a peasant whose property had been damaged by the royal hunt or to the poor during time of famine. When relaxed, he joked with his intimates or called for needle and thread to mend his own clothes. He was tolerant of Jews and heretics, but not homosexuals, once authorising torture for some Templars accused of sodomy. Much of his legislation is a model of justice, while his forest laws were vindictively cruel.

Indifferent to food, he contented himself when necessary while travelling with gruel or bread and expected his companions to do the same. If he thought that this lifestyle might drive Eleanor to retire from the erratic progress and wait for him in the comital palace at Poitiers, he was wrong. The woman who had ridden across Turkey on the Second Crusade was tougher than that. Rising to every challenge, she was determined to establish her own position in the marriage from the outset, while quickly realising she would never have a fraction of the influence over her new husband that she had enjoyed over Louis.

Hyperactive, Henry rarely sat down except for a game of chess or to eat, and would be on the move again as soon as hunger was sated or the game over. Even during Mass he fidgeted continually, giving orders to his clerks or taking aside someone with whom he wished to talk. He dressed in costly but carelessly worn clothes, taking no interest in his appearance. His reddish hair was kept cut unfashionably short for the good reason that long hair became tangled by rubbing against the leather liner of a helmet of a man forever ready for combat. His nickname, Henry Curtmantle, referred to his habit of wearing a very short coat that gave little protection from the weather but made it quicker to mount and dismount.

His curiosity was insatiable. Never accepting another man's word for anything, he had to see, touch and try it out for himself, whether a horse, a dog, a jewel or piece of material offered by a merchant, a vassal's hawk, a weapon or an idea.[7] A genial enough companion for the few with the intellect to amuse him, he rapidly lost interest when they could no longer be of service or entertainment value. If thwarted or defied, he went literally berserk, foaming at the mouth and hurling himself at anyone within reach, or falling to the floor and rolling in the soiled reeds and refuse of an audience hall, groaning like an animal in agony.

Yet there was nothing haphazard about his apparently erratic habits. His hectic itineraries were an important factor in his later ability to govern very successfully the enormous spread of territory on both sides of the English Channel known as the Angevin Empire. While keeping everyone around him in the dark, he himself knew exactly what he was about; he was simply too paranoid to tell anyone else.

During the long *chevauchée* with Eleanor that lasted well into the autumn of 1152, he showed that England was never far from his mind by taking a close interest in the large number of ships and men employed in fishing along the Gascon littoral, who could be useful in crossing the Channel. However, before facing the risks of that invasion he wanted to teach Eleanor's vassals the same lesson he had given to Louis' coalition, and so lessen the likelihood of a rebellion in the south-west during his absence the following year. On the journey north, in Limoges for his coronation as duke of Aquitaine, the opportunity he wanted presented itself.

The Limousin capital was composed of the lower town, including the abbey of St Martial and the viscount's palace, and the upper town or citadel with the cathedral and the bishop's palace. After being welcomed by the populace and in great pomp by the abbot and his monks, the new duke of Aquitaine demanded by feudal right provisions for all his retinue. The abbot refused on the grounds that his obligations were to provide food and lodgings while the duke was inside the walls, whereas Henry was encamped outside the town with his followers.[8] The dispute had more to do with the numbers involved than where they were actually billeted, but fights broke out in the streets of the town between the citizens and Henry's soldiery, some of whom were wounded.

The outraged duke gave orders for the recently built walls of the town to be razed to the ground so that it was impossible to be inside them or outside. The new bridge over the River Vienne was likewise torn down.[9] His depredations were only stopped by encouraging news from Matilda's supporters in England that caused him to hurry north. On 8 January 1153, he defied the winter storms by setting sail from Barfleur with a small fleet of twenty-six vessels,[10] leaving Eleanor pregnant in France.

The following day he landed an army of around 3,000 men in the country where he had spent part of his childhood acting as figurehead to Matilda's supporters in the civil war with Stephen of Blois and being groomed to wear the crown of England. Despite widespread dissatisfaction with the raping and looting of Stephen's Flemish mercenaries, Henry's position as the most powerful man in France was not enough to bring the Anglo-Norman nobility as a whole over to his side. With the same tenacity his mother had shown, he settled down to a long campaign, considering that he had little to fear from a rebellion in his French domains with her in control of Normandy and Eleanor acting as regent for his other domains.

The two women kept their distance. Regarding Normandy as hers, Matilda was not prepared to quietly step aside as Adelaide de Maurienne had done when Eleanor arrived on the Ile de la Cité. A pious autocrat, she accepted the political necessity for her son's marriage, but had no welcome for a daughter-in-law fresh from another man's bed and within the prohibited degrees of consanguinity. Nor was Eleanor inclined to curry favour from so hostile a mother-in-law.

Leaving her uncle Raoul de Faye to govern Aquitaine, she moved into Henry's territory by setting up in his capital city of Angers the first of her own courts where comfort and pleasure meant not just good food and wine but all the other civilised pleasures of the day. In Rouen, all was sobriety and pious learning at the empress' court; in Angers, men played the gallant or were sent away until such time as they learned to. However valiant they might be in the field, Eleanor required them to speak eloquently, dress well and have their hair properly cut when in her presence.

Western Europe was still groaning under the heavy taxes to repay the borrowing of the Second Crusade. In Normandy and Anjou, much good land had been laid waste during the brief war with Louis' coalition, leaving the knightly class impoverished and the peasants once again facing starvation after the drought of the long hot summer of 1152. Those great patrons of the arts Henry Beauclerc, Thibault of Champagne, William IX and Geoffrey the Fair were all dead. To rid himself of one more memory of Eleanor, Louis had banished from his court the *trouvères* and other entertainers she had employed and whom he accused of distracting men's minds from their faith.[11]

In these conditions, it was not hard for the largesse of the richest woman in France to attract the most talented troubadours to flatter and amuse her with their verse. They could not have found a more appreciative employer than the granddaughter of William IX, who had seen for herself the settings in Byzantium and the Holy Land of the great *chansons de geste* and whose catholic appetites in music and poetry covered everything from the Arthurian legends to love songs and *sirventès*.

At her court in Angers, she and her intimates were entertained by the best of European poetry and music.[12] The code of courtly love may or may not have originated there, but never was it better practised. As equal partner in the marriage with Henry, Eleanor reigned supreme in his absence. What better way of demonstrating this than by turning upside down the convention that every woman of whatever rank owed deference to her father, brothers and husband? At Angers it was men who were the supplicants and the ladies of the court who sat in judgement on them, and set convoluted tasks to test their admirers' sincerity.

It used to be thought that the cult of courtly love spread from Eleanor's courts at Angers and later in Poitiers through her daughter Marie de Champagne being called to run the household in Poitiers during 1168–73. Recent studies indicate that mother and daughter probably never met or even corresponded after the divorce from Louis. If their courts had much in common, it was because the two women exemplified the many twelfth-century noblewomen who evolved their own lifestyle during the absence of their husbands on campaign, pilgrimage and crusade. The role-reversal of courtly love, the poetry and songs, were an antidote to the emotional aridity of their lives, spent in politically arranged marriages, with sons sent away to be brought up by others and daughters dispatched as child brides, never to be seen again.

Since Eleanor's troubadours were writing to please her, their verses represent an indication of her personal feelings, particularly valuable in the case of a twelfth-century character who left no personal letters. Though she could be as tough and ruthless as the Empress Matilda, Eleanor was not all piety and politics like her mother-in-law. She had another side to her personality that yearned for all the joys forbidden by her station in life – the joy of imagining herself the April Queen, abandoning herself to the caress of an adoring lover.

Who were these troubadours? The image of a penniless songsmith making his way from castle to castle with nothing but his voice, an ear for a good tune and a lute slung over his shoulder is misleading. Itinerant minstrels or *jonglars* scratched a living by travelling from one castle to the next, singing traditional and popular songs of the day, but the troubadours[13] who composed the songs and poetry were mostly of knightly families. What counted, however, was not noble birth, but nobility of soul. Guilhem Figuera was a tailor's son and Bernat de Ventadorn the son of a sergeant-at-arms and a kitchen maid working in the bakery of the castle of Ventadorn.

Lowly birth did not mean they had anything to learn from the rules of courtly love as later codified by Andreas Capellanus at the court of Marie de Champagne. Rule XV: Every lover turns pale in the presence of his beloved. Rule XVI: When a lover suddenly catches sight of his beloved, his heart palpitates. Bernat knew this by instinct:

> *Quant ieu la vey, be m'es parven*
> *als huelhs, al vis, a la color –*
> *quar aissi tremble de paor*
> *cum fa la fuelha contre'l ven.*
> *Non ai de sen per un efan . . .*

[When I see her, it always shows / both in my eyes and my pale cheek. / What is this fear that makes me weak? / Trembling like a leaf when the wind blows / I'm reduced to a child again . . .]

And the mistress for whom he wrote his first poems replied:

> *. . . e'il domna deu a son drut far onor*
> *com ad amic mas non com a senhor.*

[. . . and the lady must honour her lover / like a friend, but not as her master.]

It was at some point during Eleanor's journey through the Limousin with her new husband that Bernat first attached himself to her household, not that Henry Curtmantle would have spared him much attention, for he was no lover of troubadours and preferred the company of learned clerics and laymen attending his court as counsellors or ambassadors.

At that moment Bernat needed a patroness badly, having been banished from Ventadorn for becoming too close an admirer of its versifying countess. Being a man who lived dangerously, he did not let the experience prevent him becoming Eleanor's intimate. Roughly her age, he was endowed with a fine voice, poetic talent and handsome good looks. For her part, how could the duchess, who had been brought up both to know about the transports of love, and also that its joys were not for her, fail to respond to a poet who wrote *Quand vei la lauseta mover de joi sas alas contre'l rai* – likening her to a swallow, its wings joyously silhouetted against the sun, so delicate, so elusive, yet so powerful as it soared so impossibly high above him in station?

> *Ailàs tant cujava saber d'amor et tant petit en sai!*
> *Car ieu d'amar no'm posc téner celui[14] dont ja pro non arai.*
> *Anc non aguí de mi poder, ni no fui meus de l'or' en çai*
> *que'm lesset en sos òlhs veser en un miralh que mìut mi plai.*

[Alas, I who thought so much to know of loving, yet know so little! /
I cannot help but love her, though she will never satisfy me. / Before
her I am powerless and really not myself at all / since the moment she
met my gaze in the mirror which put me in her thrall.]

The eventual reward for Bernat's devotion was cruel. Rumours of his
intimacy with Eleanor having reached Henry's ears in England, the
poet was summoned there and went unwillingly:

> *Aissí'm part d'amor e'm recrè. Mòrt ma per mòrt li respond*
> *e vau me'n, pos ilh no'm reten, chaitius en eissilh no sai ont.*

[I must leave my love and go away, banished I know not where / for she
does not bid me stay, though this cruel exile I cannot bear.]

After singing different songs for his supper for the amusement
of Henry's hectically peripatetic court in England, Bernat contrived to
sneak back across the Channel and turned up again in Angers
to address new compositions to Eleanor, ignoring his master's orders to
return. But Eleanor had more important matters on her mind and
left him behind in Angers to pine in verse for his lost love when her
court moved on.

On 17 August 1154 she gave birth to a son, her relief doubled by the
knowledge that she had erased forever the stigma of having given Louis
only daughters. She christened the boy William, after her father and
grandfather and all the other Williams in her family, and honoured him
with the courtesy title duke of Aquitaine[15] without asking Henry's
opinion. Learning of the birth in Paris, Louis saw it quash the last
chance of either of his daughters inheriting the title to Aquitaine
through her mother.

Never had Eleanor felt more secure, having every reason to believe
that she had forfeited none of her independence in return for her new
status. Many minor events bear this out. When signing in her own name
for Abbot Robert of Vendôme a charter confirming the liberties of his
priories in the Saintonge that had been harassed by her agents, she
included no mention of Henry in the way that Louis' decrees during
their marriage had carried a line indicating her assent. Second, when

Pope Anastasius IV confirmed by a papal bull the privileges of the foundation of Notre Dame de Saintes on 29 October of that same year, the list of donors includes Geoffrey of Poitou, Louis of France, Eleanor and Aelith, but of Henry there is no mention. Even that wily churchman Geoffroi de Lauroux, forever sniffing the winds of change, went on record by stating in a charter of 25 September 1153 that Aquitaine acknowledged only the authority of its duchess.[16]

A few days after the birth of William, Eleanor received news that King Stephen's son Eustace of Boulogne had choked to death during a meal near Bury St Edmunds on 18 August. Worn out with strife, and in the hope of avoiding another civil war, the grieving king of England formally accepted Henry fitz Empress as his legal successor after protracted negotiations that dragged on into mid-November. At Christmas of that year Archbishop Theobald of Canterbury enshrined the arrangement in a treaty witnessed at Westminster by fourteen bishops and eleven earls of the realm. Since Stephen of Blois was in his late fifties and thus an old man by the standards of the time, Henry was certain to be the most powerful monarch in Europe within a few years. It was a wonderful stroke of good luck for an ambitious young man of twenty-two.

Returning to France in high spirits, he summoned Eleanor and his infant son to Rouen, where they moved into the palace built by his grandfather. Biding his time, Henry now made peace with Louis. In consideration of 1,000 silver marks as a 'fine' or gift, Louis ceased to include 'duke of Aquitaine' among his titles, which he had been doing since the divorce on the strength of the argument that Duke William X had given his patrimony to Fat Louis when asking him to arrange his daughters' marriages and that Eleanor had become duchess by virtue of her marriage to him as Fat Louis' successor. In Bordeaux during September 1154, Geoffroi de Lauroux sniffed the wind again and proclaimed that the master of Aquitaine was henceforth Henry of Anjou.[17]

Under the obligations of homage for his domains, the duke of Aquitaine had to perform military service for his king when called upon. After recovering from some unspecified but severe illness, Henry rode at the head of a large body of men to help Louis pacify the ever-restless Vexin. It was during this time that messengers from Archbishop Theobald arrived a few days after Stephen's death on 25 October to announce that the duke and duchess of Aquitaine and Normandy could now add 'king and queen of England' to all their other titles.

Stunned at Eleanor's rapid rise in the world, Louis left Paris on pilgrimage to Compostela. He did not ask her and Henry for the safe conduct to which he was doubly entitled, both as a pilgrim and as their liege as far as their continental possessions were concerned, but travelled by a roundabout route, via Montpellier and Catalonia,[18] which had the advantage of giving him the opportunity to con the Christian courts of Spain for a new wife.

Neither Eleanor nor Henry could have cared less what he was up to at the moment. In a fever of impatience to claim the crown of England, Henry assembled within less than a fortnight a fitting host that included Eleanor's now widowed sister Aelith, his younger brothers Geoffrey and William, and the chief barons and prelates of Normandy. Diplomatically, in order not to alienate the many enemies she had made across the Channel, the Empress Matilda was not included in the party, but left to keep the peace in Normandy.

By now Bernat de Ventadorn was accepting of his fate, for did not *fin amar* require the lover to submit to his mistress' will, however much it hurt?

> *Domna, vostre sui e serai*
> *del vostre servizi garnitz*
> *Vostr'om sui juratz e plevitz*
> *e vos etz lo meus jois primers*
> *e si seretz vos lo derrers*
> *tan com la vida m'er durans.*

[Sworn to your service / I am and ever shall be, lady. / You have no truer man than me / for of all joys you are the best. / My love will never fail the test / as long as life is in me.]

Two years later, comforting himself with the knowledge that she still heard his songs, albeit sung by other voices, he was still proposing himself in verse as her valet and devoted bedroom slave, asking in return no greater favour than the privilege of drawing off her boots when she undressed.[19]

With no intention of letting the twenty-year anarchy of Stephen's reign continue a day longer than necessary, Henry intended arriving in England in a manner that would show the Anglo-Norman magnates from the outset the way they were to behave in future. Thus, with only a small retinue of personal servants, Eleanor found herself on arrival at Barfleur seven months pregnant, surrounded by eminent nobles and churchmen who had been on the Second Crusade and witnessed at first hand her disgrace after the massacre on Mount Cadmos and her humiliation after the abduction from Antioch. This was her moment of triumph, looking each of them in the face, and requiring the proper deference due to the mother of their overlord's son, about to produce another child by him – and not a mere consort like any other but a queen/duchess/countess whose own possessions far outweighed theirs.

For a whole month, this uneasy court-in-transition marked time in the little Norman seaport near Cherbourg. As though to remind Henry that his might was only temporal, November gales blew in from the Atlantic day and night, making it impossible to put to sea. His frustration can be imagined. They were still stormbound on 7 December when, determined to celebrate Christmas wearing the crown of England, he ignored the lesson of the *White Ship* sinking in that very place and embarked himself, Eleanor and the infant Prince William in a virtually identical clinker-built vessel with high bow and stern, and rigged with a lateen sail that enabled them to cross against the westerly swell, rolling and tossing on a grey sea under a leaden sky. It was for Eleanor a replay of her storm-tossed voyage across the Mediterranean on returning from crusade.

The weather was still so bad that even with sails reefed the convoy was scattered before nightfall, after which the usual station-keeping devices of horn lanterns and bugle calls were useless. For more than twenty-four hours, humans and horses were buffeted by wind and tide until the individual vessels made land in harbours widely separated. Henry and Eleanor first set foot on the land of their new kingdom in the New Forest near Lyndhurst, where William Rufus, after a reign of four years, had been assassinated under cover of a hunting accident, permitting Henry's grandfather to seize the crown a few days later.

Their first call was at Winchester to secure the royal treasury, commandeering fresh horses on the way and gradually acquiring a cortège of Anglo-Norman prelates and nobles, drawn to Henry's banner by the news of his apparently miraculous arrival, borne on the wings of the storm. From Winchester they progressed to London without a hand lifted or a sword drawn in protest, thanks to Archbishop Thibault of Canterbury, who had assembled the bishops of the realm to acclaim their new monarch.

The abbey at Westminster[20] upriver from London was the traditional place for coronations, but had been vandalised by Stephen's mercenaries during the civil war. The adjoining palace, built by William Rufus for his scandalous court on the site of an earlier Saxon palace, was uninhabitable for the same reason. So Henry and Eleanor set up court south of the River Thames in Bermondsey. On the Sunday before Christmas, they were crowned king and queen in a curious mixture of pomp and squalor in Westminster Abbey, walking out of it to the English cheers of the Anglo-Saxon lower orders and the Norman-French and Latin acclamations of the nobility and clergy.

The Jersey poet Robert Wace, who shortly afterwards wrote *The Story of Britain*,[21] based on Henry of Monmouth's fanciful history of the kings of Britain and dedicated to Eleanor, most probably based his depiction of the legendary King Arthur's coronation feast on hers and Henry's. There was no shortage of food for the upper stratum of Anglo-Norman society. While mutton was not much in favour, beef, pork and game were consumed in large quantities. Game could be fresh all the year round, but beef and pork had to be salted for winter consumption when the animals not required for breeding were slaughtered in what the Norsemen had called 'blood month', or November. As a result, dried herbs, pepper and other imported spices were used heavily in stuffings, sauces and marinades to disguise the saltiness and cover the unpalatable taste of rotten meat.

Most bread was wheaten or rye, the cause of the disease called St Anthony's Fire when made with ergot-infected flour, causing convulsions, miscarriages, dry gangrene and death. Omelettes, stews and pies were common, and fish was consumed in quantity, with palaces and monasteries having their own fish farms to guarantee a supply for Fridays, Lent and the many other meatless days. To cleanse the palate there was a wide range of sweet desserts – fruits fresh, stewed and candied, jellies, tarts, waffles and wafers. While the natives preferred to drown their sorrows in ale and beer, their masters preferred wine.

The waferers, whose speciality was making and serving the thin pastries eaten at the end of the meal with sweet white dessert wine, were also the cabaret.[22] Henry's personal waferer, Godfrey, was rewarded for his services with the manor of Liston Overhall in Essex, which remained in his family for several generations. There were tumblers of both sexes, storytellers, conjurers and jugglers, farters, singers and musicians playing bowed and plucked stringed instruments, harps, lyres, flutes of various kinds, shawms, bagpipes and other instruments. Chrétien de Troyes describes a wedding at which girls sang and danced. There were chess and backgammon boards for those who wished to gamble fashionably, and dice for those whose taste was less refined. ·

While many court entertainers were rewarded only with clothes and food, Roger de Mowbray, earl of Warwick at the time of the coronation, was more generous, bestowing land on several of his favourite entertainers. One who was both viol-player and *joculator* was rewarded with a life-interest in a small estate in Yorkshire for the annual rent of one pound of pepper. Henry's jester Herbert was given thirty acres in Suffolk. Roger the Fool doubled as keeper of Henry's otter-hounds in 1179, for which he was given a house in Aylesbury.[23] They and other jesters, whose predecessors' function had been retelling the *res gesta* or great deeds of past heroes, were now jokers whose irreverence was indulged so long as their wit was faster than that of their masters. There were also some female comedians, known as *joculatrices*.

The coronation festivities over, Eleanor at the age of thirty-two was the consort of the man who ruled from the Scottish border to the frontier of Spain. Mother of his son and heir, and conscious how great a part her wealth and possessions had played in his rise to this position of power, she had every reason to feel secure in her marriage to Henry.

TEN

Court Life with Henry

Nine decades after William the Conqueror imposed his Norman followers on the population by dispossessing the native nobility, England was still an occupied country ruled by an elite of 200 Anglo-Norman families, all related in easily traceable degree.

Although they complained that it was impossible to tell any longer who belonged to which race because of the intermarriages that had taken place with girls of native stock, the gap between the French-speaking equestrian classes and their Anglo-Saxon underlings was painfully obvious from the viewpoint of the conquered.[1] The replacement of the slavery prevalent under the Saxon kings by serfdom was a legal improvement in the lot of the most wretched, but in practice the only significant difference was that a slave could be sold separately, while serfs were tied for life to the land on which they were born and could only be sold with it.

French continued to be the language of the law courts and of the royal court for another two centuries, although legislation was couched in Latin for greater precision. Among the upper classes, those who spoke 'proper' French despised others with an English accent and usage. Clemence, a nun at the aristocratic convent of Barking who wrote a life of St Catharine shortly after Eleanor's arrival in England, apologised to her patrons – probably the new king and queen – for using 'a poor English kind of French'.[2]

The higher one's class, the less likely it was to have an English name, or if christened with one, to use it. Even the religious conformed to this snobbery, like the ten-year-old oblate to the monastery of St Evroul in Normandy, who lost his embarrassing English baptismal name to become Ordericus Vitalis. Ecclesiastical re-baptism like this could pose theological problems: Augustine, who had been 'Henry', worried that prayers for the salvation of his soul could go astray if incorrectly addressed.

So fashionable were the names of the Conqueror and his barons[3] that a William, Richard, Robert, Roger or Hugh needed to add a nickname, toponym or the patronymic *fitz* to distinguish himself from all the others. At the highest level of society even Henry I's native first consort, whom he married to bridge the gap between what remained of the old ruling class and their Norman conquerors, had been obliged to change her name from Edith to Matilda to avoid open mockery at court.

Her tapestry of the Conquest at Bayeux shows Norman knights clean-shaven with short hair while English warriors had longer hair and sported moustaches. Nearly a century later, facial hair was still a sign of uncouth Englishness. Men wore their hair shoulder-length. Women's hair was longer, uncovered before marriage and bound or concealed by a veil or wimple afterwards. Among the fashion-conscious and the flatterers, Henry's short cloaks now ousted the ankle-length cloaks that had been popular under Stephen. Fur being a mark of luxury, sable and ermine were reserved for the very rich while nuns showed poverty by keeping warm with cat- and lamb-skin. Bathing was not an English habit. After John's coronation in 1199 his bath attendant William Aquarius was called to wait upon his master once every three weeks, which was considered excessive indulgence by his unwashed, silk- and fur-clad courtiers.

In Eleanor's London, God and Mammon were neighbours. Walter Map found it a haunt of pimps and whores, while his fellow courtier William fitz Stephen judged it a noble city. It boasted 126 parish churches and thirteen monastic houses built of stone among streets of shops displaying native produce and luxury imported goods, like silk, brocades and spices from the East, exquisitely worked enamels from Limoges, wine from the Rhine Valley. Trades and crafts tended to cluster, hence Bread Street, Milk Street, Ironmonger Lane and the like. So closely built were the shops and houses, wood-framed with lath and plaster infill, that fire was an ever-present urban danger. One had destroyed St Paul's Cathedral and a large area around it only seventeen years before Eleanor's arrival. Not until the next century would London's building regulations forbid thatched roofs to make houses more fire-resistant.

Paris counted only 25 acres within the walls, but London Wall enclosed 326 acres. There were seven double gates leading north, east and west. At the eastern or downriver end of the Roman wall stood William I's Tower of London. Two other fortresses, Baynard's Castle and Montfichet Castle, housed the garrison. To the south, the river wall was in disrepair and London Bridge was a ramshackle wooden structure that served also as a toll-point and barrier to possible invasion fleets. Replacing this in stone with a drawbridge to permit the passage of tall-masted ships was not begun by Henry until 1176, and took three decades to complete.

The left-bank waterfront was a thriving mercantile area where, among the taverns and pot-houses, there was at least one take-out restaurant catering at any hour of the day or night to the hunger of those wanting to eat at home but with no servants to cook for them. It was here that Eleanor invested in a wharf known as Queenshythe, whose construction had been financed by Henry I's consort Matilda, whose other philanthropic works included the city's first public lavatories and bath house. Less generously, Eleanor developed Queenshythe as the centre for importing wines from Poitou and Gascony, including those from her own estates. 'Vintry', as the area was called, was also the site of the king's bonded warehouses, where all wine entering the country was assessed for duty.

While making their money in the city, some richer Londoners preferred to live outside the walls, in garden suburbs around Clerken Well and St Clement's Well, where cleaner water was available. Beyond these lay fields, pasture and woodland. As coal was not worked in any quantity, wood and charcoal were the principal fuels for heating and cooking. Unusually in England, where monarchy guarded its hunting with vindictive ferocity, London's citizens had the right to hunt with hawk and hound in Middlesex, Hertfordshire, the Chilterns and into Kent as far as the River Cray.

Every week on the smooth field that came to be called Smithfield, a livestock market was held, with the spectacle of horses being put through their paces by prospective buyers providing an impromptu entertainment for the public, even the poorest of whom knew enough abut horses to express an opinion. At weekends and on feast-days amateur jousts were held, with borrowed or improvised body armour and padded lances. More or less organised entertainments included a form of football played in the streets on Shrove Tuesday and cockfights for gambling. The baiting of bulls, bears and boars by starved and goaded dogs was a regular winter entertainment.[4] When the marsh fields or Moorfields north of the city froze over, young men with animal shin bones tied to their shoes used iron-spiked sticks to propel themselves across the ice in a cross between skating and Nordic skiing.

The bustling metropolis on the Thames made even Paris seem provincial, except in learning, and Poitiers and Bordeaux very small indeed. To Eleanor's ears the language of the natives was a grotesque and guttural babble, but learning it was unnecessary because those Anglo-Saxons with whom she came into contact, as servants and tradesmen, could all speak enough French to get by.

The manner of occupation was not colonial, as under the Romans, who had used the existing aristocracy to rule subject races. Virtually the whole of England was directly in Norman hands. Stemming from the original idea of a war-leader sharing out the booty with the warriors of his band, the king theoretically owned all land but bought the loyalty of his vassals by making them tenants-in-chief of huge estates. In return, they owed him taxes and knight service commensurate with their holdings, and support in council when required. The range of wealth among tenants-in-chief was enormous, with the count of Mortain one hundred times richer than Robert of Aumale. Even the term 'baron' is vague. Not all held land directly from the king; many were vavassours. The earl of Gloucester regularly addressed his charters to 'all my barons'.[5]

Roughly half of England was held by the barons, the rest being divided between Crown and Church. At the time of the Domesday tax census in 1086 William I had directly possessed more than 18 per cent of the land in the kingdom, reckoned by value. In four shires he had retained over 30 per cent of all the land, and more than 20 per cent in another eight. The Crown had been extracting both goods in kind and rents from every part of the kingdom and the royal presence this implied overall had been a part of the force of government, unlike the situation in France and Germany, where there were whole regions in which the king or emperor directly owned nothing at all.[6]

In addition, it was feudal practice for the Crown to hold in trust the estates of sees whose bishops had died until their successors were elected and also any estates whose heirs were under-age or unmarried women. The original principle was that kings alone could protect the integrity of the estates, which would otherwise be annexed by predatory neighbours. Inevitably, kings extended the period of custody in order to continue enjoying the revenues for as long as possible, and then in the case of lay estates conferred them on favourites by arranged marriages.

The audited royal income in 1130 – the sole year of Henry I's reign for which the Pipe Rolls survived – was £24,500. More than 40 per cent of this came from the royal domains in produce and rents, and the rest was made up from feudal dues, taxes and justice fees. Henry's immediate problem as king was that, after the years of civil war, Crown revenues amounted to only a third of that sum, without allowing for inflation.[7] His most urgent need was therefore for an efficient and trustworthy chancellor with a brain as quick and an appetite for work as relentless as his own.

As churchman and politician, Archbishop Theobald had done everything to ensure a peaceful succession. Aware that the gratitude of kings was short-lived, he now offered a solution to Henry's problem that seemed to guarantee the Church's long-term reward for the parts it was playing,[8] and brought to that first English Christmas of Eleanor's at Bermondsey an ambitious Londoner in his early thirties. Thomas Becket was four years older than the queen and therefore almost old enough to be Henry's father. Did Eleanor's instinct for people warn her how dangerous his introduction at court would be for her? Since he did everything to ingratiate himself to the royal household from the outset, it can only be because he received no encouragement from the queen that there was never the slightest evidence of friendship between them.

Tall, bright-eyed, well-built and dark-haired, with the pallor of a schoolman but no scholarly hunger for the disinterested pursuit of knowledge, Becket was no longer the eager student whose path had crossed hers in the schools of Paris. Having developed the smooth manners of a courtier during twelve years at the archbishop's court,[9] he was in every way a product of the century, belonging to neither the knightly classes nor the feudal peasantry. Apart from a susceptibility to stress-related illness, he had a tendency to stutter which he sometimes exploited to give himself time to think.

His surname was a toponym, the family coming from the village of Bequet in Normandy, although Thomas preferred to refer to himself as Thomas of London, which sounded classier. Born in Cheapside, the son of a prosperous merchant who was also a port-reeve or deputy mayor, he was educated by the Augustinians at Merton Priory and at a grammar school before going to Paris. His début in the adult world was either as a trainee sheriff or as an accountant with a London banker by name of Osbert Huitdeniers.[10]

Having travelled to Rome with Archbishop Theobald, who sent him to study canon law at Auxerre and Bologna and entrusted him with diplomatic missions both in England and abroad, Becket was equally at ease in a royal court or the Roman curia. Appointed provost of Beverley and archdeacon of Canterbury in 1154, he was comfortably wealthy by the time the archbishop brought him to the king's notice and enjoyed a high reputation for integrity and sobriety, which Henry's suspicious nature must have tested more than once.

Becket rapidly fulfilled the mission with which Theobald had entrusted him. As a good courtier, he spared no effort in becoming the boon companion for the king's leisure time, sharing his pleasures with horses, hawks and hounds at any time of the day and working long into the night with Henry or amusing him in a game of chess or with learned conversation.[11] The only activity he did not share was the king's incessant womanising.

As a first test of his managerial skills, Henry entrusted to him the rebuilding, restoration and furbishing of Westminster Palace, to make a more fitting setting for the royal court than was afforded by Bermondsey, surrounded by swampy flatland. Immediately, Becket set several hundred skilled artisans and labourers to work round the clock at Westminster in a din so loud that no one could be heard at less than a shout.[12]

Eleanor gave birth at Bermondsey on 28 February to a second son, named after his absent father. Henry was in the north, straightening out some recalcitrant barons who thought that distance from London meant they could ignore the new king and his laws. On return, he honoured the newborn by naming him heir to the county of Anjou.[13] On 10 April 1155, to avoid any ambiguity about the succession, he borrowed a constitutional device of the Capetian kings and formally declared Prince William his successor as king of England; in the event that the boy predeceased his father, Prince Henry would succeed.

By Whitsuntide, the palace of Westminster was ready for occupation. On moving in, Eleanor found that in addition to her own two sons, her household was to include Henry's bastard Geoffrey by his Saxon mistress Ykenai. What she thought about this arrangement is unknown but she was on good terms with her own illegitimate half-brothers and Henry I had also raised bastards in his household.

With Becket named chancellor, the king appointed as his chief justiciar for the realm the experienced Richard de Lucé or Lucy, who had been a county justiciar under Stephen. Robert de Beaumont, second earl of Leicester, was to serve jointly with him. Eleanor did her best not to be displaced by these competitors for Henry's ear.[14] Charters given at this time show her name as witness, alongside those of Becket and Lucy.

Henry had been aware that events would soon force him to return to France. Before that happened, it was imperative to do for the administration of justice what Becket was doing for the Exchequer. That required extensive travel throughout the southern parts of the realm,[15] putting barons and bishops back in their places by ordering the destruction of adulterine castles and forcing the payment of overdue taxes. He also revived Henry I's system of travelling judges, to replace the idiosyncratic justice of his vassals by the royal justice applied uniformly throughout the realm.

First Seal of Henry II.

Dating from 1135 when Stephen of Blois ascended to the throne, the organisation of the king's household[16] listed more than one hundred permanent royal servants, plus huntsmen, falconers and the rest. But Henry's court on its travels was often twice as large.[17] If not all the royal servants were present at any one time, the numbers were swollen by the knights and men-at-arms of the royal escort, plus a haggle of vassals manoeuvring for power with their attendant knights and households and a bevy of hangers-on, ambassadors, visiting prelates and merchants intent on catching the eye of potentially the richest clients in the kingdom.

There were billeting officers, messengers coming and going, cooks, grooms, dog-handlers, washerwomen, chambermaids and the whores to which Walter Map took exception. In addition to all these humans there were dogs, falcons, the baggage train of pack animals and wagons carrying bedding and chapel furnishings, the ridden palfries and led remounts and destriers of the knights.

Within this mobile *familia* or household, each royal servant had his jealously guarded area of authority and responsibility, with his own servants. The household administrative machinery ensured that everyone received the right daily allowances of money, food, drink and candles. The chancellor was given five shillings a day, plus three loaves, four gallons of fine wine and four of table wine, a large candle and forty candle ends. Further down the ladder, a chamberlain got two shillings and one loaf, plus four gallons of table wine, one small candle and twenty-four candle ends. On the bottom rung, the lowliest attendants received only their food and some clothing from time to time. Some offices became hereditary, as with William the Marshal, whose father and grandfather and brother also served as marshals to their kings.

It has been calculated[18] that King John's court moved thirteen or fourteen times in an average month, making it rare to sleep in the same place more than two or three nights in a row. Henry, who cared little for physical comfort, was even more restlessly mobile, and it must have come as a relief to Eleanor and her ladies when he decided to enjoy his favourite sport at one of the royal hunting lodges or the court tarried in one of the palaces at Westminster, Winchester, Windsor, Northampton or Woodstock. There, in addition to the legendary maze, was a zoo of lions, leopards, lynxes, camels and other exotic presents from foreign rulers.

For Eleanor, court life was devoid of privacy, whether at one of the royal palaces or on the road. The very desire for solitude was considered aberrant in lay people and a sign of piety in anchorites.

Until recently all the court had slept in one great hall. Twelfth-century manor houses where Eleanor stayed on her travels were, like Oakham Hall in Rutland, one huge undivided space with a solar at one end where she and Henry could sleep when his interest did not take him elsewhere. Even there, they were never alone, and anyone entering or leaving could plainly be seen by everyone in the main hall.

Under normal circumstances the distance the court travelled in a day was limited by the sumpter train to twelve or fifteen miles over roads that had not been paved since the Romans left Britain and were often no more than potholed tracks. The main roads were collectively the king's highway, with those lords through whose territory it ran responsible for its upkeep; they were wide enough for two wagons to pass or a dozen horsemen to ride abreast.

The provisioning in fodder and perishable foodstuffs like milk and meat was a considerable forward-planning operation. The royal *bouteiller* or butler had 700 tuns containing 20,000 gallons of varied wine to move around the country to where it was needed. Henry's bakers numbered four, but were split into two teams, so that two men and their helpers were always one stage ahead to ensure the provision of sufficient wood and heat the ovens long before the court arrived, by when it was already too late to begin baking. Whenever the king changed destination en route, there was no fresh bread that night.

Henry's erratic progresses were in complete contrast to those of his grandfather Henry I, who always stuck to published itineraries so that petitioners and merchants and vassals knew where to find him and the business of the realm could be conducted in a calm and measured manner. The land through which Eleanor and her husband travelled had suffered greatly during the civil war. Although the weather was mild during the medieval warm period, and the upper limit of cultivation extending to the 1,000-foot contour, many manors that had been assessed in Domesday as fertile and productive farmland were producing no revenue and therefore no tax. Pastureland had gone to scrub, the livestock driven off by one side or the other, the herders also driven away or dead.

In towns, trade was poor. The forests were infested by dispossessed peasants with a price on their heads if for no other reason than their defiance of the forest laws that made a crime of collecting dead wood for a winter fire, let alone killing for food a deer reserved for the sport of their Norman oppressors. While Eleanor's legendary contemporary Robin Hood may never have existed, the fourteenth-century ballads casting him as a Saxon hero resisting Norman oppression give a fair picture of life in occupied England a century after the Conquest.

The court being often far from London, Becket's house there became the place for the fashionable and ambitious to be seen. Although drunkenness and lechery were discouraged by its puritanical master, his generous table and well-stocked cellar attracted a constant stream of visitors, who complained about the comparatively sparse fare Henry considered adequate for himself and his guests – half-baked bread, sour wine, stale fish and meat.[19] As his influence grew, Becket's household became swollen with sons of the nobility, sent to learn the ways of the world in the expectation that they would return as belted knights.[20] Newly arrived emissaries from Paris and Rome called first on England's powerful chancellor, not for the good cheer to be had at his table but to learn the king's mind from the man who knew it as well as he did himself.

Becket had a staff of fifty or more clerks and accountants working all hours under him, and his house so rapidly became the political centre of England that Henry complained of feeling deserted. Yet such was Becket's usefulness that he continued to receive presents and privileges from his master, one of which was a political time-bomb in the form of an exemption from the requirement to keep full accounts for revenues from estates held in trust by the Crown.

In September, Eleanor moved her main home yet again – this time to Winchester, the old Saxon capital, in order to be nearer Henry, who was spending several weeks hunting in the New Forest with Becket. His nights were not spent in idleness but planning the next stage in his strategy. At the end of September, a Michaelmas council of the barons was summoned to discuss his plans to invade Ireland, a venture blessed by Pope Adrian IV – otherwise Nicholas, the only Englishman ever to occupy the papal throne.

Henry's purpose was to impose the supremacy of papal rule on the westernmost province of Europe, which had been so important for the early Church. What he hoped to gain, apart from Adrian's gratitude, by invading territory that represented no menace to England and would contribute little to the Exchequer, is hard to say. He was at the time only twenty-two years old – an age at which a mother like his sometimes still knows best. Empress Matilda arrived in England to discourage the Irish expedition with news that could not be ignored: her second son Geoffrey was preparing to take by force his legacy of Anjou, Maine and Touraine.

Henry's territory, so extensive north to south that a month was required to travel from one end to the other, was perilously slender east to west at precisely that point. The journey from Tours to the border of Brittany was no more than a day's ride. Geoffrey's triangle of land, with its three great castles of Chinon, Loudun and Mirebeau, was therefore a wedge that might easily be used to split the fragile new empire in two. Matilda won her point: the Irish project was shelved.

By the time of the Christmas court at Winchester, Eleanor was pregnant again. On 10 January 1156 Henry left England in the care of Becket and the justiciars, with Eleanor and his children under the protection of Archbishop Theobald and John of Salisbury. Crossing from Dover to Wissant for a meeting with Louis, he belatedly paid homage for his French possessions. Continuing to Rouen, he listened to the arguments of his brother Geoffrey that the oath Henry had sworn after Geoffrey the Fair's death should be honoured.

Henry's reply was to attack Geoffrey's trio of castles just after Palm Sunday on 8 April. He took Chinon and Mirebeau without difficulty, leaving his brother in possession of Loudun alone. As compensation for the others, he promised Geoffrey a generous pension of 1,000 English pounds and 2,000 pounds Angevin annually, not all of which was ever paid.[21]

That situation temporarily resolved, Henry turned his attention to the Vexin around Bayeux, which had been bartered by his father to Louis in the year of Eleanor's divorce. Another area of concern was Berry, on the eastern border of Poitou, which belonged to those enemies in the house of Blois who might well have been the ones to tap the wedge that could have split his domains in two.

Direct action in either case meant pitting himself against his feudal overlord, something for which Henry was not ready. The next months were therefore spent strengthening Rouen, the Norman treasure castle at Caen and the Angevin treasure castle at Chinon. The important Loire crossing at Tours was re-fortified and border castles everywhere overhauled and garrisoned with men loyal to him. Since loyal often meant 'mercenary', this generated a new round of taxes to pay his soldiery.

Like the whirlwind, Henry was always on the move, promising rewards to the obedient that had them redoubling their efforts, and handing out penalties to the disobedient. Regarding the Church on his domains as being as much his as the land its buildings stood on, wherever a see became vacant he sought to appoint a docile prelate of his own choosing.

In England, although Eleanor held no writ of regency as such, she travelled widely and in comfort, signing numerous charters that show she was far from being a stay-at-home wife and mother. The Pipe Rolls show her receiving allowances for herself and her sons, also for Aelith and her two illegitimate half-brothers, William and Joscelin. At Winchester, she introduced innovations like fireplaces and had glazed windows installed. At Clarendon, she had a kiln built by tilers especially brought from Aquitaine for the firing and glazing of elaborately designed multicoloured tiles for her apartments.[22] The intricately patterned floors show the same Moorish influence to be found at twelfth-century abbeys in Aquitaine, and hint at her pleasure in fine living, as do the mentions in the Pipe Rolls from time to time of silk hangings, carpets, cushions and other comforts. Many of these were transported on her travels, to convert her temporary accommodation into fit places for a queen to spend the night.

Now was she content just to plan the décor of castles and palaces. Queens and noblewomen operated networks of influence through arranged marriages. By betrothing one of her wards to a knight of Henry's household, Eleanor gained ears and a voice in his council. By granting land to knights married to her women, she had their children raised with hers to ensure a continuity of loyalty. And her influence in the marriages arranged for her own daughters was of even greater importance. Once implanted in a foreign court, they could serve as diplomatic channels between country of birth and the new homeland, as Eleanor's namesake daughter the queen of Castile did for her husband Alfonso VIII and her brother King John.[23] And her daughter Blanca or Blanche conveyed messages between him and her father-in-law Philip Augustus.[24]

In June 1156 the queen was back at Winchester for the birth of a daughter, baptised Matilda in honour of the empress by Archbishop Theobald at Holy Trinity in Aldgate. Shortly afterwards, the young Prince William died and was buried beside his great-grandfather in Reading.[25] As soon as she was fit to travel again, Eleanor crossed the Channel with both surviving children to catch up with Henry in Poitiers, where Geoffroi de Lauroux was waiting to petition her for the confirmation of the liberties of the churches of Sablonceaux and Fontaine-le-Comte, granted by William X and confirmed by Fat Louis but severely infringed by Henry's administrators of late. That the archbishop waited for his duchess' arrival implies a certain wariness about approaching Henry with his request.

It was one of many Eleanor granted. The official history of the abbey of La Sauve Majeure noted among the glittering retinue of barons and bishops in attendance on her and Henry the presence of 'Thomas of Canterbury', as Becket was later called.[26] Eleanor's seal, attached to the original deed confirming the abbey's privileges, showed her crowned and with a sceptre in her right hand. In her left, she held an orb with the peacock of Aquitaine perched on the cross, the legend reading 'Eleanor by the grace of God, Queen of the English'.[27] On the reverse, she held in the right hand a lily symbolising the Virgin and another orb and peacock in the other hand, while the legend confirmed her as 'duchess of Aquitaine, duchess of Normandy, countess of Poitou'.[28]

The insult to Henry four years earlier in Limoges still rankled. Shortly before Martinmas on 11 November, he returned there to raze the castle walls, recently strengthened to keep the dissident

Seal of Eleanor reconstructed from fragments in the Archives Nationales de France and elsewhere

townsfolk at bay. As guarantee of future good behaviour he took hostage the young Viscount Aymar and entrusted the government of the Limousin to two Norman vassals, who did indeed keep the peace for three years. He also punished Geoffrey of Thouars for siding against him in the dispute with his brother two years previously. So swift was the fall of Thouars that rumours began to circulate of treachery, when the real reason was his lifelong rule of moving fast and striking before the enemy saw him coming. To make the point that Henry's authority as duke of Aquitaine came from the marriage to her, Eleanor was present as the walls of Thouars Castle were torn down,[29] its seigneur banished and replaced by a trusted castellan.[30] It seems to have been her idea to force the captives taken in this adventure to make donations to her favourite religious foundations, as an alternative to being held to ransom.

After the Christmas court in Bordeaux Henry and Eleanor rode north separately, she receiving petitions and dispensing justice on the way. From the list of witnesses to a charter signed at Ruffec, it can be seen that she was attended by her own ducal entourage of vassals and a chancery headed by her clerk Matthew. Notably absent were Henry's intimates like Becket. Having abandoned his former allies of Thouars to Henry's mercy, Geoffrey of Anjou was enabled by the largesse of his pension to live in such generous style that the citizens of Nantes, who had just deposed the count of Brittany, offered the title to him instead.[31] With Henry's agreement, he accepted.

At some point on the journey north, the two households must have met, for Eleanor was pregnant again when she returned to England in February 1157, leaving Henry in France. He followed shortly afterwards, to counter the Welsh threat to Chester, but was foiled by the terrain and tactics that had frustrated the Roman legions. After a truce had been agreed, Becket, Lucy and Beaumont were summoned to join him for an extensive tour of the realm, during which Eleanor caught up with them at Oxford.

Henry I's palace there, called the King's House, was among the more comfortable of her temporary homes, with its great hall decorated with murals, and its chapels, cloister and private quarters for the queen. On 8 September she gave birth there to yet another son, destined to become England's most famous king. Named Richard, he was designated in William's stead as Eleanor's heir to the county of Poitou and therefore the duchy of Aquitaine. With nurses and maids – including Hodierna, the wet-nurse to whom Richard remained deeply attached throughout his life – to look after her children, Eleanor was free to travel with Henry. This was not to keep his roving eye in check but because she was inured to the discomforts of feudal travelling since childhood and loved the business of state.

For the Christmas court of 1157 held at Lincoln there was time for the queen's maids- and ladies-in-waiting and their servants to unpack their wardrobes from the travelling chests and leather sacks in which they had been growing mouldy during weeks of one-night stays. Henry too would dress up on these occasions, so that the royal court provided a glittering contrast to the penury and misery of the common people.

Christmas over, Henry headed north to secure the border with Scotland, Eleanor catching up with him at Blyth in Northumberland and accompanying him to Nottingham. From there began a relentless itinerary amounting to over 3,000 miles in twelve months. At Mass on Easter Day in Worcester Cathedral the king and queen removed their crowns in a mysterious ceremony whose symbolism remains unexplained, laying them on the shrine of St Wulfstan[32] after swearing never to wear them again. Through Shropshire, Gloucestershire and Somerset they headed before going north again to Carlisle in June.

At some point in the progress they learned from Paris that Queen Constance had been delivered of a daughter christened Marguerite, leaving poor Louis pacing the corridors of the palace on the Ile de la Cité muttering about the frightening number of princesses with which God had blessed him.[33] Betrothing Young Henry to her seemed to Eleanor and Henry a way of bridging the rift between London and Paris. The complication was that few of Louis' advisers would look favourably on the marriage of the infant princess to a son of the Whore of Aquitaine.

Overcoming their resistance was a job for a master diplomat. Becket rose to the occasion, setting out from the Norman capital of Rouen at the beginning of summer to charm the French capital. He entered Paris with a show of pomp and affluence that was never to be excelled. Eight wagons were laden with his personal effects and wardrobe, another carried his chapel and devotional objects, another the linen and coverings of his bedchamber, another the utensils of his kitchen. Drays followed, lurching under casks of good English ale to quench Parisian thirsts, and covered wagons stuffed with more bags and chests of clothing, carpets and hangings. Twelve packhorses bore so much plate to grace his table, together with his library of books and scrolls, that armed guards prowled alongside to prevent theft. Grooms led finely bred hounds on the leash and hawkers strutted among them with falcons on their gauntleted wrists.

As if that were not enough to impress the inhabitants of Louis' capital, there followed a spectacle worthy of an Olympic Games opening ceremony: groups dressed in traditional costume from every region subject to Henry, each singing in its own language. Next came knights in full armour and bishops no less grand, followed by squires bearing their shields, and clerks. Last came Becket, more magnificently apparelled than any who had preceded him. If this was only the Chancellor of England, the Parisians whispered, how far more splendid his master must be![34]

With no accommodation inside the walls large enough to house his entourage, it was only in the Templars' splendid new halls outside the city that Becket could find a setting grand enough for his embassy.[35] When he visited the shrines, he charmed all who came within reach of his generosity, whether an abbot with hand outstretched or a wayside beggar or the citizens of Paris who ate and drank their fill at his table. Gifts of fine clothes, jewels, horses, hawks and hounds flowed from the chancellor to every Frankish noble he met; to the common people went his generosity in food and wine; to the English students at the schools, of which he had been one, went purses of coin to fill their bellies with food and their minds with books for months after his departure. Asking nothing in return, Becket contented himself with implanting the message that the daughter of Louis' Spanish queen would be the instrument to reverse the disaster of his first marriage to Eleanor.

Before the end of the long progress through England, Henry had learned of the sudden death on 26 July of his brother Geoffrey, aged twenty-four. On 14 August he crossed to Normandy, leaving England in the hands of a heavily pregnant queen and Lucy the justiciar. Under the pretext of swearing fealty for Geoffrey's interest in Brittany, he met Louis on the banks of the Epte, an otherwise unimportant river that divided the Frankish Vexin from his own Norman Vexin. There he confirmed Becket's proposal to betroth Princess Marguerite to four-year-old Prince Henry, the marriage to be celebrated when she reached puberty[36] and her dowry of three castles in the Vexin to be held in trust by three Templar castellans until then. Louis stipulated only that his daughter should not in the normal way be raised in Eleanor's household, but in Normandy with a family to be mutually agreed.

On the face of it, the match was a good one whereby the house of Capet bestowed a superfluous princess on the eldest son of its most important vassal in the reasonable expectation that her children would rule the whole of western France and England too. The two daughters Eleanor had left behind in Paris had already been used to cement the alliances of the house of Capet with those of Champagne and Blois – a family that had suffered so much from Matilda and Henry during the civil war in England and had every reason to keep the border between Berry and Anjou in a state of unrest.

Louis considered that the engagement of Princess Marguerite to Prince Henry enabled him to play the game both ways. Equally satisfied that he had won this round of the betrothal game, which could win the throne of France for a grandson of his, Henry accepted Louis' invitation to collect the infant princess in Paris. First, however, he had to stake his claim to Brittany, now that Louis had legitimised it. In Nantes, the Breton capital, the citizens acclaimed Count Conan IV as his vassal in the hope that their new overlord would usher in an era of peace.

In early September Henry returned to Paris with a modest retinue. Dressed like any other noble pilgrim, he visited shrines and distributed largesse to the poor, to lepers and to religious foundations. Like all his visits, it was brief.[37] Within the week he rode away with Princess

Marguerite to Nantes, where she was given into the care of Robert of Neubourg, the pious justiciar of Normandy, to be raised and educated by him. For Queen Constance to thus hand over her six-month-old daughter according to feudal custom was as good as giving her away to strangers with no expectation of seeing her again. Across the Channel, on 23 September, Eleanor, continuing her joint regency with Lucy, gave birth to her fourth son, christened Geoffrey after his late uncle and designated duke of Brittany.

Louis, still a monk at heart, accepted an invitation to visit Mont St Michel as Henry's guest, which enabled him to visit the new home of Princess Marguerite at Neubourg and the city of Avranches, which Henry had promised would be one of her honours. At Le Mans a retinue of high churchmen was assembled to accompany the two kings to the shrine together. There, cut off by the tide, they heard Mass together and dined with the monks in the refectory, as Louis loved to do.[38]

At low tide they rode back to the mainland, spending a night at Bec, where Louis offered prayers to the memory of Anselm and Lanfranc, who had preceded him there. On Henry giving up his own bed for his suzerain, Louis exclaimed to all within earshot that he loved no man more than the king of the English. He returned to Paris confident that the betrothal of Marguerite and Young Henry had ushered in a new era of fraternal love between their fathers.

As though the excess of piety that had seduced Louis was too much for him to stomach, Henry showed a different face to the canons of Bordeaux Cathedral meeting to elect a successor to Geoffroi de Lauroux, who had died in July. Unable to agree, they delegated the decision to the bishops of Aquitaine, who met in the spirit of the freedoms granted by Louis and his father, as confirmed by Innocent II, Lucius II, Eugenius III and the new Pope Adrian IV.

In the middle of the bishops' conclave, Henry burst into the room, ordered them to elect a pliable schoolman from Poitiers nominated by him and added menacingly that he would remain during the vote. The prelates were silent until the bishop of Angoulême rose and announced that their deliberations could not continue until he left.[39]

Surprisingly, Henry accepted defeat. He had bigger things on his mind.

ELEVEN

King, Queen, Bishop

Among the many inducements for Henry to marry Eleanor, not least was her claim to the county of Toulouse, lost to the duchy of Aquitaine by William IX mortgaging his second wife's dowry as a way of financing his departure on the First Crusade.[1] If the former boundaries of Aquitaine from the Atlantic to the Mediterranean could be restored, uniting the two great cities on the River Garonne, trade would benefit enormously. Important customs dues would come from the resultant traffic in precious commodities like silk and glass and spices, shipped across the Mediterranean to Narbonne, up the River Aude to Toulouse and down the Garonne Valley to Bordeaux and from there by sea to England along one of the great natural trade routes of Europe.

Henry had an additional reason to covet this avenue to the Mediterranean. At what point he confided this to Eleanor is unknown – it could have been broached during Geoffrey the Fair's secret talks with her – but all the evidence points to him having a grand design, in which Toulouse had an important part to play.

A crafty chess-player, whether on the two-dimensional board or in the four-dimensional world, he could bide his time before a crucial move until he was assured of success. With England firmly in his grasp and the Welsh and Scottish borders stabilised, and with his continental possessions as peaceful as they were ever likely to be, the time seemed ripe to move against Toulouse in August 1158 when Count Berenger of Barcelona allied himself with his neighbours of Béziers and Montpellier and the formidable warlady Ermengarde of Narbonne.[2] If Henry joined them, Toulouse would be surrounded by enemies on three sides.

After the Christmas court at Cherbourg, for which Eleanor crossed over from England, the Catalan count was invited to an Easter meeting at Blaye on the Gironde estuary, where Eleanor's presence gave legitimacy to Henry acting as duke.[3] Together, they tied the knot of friendship by engaging eighteen-month-old Prince Richard to the count's daughter Berengaria.[4] Seemingly unaware that not all Henry's betrothals ended in marriage, Count Berenger was delighted at the idea of his daughter one day becoming the duchess of Aquitaine.

Since Count Raymond V of Toulouse and St Gilles was not only Louis' vassal, but also his brother-in-law, the next move was for Eleanor to send him a demand that the county be handed over to her. That refused, Henry gave instructions for his vassals in England and France to assemble with their knights at Poitiers by Midsummer Day, ready to move south. In default, they were to pay scutage. In addition, his seventeen-year-old ally Malcolm IV of Scotland – known as Malcolm the Maiden because he died before marrying – promised an expeditionary force.

Seeking to give the enterprise some legitimacy, Henry sounded Louis out during a meeting in Tours, but the last thing Louis wanted was any further expansion of the Angevin possessions. Remembering all too well his own abortive expedition to Toulouse when married to Eleanor, to whom he certainly owed no favours, he retorted that he would not sanction a war launched by one of his vassals against another who had given no offence – and who also happened to be his sister's husband.

In a series of meetings at Heudicourt in Normandy on 6, 7 and 8 June 1159, Henry failed to change Louis' mind. A week later, the die was cast when a fleet of forty vessels disembarked Malcolm's small army in Normandy to join the coalition. Together, he and Henry moved south, gathering other forces as they went, among them Thomas Becket at the head of an impressive contingent of 700 knights equipped and provisioned by a special and very unpopular tax he had levied on Church lands in England, the shortfall made up by a loan of 500 marks from a Jewish moneylender.[5] In this martial enterprise, Becket was being trained for even higher things.

Meeting up with the Aquitain and Angevin elements at Poitiers, where Eleanor seems to have remained during the expedition, the entire force reached Périgueux on the frontier with Toulousain territory at the end of June. Henry's logistics had run like clockwork, but his allies were way behind schedule. When they failed to show up at Agen, three or four days' march to the south, there was a limit to how much time could be passed in feudal niceties such as tournaments and ceremonies with Henry dubbing Malcolm a knight and Malcolm in return dubbing twenty or thirty of Henry's young nobles. Time was spent threatening the important river crossing and town of Cahors, whose citizens accepted the coalition rather than see their homes destroyed.

Elsewhere, crops were being laid waste and vineyards destroyed as everything that could be carried or driven off was taken and the rest burned to deny it to the enemy. For the troubadour Bertran de Born, lord of the castle of Hautefort in Périgord, this was the stuff of life:

> *Tot jorn contendi e m'baralh,*
> *M'escrim, e m'defen e m'tartalh*
> *E m'fon hom ma terra e la m'art*
> *E m'fai de mos arbres essart . . .*

[I'm always in the thick of the fray. / Skirmishing and fighting, that's my way. / They waste my lands, leave my fields burnt brown. / Now they're hacking my trees all down . . .]

Not until the beginning of August did the combined allies reach Toulouse,[6] by which time the commander of the city was not the weak and idle Count Raymond. Goaded into action by Henry's lobbying, which had soured the memory of the joint pilgrimage to Mont St Michel, and already regretting the betrothal of Princess Marguerite to Young Henry, Louis had ridden at full speed from Paris with only a small entourage in order to stiffen the resolve of his brother-in-law, whom he suspected of being all too likely to seek terms at the outset of hostilities.

Once in Toulouse, he showed unusual powers of leadership, motivating the garrison and strengthening the walls, as a result of which Henry's usual blitzkrieg tactics failed at considerable cost to the attackers. Among the casualties was William, the last surviving son of Stephen of Blois. For once, Louis had done everything right, and even provisioned the city to withstand a siege of many months. Stingy as ever, Henry had contracted his mercenaries for only thirteen weeks, and his purse would be empty long before the Toulousains' larders.

To everyone's surprise, he announced that he had only come from loyalty to his Catalan allies, and would give a good example of feudal duty to his own vassals by refraining from attacking the city so long as his suzerain was present there.[7] With Becket's contingent left behind in Cahors, Henry withdrew and the coalition melted away, leaving the peasantry contemplating the bleak prospect of a winter famine with their crops destroyed. As wars went, this was a small one, but what Bertran de Born saw as heroic had a very different look to Aimeric de Pegulhan:

> Quare de guerra ven tart pro et tost dan
> E guerra fai mal tornar en peior
> en guerra trop, per qu'ieu non la volria
> viutat de mal, et de ben carestia.

[The fruits war seeds are wormwood and gall. / Life, already hard, gets only worse / for all our problems stem from this curse / that brings great grief – of good, nothing at all.]

Eleanor's disappointment at the failure of the campaign was tempered by knowledge that Henry had an alternative plan which did not involve sharing Toulouse with any allies. They spent the time of the grape harvest and vintage on her estates in Poitou,[8] after which he headed north with Malcolm early in October. That he did not tarry in the renowned hunting forest of Talmond was due to Louis' brothers Count Robert of Dreux and Bishop Henry of Beauvais having taken advantage of his preoccupation with Toulouse to invade Normandy. There, fighting dragged on into December, when the two sides agreed to a truce negotiated by the bishops, which was to last until Whitsun.

Eleanor rejoined Henry at Falaise for the Christmas court. Short of funds after the abortive Toulouse campaign, Henry sent her to England to bring back the money he desperately needed. She set sail on 29 December in his ship Esnecca,[9] rode to Winchester, secured the bullion and coins and then escorted the precious consignment back to Barfleur before returning to England – all this in the throes of midwinter weather.

Her reward for this arduous errand was to be Henry's regent there for much of the next three years, with Beaumont as chief justiciar, while Becket stayed initially in Normandy with Henry. The Pipe Rolls reflect her progress from castle to city to castle, living in some style as she travelled extensively throughout southern England. In Winchester she had repairs carried out to the palace, the chapel and the walls and garden, and drew on the Exchequer for the considerable sum of £226 for herself and £56 for Prince Henry. As well as her children and servants, her household included maids- and ladies-in-waiting. If the married ladies spent short periods in her service, for which some were rewarded by money and some by gifts, a maid-in-waiting could often be a ward of the Crown for years.

In addition to her duties of state, Eleanor found the time and energy to polish the dull cultural scene in London by importing the latest fashions in poetry and music. Prone to send away from her Thameside court with a flea in his ear any man who appeared badly dressed or with hair uncut, she expected her ladies to follow her example in the latest continental fashions. For their amusement, Arthurian legends had to compete not only with *chansons de geste* recounting the deeds of Roland, Charlemagne or Godefroi de Bouillon on the First Crusade but also the legends of Greece and Rome and the poetry of favourite troubadours. It was arguably at Eleanor's short-lived London court that European literature, whose business had hitherto been instruction, first developed the entertainment form it has never lost.

Romances were dedicated to her. There was no public theatre, but plays performed at court included a lost tragedy *Flora and Marcus*, written by the brother of Peter of Blois. Chrétien de Troyes may have been another of the queen's protégés; his habit of describing himself as 'of Troyes' indicates a knowledge of English and he did later frequent the court of her daughter, Marie de Champagne. And the mysterious poetess Marie de France – whose topical *lais* include the 1,184-line poem *Eliduc* about a devoted wife whose husband brings a second wife home from overseas – also appeared in England at about this time, to be patronised by Henry's bastard William Longsword and probably the queen also.

Both John of Salisbury and Walter Map complained that all these entertainments were distracting men's minds from more serious matters and that Eleanor's regal but flirtatious southern ways were effeminising the men of her court. To them, such devices as the shepherdess seduction theme of the *pastorela* were a perversion that romanticised the rutting of peasants. If Map was simply sarcastic, Salisbury went so far as to suggest excommunication of all who earned their living as entertainers in Eleanor's London – an attitude that persisted in the long denial to the acting profession of burial on consecrated ground. Even Eleanor's music, embracing the concept of harmony that had pleasured her ear in Byzantium, had been condemned by such as Abbé Bernard, who complained that the human voice was given to man for no other purpose than to praise God without any of the devil's artifices of harmony and counterpoint getting in the way.

Yet Gerald de Barri – better known as the Welsh chronicler Giraldus Cambrensis – had to admit later that the cultural revolution brought about by Henry's queen made the royal court at Westminster interesting enough to compete with the attractions of Becket's house in the city. Jealous tongues wagged until inevitably the same accusations of loose living that had been levelled at Eleanor on the Ile de la Cité were soon heard in the cloister at Canterbury and the streets of London. Innocent Louis had probably never heard the rumours before departure on crusade, but had there been any substance to them in London, there is no doubt Henry would have known. A king whose constant curiosity and perpetual paranoia drove him to quiz every newly arrived messenger not only about the state of the roads over which he had travelled but also the latest news from Jerusalem and Rome, could not have failed to learn of misconduct by his queen. And had he learned of such, he would have locked Eleanor up without any qualms, as later events were to prove.

Being an Angevin, he understood that what to the Anglo-Norman eye looked like scandalous intimacy between a troubadour and his adored mistress was no more than a game by which the frustrations of ladies married off for reasons of state could be sublimated without any harm to them, even if from time to time an importunate poet like Bernat de Ventadorn did become a casualty of the game. So long as Eleanor performed her duties as his queen and provided sons for the succession and daughters to use as pawns, it mattered little to Henry that she took her pleasures thus, so long as things went no further. Others were less tolerant: in disapproval of this neo-pagan society centred on the queen's court, in the summer of 1160 the archbishop of Canterbury begged the king to return to England on the grounds that the growing princes needed their father's moral guidance.

In September Henry ordered Eleanor to bring Prince Henry and Princess Matilda back to Normandy, not out of paternal sentiment[10] but for another round of betrothals. At a cost of seven English pounds, according to the Pipe Rolls, the queen hastened to cross the Channel. For diplomatic reasons she was not present when Henry witnessed Prince Henry's act of homage to Louis for the duchy of Normandy, given on bended knee to make amends for his father's invasion of Toulousain territory and because Henry had in mind to betroth Matilda to the child about to be born to Louis and Constance, should it be male.

The next step in the plan went awry as misfortune struck the king of France yet again. In giving birth to his fourth daughter, Queen Constance died. Forty years old, the widowed father of four girls and no sons, Louis was desperate for an heir. His counsellors advised strengthening the house of Capet by taking a wife from the house of Champagne, despite his late brother Philip having been denied a bride from that family on the grounds of consanguinity. Less than a month after Constance's death, Louis risked that sin by marrying Alix or Adele of Champagne, who was a sister of his future sons-in-law, the counts of Champagne and Blois![11]

To Henry, this smelled of conspiracy. Assembling the whole family at Neubourg, he took advantage of the presence of two papal legates soliciting his continued support of the new Pope Alexander III against the German Emperor Frederik Barbarossa, who supported the anti-pope Victor.[12] Princess Marguerite, now three years old, was married by Cardinal Henry of Pisa to five-year-old Prince Henry[13] in defiance of the requirement to obtain a papal dispensation for the marriage of minors and in total disregard of the oath of fealty the boy had sworn so shortly before.

What had this to do with Toulouse? It seems that Henry's support for the pope was also part of his grand design.

Neubourg was perilously near French territory. Lest Louis should be tempted to kidnap the two children and find grounds for the dissolution of the unconsummated marriage, they were whisked away to the safety of Eleanor's household despite the specific undertaking to Louis that Marguerite would not be brought up by her. By advancing the marriage a decade, Henry legitimised to his own satisfaction the plan to take possession of Marguerite's dowry castles straight away. The three supposedly neutral Templar castellans chose to comply with his imperious demands,[14] given the appearance of papal sanction by the legates' presence.

In retaliation, furious at having been again outwitted, Louis expelled all the Templars from his domains and began massing his forces, plus those of Champagne and Blois, on the borders of Normandy. With the speed of a snake Henry struck first, capturing the castle of Chaumont from Thibault of Blois before Advent ended campaigning for the year. The Christmas court of 1160, held by Henry with Eleanor in Le Mans, was in celebratory mood.

On 18 April next Archbishop Theobald died unmourned by either the protégé he had raised so high or the king for whom he had done so much. It is significant that he knew Becket's character too well to propose him as successor. Indeed, few in the Church hierarchy seriously considered him for the office. Yet, with Henry's record of interfering in Church matters on both sides of the Channel, the canons of Canterbury Cathedral had little hope that he would allow them to choose their new archbishop.

Henry saw in this important appointment a chance to curb the political power of the Church in England and, in particular, to end what he regarded as gross abuses of clerical privilege, by which a 'criminous clerk' could claim benefit of clergy and escape the penalties of his actions under the law of the realm by demanding to be tried before an ecclesiastical court, where he would receive preferential treatment.

Second, there was the grand design, in which the appointment of a new archbishop was *the* crucial move – so crucial that Henry pondered it for a whole year, during which he was also working on his strategy to secure Toulouse by means other than warfare, which included improving the comital palace at Poitiers as a base for his operations and a general tightening of his grip on the duchy of Aquitaine by installing his own northern administrators – the same error that Louis had made.

One tightening of the screw too many resulted in a group of Eleanor's resentful vassals approaching the papal legates with a family tree showing how she and the king were related, probably at the meeting in early September at Toucy-sur-Loire between Louis and Henry under the aegis of the exiled pope, settled for the time being in Sens. Diplomatically, the cardinals showed no interest in separating the king from his wife, who was expecting a child any day. Later in the same month Eleanor gave birth for the ninth time at Domfront – to a girl, baptised Eleanor after her mother by Cardinal Henry of Pisa, with the chronicler Robert de Torigny as godfather. As thanksgiving, her mother joined Henry in financing the construction of the cathedral of St Pierre in Poitiers.[15]

The archbishops of Rouen and Canterbury were not alone in saying that it was time for Young Henry's formal education to begin. To whom could a prince better be entrusted than to Becket, already responsible for a cluster of noble lads? After the Christmas court of 1161 at Bayeux, and impelled by another illness that gave the matter urgency in his mind, Henry sought to kill two birds with one stone. While honouring few of the obligations he entered into, Henry had an obsession with the renewal of pledges by others, and decided to avoid any disturbance to the realm consequent upon the announcement of his candidate for the prelacy by having the barons of England first renew their pledge of allegiance to Young Henry, given at Wallingford in the year after his own coronation.

At the Easter court in Falaise, Becket was therefore instructed to take the prince back to England, have a suitable golden coronet and sumptuous ceremonial robes made for him and convene the barons and bishops in Winchester to renew their recognition of the prince as the next king of England.[16] At the last moment before they set out for Barfleur, Henry took his chancellor aside and told him apparently for the first time of his plan to set him on the throne of Canterbury. Instead of thanking his monarch for yet another great honour, which can hardly have taken by surprise someone so astute, Becket implored him to reconsider, quoting the Gospel of Matthew (6: 24): 'No man can serve two masters. For either he will hate the one and love the other, or else he will hold to the one and despise the other. Ye cannot serve God and Mammon.'

To deflect Henry's displeasure at this reaction, he jokingly plucked at his costly brocaded sleeve and asked how such a worldly garment would look, if worn by the humble shepherd of Canterbury.[17] But Henry would not take no for an answer even when Becket proposed a list of other candidates, whom he considered better suited for the primacy.

While Chancellor Becket was dutifully convening the barons and bishops in Winchester at Whitsun, the imposing Chapter House at Canterbury was in uproar at the announcement of the king's plans for the succession to the see. The most obvious objection to Becket was that he was ineligible, having only taken minor orders. Meanwhile, the future archbishop was on his bended knees, not before an altar but pledging his homage to the boy of seven, whose father was about to make the worst miscalculation of his career.

Just over a month later, Becket was consecrated priest, bishop and then archbishop in the space of two days by Henry, the compliant bishop of Winchester who had crowned Stephen of Blois.[18] The city of Canterbury, half of which was owned by the cathedral priory, had been ravaged the previous year by a fire in which most of the houses were destroyed, so the magnates and fifteen diocesan bishops and all the knights and attendants in their retinues were accommodated in a huge tented camp outside the walls like some army on campaign. In the presence of the justiciar and Young Henry, Becket renounced all his worldly offices and gave up the chancellor's seal.[19] It was the news of this which caused Henry to wonder for the first time whether his plan was going to work.

Becket took to wearing a horsehair shirt, constantly irritating the skin beneath the fine clothes he still affected, and followed a strict *horarium* with midnight prayers, rising at dawn to wash the feet of beggars and distribute food to the hungry. He also ordered for himself daily penitential floggings. Yet many of the bishops were unimpressed by this ostentatious conversion, their attitude summed up by the wry comment of Gilbert Foliot, bishop of Hereford and abbot of Wells, that the king had worked a veritable miracle in so swiftly translating a soldier and courtier into a priest. And even when Becket visited his old school at Merton and adopted the sober black habit of an Augustinian canon over the hair shirt, his ecclesiastical critics still pointed to the lavish lifestyle he was unable to put aside. Among the sceptics must have been the king, who wrought the miracle, for had he not shared all the pleasures of life with Becket, except women?[20]

Henry had intended holding his Christmas court in England but, weather preventing a departure from Barfleur, it was from Cherbourg that he and Eleanor eventually set sail on 25 January 1163, three stormbound weeks after holding the Christmas court there with several of their children. Waiting at Southampton to welcome the king back to England after an absence of three and a half years was Becket. Young Henry, who was still living in his household, emerged from the shelter of the archbishop's cloak[21] to greet his parents and sisters.

Far from sorting out the ecclesiastical excesses of which the king complained, Becket had in the months since his ordination clawed back from the barons many former Church properties they had seized during the unrest of Stephen's reign.[22] Henry I's travelling justices, reinstated after the civil war with the help of Becket himself, were already complaining at the spate of clerks now avoiding the law under the umbrella of ecclesiastical protection. These early excesses have been interpreted as Becket's way of ingratiating himself within the Church hierarchy, but they bear more the stamp of a once-brilliant subordinate unable to handle the top job. Or had he got cold feet after being taken fully into Henry's confidence about the true reason for his appointment?

According to Herbert of Bosham, there were harsh words from Henry at the first meeting on the quayside in Southampton, but the following day the two men, who had been bosom friends, rode side by side to London, with the king gnawing at a solution for the problem he had created: if Becket would not bend, he must be broken.

Henry's return marked the end of Eleanor's interrupted regency in England. What he saw as Becket's betrayal inflamed his paranoia so much that he gathered to himself all the reins of power before departing to renew hostilities against the Welsh, this time with greater success that ended with all their princes swearing fealty to him. Meanwhile, Eleanor was reduced to making preparations to celebrate Young Henry's eighth birthday in a style befitting a crowned king of England.

What she had thought of Henry's idea of making Becket archbishop, we do not know. But the Empress Matilda had gone on record as speaking out against it[23] for the good reason that she had, during her years as German Empress, seen the same device fail when Archbishop Adalbert of Mainz decided to serve his Church and not the temporal overlord who had appointed him. She was wasting her ink, for Henry could point to a more recent precedent, when Frederik Barbarossa had appointed his chancellor Rainald von Dassel archbishop of Cologne only two years previously.

If he had hoped to win over his own ex-chancellor by soft words, he had a rude awakening. Returning from a meeting with the pope at the Council of Tours in May 1163, Becket took up the cause of the English bishops who were protesting against the interference of agents of the Crown in Church matters and the diversion of what they regarded as ecclesiastical funds. It was one affront too many for the king, who called a Great Council at Westminster on the first day of October, at which he harangued the prelates present for the liberties they were taking and demanded an undertaking to comply with his will.

The tactic having failed, he stormed out of the meeting, to summon Becket the following day for a personal humiliation in which he was dispossessed of the chief sources of his wealth – the manors of Eye and Berkhampstead. As an additional slap in the face, Young Henry and his child bride were removed from Becket's care, with the prince being given a household of his own. From the pope – in Paris to lay the foundation stone of Notre Dame and in Henry's debt for continuing political support – came no encouragement for the contentious archbishop; Becket was urged by the pontiff to make peace with his king.

On 13 October Henry was present in Westminster Abbey when Becket officiated at the translation of the remains of Edward the Confessor – an event of greater symbolic importance to Henry because the Emperor Frederik was arranging with the new anti-pope Paschal III for the canonisation of one of his predecessors, the Emperor Charlemagne.

About this time Henry decided to marry his surviving brother William to Isabella de Warenne, the widow of Stephen of Blois' son who had died at Toulouse. Becket forbade the match on the grounds of consanguinity, and when William died shortly afterwards, there were many among the archbishop's increasing number of enemies who said the king's brother had had his heart broken by the prohibition that denied him his true love. True or not, it was one of the accusations hurled at Becket by Henry's knights on the night of the murder in Canterbury Cathedral.

With the pope firmly aligned on the king's side, many English bishops began to worry where Becket was leading them in this dangerous test of strength. Even the archbishop's most loyal supporters begged him to find some compromise, and many bishops who had resented his manner of raising the tax for the invasion of Toulouse were openly hostile to their spiritual overlord for the troubles his inexplicable arrogance was bringing upon them all.

To concert the opposition to him within the Church hierarchy, headed by Roger, the rival archbishop of York, Henry appointed Gilbert Foliot bishop of London. It was a move that required, and received, a special licence from the pope. When Becket demanded the new bishop's homage for his see, Foliot refused, saying that he had already given it when bishop of Hereford.

At the palace of Woodstock in December, Becket appeared to back down, to the bishops' great relief. But Henry's blood was up. To show the world who ruled England, he announced that the Christmas court would be held at the castle of Berkhamsted, where he took a vicious pleasure in working with Becket's former assistants in what had been Becket's luxurious private palace on the drafting of what would become the Constitutions of Clarendon.

As though in compensation for the difficulties caused by Becket, at the end of Advent 600 miles to the south the bellicose new archbishop of Bordeaux, Bertrand de Montault, was doing his best to make up for Henry's failed invasion of Toulouse. He took advantage of Count Raymond's indolence to lead his own knights and a number of Eleanor's other vassals in ravaging the disputed country around Rodez, getting to within a trebuchet's range of the city of Toulouse itself after destroying several castles, burning and looting churches on the way and departing with prisoners to be held for ransom.

The council held at Clarendon on 25 January 1164 had as its purpose the restoration of the 'former customs' of the realm by which power had traditionally been shared between Church and Crown. Henry made sure that the archbishop who had been so well schooled as a lawyer did not receive an advance copy of the lengthy document, but was confronted with it in plenary session.

The sixteen articles of the Constitutions defined the relationship of Church and State in a manner going far beyond any former customs.

The king was to receive the revenues from all vacant sees and monasteries, which could be filled only with his consent. Cases of advowson or Church patronage, debts and disputes over land held in lay fee were reserved to the secular courts, as was any property dispute between a layman and a churchman. Benefit of clergy was to be abolished, with 'criminous clerks' subject to the king's justice like anyone else. Even the right to appeal to Rome, or to leave the country on pilgrimage, became privileges to be accorded or withheld at the king's whim.

The bishops reluctantly assented with the face-saving proviso *salvo ordine* – 'saving their order'. To their amazement, Becket capitulated in the face of Henry's unconcealed fury and agreed to everything, although refusing to set his archbishop's seal to the document. As Gilbert Foliot commented acidly, it was the captain who ran away while the troops stood firm. In penance for his hypocrisy and the perjury he had committed at Clarendon, Becket ceased removing at night his hair shirt, which rapidly became vermin-infested, increasing his discomfort, but had a slit made in the back, tied up with tapes that could be undone to permit his daily floggings.

When Pope Alexander read the Constitutions, he condemned them but sent contradictory letters to Henry and to Becket, each explaining away some concession granted to the other as he swayed in the political winds blowing across Europe.[24] However, the gist of Alexander's advice to the archbishop was that he could expect no gesture of support that might upset the king, whose political support continued to be vital to the papacy.

To make the point that even the most senior churchman in England was subject to his laws, Henry had Becket arraigned on a trumped-up charge.[25] Fearing for his life, the archbishop rode secretly the 30 miles from Canterbury to Dover only to find that he who had formerly only to lift a finger for the king's captains to weigh anchor with as many vessels as he desired was now denied passage on the humblest fishing smack. It was not the first time he had planned to flee and been turned back. Passports were now required to enter or leave England, in a net of laws designed to catch one fish.

Arriving at Northampton on the day in October appointed for the court hearing, Becket found himself denied suitable lodgings in the town, with the plaintiff still in London and the king amusing himself with hawk and hound somewhere en route. Next morning after Mass, he attended early at the castle, to be left waiting in an ante-room while Henry slumbered on, or pretended to.[26] Rising to his feet in respect as the king strode past him to hear Mass in his private chapel, the archbishop was ignored and then ignored again when Henry returned to take his breakfast.

The court finally in session, Becket found himself facing a different charge of misappropriation, for which he was fined £300.[27] The bishops present stood surety but no one could be found to inform the accused of the verdict until the ageing turncoat bishop of Winchester went out and broke the news to the man he had consecrated archbishop sixteen months before. His appetite for revenge whetted by that first humiliation, Henry now demanded another £300, which he alleged Becket had illicitly removed from the funds of the manors of Eye and Berkhamsted. For this amount, too, sureties were found among the bishops present.

On the following day, Henry's first demand was for the repayment of 1,000 marks alleged to have gone missing from the tax Becket had raised for Toulouse. Sureties were again found, but this time among lay people. Then the king demanded detailed accounts for the enormous rents Becket had received on his behalf from vacant sees and other religious properties – a sum in the order of 30,000 silver marks was mentioned.[28] Becket truthfully replied that he had been exonerated from all worldly obligations when he was consecrated at Canterbury – and this before witnesses who included Young Henry.

However, the sureties melted away, for who could tell what the furious monarch would demand next? Some of the bishops begged Henry on their knees to have mercy, but he was adamant. That night the archbishop's entourage was divided, with many proposing that he should resign before the king's wrath embraced the entire Church. Next day, in agony from an attack of renal colic, Becket was physically unable to attend the court, but roused himself twenty-four hours later to attend the resumed hearing. Dissuaded by some Templars from going barefoot as a penitent, he decided to put on the full panoply of Canterbury, but was persuaded not to, in case that irritated Henry even more. It was with a simple cloak over his black Augustinian canon's surplice that he arrived in court, clutching his primatial cross before him as though to ward off the foul fiend himself.

With his legal background and familiarity with the workings of Henry's mind, he cannot have been surprised at the ruling that he was to make no appeal to Rome, nor give any instructions to his suffragans, and that he was to submit full accounts for the 30,000 marks which the king alleged had gone missing. To this, Becket gave a lawyer's reply, saying that he had come to court to answer the first charge and none other. Nor would he offer sureties. Instead, he would appeal to God and the pope for himself and for the Church of Canterbury.[29] Confronted with a new writ from Henry being served on him by the earl of Leicester, he declared that his travesty of a trial was without any legal basis and that he was not subject to the royal justice.

In turning to sweep out of the astonished court, his grand gesture turned to farce. The castle courtyard was so packed with the many hundred mounts of all the magnates, bishops, knights and their attendants that there was a parking problem. The archbishop's horse was disengaged, as were several others, but Herbert of Bosham's was so hemmed in that he had to jump up on the crupper behind Becket or risk being left behind. Then came panic: the gate was locked and the gatekeeper nowhere to be found. Becket's party naturally assumed that Henry intended to imprison them all, there and then.[30] But the key was found hanging on a hook, and the archbishop's retinue made an undignified retreat, amid insults from the castle riff-raff who then beat up their unfortunate servants, abandoned in the hasty departure.

Knowing that nothing less than his death would sate Henry's hunger for vengeance, Becket spent the night in sanctuary, praying for part of the night at the altar of the priory where he had been lodging. The monks crept in for Compline, believing that the huddled form behind the altar was the archbishop asleep, but it was just a dummy made from cushions and cloaks. Becket had left Northampton before daybreak, a man on the run scurrying from one religious house to another, frightened to spend two nights in the same bed.

A week later, after making the 30-mile Channel crossing in a small rowing boat from the less frequented port of Sandwich, which was Church property, he was a fugitive in exile. At a monastery near St Omer, the faithful Hubert caught up with him, bringing clothing, horses and a small amount of money and plate from Canterbury to meet his immediate needs. Passing through Compiègne on the way to meet Pope Alexander in Sens, Becket was reassured on meeting Louis[31] to hear that he was welcome on Capetian territory.

It was a refrain that all Henry's enemies, including his sons, would be hearing over the years to come. Whether truly seeking to reconcile Becket and his monarch or to rub salt in Henry's wound, Louis tried a dozen times during the archbishop's six-year exile at Pontigny and Sens to arrange meetings of reconciliation between him and Henry. Each time they met, failure was the outcome.

On 24 December 1164 Henry was at Marlbrough with Eleanor for the Christmas court when the ambassadors he had sent to present his side of the dispute to the pope returned with the news that Becket had got there first with Louis' help. Having heard him out, Alexander was threatening to excommunicate the king of England. This triggered one of Henry's legendary berserker rages, in which he threw himself about, rent his clothes, tore the bedding and chewed the straw of his mattress.

There was little of festivity next day for Eleanor and her children, but the following day was worse. Invoking the Germanic principle of *Sippenhaft*, Henry ruled that everyone related to Becket shared the archbishop's guilt. As a result, 400 innocent men, women and children were forcibly deported to Flanders and left there homeless in midwinter with only the clothes they stood up in.[32]

In February, leaving Eleanor at Winchester, the king returned to Normandy and welcomed to Rouen Archbishop Rainald of Cologne with a view to worrying Louis, who rightly feared his enemies from east and west uniting against him. It was also a way of showing his resentment of the pope's support for Becket. There was even talk of Princess Eleanor being married to the emperor's infant son, Frederik, but at the same time Henry was negotiating for the marriage of Princess Matilda to Henry the Lion of Saxony, a cousin of the emperor who had been giving him much trouble lately.

Eleanor spent the spring of 1165 with all the children but Young Henry at Winchester without apparently exercising any real power. With her household and children she stayed for a while at Sherborne and on the Isle of Wight before moving back to Westminster, where Archbishop Rainald was introduced to the princesses and where she summoned a council on the king's instructions to announce the new alliance. On the Sunday after Easter, Henry and Louis met at Gisors for an inconclusive meeting, after which he ordered the queen, now pregnant again, to meet him at Rouen with eight-year-old Richard and Matilda, aged nine.

However, his plan as part of the grand design to marry the princess there and then to Henry the Lion was put on hold either due to the schism or because it was Henry's nature to promise but not deliver. Leaving Eleanor to oversee the continental domains, which can be read as an indication of her regained status now that Becket was out of the way – or at least of Henry's renewed need of someone to rely on in addition to the ageing Empress Matilda while he was on the other side of the Channel – the king departed on another campaign against the Welsh for which there was scant enthusiasm among the English knighthood, causing him to institute the inquiry to establish exactly what knight service his vassals-in-chief owed him and were in turn owed by their vavassours. The essential lien of vassalage had so fallen into disuse in England that many barons could give no clear answer to the inquiry before consulting the aged inhabitants of their fiefs.

There was even less enthusiasm for his continental expeditions because the English barons argued that they owed homage to him as king of England for their mutual support, but not to him as duke of Normandy or Aquitaine in pursuit of his ambitions on the continent.

Henry's mood is indicated by his ordering during this campaign that all the Welsh male hostages be blinded and castrated; the females had their noses slit and ears cut off.[33] Such violence was not reserved for enemies of the Crown. A small group of proselytising religious dissidents from Germany arrived in London and openly denied the sacraments. To show that he was not hostile to the Church *per se*, the normally tolerant king had them brought for trial before him and his bishops in council at Oxford. Sentenced to be branded and flogged before being outcast among a population forbidden to give them food or shelter, the Germans starved to death, their solitary English convert having recanted.

Reviving her first court of the marriage in Angers, Eleanor received from Becket a plea for her support in the quarrel with Henry. Whether she replied is unknown, but the bishop of Poitiers told him he was wasting his time in such an approach and hinted darkly that Eleanor's hostility was the result of the undue influence of her uncle Raoul de Faye, who was acting as her chief counsellor. Once again a celibate used the oldest slur to demean the queen, hinting broadly that there was something illicit in the relationship of uncle and niece. At the time Eleanor was four months into her eleventh pregnancy.

On 22 August 1165, Louis at last had a son and heir to the throne of France. Giraldus Cambrensis, then a student on the Ile de la Cité, was awoken in the middle of the night by the ringing of every bell in the city. Sticking his head out of the window, he learned from some women passers-by that France now had a prince who would one day put the Angevins in their place. Baptised Philip after his dead uncle and Augustus for the month, Louis' son was also called Dieudonné – the God-given. Hearing the news in Wales, Henry knew that his plan to claim the crown of France through Young Henry as husband of Marguerite would never come to fruition.

In October Eleanor gave birth to a third daughter, christened Joanna. Taking advantage of the queen's indisposition and Henry's problems with the Welsh, the barons of Maine and Brittany had risen up against Angevin domination. Despite the dispatch of a punitive force under the Constable of Normandy, the rebellion simmered on. For the first time Eleanor and Henry celebrated Christmas apart: she in

Angers and he at Oxford. Romantically inclined historians have interpreted the separate Christmas courts and his relative immobility as evidence of obsession with Rosamund Clifford, despite there being no evidence that he cared more for her than several other mistresses like Rohese, a daughter of the De Clare family, with whom he had had a liaison three years earlier.

Eleanor, like all noble and royal wives, was supposed to shut her eyes to these adulterous adventures, of which the chroniclers kept a lick-smacking tally. Giraldus Cambrensis delighted in quoting the Latin puns on Fair Rosamund's name: not Rosamunda but *rosa immunda*, the unclean rose – and not *rosa mundi*, the rose of the world, but *rosa immundi*, the rose of filth or unchastity.[34]

He offered no suggestion how the beautiful teenage daughter of Walter Clifford, a Norman marcher lord performing knight service for Henry during his forays into Wales, could have rejected the advances of the king, whose vassals and tenants went to great lengths to keep their wives and daughters away from his lascivious gaze,[35] unless they sought to gain something from satisfying his desires. As so often, it was the helpless female victim who was assumed to have seduced the powerful male perpetrator unwilling to control his lust.

Of one or more rumoured bastards by this liaison, nothing is known. Rosamund may have been discarded by Henry when Richard's child fiancée Princess Alais came of an age to share his bed, for she died young in pious retirement at the convent of Godstow, where she had been educated. Henry paid for a lavish tomb in the convent church, on which the charitable nuns who had known her better than any gossipy celibate chronicler honoured the memory of the king's ex-mistress with daily floral tributes until Bishop Hugh of Lincoln was scandalised on a visit early in the 1190s. On his orders, the tomb was resited less publicly lest the pious should cease to fear the dreaded consequence of such a life of sin as she had led.[36]

Resited in the nuns' chapter house, the new tomb was ornamented with an admonitory inscription:

> *Hic jacet in tumba*
> *rosa mundi, non rosa munda.*
> *Non redolet, sed olet,*
> *qua redolere solet.*[37]

[The rose of the world lies here / but not too clean, I fear. / Not perfume, but stenches / she now dispenses.]

The legend inspired by her early death has Fair Rosamund kept by Henry for his pleasure in a secret bower within the maze at Woodstock Palace, where 'Dame Ellinor the furious queene' discovers her and offers her young rival a choice between poison and the knife. Even if Eleanor had arrived unexpectedly at Woodstock and found Henry's young paramour on the palace estate, she would not have demeaned herself in this or any other way. No detractor ever accused her of lacking queenly dignity; nor would she have been particularly surprised, having known at least two of Henry's bastards personally. As to the poison and the knife, she would be under lock and key as his most closely guarded prisoner at the time of Rosamund Clifford's death.

TWELVE

Rift and Separation

D uring the Easter court of 1166 at Angers Eleanor became pregnant for the eleventh time, possibly as a last attempt to keep some kind of relationship with Henry despite her resentment at being shown by him none of the respect due to the queen of England; in recent years, all he had used her for was to beget more sons and daughters he could trade in some alliance. With the menopause approaching, she knew she would be completely discarded.

The widening rift between them may have been triggered by his giving her a venereal infection, caught from one of the many whores he used. Gonorrhoea and chancres were common. Although syphilis was not formally identified in Europe before contact with the Americas, what was called sexually transmitted leprosy was a condition which, in symptoms and treatment, had much in common with syphilis. Before returning to France on 16 March, Henry had been very inactive for six months, apparently due to ill-health. He was only thirty-three years old, but in later years limped badly from a leg broken when a horse kicked him and badly set, so this may have been the cause. But after Easter he was ill again at Chinon and did not recover until July.

He suffered increasingly debilitating bouts of malaria, but may also have had other health problems. Whatever this one was, his being ill meant that Becket could not include him when, at the great pilgrim church of Vézelay, he excommunicated just about everyone else involved in framing the Constitutions of Clarendon. At Henry's request, Pope Alexander annulled the excommunications and warned Becket to desist. His health improving, Henry turned his attention to Brittany, forcing Count Conan IV to abdicate in favour of his daughter Constance and betrothing her to eight-year-old Prince Geoffrey.

Eleanor had put up with much to be Henry's partner in building an empire, but her pride would not let her sink to being 'just another vassal'. Determined to bend her to his will, he issued a summons from Caen, calling all her vassals of Poitou and Aquitaine to meet him at Chinon on 20 November. There he announced that he would hold a Christmas court in Poitiers, at which they would be required to swear allegiance to Young Henry as nominal duke of Aquitaine in addition to the titles to England, Normandy and Anjou which he already held.

Eleanor was furious at this dispossession of Richard. Returning with him and Princess Matilda to England, she spent a troubled Christmas at Oxford with all the children except Young Henry, whose Channel crossing with a considerable retinue to impress her vassals in Poitiers had cost £100. On 27 December 1166 at the age of forty-four she gave birth in Oxford to the last of her brood, christened John after the Baptist, whose feast-day it was. Within a few hours of the birth Henry was forcing the barons of Aquitaine to swear fealty to Young Henry in Poitiers. The anger Eleanor felt coloured her attitude to John from birth, for she never liked him. In Aquitaine, Henry's latest high-handedness lit the fire of a rebellion led by her uncle William Taillefer. Its swift repression did not stop another dissident vassal, the count of Auvergne, from appealing for feudal justice directly to Louis.

Heading east to put him in his place, Henry met Count Raymond of Toulouse at the monastery of Grandmont. In order to marry Richilde, widow of the count of Provence, Raymond had just divorced Louis' sister, who had been very popular with the citizens of Toulouse. Furious at this insult, Louis was threatening armed intervention. The count therefore placed his domains under Henry's protection by declaring himself a vassal of the duke of Aquitaine. In this roundabout way, Eleanor saw the breakaway county temporarily re-attached to Aquitaine, ironically at a time when her hold over the duchy was at its weakest.

This was the excuse for Louis to reopen hostilities against Henry in Normandy, ostensibly over a long-running dispute as to how the money raised in both their territories by the current crusade tax should be spent.[1] Hardly had a truce been arranged in August 1167, to last until the following Easter, than Henry marched west to subdue some independent Breton lords who refused to recognise Prince Geoffrey. That campaign was cut short by the news that the Empress Matilda had died on 10 September. Aged sixty-five, she had been politically active to the last, firing off letters urging bishops to arrange a truce in Normandy and castigating Becket for his ingratitude to the king who had raised him to greatness.

It is indicative of the emotion and respect Henry still felt for his mother that he executed Matilda's will to the letter and did not filch property or wealth from her estates. In poor health once again, he attended her funeral with a frigid Eleanor. The rift between them had gone too far to be bridged. With Becket his sworn enemy, the Empress Matilda dead and Eleanor irrevocably alienated, Henry was without any close advisers.

To ensure that Princess Matilda's long-delayed marriage to the Lion of Saxony did take place, Eleanor took her back to England. The first of the princesses to be married off, she was given a suitable dowry and a regal send-off that together cost around £4,500, or a quarter of the realm's annual revenue. By feudal custom, this money was raised by an *auxilium* tax levied for the occasion. In addition to a trousseau that cost £63, the twelve-year-old princess was provided with luxuries such as scarlet saddles with gilt fittings for her palfries and a train of thirty-four packhorses to transport her belongings. All this was to enable her to arrive in fitting style in Saxony, where the wedding was eventually celebrated at the beginning of 1168.

After accompanying her to Dover for embarkation on a German ship, Eleanor busied herself assembling her own movable property with the intention of leaving England for good. Historians have argued that it was Henry's plan for her to take over the government of Aquitaine in order to leave him free to govern his northern domains, but that would not have involved moving seven entire shiploads of her furniture and other belongings across the Channel.[2] Nor would weakening her authority by replacing her appointee Richard with Young Henry as titular duke have been an intelligent move on Henry's part if he intended Eleanor to resume direct rule of the duchy.

Of the fourteen and a half years since the May wedding in Poitiers, she had spent the equivalent of six entire years pregnant, bearing

Henry five sons, of whom four were still living, and three daughters. This was after the three pregnancies by Louis that produced his first two daughters, and in an age when every pregnancy could be lethal, the slightest complication resulting in agonising death.

When she married for the second time, she was no manipulable under-age bride dominated by an older husband, but a woman of thirty with fifteen years' political and life experience behind her – and the strength of will to break free from Louis and his powerful clerical and lay advisers. She knew many examples of royal and noble ladies who had chosen not to have large families, whatever their husbands wanted.

Henry's own mother had grudgingly borne three sons before refusing to produce any more. His maternal grandfather had married Edith-Matilda, daughter of St Margaret of Scotland, and found her more interested in good works, like washing the feet of lepers and kissing them on the lips, than in sharing his bed. After dutifully producing a son and a daughter in the first three years of her marriage, she 'ceased to become pregnant or give birth, and tolerated with equanimity that the king was occupied elsewhere'[3] while her husband proceeded to father more bastards than any other English monarch.

Apart from abstinence, contraceptive methods included magical spells that worked as often as the law of averages allowed. Clemence of Burgundy, the wife of Count Robert II of Flanders, practised 'womanly arts' after producing three sons in three years, according to Hermann of Tournai.[4] Mechanical methods included tampons soaked in vinegar, olive oil and other liquids. By observation, the so-called rhythm method was known, if unsuccessfully practised. Prolonged breast-feeding never lost its reputation for preventing ovulation, although the conditions under which it has an acceptably low failure rate were not understood. Anal and intercrural intercourse, coitus reservatus and coitus interruptus were penalised by confessors, who considered abortion and infanticide as murder, but the penalties show that the practices existed. In addition, the Church proscribed intercourse for pleasure, during pregnancy and menstruation, on the Sabbath and a whole list of feast-days and during Lent.

Henry's own register of wards and widows compiled in 1185 and covering 112 large noble families in England gives an average of less than four children per couple. By one means or another many noble and royal wives succeeded in limiting the number of children they bore, in order to avoid exactly the problem by which Henry was hag-ridden into his early grave: too many sons fighting over their patrimony.[5] For an example, Eleanor needed to look no further than Henry's great-grandfather William the Conqueror, who fathered nine legitimate children, only to die while one son was in armed rebellion against him, leaving an empire over which the three surviving legitimate sons fought bitterly. After William Rufus' death, Henry I kept his elder brother Robert Curthose in prison for twenty years to debar him from the throne.

So why did Eleanor want all those sons?

Given Henry's promiscuity, she had every excuse after producing a couple of sons to take refuge in real or feigned religious vocation or simple frigidity and tell Henry she had done her duty and was no longer interested in bearing more children. But she chose not to. And since she was aware of the problems of dynasties with too many sons, one has to ask, why?

The only satisfactory answer to the question also unlocks another great mystery: why did Henry appoint Becket archbishop? The standard answer of contemporary chroniclers and modern historians is that he needed a compliant prelate through whom to curb the independence of the Church. But if Henry was at times violent, cruel and arrogant, he was also one of England's more intelligent monarchs, and such a move was unworthy of a chess-player of his intellect. With many years' experience of interfering in ecclesiastical elections in England and in France, he could have manoeuvred any of several ambitious and compliant churchmen into the post – Roger of York, Henry of Winchester or Gilbert Foliot, to name only three. So why throw away his versatile and extremely competent chancellor and companion to do the job that one of them could have done?

Becket had also served him in the field on the Toulouse expedition and during the Vexin campaign of 1161, when he had acquitted himself well in command of Henry's vanguard totalling 6,000 horse and foot. So, in chess terms, appointing him to the see of Canterbury was the equivalent of trading more than a knight and a castle in order to have only a bishop on the board, albeit the chief bishop of England – unless there was more to the move than meets the eye.

Historians have seen the dispute between king and primate as the turning point in Henry's fortunes. The clerical chroniclers portrayed the problems of his later years as divine retribution for his part in Becket's martyrdom, but the downturn came *before* the murder in the cathedral. Their difficulty in discerning Henry's game plan lay in a tendency to present success and failure, health and illness, riches and poverty in terms of divine reward or retribution – and in medieval maps, adequate as route planners but not for reading strategy in Henry's league.

An alternative analysis of the evidence is that Becket's appointment was intended to be a once-in-a-lifetime game-winning move, so that when his hitherto obedient lieutenant refused to play the role allotted, Henry knew that the endgame for which he had worked so long was lost. The sustained fury with which he persecuted Becket was curiously similar to the fury he directed against Eleanor.

It was no secret that Henry had had frequent trafficking with papal legates for years before the break with Becket. According to the nineteenth-century French historian Alfred Richard, who spent his life immersed in the medieval charters of the Limousin region of Aquitaine, these negotiations were in furtherance of Henry's ambitions *ultra montes*, that is, south of the Alps, where he had been seriously considering an invitation to become king of Lombardy[6] as a springboard for all Italy.[7]

His obsession with the return of Toulouse and the alliances with the northern Spanish kingdoms, his support for Popes Adrian IV and Alexander III in the schisms of the Church, the marriage alliances he effected with Saxony, Castile, Maurienne and Sicily, and the placing of Becket on the throne of Canterbury, can all be seen not as disconnected ploys but parts of a unified grand design if Becket's appointment was not an aim in itself, *but the vital step in him becoming pope.*

There is nothing far-fetched in that. Pope Adrian IV was English and had been rejected by the first monastery he applied to join because he was a Saxon, illiterate in Latin. If an illiterate Saxon from St Albans could make it to the top without any patronage, it was entirely within the bounds of possibility for an astute, politically experienced Anglo-Norman with Becket's background to gain the see of St Peter.

There was no way Henry could foresee that Adrian's successor Alexander III would turn out to be the longest-serving pontiff of the twelfth century. For the most part appointed elderly, patriarchs tended not to be long in office. Within the century, six lasted a year or less. By making a man as accomplished as Becket Archbishop of Canterbury in 1162, Henry could reasonably have expected him to be elected pope in a few years' time, given the backing of one of the two most powerful monarchs in Europe.

After this, with Becket's military experience directing the considerable forces of the papal territories with their castles and wealth, Henry would have had in the spiritual leader of Europe a temporal ally, enabling him to secure that part of the long peninsula of Italy subject to the German Emperor and link up with the Norman presence in Sicily, Puglia and Calabria. And having done that, what

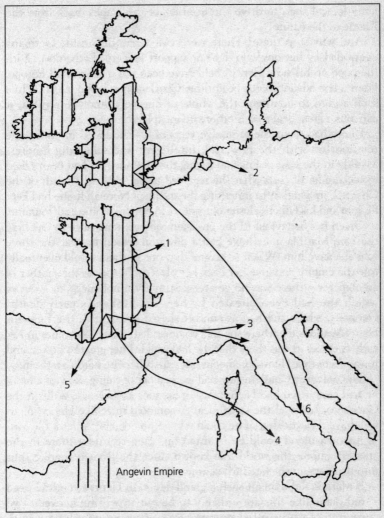

Was this Henry's grand design? 1. Young Henry and Marguerite. 2.
Princess Matilda and Henry of Saxony. 3. Re-attachment of
Toulouse/Prince John and Alix de Maurienne/the Crown of Lombardy. 4.
Princess Joanna and William II of Sicily. 5. Princess Eleanor and Alfonso of
Castile. 6. The winning move: Becket to Pope.

more logical than to drive the frontiers of the empire back from the Rhône to the Rhine?

And why stop there? There were vast territories inside Germany controlled by bishops who did not support Frederik Barbarossa. With the pope on his side, Henry could have been the master of all Europe. From a less advantageous beginning, Charlemagne had done it. While such a plan to dominate the whole of Europe cannot be proven, it explains a great deal that is otherwise inexplicable.

Henry had spent the formative years of his childhood in an intense relationship with the powerful, intelligent and scheming Empress Matilda in the west of England during the civil war. He had been raised to reclaim at all costs what she regarded as her birthright north of the Channel, in addition to inheriting the duchy of Normandy she had kept for him and his father's cluster of territory in Anjou, Maine and Touraine.

Given her behaviour in the on-again, off-again marriage to Geoffrey the Fair, Matilda must have had a powerful reason to bear the three sons she gave him. Was it to ensure that one of them would eventually rule the empire and give her back her place in history as the mother of an emperor – there was no greater destiny for a noblewoman – out of which she had been cheated by her first husband's early death? Germany, where she had as consort shared power with the Emperor Henry V and Italy, where she had commanded Henry V's armies in her early twenties. It was there that she had wielded her greatest power, and it was there that Henry's manoeuvrings are otherwise hard to fathom.

The only way Charlemagne had worked out of ruling the vast empire he had conquered had been by using his sons as viceroys. William the Conqueror had had the same idea. A paranoid ruler like Henry might well have thought that, if he could rely on no one else, at least the sons of his own blood could be counted on, each to rule a share in the greatest empire the world had known since the Roman Empire split into two parts in the late fifth century.

If Matilda did implant such a grand design in Henry's youthful head – and plans like this are unlikely to be put in writing between two conspirators who trusted no one else – it would go a long way to explain all those sons and Eleanor's bitterness at being discarded now. It would also explain why she was to support her sons against him after Becket's obstinacy had aborted the grand design, and made it unlikely ever to be primed again.

The Christmas court in Argentan was a frigid affair. Just over a month later, on 1 February 1168, Princess Matilda was married in faraway Brunswick to Henry the Lion of Saxony. Before Eleanor could continue her journey south, encumbered by the seven shiploads of belongings and furniture, her vassals of the houses of Lusignan and Angoulême, knowing that Henry was overstretched, renounced their allegiance to him and appealed to Louis to accept their fealty directly. While he vacillated, among the Poitevin strongholds Henry stormed and razed to the ground in violation of both the Truce and the Peace of God was the castle twenty miles south-west of Poitiers belonging to Hugues le Brun, a prisoner of the Saracens in the Holy Land, where he had been on crusade since 1163.

Before Easter Henry departed for Normandy, leaving as Eleanor's constable or guardian Count Patrick of Salisbury, who took his orders directly from the king. With Eleanor's encouragement, Patrick made a quick pilgrimage to Compostela, after which he was escorting her near Poitiers on 6 or 7 April when they rode into an ambush sprung by the Lusignans in retribution for the loss of their fortress. After conducting his charge to safety in a nearby castle while his men kept the intruders at bay, Patrick returned to the scene of the fighting.

Possibly they had been out for a day's hunting or hawking, for which he had left his armour behind in Poitiers. Alternatively, it would have been normal on a hot day to remove his mail cotte and leggings, to have them transported on one of the packhorses in what should have been safe territory – just as the four knights who arrived to kill Becket on 29 December 1170 first checked that he was in the palace by the cathedral before going outside to put on their armour, packed away for the journey.

Mounted on a palfrey and not his charger, Count Patrick was at a triple disadvantage, lacking the manoeuvrability of his destrier and the protection of the high-cantled and -pommelled war saddle as well as any body armour. Stabbed in the back by either Guy or Geoffrey de Lusignan, he fell to the ground mortally wounded. The last thing he saw was his nephew William also cut down in attempting to save him.

Taken prisoner and denied treatment for his wounds by his captors, the young knight was ransomed by Eleanor, who rewarded his courage and loyalty with gifts of arms and armour, horses, money and clothes, setting the man who would become famous as William the Marshal on a long career of loyal service to Henry and her sons, during which his path would cross hers many times. She could have kept him in her household. Instead, she commended him to the king as a suitable master-at-arms to teach the skills of war to Young Henry and keep him out of trouble – which gave her, as his patroness, a useful pair of eyes and ears within the Young King's household.

William epitomised Chaucer's 'parfit gentle knight' before the concept of chivalry was generally accepted. Tall, brown-haired and with an open and frank demeanour, he was a grandson of Gilbert, Marshal to Henry I. His father had at various times been Marshal to Henry I and Stephen of Blois. At the age of five or six William had been given as a hostage during the siege of Newbury Castle, and narrowly escaped being hanged when his father cheated on a truce to bring in reinforcements.

King Stephen was not a vindictive man. He offered to hand back the young hostage if his father would surrender the fortress. John Marshal refused, adding that his son's fate was of no great moment, since he still had 'the hammer and the anvil to forge better ones'. By way of reply to this insolence, some of the besiegers advised catapulting the boy alive into the fortress from a siege engine, but Stephen placed him under his personal protection. How often gallantry begat gallantry is a moot point, but this was an auspicious start to the career of the noblest warrior of the twelfth century, which would peak when he was appointed regent for Eleanor's grandson Henry III in 1216.

Exactly how the Lusignans knew where Eleanor would be that day in April 1168 is an interesting question. Plainly Patrick thought there was no danger. Since his death paved the way for Eleanor to surround herself with her own advisers, there was conceivably an element of guilt in her lavish provision for Masses to be said at St Hilaire in Poitiers for the dead constable's soul. The charter bore both her seal and the autograph crosses of the members of her immediate entourage, whose names recur many times in the coming years: Hugues de Faye, the viscount of Châtellerault, her seneschal Raoul de Faye, her constable Saldebreuil, her steward Hervé and her chaplain and secretary Pierre.

Before Henry could intervene, he had to march again into Brittany, where the latest unrest had been sparked by his own lust. Having taken as hostage Aelis, the daughter of Conan IV, he was now accused by her family of having abused her, for the good reason that she was pregnant and about to give birth to his child. Embroiled in this entanglement, he had to hurry back to Argentan when Louis invaded Normandy yet again.

Count Patrick's death, accidental or otherwise, suited Eleanor's plans to regain control of her inheritance. Like her father and grandfather, she travelled widely, receiving homage in Niort and Limoges and as far south as Bayonne, meanwhile dismissing a number of Henry's administrators, renewing former rights and privileges that he had abolished and restoring many of her vassals whom he had dispossessed.

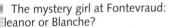

1 The mystery girl at Fontevraud: Eleanor or Blanche?
2 Queen of France, aged fifteen: Eleanor's hidden head in Bordeaux Cathedral.
3 The proud pagan queen: Eleanor in her early twenties at Chartres Cathedral.
4 Eleanor, Henry's prisoner, aged fifty-two.
5 The tragic head at Fontevraud: Eleanor aged seventy-eight.

6 The ill-matched couple: Eleanor and Louis in the Portail Royal at Chartres.

7 The golden Virgin of Beaulieu, paragon of twelfth-century feminine virtue.

8 Louis on his wedding day: Eleanor's 'I married a monk' says it all.

9 Geoffroi de Lauroux savouring his political triumph at the royal wedding in Bordeaux.

11 Eleanor's state apartments in the Maubergeonne Tower at Poitiers.

10 Polychrome enamel funeral plaque of Henry's father, Geoffrey the Fair.

12 The magnificent audience hall built by Eleanor and Henry for the court in Poitiers. The doorway on the left at the head of steps leads to Eleanor's apartments.

13 The richly carved porch of Poitiers Cathedral, built under Henry's and Eleanor's patronage.

14 Eleanor's décor: these twelfth-century floor tiles from Aquitaine resemble those the queen commissioned for the palace of Clarendon.

15 Altar cross in Limoges enamel from La Sauve Majeure, given to the abbey by Eleanor or Richard.

16 The contemporary fresco in St Radegonde chapel, Chinon depicting the end of rebellion in 1174. Henry leads away Eleanor, his prisoner; Joanna pleads for peace between her parents.

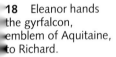

18 Eleanor hands the gyrfalcon, emblem of Aquitaine, to Richard.

17 Henry triumphant.

19 Eleanor's sons desert her: Richard takes the falcon, and Geoffrey copies his father's gesture, meaning, 'I obey you'.

20 Chinon Castle. The Tour du Moulin, probably Eleanor's first prison, is on the far left.

21 The ruins of Châlus Castle, with its circular keep on right, from where the fatal crossbow bolt was fired.

22 Aerial view of Old Sarum, where Eleanor was locked up for the best part of fifteen years. The castle ruins are in centre; the foundations of the first cathedral are visible within the outer fortifications.

23 Killed by greed: the Lionheart's effigy at Fontevraud.

24 England's first virgin queen? Berengaria's effigy at L'Epau, the abbey she founded near Le Mans.

25 Effigy at Fontevraud of Isabella of Angoulême, the sensual young bride by whom King John was obsessed and whom the chroniclers castigated as 'an animal'.

26 Eleanor's son John, outmatched by Philip Augustus: effigy in Worcester Cathedral.

27 At rest in Cistercian simplicity: the Plantagenet effigies at Fontevraud Abbey.

28 Testimonial to a sad life: the nuns' kitchen at Fontevraud, built with Joanna's bequest.

29 Together in death as so rarely in life: the effigies of Eleanor and Henry at Fontevraud.

After a decade and a half of being the perfect feudal wife and queen for Henry and doing in public everything that he demanded – and fifteen years before that during which she had visited Aquitaine as wife of Louis, similarly exercising the ducal powers that marrying her had conferred on him – Eleanor was determined to enjoy the years remaining for herself. Her personal wealth enabled her to dispense great largesse to her relatives and favourite individuals and charities, one of which was the Benedictine abbey of Fontevraud, geographically in Anjou but within the see of Poitiers. Founded by Robert d'Arbrissel on the principle that women – especially elderly widows – were morally better than men, its rule provided for an abbess to rule twin communities of monks and nuns totalling several thousand, divided into the houses of Grand Moustier, La Madeleine for repentant prostitutes, St Lazare for lepers and St Jean de l'Habit for male religious.

Similar thinking made Eleanor respectable at last. A spin-off of Hippocrates' theory of the uterus moving about in the body was the current medical–philosophical view that women were fouled by their own menstrual blood. For either sex, attaining what we should call middle age was in itself an achievement when so many died young, but women who lived through the menopause were afterwards considered purified, as though infertility turned them into quasi-men, just as the clerical gown excused men from proving themselves as such.

Poitiers was a fitting city for Eleanor's capital. The palace itself had been extended from its original Merovingian confines by a suite of chambers unlike the comfortless quarters Henry inhabited most of the time. Clustered at one end of the spacious new audience hall – still magnificent as the *salle des pas perdus* or concourse of the law courts – these rooms afforded space and privacy and comfort to Eleanor and her ladies, which makes it a reasonable assumption that they were built to her design in the first place, for Henry would have had no use for them (plates 11, 12).

Not for the countess of Poitou as mistress of her own house the dirt of horses, dogs and hawks, the noise of armourers and blacksmiths, the stink of unwashed sweaty bodies, the ribaldry of soldiers and whores, the discomfort of unglazed windows and public halls heated, if at all, by smoking central fireplaces. This, by the standards of the age, was comfort and elegance such as she had not known since her sojourn in Byzantium and Antioch, whose oriental architecture was echoed in the neighbouring church of Notre-Dame-la-Grande, its ornate triple façade crowded with statues illustrating biblical or moral stories for the illiterate believer.

The city walls had been rebuilt and extended after being partly demolished to make way for the palace extensions. Formerly outlying parishes were now within the walls, providing space for new churches and collegials but also the shops and craftsmen's workshops and market space that constituted the secure facilities necessary for the development of a prosperous merchant class. The cathedral under construction was fittingly enriched for the seat of a palatine count, with a huge window above the altar depicting Henry and Eleanor in suitably pious poses.

At Montmirail in January 1169, she gained a significant victory when Henry acceded to her pressure to give Aquitaine back to Richard. Eleanor's favourite now swore loyalty for the duchy to Louis, while Young Henry did homage for Maine and Anjou, after which Louis assented to Prince Geoffrey's betrothal to Constance, Countess of the Bretons, who was also a hostage in Henry's keeping. Although the match was consanguineous, Henry had obtained a papal dispensation. By Geoffrey swearing fealty for Brittany to Young Henry, Louis retained suzerainty by subinfeudation.

Henry's main achievement in this exercise was to persuade Louis to give him another of the 'superfluity of princesses'. This was nine-year-old Princess Alais, who was now betrothed to Prince Richard.[8] Her dowry was the Berry, which lay between Aquitaine and Burgundy, a piece of land Henry had long wanted to strengthen his eastern frontier. Louis had now given away two princesses in the hope that one would become queen of England and the other duchess of Aquitaine.

Thus, as a respectably sterile dowager duchess-queen Eleanor became the guardian of offspring by both her husbands and many other great families west of the Rhine. Young Henry's seventeen-year-old wife Marguerite Capet, her younger sister Alais, betrothed to Prince Richard but destined to become yet another of the king's entrapped mistresses, Constance of Brittany, now betrothed to Prince Geoffrey and Alix of Maurienne, betrothed in infancy to Prince John. All of these young people spent time at the court of Poitiers, which must have seemed to them afterwards like a glorious extended summer day. In addition, Eleanor's own namesake daughter and the Princess Joanna graced the Poitevin court, as did their brothers Richard and Geoffrey. Even Young Henry came on occasion.

Historians have criticised Eleanor for showing little affection towards her offspring, but in this they have been perpetuating the bias of their sources, themselves all too eager to retail gossip and scandal and impute to a woman of whom they disapproved the ultimate opprobrium of failing to live up to that paragon of motherhood, the

Virgin Mary. The accusation that she chose to abandon her two eldest daughters in Paris on leaving Louis is unfair because she had no choice in the matter: they were assets of the French Crown, who would have been brought up by others and used in the same way, whether she had stayed with Louis or not.

There were certainly long periods when she did not see individual sons and daughters of her second marriage, but many of these separations were necessitated by her duties and Henry's require-ments for them to be where she was not. Her often-exhausting travel schedule and the fashion of putting children to live with tutors, like Prince Henry with Becket, meant that even when they were near her, little time was actually spent together. With layers of nurses, maidservants, tutors and grooms between her and the royal children, there was a lack of intimacy, but that did not mean she failed to care about them.

During much of the period 1168–73, which she spent in Aquitaine, various of the princes and princesses were with her or lodged at Fontevraud Abbey, where Henry considered them safely on his land, but where she visited and from where they could easily be brought to her. Nor were Eleanor's daughters sent away to husbands at very tender ages, despite their father's penchant for infant and child betrothals. Princess Matilda was twelve at the time of her postponed marriage to the 36-year-old Lion of Saxony; Eleanor the middle daughter departed to live in the household of her Castilian fiancé at the age of nine; Joanna, the youngest of the three girls, was not dispatched to her fate in Sicily until she was thirteen.

Of the princes, Young Henry was a profligate spendthrift, quickly bored when accompanying his father on the endless tours of inspection and justice, balancing the income and expenditure of the realm. Tall and endowed with the good looks of his paternal grandfather Geoffrey the Fair, the Young King dressed and lived with style. His easy charm drew a large circle of friends of his own age who enjoyed his open-handed generosity.

His greatest passion was for the tournament, that lethal mock battle said to have been invented by the Angevin knight Geoffroi de Preuilly,[9] who died in the year of the Conquest. This was not tilting, that bloodless test of skill and horsemanship in which a revolving board was struck with the lance at full gallop, nor the sanitised joust, with two knights separated by a stout wooden barrier attempting to unseat each other at one pass. In the mêlée, no blows were barred and being unseated could mean death from being trampled on by one's own and all the other horses, as one of Eleanor's sons was to find out firsthand.

So popular were tournaments that several hundred knights converged on a chosen venue in northern France and Flanders to show their prowess twice a month during the season from Pentecost to Midsummer Day. These lethal entertainments were banned in England by Henry because he feared that so many knights coming together armed and equipped for war might mask the start of a rebellion. Louis banned them in France because of the damage to property. They had been outlawed by the Church at the Council of Clermont in 1130 and were theoretically forbidden throughout Christendom[10] because they resulted in the death of so many knights and warhorses who might otherwise have gone on crusade to kill the Saracen.[11]

Starting with the confrontation of two armed bands before spectators in a town square, a mêlée often continued in wild pursuits across country involving damage to property and crops. Once broken on impact, lances were discarded and combat continued with swords, maces and other close-combat weapons. The custom of bearing heraldic arms on a shield arose out of the need to identify immediately as friend or foe in the confusion of the mêlée another knight whose features were concealed behind the face-piece of his all-enveloping pot helmet.

The aim of each team was to batter into submission and take captive as many as possible of the opposing knights, who were then held for ransom with their mounts and armour. It was a practice for battle that also satisfied the urge to gamble, for a poor knight could make his fortune or be ruined financially, his destrier alone being worth a year's income.

Of acceptable prowess at arms himself, Young Henry relied on William the Marshal to keep him out of trouble in the field and also to top up his over-spent allowance by taking for ransom other knights and their horses when the princely purse was empty – with many a loser left to walk home, deprived of even his sword and armour. With a quick brain, a sure hand and eye, and the skill and strength of an Olympic athlete, William took in his first season over 100 captives, and went on to claim more than 500 in his career. Nagged on his deathbed to hand over to the Church a sum equal to all those ransoms, he politely but firmly declined.

Chivalry as a code of honour did not then exist. Whole fiefs changed hands in the space of a mêlée and so many vavassours were held as surety for their overlords' losses and imprisoned when debts were not honoured that Henry enacted a law making the practice illegal in his territories. Another decidedly unchivalric aspect of the sport was when unscrupulous tourneyers agreed beforehand with opponents to allow inexperienced but wealthy knights on their own side to be captured, so that they could share in the ransom.

The main attraction was surrounded by a horse fair, displays of arms and armour and performances by *jonglars* of songs celebrating great deeds against the Saracen. Smiths and armourers worked night and day repairing and improving equipment to be tested at risk of life and limb on the morrow. Huge feasts were set out in the open air and paid for by wealthy patrons like Young Henry.

It was a man's world, where women of whatever rank came to be thrilled by death, broken limbs and lost fortunes. As might be expected, Betran de Born loved the whole tournament scene:

> *Bela m'es pressa be blezos*
> *coberts de teintz vermelhs e blaus*
> *d'entresens e de gonfanos*
> *de diversas colors tretaus*
> *tendas e traps e rics pavilhos tendre*
> *lanzas frassar, escutz trancar e fendre*
> *elmes brunitz, e colps donar e prendre . . .*

[The mêlée, with its thousand charms: / shields vermillion and azure / standards, banners, coats of arms / painted in every bright colour, / the pavilions, the stands, the tents, / shattered lances, shields split and bent, / blows given, taken, helmets dented . . .]

One of the backhanded compliments the chroniclers dreamed up for Eleanor was that she was wise but unstable.[12] The second adjective, but not the first, fitted Young Henry like a glove. Forever dragging his friends into wild ideas soon dropped,[13] he was subject to mood swings from elated defiance to abject submission, from baseless optimism to dark depression. Some said that he never recovered from being abruptly wrenched away from Becket's household at age nine to be given the falcon treatment throughout his adolescence by the very man who had his foster-father murdered. What is certain is that he resented bitterly being kept on a leash by his father when his younger sibling Richard appeared to be enjoying real freedom with Eleanor in Aquitaine.

It was Richard who was coming to most resemble, physically, not his father as he now was – limping, bandy-legged, prematurely grizzled and bent from all those long days spent in the saddle – but Henry as he had been at the May wedding in Poitiers. With the same trained warrior's stance, the same reddish hair and burly build, Richard preferred the hunt and real warfare to the make-believe kind on the tournament field, but when he did appear in the lists he was ruthless. The other side of his complex character included a love of music and poetry. Like his great-grandfather William IX, he could turn out a neat *sirventès* to plead a case, and loved to sing with gusto in church, exhorting his fellow choristers to give their all and admonishing by voice and a blow monks who sang too quietly or out of tune.[14]

In adolescence and later life he could be impulsively generous to his friends of the moment, and was soon predictably surrounded by young nobles whose pleasures were his: campaigning and, in between, the good life and the hunt. The moments of generosity were unpredictable. Cooks were important members of a noble household because their mistakes or ill will could kill their masters. On one occasion Richard elevated his to the nobility after a particularly good meal and made the post a hereditary fief. Yet the dark side of Eleanor's favourite son was a love of slaughter and a greed for gold that would literally be the death of him.

Prince Geoffrey was of smaller build, and darker-complexioned. While fond of the tournament scene, he fought only when he had to, but had the best brain of the four sons. Saved by having a younger brother from being put into the Church, he would in fact have made an excellent cardinal, for he had a lawyer's gift with words and the smooth-talking ability to make black seem white that convinced even those who well knew his reputation for untrustworthiness.

The last of the brood, Prince John resembled Geoffrey in looks, shorter and darker than the two oldest princes. But he lacked Geoffrey's intellect, Henry's generosity and Richard's undoubted physical courage. To his father he served primarily as a way of annoying his older brothers; to his mother, he was the runt of the litter. Left out of the arrangements announced at Montmirail because there was no remaining Plantagenet territory to which he could be entitled, he became known as John Lackland or Jehan sans Terre, and suffered the fate of so many other landless younger sons, being put into the Church – in his case as an oblate at Fontevraud. The experience inculcated in him a lifelong loathing of religion and priests. Growing up envious and scheming, he was convinced from an early age that he had been deprived of his rightful share of the double realm. Cursed with a generous measure of the Plantagenet paranoia, he was an unloved and unlovable prince.

Henry once had a wall painted depicting himself as an eagle being attacked by four eaglets; a better image would have been that of a huntsman holding four hounds on intertwined leashes, he curbing them at every turn and they forever snapping and snarling at each other, each ready to take a bite of one of the other dogs or even the huntsman himself when the occasion offered. With John in the cloister at Fontevraud, why did the king not make some space by sending Geoffrey or even Richard to carve out his own place in the sun, in the Holy Land? Was he still hoping that the grand design would one day see the Angevin Empire so vast that it would need to be divided between four kings of his own blood?

Since feudal law proscribed marriages without the prior approval of the spouses' suzerain, and since Eleanor was the overlord of Aquitaine, her court became a marriage mart. The princes were far from being the only young men to amuse the noble maidens and older ladies – numbering as many as sixty on occasion – in the glittering palace dominating the high ground above the confluence of the Clain and Boivre rivers. Of course, it mattered that the young bloods had proved themselves by sword or lance, knew how to set a balking lanner falcon on its prey and ride a destrier centaur-like, as though of one flesh, in the mêlée of battle or tournament. But the prizes at Eleanor's court went to men who had manners, dressed well, showed gallantry, could pluck a lute or turn mere words into poetry.

> A l'entrada del temps clar,
> per jòia recomençar e per gelós irritar
> vol la reina mostrar qu'el' es si amorosa.
> El'a fait pertot mandar
> non sia jusqu'a la mar pucela ni bachelar
> que tuit no vengan dançar en la dança joiosa.

[In spring the queen of romance / summons to her from far and wide / every unwed knight and maid / to join her in the joyous dance / and worries her husband by these proofs / that she still knows what love is.]

La reina aurilhosa, the April Queen was back where she belonged. Among the troubadours who flocked to her side was Bernat de Ventadorn, lean after his years in disfavour but later recounting how his lady read and rewarded the new compositions he wrote for her. Life at the court in which Prince Richard spent his adolescence was such fun that he continued to regard Poitiers as his home for the next twenty or so years, and was happy to be known by the traditional title of count of Poitou, rather than duke of Aquitaine, until he was crowned king of England in 1189.

The lavishness of court life in Poitiers was criticised by Bernard of Clairvaux, who commented sarcastically on the excesses of make-up and dress. Although he criticised the long trains and floor-length sleeves of the fashionable gowns, according to the chronicler Geoffroi du Vigeois, so great was the surge in demand for furs and fine cloth at this time that prices doubled in the south-west, with even bishops and viscounts taking a new interest in their appearance and blushing to be seen in clothes their fathers might have worn, slashing their outer garments to show off the precious stuff below and wearing sleeves so long they had to be knotted up out of the way most of the time.

But life was not all dress and show. There were the courts of love, with noble ladies imposing tasks on lovers and judging them worthy or not of favours, such as a handkerchief to sport on helm or lance in a tournament, in a fantasy reversal of reality. In the famous canon of *amour courtois* that love cannot exist between spouses lies the plight of the noble wife, for whom 'being married does not prevent one falling in love (with someone else)'.[15] According to Andreas Capellanus, even Eleanor in a wistful moment expressed the thought that it would be a fine thing if a wife could find love and marriage consonant. To ladies even as highborn and beautiful as Eleanor, who were locked in marriages over which they had little or no say, an anonymous troubadour offered the beguiling dream of being able to escape into the haven of a lover's arms:

> *En un verger, sotz fuelha d'albespí*
> *tenc la domna son amic còsta sí . . .*
> *Bèls dous amics, baisem-nos ieu e vos*
> *aval els pratz on chanto'ls auzelós.*
> *Tot o façamen despiech del gilós. . . .*

[In an orchard, beneath the hawthorn tree / the lady holds her lover lovingly. / O, sweet my friend, let us kiss in bliss / while down in the meadow birds sing this / sweet defiance of my jealous husband. . . .]

The *trobairitz* Clara d'Anduza yearned for a lover to tell her, 'I shall always be true . . .

> *. . . si'm pregavon d'autras dònas un cen*
> *qu'amors que'm ten per vos en sa bailia*
> *vòl que mon còr vos estui e vos gar.*

[. . . though a hundred other ladies / begged me for the love that keeps me yours / and makes me guard my heart for you alone.']

And what could be more deliciously seditious that a man on his knees, a slave to love?

> *Ma belha dompna, a vos me valha Deus!*
> *Que mil aitanz soi melh vostre que meus*
> *obedïent plus que serf ni judeus*
> *e de vos tenc mon aloc e mos feus.*

[God save me from your power, O lady fair! / I'm a thousand times more yours than mine, I swear / and more your slave than any Jew or serf. / 'Tis from you I hold both allod and my fief.]

Appropriately, the church onto which Eleanor looked from her apartments in the Maubergeonne Tower was consecrated to the Virgin, for what was happening in Poitiers was a rebellion against the bloody masculine business of war and the tournament and the harrying and killing of beasts with hawk and hound in favour of the subtler pleasures of life – fine clothes, good conversation, poetry, music and all the *gai saber* of Mediterranean civilisation. In a very short time Eleanor re-created a way of life essayed during her reigns in Paris and London. On the banks of Seine and Thames she had been merely a consort, and yet had introduced fashions and comforts and entertainments, in some cases with lasting effect. Here, where she had grown up to the sound of lute and laughter, she was more a queen in her own right than any other woman in the world.

THIRTEEN

Rebellion and Betrayal

Aside-issue of the meeting at Montmirail on 6 January 1169 was Louis' persistent endeavour to reconcile Henry and Becket. Henry had agreed to their first meeting in the four years since his archbishop's furtive departure from Sandwich in a humble rowing boat. But Becket was so obstreperous that when Henry walked out of the meeting in a fury no one blamed him; even in the archbishop's own entourage everyone considered it time to make some concessions and end the long dissension. As a lord of the Church, Becket owed a duty to listen to his counsellors, but would not.[1]

Leaving the Young King with William the Marshal to keep order in Normandy, Henry rode south to reimpose his authority in Poitou and Aquitaine. The two Henrys met again at Angers in August and spent some time hunting together before travelling north to Bayeux, where papal legates tried again in vain to patch things up between the king and Becket. There was a subtext to their comings and goings: with the crown of Lombardy on hold for the moment, Henry turned his attention further south, betrothing Princess Joanna to William II, King of the Two Sicilies. At the Hill of Martyrs, now Montmartre, Louis again tried again to reconcile king and archbishop.

The concession came from Henry's side: on 18 November 1169 at St Germain-en-Laye, south of Paris, he restored Becket's confiscated property in England and asked him to officiate at the coronation of Young Henry. This was not strictly necessary; since the Conquest the rival archbishops of York and Canterbury had both officiated at different coronations.

In addition to the verminous hair shirt and his daily flagellations, Becket had contracted osteomyelitis of the jaw while locked with a tooth abscess into the sewers of the monastery at Pontigny as self-imposed penance for sexual desires, and been operated on without anaesthetic by a monk known as Guillelmus Medicus to remove two splinters of bone from the jaw.[2] Whether from the pain or simply to frustrate Henry, he failed to grasp the olive branch that could have ended the dispute between Church and Crown there and then.

The Christmas court was held with Constance and Geoffrey at Nantes to emphasise to the Bretons that he really was their duke, but the festivities did little to appease Henry's anger with Becket. Resolving to have Young Henry crowned anyway, he crossed from Barfleur to Portsmouth on 3 March 1170 in a mood so foul that he insisted on setting sail during a gale that sank the largest ship in his convoy with the loss of some 400 souls.[3]

Knowing how often Henry reneged on promises, Eleanor held her Easter court of 1170 in Niort, where she summoned the chief Poitevin vassals to swear fealty to Richard.[4] At twelve, he was already tall and well built, schooled to speak and write Occitan and Latin fluently as well as *langue d'oïl*. Having shown prowess in riding, hunting and the use of weapons from an early age, he was in every sense a warrior-poet in the making – the first duke of Aquitaine in thirty-three years of whom his vassals could, at least to begin with, approve.

After Niort she took him to Poitiers, where he was, in accordance with comital tradition, proclaimed abbot of St Hilaire, with the archbishop of Bordeaux and the bishop of Poitiers presenting him with the lance and standard that signified his authority as count of Poitou. The ceremony ended with a huge procession in his honour, in which everyone sang the responses, 'O princeps egregie!'[5] An extraordinary prince indeed. . . .

From there, Eleanor took her son to Limoges to be proclaimed duke of Aquitaine at a symbolic ceremony designed to seduce the volatile citizenry into accepting Richard as one of their own. Geoffroi du

Vigeois, then a monk at the abbey of St Martial, described how the bishop placed on the finger of the young duke the ring of martyred St Valérie, patron saint of the city, making Richard her symbolic bridegroom.[6] Despite Geoffroi's sour comment that the Poitevins had stolen '*O princeps egregie!*' from the liturgy of St Martial,[7] this heady moment for the prince must have caused his mother's heart to swell with pride. But there was more than mere maternal emotion involved in these moves: having Richard swear fealty to Louis and formally installing him in these three important cities made it more difficult for Henry to reverse the restoration of Aquitaine to him.

Shortly afterwards Eleanor travelled north to Caen, in anticipation of the coronation of her eldest son, at which her attendance would have been normal. To spite her for securing Richard's titles, she was not invited to the ceremony. Nor was Princess Marguerite in her husband's entourage when Young Henry crossed the Channel on 5 June, escorted by the bishops of Sées and Bayonne. Knighted by his father soon after arriving in England, he was crowned in Westminster Abbey by Archbishop Roger of York on Sunday 14 June 1170,[8] a step in the grand design freeing his father for the next move,[9] shortly to be pre-empted by his own sons.

To counter the very real danger of an emissary from Becket crossing to England and forbidding the coronation, the Norman justiciar Richard fitz Richard of Le Hommet had been ordered to close all the Channel ports on the French side. The fish caught in this net was a cousin of the king, Bishop Roger of Worcester, who was compelled to kick his heels in Dieppe instead of preventing the coronation by the threat of excommunications as Becket had instructed him to do. Among the six bishops present at the coronation were Becket's enemies the bishop of Salisbury and Gilbert Foliot, immediately excommunicated by the exiled primate. In Foliot's case, this was a second anathema, the first having been absolved after he had struggled in midwinter halfway across Europe to present his petition in person to the pope.

From the moment of his coronation, Prince Henry was known to his contemporaries as Henry III or Henry the Young King, and his father was referred to as 'the old king' although only thirty-seven years old. Like many another fifteen-year-old born with a solid gold spoon in his mouth, once endowed with his own household and seal the Young King was often carried away with his own importance. At the coronation feast his father, in a typically informal moment, carried in the platter bearing the *plat de résistance*, a stuffed boar's head. Young Henry made a disparaging remark which the archbishop of York tried to smooth over by observing that it was a privilege to be served by a king, at which the arrogant Young King joked that he saw nothing wrong in the son of a count waiting on the son of a king. In a society where breeding and pedigree counted for so much it was an insult to remind his father of his comparatively lowly origin.

Another insult – this time to the house of Capet – was the exclusion of Princess Marguerite from the ceremony. At a meeting arranged by him and Archbishop Rotrou of Rouen with Becket on 22 July at Fréteval, Henry agreed to have her crowned as soon as he returned to England and went as far as he could to build a bridge for the exile's return, admitting that the coronation had been a mistake and asking Becket to re-crown Young Henry – this time with Marguerite – in England.

In an additional effort to prevent his erstwhile bosom friend from persuading the pope to place all England under interdict, Henry offered to go on crusade as a penance for his behaviour[10] and to entrust Young Henry and the country to Becket as regent during his absence. What more could he do? The contentious Constitutions of Clarendon were not mentioned. Becket agreed to return, but Henry refused him the kiss of peace, saying that he would get that once back in England.

Two weeks later, on 10 August, Henry was ill in Domfront with a high fever, possibly malaria. Rumours of his imminent death ran throughout Christendom after he dictated a last will and testament confirming the division of power as at Montmirail.[11] Nearly two months passed before he could celebrate his recovery by a pilgrimage of thanksgiving to the shrine at Rocamadour in Quercy.[12] Grateful to be still alive, Henry was in a less rancorous mood than for a long time when he and Eleanor discussed betrothing Princess Eleanor to Alfonso, the fourteen-year-old king of Castile, because his manoeuvring with Saxony, Lombardy and Sicily had so alienated the German Emperor that her betrothal to his son had been broken off.

In October, Becket had another meeting with Henry at Chaumont near Amboise before deciding to return to Canterbury under safe conduct. In pain at a level that blocks rational thought, he was issuing letters of excommunication right up to 30 November, the day before he landed at Sandwich. On 2 December he was back at Canterbury, heavily in debt but bringing with him a library of books and scrolls weighing half a ton and a whole shipload of wine that was hijacked by ill-wishers somewhere between the coast and Canterbury. The exile's return made him more intractable than before. His continuing provocations of Henry included further excommunications of royal officers and a refusal to rescind his excommunication of the English bishops.

Summoned like any other vassal to Henry's Christmas court of 1170 at Bures to account for her stewardship of the duchy, Eleanor was present when Foliot and two other excommunicated prelates protested about Becket's continuing excesses. Young Henry was holding his own Christmas court at Winchester, but the other princes and Joanna were all at Bures. Not unnaturally, Henry was furious to hear that Becket was still defying him, despite all the concessions made. Such was his anger that his chamberlain Ranulf de Broc[13] incited four household knights – Hugh de Morville, who had been an itinerant justice in the north of England, Reginald fitz Urse, Richard de Brito and William de Tracy, a former chancellor of Becket – to travel to England and rid the king of his most troublesome subject.

After the four knights arrived in Canterbury with obviously murderous intent, Becket was accused by his secretary John of Salisbury of having brought the situation upon himself. An archbishop owed a duty to listen to his advisers in council just as a baron listened to the advice his vassals were required to give. In this Becket was constantly remiss, according to his own secretary.[14] When it became clear that his master was set on a martyr's death, John pointed out that he and the other members of the archiepiscopal household were sinners, not yet ready to meet their Maker. He saw no one else present who *wanted* to die.[15]

In that eyewitness account may lie the key to Becket's intransigent provocations. Since he was never reported to have any other sexual inclinations, he may have been a pathological masochist who, once launched on the progression from hair shirt to daily floggings, could not stop escalating the doses of pain until the final overdose.

Begged by his household to claim sanctuary in the cathedral, Becket refused. He had to be pulled and pushed against his will through a narrow tunnel leading out of the palace and into the cathedral via the cloister. Protesting all the way, Becket made sure the door was left unlocked, so that the pursuing knights could enter. The service of Vespers had not yet ended when some of his servants ran through the choir in panic, interrupting the singing. Some monks came to see what the shouting was all about. Becket ordered them back to their stalls. Manhandled this way and that by servants seeking to protect him, he tried to leave the sanctuary and met the four knights, accompanied by one other, on the stairs leading up to the choir.

The killing was a messy affair for men whose business was arms. Becket was first beaten and insulted. They tried to carry him out of the building, to commit the deed in the cloister, but he fell. His crossbearer thrust the primatial cross out to shield him and had his arm severed at the elbow by a sword-cut. Many blows later, Becket lay dead, his brains a mess on the flagstones.

When his body was stripped after the murder, it showed not only great emaciation concealed under his many layers of clothing, but tunnels made by the vermin through the lacerated flesh of his back. In the stained-glass window of the cathedral made shortly afterwards, the prematurely grey-haired martyr's face is not blissful, but haggard with pain, as it is in Herbert of Bosham's 'great glossed psalter'.[16]

Hagiographical accounts of the martyrdom were bound to portray Becket as a man of vocation defending the Church from a rapacious monarch when, in fact, he had never shown any sign of vocation during his years in the schools of Paris, nor during the twelve years in Archbishop Theobald's service when there were many opportunities to take further orders, had he the inclination. On the contrary, during his time as Henry's chancellor, he had shown hostility to the Church on many occasions. And far from defending it during his archbishopric, he had constantly placed it at risk for little gain by his personal feud with Henry. This was in blatant contrast with his mentor and predecessor, for Theobald had been a model primate, serving both the Church and society throughout the civil war and working hard to make a stable relationship with Henry, whose accession he had done so much to facilitate. Being a shrewd judge of people, he had, of course, *not* suggested Becket as his successor.

At Argentan on 31 December or 1 January Henry greeted the news of Becket's assassination with an awesome display of rage and contrition that lasted six weeks, during which he sent messages to Pope Alexander III protesting that he had sent messengers after the five knights[17] in a fruitless endeavour to stop the murder, in which he had had no part. But this seems to have been an exercise in plausible denial, for neither then nor later did he punish anyone involved in the plot.

Everyone present at the Christmas court, including Eleanor and her children, must have been aware of what was happening. But she had no reason to love Becket, and returned to Poitiers after the court more determined than ever to act as her father and grandfather had done, sealing charters in her own name with Richard's appearing secondarily.

An important principal was dead, but the grand design was still in play – just. Having second thoughts about his oblate son's obvious unsuitability for an ecclesiastical career, Henry had opened negotiations with Count Humbert of Maurienne through Abbot Benedict of Chiusa for the betrothal of Prince John to Humbert's daughter Alix. The importance of Maurienne was that the county stretching from south of Lake Geneva to the borders of Italy and Provence included the important Alpine passes vital for any invasion of the peninsula.

At Easter the pope at last excommunicated the four guilty knights, who took refuge at Knaresborough Castle in Yorkshire for the rest of the year. Hugh de Morville was eventually absolved of his guilt after making pilgrimage to the Holy Land. William de Tracy also departed for Outremer after giving his Devon manor to Canterbury Cathedral, but died on the way.

For three and a half centuries after the events of the fateful evening, the Church prospered from the major pilgrimage site north of the Channel, as enduringly reported by Geoffrey Chaucer in *The Canterbury Tales*. It was presumably reasoned by advocates of the newly elaborated doctrine of transubstantiation that a saint's blood, like the True Cross, was infinitely divisible by virtue of its sanctity; for many years, the best-selling pilgrim's souvenirs were the small flasks of diluted fruit juice, allegedly the blood spilled at the martyrdom, for believers to drink on the spot or take home with them. The cult lasted until Henry VIII had Becket's name erased from prayer books and the shrine despoiled in June 1538.

After courting papal legates for years for his own political reasons, Henry for six months avoided those sent to negotiate terms under which he might be absolved of Becket's murder because he had in mind a different way of winning papal support. On 6 August 1171 he returned to England to plan the long-delayed invasion of Ireland, borrowing a considerable sum from the Jewish merchant Joshua of Gloucester to pay his mercenaries there, despite criticism from the Church that in using the profits of usury even a king made himself an accomplice to the forbidden practice.[18] To escape the need for repayment, Joshua was ordered to recover the loan for himself out of the proceeds of tax farming.

On 16 October the army embarked at Milford Haven, landing next day at Waterford and setting up winter quarters at Dublin. With two stretches of sea between her and Henry, Eleanor rode south to hold her own Christmas court in Bayonne with Richard, but fell ill on the way.

It was not until 17 April 1172 that Henry returned to England – for less than a month. On 12 May he was back in France, bringing with him the Young King and Princess Marguerite, still uncrowned. To the papal legates waiting at Savigny, Henry played on Alexander's gratitude for the conquest of Ireland and repeated his protestations of innocence in the assassination. However, his own bishops would not let the matter drop because the surge in popularity of the martyr he had created was making their temporal overlord dangerously unpopular both in England and on the continent.

At Avranches, across the bay from the holy shrine of Mont St Michel, Henry finally admitted that he just *might* have been the indirect cause of Becket's death by allowing the late archbishop's provocations to upset him too much. Maintaining that the assassination had nevertheless

Second seal of Henry II

grieved him more than the loss of his own father, he offered to go on pilgrimage to Rome, Compostela or even the Holy Land if proven guilty of having ordered it. To impress the legates he knelt outside the cathedral, where sinners and excommunicates belonged, and stripped off his outer garments to reveal a hair shirt. This too removed, he submitted to a scourging by relays of monks. Among the witnesses was Young Henry.

From Avranches, he was dragged by his father to Montferrand, now Clermont-Ferrand in the Auvergne, for a pre-arranged meeting with Count Humbert and the neighbouring count of Vienne, whose lands were equally important for an invasion of Italy. The alliance with Maurienne was concluded by the betrothal of six-year-old John Lackland to Humbert's eldest daughter Alix, the marriage to be celebrated when John came of age. Alix's dowry included the strategic Alpine valleys of Novalaise and Aosta and John was to inherit the entire county of Maurienne should Humbert die without leaving a male heir. In return, the count was promised 3,000 silver marks in instalments.[19]

It was at this summit conference that Raymond of Toulouse confirmed himself the vassal of Richard, duke of Aquitaine[20] and agreed to do homage with 100 knights for forty days. In addition, he was to make an annual payment of 100 silver marks per annum or give in lieu ten trained warhorses, each having a value of not less than 10 marks, or £7. Since Richard was absent, the ceremony of swearing fealty was postponed until Whitsun.[21]

When Henry headed back to Limoges, Humbert accompanied him in the hope of finding out what exactly were the possessions of Prince John. Henry's announcement that they would be the castles of Chinon, Loudun and Mirebeau infuriated Young Henry, who considered them his and declared his father had acted *ultra vires* in giving them to John. To placate him, the king arranged a second coronation – this time with Marguerite installed beside him. Because the archbishops of London, York and Salisbury were still under the cloud of excommunication and no new archbishop of Canterbury had yet been appointed, it was the bishop of Evreux who officiated at Winchester on 27 August. Neither Eleanor nor Henry was present, she being in Poitou and he back in Brittany.

In November Young Henry again demanded to be given absolute power. This being refused, he flounced off to Paris, where Louis welcomed him and Marguerite and listened to his son-in-law's complaints about his father's parsimony and unwillingness to share power. To put a stop to this, Henry summoned his son back to Normandy, but the Young King showed his independence by avoiding the Christmas court on the excuse that he was giving a banquet for knights called William, of whom 110 arrived while all his differently named friends were turned away that day.

Not amused, Henry spent Christmas at Chinon with Eleanor, Richard and Geoffrey. In the draughty castle perched high above the River Vienne, it was not just the wind that was cold. From Rome came news that Becket was to be canonised on 21 February 1173. Miracles had been claimed by the thousand in his name, a hospital dedicated to him in London and numerous churches named for him. But none of this bothered Henry. On that day he and Eleanor were at Limoges entertaining the Spanish kings Alfonso II of Aragon and Sancho VI of Navarre on pilgrimage to the tomb of St Martial.[22]

With Eleanor came Richard as duke. With Henry came Young Henry, fast becoming a figure to whose banner the growing mass of barons both in France and England who resented his father's high-handedness could rally with a show of legitimacy. Had Henry not been preoccupied with tying the knots of the grand design, he might still have nipped the rebellion in the bud, but during the week-long festivities in Limoges, his main concern was finalising with Count Humbert the betrothal of Prince John and Alix of Maurienne, which ended with four-year-old Alix given into Henry's keeping, her upbringing entrusted to Eleanor.

However, a conspiracy had been born. Had it been restricted to a few barons who acted fast enough, it might have succeeded, but the king's spies were everywhere among his sons' advisers and friends. Learning of it from Raymond of Toulouse, who considered that of his three oaths of loyalty it would pay best to honour the one made to the father of his immediate overlord,[23] Henry made the pretext of leaving the city with Raymond, ostensibly for a day's hunting.

Making a lightning tour of all his castles in the region and ordering his castellans to put them on a war footing, Henry appointed Abbot William of Reading to replace Archbishop Bertrand of Bordeaux, who had died the previous December, and sent him off to pacify Gascony before himself returning to Limoges, whence the barons had departed to raise their troops for the rebellion. To pin the snake by its head, he dismissed the Young Henry's household knights[24] and ordered the sullen prince to accompany him back to Normandy at the beginning of March, leaving Eleanor in Poitiers with Richard and Geoffrey.

For once, he was not vigilant enough. While his father was still sleeping at Chinon on the way north, Young Henry crept out of their shared bedroom and escaped from the castle early in the morning of 6 March, heading off at speed through the dawn mists via Le Mans and Alençon to Argentan. Henry was roused in a fury, to thunder in pursuit in a chase scene worthy of Hollywood. The terrified prince rode horses into the ground, as did his furious father, following closely behind.

Hearing that Louis was at Mortagne, Young Henry sought asylum there on 8 March, while his father was still taking stock of the situation back in Alençon.[25] It was both a filial betrayal and a feudally proper thing for the invested duke of Normandy to place his dispute with the count of Anjou before their mutual overlord the king of France. When Henry's emissaries arrived in Paris saying they were sent by the king of England, Louis affected surprise on the grounds that his guest was the crowned king of England and that the 'old king' had resigned, as everyone knew.[26]

He also had a replica made of Young Henry's seal, left behind in Rouen. This was used to validate charters bestowing gifts of Angevin possessions on the barons who flocked to the cause. Philip of Flanders was rewarded with Dover Castle and the county of Kent; his brother the count of Boulogne with the county of Mortain. William of Scotland, whose men were already raiding the north of England, got Northumbria; his brother David the shires of Huntingdon and Cambridge. All these allies argued that Young Henry needed his brothers to declare for him – with Richard would come Poitou and Aquitaine, while Geoffrey would bring Brittany to the coalition.

When he rode to Poitiers to enlist them in his cause, the result was by no means certain. Henry's practice of forever playing his sons off against each other had made the Young King resent Richard and Richard hate him. In addition, Eleanor's favourite was already so unreliable that he merited Betran de Born's nickname for him: Richard Aye-and-Nay.[27] Friends and allies never knew where they stood with him, nor with Geoffrey, who was known for being 'as slippery as an eel'. He was now fourteen and a half, and Richard one year older. Both were regarded as adult at the time.

Eleanor listened to the Young King's assurances of the support of so many of Louis' vassals and allies. It seemed there would never be a better time to strike against the husband and father they had all come to hate. And if the rebellion was going to happen anyway, it was better for it to have all the support possible, including hers. So she put her considerable powers of persuasion to work to reconcile the three princes and opened her treasury for them.

Off they went to Paris, eager to overthrow the father who had manipulated them all their lives. With hindsight, Eleanor should have gone with them, but she was too proud to throw herself on the mercy of a divorced husband whom she had not seen for twenty years. So she stayed in Poitiers to brave it out in the heady atmosphere of her court, where the young gallants were cock-a-hoop at the opportunity to test military skills they had spent years acquiring.

Damning his sons for ingrates, Henry ordered all his cities and castles to be on the defensive. The uprising began on the Sunday after Easter, 15 April 1173, when all the Angevin possessions south of Normandy rose against him – from Maine and Brittany through Anjou to the south of Gascony. The earl of Leicester even landed in Suffolk with a force of Flemings said to number over 3,000. In Eleanor's Aquitaine and Poitou, the list of rebels read like a directory of the nobility: Faye, Lusignan, Ste Maure, Aunay, Montevrault, La Guerche . . . and among them Geoffroi de Rancon, the ageing catalyst of her disgrace in Turkey.

Epitomising the unchivalrous nature of 'knightly warfare', the princes' ally Count Philip of Flanders ordered his troops to burn and destroy *everything* and leave nothing for the enemy's dinner.[28] By fire and sword they ravaged the territory that had declared for Henry, with the exception of those places too strong to take, like the prosperous sea-girt port of La Rochelle, whose prudent burgesses sat out the conflict behind their double fortifications in the shrewd expectation that 'the old king' would win this war.

Realising that he could count on his supporters only so long as he held the upper hand, for few had any reason to love him, Henry recruited 20,000 mercenaries from Brabant – the area around Brussels. The coalition forces ranged against him looked impressive on paper, but they had too many chiefs. The Young King, Richard and Geoffrey lacked experience and were simply figureheads, while Louis had never been much of a general.

Most of their early attacks were directed against Normandy, substantially loyal to Henry. Gradually during the summer, he won the upper hand. Negotiations were opened at Gisors on 24 September, where he offered to share out all his possessions: Richard, for example, was to receive half the revenues from Aquitaine, in return for which Henry asked for only four castles in the duchy. Behind the princes, whose youth and inexperience might have inclined them to fall for this approach, was Louis, who had learned the hard way not to trust Angevin promises. As he explained to them, the fact that Henry was making these offers *now* was proof that the titles he had previously given them with such pomp were in name only and that he had always intended to keep the revenues from their lands for himself. Following his advice, the three princes rejected Henry's terms.

Diplomacy and negotiation having failed, he returned to the attack stronger than before. In the south, Richard, recently knighted by Louis, was attempting to rally the Gascons, whose pugnacity was hampered by lack of a military leader to impose a coordinated strategy. They flocked to Richard's colours less from loyalty to him than from hatred of his father.[29] With a few exceptions such as La Rochelle, the whole of western France was once again a lawless wasteland of burned crops and razed castles, traversed by armed bands of looters. The Church particularly suffered.

Henry ordered Eleanor to leave Poitiers and join him, to lend her name to his side in the struggle. Penned by Peter of Blois, a letter from Archbishop Rotrou of Rouen threatened her with excommunication if she did not repent:

To the Queen of the English, from the Archbishop of Rouen and his suffragans, greetings in the cause of peace.

No Christian can fail to know that marriage is a firm and indissoluble union. . . . Thus, a woman is at fault if she leaves her husband and does not observe this social bond. . . .

We know that unless you return to your husband, you will be the cause of widespread disaster. Although you alone are at fault, your actions will bring ruin on everyone. Therefore, O illustrious queen, return to your husband and our master. . . .

If our pleadings do not move you to do this, at least let the sufferings of the people, the threats of the Church and the desolation of the Kingdom do so. Certainly this desolation cannot be prevented by the King, but [only] by his sons and their allies. Against all women and out of childish counsel, you give offence to the lord King, to whom however powerful kings bow the neck. . . .

Truly, you are our parishioner, as is your husband. We cannot fail to exercise justice. Either you will return to your husband, or we shall be compelled by canon law to use ecclesiastical censures against you. We say this reluctantly, but unless you come to your senses with sorrow and tears, we shall do so. Farewell.[30]

Being treated like some wayward wife who had left her husband on a whim, when it was Henry who had rejected and insulted her before and after John's birth, simply stiffened Eleanor's resolve. But one after another the rebel fortresses fell to Henry and his Brabanters: La Haye, Preuilly, Champigny and Chinon. Raoul de Faye's treasure castle, where the taxes squeezed out of the Poitevins were held, was burned and razed to the ground. The winter of 1173/4 saw another truce concluded between Henry and Louis, to last from mid-January to Whitsun.[31] Richard's mood in Poitou during the spring of 1174 was optimistic, but when Henry's mercenaries took Le Mans, marched through Anjou and captured Poitiers on 12 May, its titular count was on the run.

Silence descended once again on the great audience hall beside the Tour Maubergeonne, the troubadours and *jonglars* were scattered or dead, the flickering fire of southern culture blown out once again. Swallowing her pride too late, Eleanor fled to seek asylum on Louis' territory. Riding disguised as a man with a small escort only a few leagues from safety, she was arrested by knights loyal to Henry, but the bitterest pill was to find that her whereabouts had been betrayed to them by her own trusted courtiers Guillaume Maingot, Portclie de Mauzé, Foulques de Matha and Hervé, her steward, whose names appear on so many of the charters she had drawn up during the years at Poitiers.[32]

There is no more dread sound than a key turning in the lock, followed by the jailer's footsteps receding outside. That, she heard the first night, probably in the Tour du Moulin at Chinon, a bleak tower in the most inaccessible part of the castle reserved for important hostages. Next morning she looked south from its narrow unglazed windows across the dawn mists in the valley of the Vienne towards the duchy she would not see again for many years (plate 20).

One can imagine her feelings when brought a captive before Henry, most probably in Rouen. History was full of sons who had risen up against their fathers, but all Christendom was against her as an 'unnatural' wife, who had stood against her husband and raised her sons in treason against him. Abandoned by her closest vassals and courtiers, she knew that if Henry won the war he would pardon the princes and continue to use them. Her only use to him lay in her lands.

With or without her treason, the pope would grant Henry an annulment if asked, for the degree of consanguinity was even closer than that which provided the spurious grounds for her divorce from Louis. However, that would involve handing back her dowry of Poitou and Aquitaine – and Henry never gave anything back, not even a son's rejected fiancée whom he kept as his own mistress. Nor would he have her killed, unless in one of the berserker rages that betrayed his part-Viking ancestry, for then Richard would enter fully into his inheritance.

He offered her a choice: she could either abdicate her titles and take the veil at Fontevraud, or be locked up for however long it took to make her change her mind. She was fifty-two years old and Henry only thirty-nine. Refusing to give in to a man almost certain to outlive her, she was facing the prospect of the rest of her life under lock and key. But she did refuse. Poitou and Aquitaine were her identity. She had given Henry everything else, but not this. Henry was in a hurry to break her will and thus shorten the war: the conditions under which she was kept must have been hard. All she had to cling to was the hope that somehow Young Henry and Geoffrey and her beloved Richard would outwit and outfight the father they hated.

But Richard was retreating southwards – all the way to Saintes at the western end of the great east–west Roman highway across central France. His preparations for a stand there were brought to nothing by Henry's speed of attack. Penetrating the defences through the triumphal arch of Germanicus then serving as a town gate, he took the Capitol and invested the cathedral which was serving as arsenal and food reserve. Never one to waste resources, he simply sat and waited until the defenders surrendered, swelling his depleted coffers not only by Richard's war reserve of money, weapons and equipment but also by no fewer than 60 ransomable knights and 400 sergeants-at-arms. However, his rebellious son was not among them, having fled to Geoffroi de Rancon's reputedly impregnable fortress on the other side of the River Charente. Not having any available siege engines, Henry left him there and withdrew northwards with his captives after carving the duchy into six regions under military governors and rewarding Porteclie de Mauzé, leader of the barons who had betrayed Eleanor, with the office of seneschal.

A consortium of French nobles under the count of Flanders judged the time right to make an expedition across the Channel with Young Henry at their head and place him on the throne with the support of King William of Scotland while his father's back was turned. On 8 July the Young King's party were awaiting favourable winds at Gravelines[33] when Henry defied the elements by setting sail from Barfleur on a fleet of forty vessels carrying several thousand of his Flemish mercenaries and his entire family with the exception of the three princes.

Eleanor, who had been kept incommunicado for months in various of his castles, was now in the bizarre position of sharing the same storm-tossed ship as her daughter Joanna, Prince John and Alix de Maurienne, the Young Queen Marguerite and Richard's betrothed Alais Capet, Constance of Brittany and Emma of Anjou[34] – all of whom Henry was holding hostage together with notables such as the count of Chester and the countess of Leicester, whom he would entrust to no other jailer.[35] Yet however unenviable the position of Marguerite, Constance and the others, their plight was roses all the way compared with the fate Eleanor knew awaited her, once across the Channel.

Not all Henry's English subjects preferred life under his harsh but ordered rule. To win over his enemies, he decided on an act of public penance at the shrine of Becket. After securing Marguerite, with Alais and Constance of Brittany in the castle of Devizes and Eleanor in Old Sarum,[36] he travelled to Canterbury along the Pilgrims' Way for his self-abasement at Becket's tomb.[37] On Saturday 12 June he dismounted at the West Gate of the city, donned a simple woollen pilgrim's robe and walked barefoot through the dirt streets to the cobbled precincts of the cathedral.

Admitted to the crypt, he stripped and knelt at the saint's tomb, to suffer three lashes from each of the eighty monks in the community.[38] Gilbert Foliot was meanwhile preaching a sermon on the king's innocence to the assembled crowd of townspeople and pilgrims. Some of the lash-wielding monks had witnessed the murder and must have taken a personal pleasure in punishing the monarch on his knees like a naughty schoolboy for polluting their cathedral with a blood crime, as a result of which services had been suspended for a whole year until 21 December 1171 when the bishops of Exeter and Chester formally 'reconciled' the building. After the flagellation, Henry spent the night on his knees in the crypt before departing next morning for London, exhausted by his three-day penitential fast.

At Westminster he submitted to the cares of his physicians and valet, dressing the cuts on his feet and back, while getting an update on the rebellion. The Scots were moving south and the count of Flanders' mercenaries had already landed in East Anglia.[39] However, the mass of the Young King's forces was still in France, awaiting calm weather for the crossing. Before the night was out, the situation had changed yet again. A messenger burst into the king's chamber with the news that William of Scotland had been captured and was held prisoner in the castle of Richmond in Yorkshire, at which reverse his forces were melting away. Deciding this was a miracle sent to reward his penance, the king ordered all the bells of Westminster to be rung in order to waken every citizen of London to the news that God was on his side again.[40]

By the end of July – a mere three weeks after Henry's return – the rebellion was over in England. With its leader, the 78-year-old duke of Norfolk, Hugh Bigod, pardoned and swearing fealty anew, the advance guard of Young Henry's army was allowed to return to Flanders from East Anglia. Abandoning his plans for invasion, he headed for Rouen, under siege by Louis, but the result was a foregone conclusion. On 8 August Henry landed at Barfleur with the ranks of his Brabanters strengthened by 1,000 Welsh mercenaries. Their arrival to lift the siege of Rouen was so rapid that Louis at first doubted the evidence of his own eyes.

Retreating to Paris, he advised Young Henry that he could not dip further into his treasury to subsidise the princes' ambitions and that now was the moment for them to extract the best terms from their father, worn out with all the travel and stress of the last eighteen months and so near the end of his resources that he had had to pawn even the ceremonial sword used at his coronation.[41]

Henry welcomed the heralds' approaches and agreed to a meeting with the Young King on 29 September as a way of isolating Richard and Geoffrey, still campaigning in Poitou and Brittany respectively. The tactic worked. Richard acted true to his nickname, abandoned all the castles he had taken and left his supporters to their fate as he rode to Montlouis near Tours on 23 or 29 September to throw himself at his father's feet in tears. Henry raised him and gave him the kiss of peace, after which they rode east together and arrived one day late for the meeting with Louis, where Prince Geoffrey and Young Henry likewise humbled themselves before their father.[42]

As the broker of the peace, Louis insisted that a treaty be drawn up, under which the princes and the barons who had supported them accepted Henry's sovereignty; in return they were to be pardoned and guaranteed possession of the lands and castles that had been theirs two weeks before the uprising. For the princes, it was a rewrite of Montmirail.[43] Young Henry was to have a generous annual stipend of 15,000 pounds Angevin, plus two castles in Normandy to call his own. Richard was given half the taxes of Poitou and two unfortified and ungarrisoned castles for his residences. Geoffrey was given half the revenues of Brittany and the promise of all of them upon his marriage to Constance. The three castles of Chinon, Loudun and Mirebeau, which had triggered the rebellion, were to remain with seven-year-old John, who was also awarded other properties on both sides of the Channel.

In addition, Henry undertook to release 1,000 of his ransomable captives, many times more than the other side had taken. The exceptions to this amnesty were some VIP prisoners detained in the castle of Falaise, among them the king of Scotland and the counts of Leicester and Chester.

Of Eleanor there was no mention in the treaty. She had inflamed the princely arrogance of her sons, but it was not she who had given them grounds to rebel. However, Henry needed a victim of whom to make an example so that they would think twice before defying him again. It suited the princes' slyness to let her accept all the blame.

In 1964 some amateur historians cleaning the twelfth-century chapel of St Radegonde near Chinon discovered a fresco hidden beneath layers of limewash (see plates 16, 17, 18, 19). The painting, dated to within a few years of the rebellion, shows a richly dressed and crowned figure identified as red-bearded Henry of Anjou making a gesture that says, I am in command. He is leading Eleanor away to her long captivity in England after the failed rebellion. The dark-haired young woman with her is Joanna, who is known to have shared the journey. She seems to be begging her parents to stop their fighting. The two beardless youths are Richard and Geoffrey, a year his junior. Eleanor is bidding farewell to Richard after giving him a white gyrfalcon, symbolic of the duchy. Geoffrey is copying his father's gesture as a sign of obedience.

That says it all. Richard and Geoffrey renewed their homage to the king; Young Henry was excused on account of his title being equal to Henry's.[44] As to Eleanor, all that was known – except by Henry and a trusted few – was that she was locked up near Salisbury in one of England's grimmest castles known as Old Sarum, and likely to stay so for the rest of her life.

FOURTEEN

From Palace to Prison

J ust north of Salisbury's city limits, one of Salisbury Plain's many Iron Age hill-forts dominates the landscape for miles around. The entire hill has been remodelled by pick and spade; its concentric rings of ditches and earthen ramparts are not worn soft with time, but still crisp. Pre-Roman hill-fort, it became a Romano-British *oppidum*, then a well-defended Saxon administrative and trading centre which was in turn refortified after the Conquest by William I, who considered it secure enough to site a mint there (plate 22).

The space within the outer ditch and rampart was the first site of Sarum or Salisbury. The houses have all disappeared but the foundations of the cathedral show up chalky white in the thin turf. Roughly in the centre of the levelled area, an inner circular rampart and ditch enclose a steep mound, on the flattened top of which stand the ruins of an eleventh-century castle built by a bishop named Roger for King Henry I. Quite a character, the bishop had in his mistress, Matilda of Ramsbury, as tough a military commander as they came. When besieged in another of her lover's castles at Devizes, she refused to surrender until the attackers paraded in front of the drawbridge with a noose around his neck a captive who happened to be her son by Bishop Roger.

Eleanor's heart must have sunk on arriving at Old Sarum with the knowledge that this grim fortress was to be her prison. Rescue was out of the question. An assailant had to climb up the hill, scale or breach the outer parapet, cross a deep ditch and break through a high parados surmounted by a formidable palisade. Having got that far, he had to cross 200 yards of flat killing ground devoid of cover before coming to the inner defences: another rampart, deep ditch and steep earth glacis surrounding the base of the castle walls. The sole gateway was reached by a drawbridge and protected by a portcullis.

So exposed is the position of Old Sarum that five days after the inauguration of the cathedral, which had taken fourteen years to build, the roof blew off in a gale, causing considerable damage to the whole structure. Standing on the motte or mound, the castle walls reached as high as the cathedral roof, and were subject to the same wind loading. The keep that was the key feature of Norman castles was higher still, to give sentries on the top visibility for miles in all directions. Although it was the safest part of the castle for storing gold or incarcerating hostages, the original royal apartments in it were too cold and miserable to be lived in from choice, even by Norman standards.

Accordingly, in the 1130s Bishop Roger built a small palace within the courtyard, where the high walls afforded some protection from the elements. Its ground-floor rooms were filled with earth as a defence against battering rams, should an enemy ever penetrate into the courtyard. Usually, for defensive reasons, access to a keep was on the first floor. The entrance to the palace was on the second floor, reached by an external stone staircase. On that level was a hall and a solar or smaller room with *garderobe* or latrine emptying into a cesspit. From here a narrow staircase inside the thickness of the walls was the only means of reaching the gloomy first-floor apartments.

In the whole of England Henry could not have chosen a more secure prison for Eleanor. Her accommodation had the advantage of being less cold and windy than the keep, but offered no view of the outside world. The horizons of the woman who had seen Rome, Constantinople and the Holy Land had shrunk to a cobbled courtyard in which she could take at most seventy paces in a straight line before being brought up short by a high stone wall, from the walkway of which sentries stared down at her. For most of her incarceration there, her prison was shared only by a small detachment of guards. Their first commander, under Henry's justiciar Ranulf de Glanville, was Robert Maudit by name – although that may not have been his real surname, for it means 'accursed'.

Eleanor's world for much of the next decade and a half was to be this grey, grim stone cage, open only to the sky. In a repetition of her lost year in the Holy Land, she ceased to exist. Her retinue was reduced to one maid, Amaria. Even her wardrobe had dwindled to the minimum, the Pipe Rolls indicating her need for something fitting to wear when occasionally summoned to court. One entry is for two scarlet cloaks and two capes and two grey furs and one embroidered bed furnishing 'for the use of the Queen and her maid', which sounds as though Eleanor and her sole retainer had to share a bed. The size of the solar in the palace makes that likely in any case. An anonymous Poitevin poet evoked her fate:

> *Piegz a de mort selh que viu cossiros*
> *e non a joy, mas dolor e temensa*
> *pueys ve la ren que'l pogra far joyos*
> *on non troba socors ni mantenensa.*

[It's worse than death for she who lives / yearning and suffering above ground / without the strength that hope could give / where no help or support is to be found.]

When Henry needed a lady to grace his public events, there was always the Young Queen, whose allowance was accordingly increased. Across the Channel in France, he kept Richard and Geoffrey as puppet-rulers, each dependent on his father's purse. In Aquitaine, as a way of demonstrating his loyalty to the hand that paid him, the prince who would become England's hero-king was enthusiastically persecuting barons who had supported the rebellion, razing their castles to the ground and having salt strewn over their lands to render them uncultivable. For the moment, Henry dared not trust the Young King out of his sight in case another coterie had it in mind to place him on the throne prematurely.

All three of the older princes were therefore summoned to the Easter court of 1176 when 'the old king' talked openly about divorcing Eleanor, for which purpose he had been negotiating with the papal legate Cardinal Uguccione or Huguezon for the last six months.[1] Grounds for dissolution were simple to find: treason, plus consanguinity closer than had been the case with Louis. First, however, Henry insisted Eleanor renounce all her titles and retire from the world, since otherwise he would have been repeating what Louis still bemoaned as the greatest error of his rule.

It was therefore up to the good cardinal to talk the queen of England into becoming abbess of Fontevraud.[2] This was a suitable job for a rejected queen of fifty-three, even if she was not yet a widow, and the abbey's position inside the county of Anjou gave Henry confidence that she would behave herself there.[3]

The only problem was that Eleanor refused. Over my dead body, was the gist of her reply to king and cardinal alike. Henry might lock her up and deprive her of all her privileges and even money for clothes, but she was determined not to give up the two trumps she still held. One was the argument that as duchess of Aquitaine she was the direct vassal of the king of France, who would never consent to her renunciation. The other was her knowledge that Henry wanted to marry again. There was talk of him wedding Richard's fiancée Princess Alais, who was his current mistress, in order to father a new brood that would enable him to disinherit her sons. Frustrating this plan seemed to her the only way of regaining their support.

Henry, however, was confident of getting his way in the end by keeping Eleanor in Old Sarum and a series of other cities and fortresses[4] under conditions which would make even the prospect of abdicating and spending the rest of her life in a convent seem attractive. In his game of cat and mouse, from time to time she was moved in the custody of high officials from Salisbury to Winchester, Ludgershall and elsewhere.

Young Henry, forever chafing at the bit, finally escaped to France on pretence of making pilgrimage to Compostela.[5] Landing at Barfleur with Marguerite at Easter 1176, he left her in Paris at her father's court, where Louis provided horses and armour to enable him to fill his empty pockets in the Flemish tournaments with William the Marshal's help. The costs of this regal indulgence, including reparations for damage to people, dwellings and crops, staggered Louis' advisers.[6]

The season ending on Midsummer Day, Young Henry rode south to Aquitaine, where Richard was campaigning against his vassals the count of Angoulême and Viscount Aymar of Limoges, both sides manoeuvring large forces of mercenaries across the tortured landscape of south-west France. The jealousy and mutual mistrust of the princes preventing them spending long together, the Young King installed himself in Eleanor's former quarters at Poitiers where, as was his wont, he charmed the barons now disenchanted with Richard.

Among his father's spies in his entourage was Adam Chirchedune, the Young King's vice-chancellor. An intercepted letter resulted in him being judged for treason[7] and escaping summary execution only because the bishop of Poitiers argued that Adam was a cleric in the service of the archbishop of York, and should therefore be given benefit of clergy. Stripped naked and flogged through the streets of Poitiers instead, Henry's spy was dispatched to prison in Argentan with orders that he be flogged through the streets of every town along the way[8] as a way of killing him without actually sentencing him to death. However, he survived and was rescued by an embassy sent from England to procure his release.

It was now the turn of Eleanor's twelve-year-old daughter Joanna to serve the grand design in a marriage designed to outflank the German Emperor in southern Italy. There were close trading links between Sicily and England, where Richard Palmer was bishop of Syracuse and his fellow-Englishman Walter of the Mill was bishop of Palermo. With Henry's clerk Peter of Blois having been tutor to Sicily's king during his minority, there was no shortage of channels of communication through which to arrange Princess Joanna's marriage to William II, the 24-year-old king of Naples and Sicily, duke of Puglia and prince of Capua.

Towards the end of August Eleanor bade farewell at Winchester to her second daughter. Dispatched to her uncertain fate in Sicily laden with presents for her future husband, she was accompanied by Bishop John of Norwich, who had been the go-between. Henry ordered the Young King to escort her from the boat at Barfleur south to Aquitaine in sufficient force to ensure that she was not relieved of her dowry of fine horses, gems and precious metals on the way.

From Poitiers, Richard accompanied his sister to Toulouse across a landscape of misery and famine while his eldest brother returned northwards, devoting himself to tournaments and little else for the next three years. Whatever Joanna's thoughts about her fate in Sicily, the progress to Toulouse was leisured and elegant. After saying farewell, Richard 'pacified' southern Gascony on the pretext that its barons were attacking and robbing pilgrims to Compostela in defiance of the Peace of God. Dismissing his Brabanter mercenaries the moment he had no more money to pay them, he unleashed another spate of misfortune when they turned to pillage and rape on their route home through the county of Limoges, which continued until the locals got together and massacred 2,000 of them on the Thursday before Easter.

The king of Sicily had been a minor of thirteen when his father died. On coming of age, he had decided to impress on his Muslim and Orthodox subjects that he was a *Christian* monarch by building outside Palermo at Monreale the breathtaking cathedral where Joanna, in a bejewelled dress that had cost the enormous sum of £114, was married on 13 February 1177. The cathedral's intact décor of marble and glittering gold mosaic gives the closest impression now available of the dazzling magnificence of Santa Sophia before the Muslim conquerors of Constantinople hacked off all the Christian decoration in 1453. The floor plan of Monreale combines features of both western and Orthodox basilicas. The styles of its magnificent decoration are, like the island's population at the time, a mixture of north European Christian, Muslim and Greek Orthodox.

Similarly, William's seal bore a Latin inscription 'by the grace of God', but his coins had an Arabic inscription on the obverse, 'desirous of being exalted by God', and on the reverse Greek letters in an abbreviation of 'Jesus Christ Victorious'. Likewise, William's court was composed of Christian, Muslim and Greek advisers. As Joanna was shortly to find out, although her husband was known as 'William the Good' because he had been the first western monarch to send aid to the beleaguered Latin Kingdom, he also spoke, read and wrote Arabic – and took his sexual pleasures in the harem of beautiful Christian and Muslim girls in his palace.

The marriage was in vain. On 24 July 1177 Henry's grand design, whose knell had been sounded by Becket's defiance, was finally undone. Despairing of the king of England ever making his move, the pope signed a treaty in Venice with the German Emperor that ended all hopes of the crown of Lombardy sitting on the head of Henry of Anjou. The 2,000 marks he had paid to the count of Maurienne had had to be written off on the death of the count's daughter. Eleanor's two sacrificed daughters – Matilda in Saxony and Joanna in Sicily – had likewise to be written off for the moment.

No longer needing England's support, the Pope sent a legate at the request of Louis to say that if Alais Capet was not married to Richard or returned to her father forthwith, England would be placed under interdict.[9] Another round of negotiations with Louis then ensued, with both kings announcing that they would take the cross and Henry agreeing to marry Alais to Richard and Louis confirming that the Vexin castles were Marguerite's dowry. Despite the trickery and deceit, when Henry returned to England in July 1178 he placed all his continental possessions under Louis' protection as a way of keeping his sons in check.

Richard's vindictiveness was alienating his vassals one by one, which pleased Henry because it rendered another rebellion less likely of support. Eleanor's favourite was now aged twenty-two and sufficiently experienced in warfare – he did little else except hunt – to demand the plenary ducal powers. For this, his mother's consent was necessary, but she still refused to abdicate her own title as duchess. So Henry tried a new tactic in the hope of alienating her from Richard.

She was released from confinement and brought to court, where Richard pleaded his case. To the courtiers it may have looked as though a family reconciliation of some kind was under way, but the queen was there on sufferance and Richard for one purpose only. In vain had a Poitevin troubadour prophesied at the end of the rebellion that Eleanor's cries of protest at her betrayal would sound loud as the trumpet to summon to her help the valiant sons who would set her free and bring her back in triumph to her own country. Confronting his mother, all Richard cared about was his title. It was this betrayal more than all Henry's punishment that nearly broke her will, until she saw in it a chance to better her position at little real cost to herself. As a reward for her cooperation in agreeing to pass title to Richard, Henry relaxed the conditions of her captivity.

Eleanor's first husband was nearing the end of his life. Health failing, Louis planned to crown his son, fifteen-year-old Prince Philip Augustus. Shortly before 15 August 1179, the date set for the coronation, the prince fell into a fever no one could cure after being lost for a day and a night in the forest of Compiègne when separated from his companions on a boar hunt. Convinced that praying at Becket's tomb would enable his anxious prayers to be heard in Heaven, Louis asked permission to make a pilgrimage to the shrine at Canterbury.

Taking ship for the first time since his nightmarish return voyage with Eleanor from the Holy Land, he was welcomed with open arms at Dover by Henry, who accompanied him to the shrine and treated him like a brother throughout the four days he was on English soil. The thought of her two husbands piously riding through the Kentish countryside on pilgrimage to the tomb of the man Henry had hated so much must have amused Eleanor, wherever she was at this time.

The prayers were heard. Six weeks later three of her sons were at the delayed coronation in Reims – Richard and Geoffrey representing their fiefs held from the French Crown and Young Henry as duke of Normandy acting as seneschal of France and bearing the crown in front of Philip in the procession to the altar.[10] The high point of the festivities was a grand tournament at Lagny on the Marne, east of Paris, where the Young King's knights were victorious, as so often with William the marshal in the team.

The coronation came not a month too soon. Shortly afterwards, news reached Eleanor that a stroke had paralysed Louis down the right side and deprived him of the power of speech. After his reign of forty-two years, of which more than a third had been shared with her, the Capetian throne was now occupied by a boy of fifteen. In September of the following year, Louis died after bequeathing all his personal property to the poor.[11] Eleanor was then fifty-seven and had been a prisoner for six years.

In July 1181 her son Geoffrey was married to Constance of Brittany, after which Henry elevated his bastard son of the same name by appointing him Chancellor instead of having him consecrated bishop of Lincoln. As a sign of displeasure with his legitimate sons for allying themselves with King Philip against the count of Flanders, Henry made Geoffrey the Bastard also archdeacon of Rouen and treasurer of York Minster, to provide him with a more than adequate income.

Shortly afterwards, Philip found a temporary solution to his pressing need for money by banishing all the Jews from Frankish territory, confiscating their houses and taking over their loans, the debtors being discharged on payment to the Crown of one-fifth of the outstanding amounts. Allowed to sell off their furniture, many of the dispossessed crossed the Channel and settled in England. The operation brought in 15,000 marks to the Capetian treasury, some synagogues were converted into churches and the space for the great covered market of Les Halles, latterly Paris' vegetable market, was found by demolishing houses in the former Jewish quarter.[12]

In Germany, the emperor's position of strength decided him to exile for seven years Eleanor's troublesome and too-powerful son-in-law, the duke of Saxony. Together with his pregnant wife and their children, he sought refuge at the Norman court with an entourage so large that Henry, mean as ever about hospitality,[13] induced him to send most of them home and even provided funds for the journey. After persuading the duke to go on pilgrimage to Compostela, Henry gave Matilda the palace of Argentan for her residence, intending her to give birth there, but she eluded him and departed for Paris, producing a son on the Ile de la Cité shortly afterwards.

When the news reached Eleanor that she was a grandmother yet again, Richard was campaigning with various vassals against other vassals and then retiring to Talmond or another of his favourite hunting forests. The two Henrys, father and son, were constantly falling out and making it up over the issue of whether the Young King had, or had not, a kingdom to rule. Finally he lost patience and withdrew to the court of his brother-in-law in Paris. Understandably, King Philip was out to seduce any disaffected Plantagenet with favours of all kinds until Henry enticed his son back to the fold with a daily allowance of £100 English for himself and £10 for the Young Queen, plus payment of the expenses of a hundred household knights to guarantee him a fitting retinue.

When the Young King joined Richard and Geoffrey at the Christmas court in Caen, also present were Matilda and her family, Henry of Saxony having returned from pilgrimage. The only member of the family not invited was Eleanor,[14] the Young Queen taking her place at the festivities. It was not, however, a happy Christmas: Young Henry and Richard demanded the right to hold their own plenary courts, but their father rejected such arrogance.

Something of the backbiting and bitchiness is conveyed by the ease with which gossips had convinced Young Henry that William the Marshal was paying court to Queen Marguerite. To vindicate himself, William challenged three owners of those wagging tongues to single combat, one after the other, himself to be hanged if he lost. He offered to cut a finger off his right hand first, but there were still no takers. Disgusted, he ignored a letter from Baldwin of Béthune confirming the Young King's pardon, and departed on pilgrimage to Cologne before staying in self-imposed exile in Germany.[15]

Bored, Richard left the court early. Unfortunately, he had brought with him to Normandy a troubadour who sowed trouble wherever he went. It would have been quite in character for Bertran de Born to be the one who whispered in Young Henry's ear the accusations against William, in order to cover up his own interest in Marguerite. Gifted poet and brave warrior, Bertran's other great talent was for causing dissension, partly because his castle of Hautefort near Périgueux was expensive to upkeep and his scant resources obliged him to depend on booty. So long as Richard was on campaign, he was happy.

> *E platz mi quan li corredor*
> *fan las gens e l'aver fugir.*
> *E platz mi quan vei après lor*
> *gran re d'armatz ensems venir.*

> *E platz mi em mon coratge*
> *quan vei fortz chastels assetjatz*
> *e los barris rotz et esfondratz. . . .*

[How I love to see skirmishers / putting the common folk to flight. / An host of armed men riding them down / is a grand sight. / It warms my heart / to see great castles under siege / and ramparts gaping at the breach. . . .]

Bertran's other passion was women. He set his cap at Matilda, comparing her beauty with that of Helen of Troy in very explicit terms.

> *Et ont òm plus n'ostaria garnisons,*
> *plus en seria envejós,*
> *que la nuech fai parer dia la gola*
> *e qui'n vesia plus en jos.*
> *Tots lo monds en gençaria.*

[When her last garment's on the floor / I'll want her all the more. / The sight of her neck changes night to day / and to see her lower down / would indeed pleasure any man.]

Matilda cannot have been disturbed by the explicit verses, for Bertran dared to reveal the identity of his adored, complaining that he would have died of boredom at the court of Argentan . . .

> *. . . ma'l gentils còrs amorós e la douça chara pia*
> *e la bonha companhia e'l respons de la Sassia'm defendia.*

[. . . but for the desirable body and sweet, kindly face / and the good company and wit of my Saxon lady.]

If he had confined himself to versifying, all would have been well. Instead, he and his *jonglar* Papiol took to fanning the fires of Young Henry's envy of Richard's comparative freedom to act as master of his own domains. To massage the Young King's ego, when the court moved on to Le Mans and Angers Henry ordered Geoffrey and Richard to swear fealty to him for their fiefs. Geoffrey complied, but Richard refused from a distance on the grounds that his title came from Eleanor and had nothing to do with his eldest brother. Moreover, he said, they were siblings of the same bed and therefore equals.[16] Encouraged by

Bertran, Young Henry retorted that the barons of Aquitaine were begging him to take over the duchy Richard was ruining by his incessant campaigning.

Henry then sent Prince Geoffrey into Aquitaine to summon the barons to witness Richard's very reluctant delayed act of homage to Young Henry on 1 January 1183. Geoffrey once remarked that the Plantagenets had from earliest times pitted brother against brother and son against father.[17] As usual, he was playing two games, having been clandestinely charged by the Young King to incite Richard's many enemies in the duchy, of whom Bertran furnished a list, to rebel against their lawful duke.

By late February Young Henry was in Limoges, the heartland of the conspiracy which was about to be joined by the duke of Burgundy and 500 knights sent by the count of Champagne. Dispatched to Paris for her own safety and to beg Philip for his support, Marguerite was unable to get a personal commitment from her half-brother, who nevertheless announced that he would not prevent any vassal taking sides against Richard.[18]

There can have been few conspiracies betrayed by a poem: secrecy was blown to the four winds when Bertran deliberately included the names of the main conspirators in a *sirventès* and then made sure it reached Henry's ears as a way of ensuring they could not retract. Travelling light, he took the road for Limoges with a small force of trusted mercenaries,[19] determined to break the Young King's conspiracy before it gathered more support. Outside the city he was attacked by a mob of armed citizens and only saved from death by an Englishman who recognised the king's banner. His *cotte* of chain-mail pierced by a sword thrust that came within an inch of drawing blood – some said by an arrow fired at extreme range from the city wall that lodged in the cloak after being stopped by the mail – Henry retired to the castle of Aixe.[20]

Young Henry arrived fully armed that evening to plead that the townspeople had not known whom they were attacking. It was a feeble excuse for an act of the highest treason, but Henry invited him to dine in the hope of talking him out of this latest foolishness. Determined on a final trial of strength,[21] the Young King refused. Henry tried to parley again next day but was almost wounded a second time, after which he remained in the castle of Aixe until Richard arrived with reinforcements, having ridden two days and two nights without rest. On the way, he missed capturing a key rebel, his vassal Count Aymar of Limoges, only because his horses were too exhausted to give pursuit.

Besieging the castle of Gorre with Aymar was a band of mercenaries who were less lucky. Many of those taken prisoner were thrown with their arms bound into the River Vienne; others were executed by the sword; about eighty were blinded and released in a countryside where everyone was their enemy[22] – all this on Richard's personal orders.

Arriving at Aixe, Richard found himself in a bizarre triangle of power with his father and his half-brother, Geoffrey the Bastard. Together they besieged Limoges where Young Henry was in financial difficulties, his allowance having ceased at the outbreak of hostilities. He borrowed from the citizens to pay his mercenaries and those sent by Philip before plundering churches of their treasures, covering this infringement of the Peace of God by giving receipts for the loot. Other bands under Prince Geoffrey pillaged St Martin in Brive and held some of the monks to ransom. In Henry's favourite monastery at Grandmont, the rebels hacked to pieces the altar vessels and distributed them as bullion. Only at Uzerche did the wily abbot outwit the rapacious prince by receiving him with such pomp and ceremony and protestations of respect that Young Henry was too embarrassed to steal the treasure.

After several months of this murderous free-for-all, in which the contingents from Champagne and Burgundy only added to the confusion and even the count of Toulouse changed sides to join the rebels, the end was in sight when Young Henry fell ill after looting the shrine of Rocamadour.[23] A few days later, after confessing his sins, receiving absolution and taking communion, he lay dying in the house of one Etienne Fabri in the town of Martel in Périgord.

When the news reached Henry, he was dissuaded from riding to Martel by Richard's reminder that the Young King had already received the last rites six years before and recovered. Should the king be killed en route by Young Henry's mercenaries under their leaders Sancho and Curburan,[24] the crown would pass straightaway to their master. Instead, Count Rotrou of La Perche and the bishop of Agen were sent, bearing the king's ring as a token of goodwill.[25]

In Martel the dying prince dictated a letter for his father, begging his mercy on Eleanor after her ten-year imprisonment, asking him to provide an acceptable pension for the widow Marguerite and to pardon Count Aymar of Limoges and the other rebels.[26] He also asked that the many thefts of Church property be made good and ended with instructions for the disposal of his mortal remains. Eyes, brain and entrails were to be buried beside the plot reserved for Henry's grave at Grandmont, but the rest of his body was to be interred beside the tombs of the dukes of

Normandy in Rouen Cathedral. After receiving the *viaticum* from the bishop of Agen, he expired two years short of his thirtieth birthday with a cross on his chest, begging his friend William the Marshal to take it on crusade to the Holy Sepulchre.[27] This, William swore to do.

The funeral cortège was a sorry sight. Young Henry having died in debt on all sides, a valuable destrier had to be sold to buy food en route and at least one of the prince's household had to pawn his shoes to buy breakfast.[28] At Uzerche, where the abbot provided bed and spartan board, himself paying for the candles at a service for the salvation of the departed soul, the collection among the dead prince's entourage amounted to twelve pence, instantly pocketed by his chaplain for food.

As the news spread, the fighting stopped. Knights, men-at-arms and mercenaries made their ways home, as did the duke of Burgundy and the count of Toulouse. The cortège progressed slowly westwards towards Limoges, Young Henry's fine friends melting away one by one, none wanting to be present when the king set eyes on the corpse of his favourite son. Finally only a few servants remained, led by the ever-faithful William the Marshal.

In the hot midsummer weather putrefaction had already set in. On arrival at Grandmont, the viscera were immediately removed and buried on the spot. Papal legates were present, bearing letters ordering a truce on pain of excommunication and interdict that were now superfluous. Before the funeral service could begin, the bishop of Limoges objected that Young Henry's excommunication for pillaging the monastery was still in force. He agreed to lift it only after the prior of Grandmont had undertaken to obtain restitution in full from the king.

Embalmed in salt and aromatic herbs, the corpse was wrapped in a white winding sheet, itself enveloped in a leather tube covered by a green cloth. The eulogies evoked the deceased's qualities of generosity and statesmanship, yet the chroniclers could not fail to observe that to die so soon after looting shrines, churches and monasteries was clearly divine retribution. Eleanor's second-born son left behind only the reputation of a playboy spendthrift who had squandered enormous sums on the tournament.

The degree of his destitution became apparent when Henry ordered William to escort the body to Rouen for burial and the Marshal explained that he was unable to obey, having himself been mortgaged by the Young King to Sancho, together with his horse, weapons and armour for 100 marks – a practice Henry had made illegal five years earlier. Redeeming the debt, Henry also gave William horses and funds for the pilgrimage to Jerusalem he had sworn to make for the good of Young Henry's soul.[29] But the body never reached Rouen, being kidnapped by the citizens of Le Mans on the way, so that it could be buried in their cathedral.

It was now the turn of Bertran de Born to pay for his role in the conspiracy. Surrendering the castle of Hautefort to Richard, he saw it given to his brother Constantin, from whom he had obtained it in the first place by trickery, endorsed by Richard before he went over to the Young King's cause. Sent under heavy escort to Henry for justice, he pleaded the slender extenuation that it would have been disloyal of him to surrender before his own overlord Viscount Aymar had laid down his arms.

What saved his life was not that argument but a *planh* or lament for the Young King that Bertran had hastily composed as an insurance policy during the siege of his castle. The grieving father was moved to tears by it:

> *Si tuit li dolh e'lh plor e'l marrimen*
> *e las dolors e'lh danh e'lh chaitivier*
> *qu'òm anc auzis en est segle dolen*
> *fossen emsems, semblaran tuit leugier*
> *contra la mòrt del jove rei engles. . . .*

[If the sadness of all the grief and tears / and the pain, the suffering and misery / that can afflict a man in a hundred years / were put together, they would seem to be / less than the death of the Young King. . . .]

Pardoned, Bertran offered to take up arms against his recent confederates, and swore to do homage for Hautefort to Richard despite having previously maintained that it was in allodium, free of feudal obligation.[30] Restored as co-seigneur with his brother, Bertran eventually sought to atone for all the mischief and misery he had caused by taking vows and dying a monk in the Cistercian abbey of Dalon. A hundred years later he was in the eighth circle of hell in Dante's *Inferno*, carrying his severed head before him like a lantern and confessing what sin had earned this fate. 'Like the biblical Achitophel who set Absolom against David,' he says, 'I set a son against his father.'[31]

The news from Martel reached Eleanor officially through Henry's messenger Thomas Agnell, archdeacon of Wells. He found her under renewed strict guard at Old Sarum – a precaution ordered at the outbreak of the recent rebellion. Rumours of the Young King's death had crossed the Channel before the worthy archdeacon, but it suited her to claim that she had been told of it in a vision. Of her sixty-one years she had spent eleven as prisoner of her two husbands. Her eldest son was dead, but he had always been Henry's favourite and not hers, so what grief she felt was tempered by the knowledge that Richard was now heir to the throne of England. With Henry's increasingly poor health, the gamble she had taken at the end of the great rebellion of 1173–4 was within a heartbeat of being won.

FIFTEEN

A Prisoner of Moment

An even more radical improvement in Eleanor's situation came when King Philip rightly insisted on the return of his widowed half-sister's dowry, in particular the three Vexin castles.

No one can have been more surprised than Eleanor when Henry declared blandly that this was impossible because Marguerite's dowry had passed to the captive queen in 1179, in compensation for her birthright passing to Richard. As 'proof' of this, she was brought from England in October under close escort[1] to take possession of Gisors in particular, spending six months in Normandy with her daughter Matilda of Saxony as companion. This was not exactly freedom, but conditions were radically better than she had known since first being locked up in Old Sarum.

Philip was playing a long game. At a meeting on 6 December 1183 in the shadow of the castle where she was living out this fiction he shelved his first demand in return for an annual pension to Marguerite of 2,750 pounds Angevin, payable in Paris, where she was living as his protégée. No abstemious monk *manqué* like his father, Philip liked to eat and live well, to dress fashionably and enjoy amusing company, but he was as persistent in negotiation and as swift in warfare as Henry. Shortly after coming to the throne he changed the title of the French monarch from king of the Franks to king of France.[2] It was an important difference. From the beginning of his reign, those who followed the fortunes of kings were prophesying that he would reverse the ascendance of the Angevin dynasty over the house of Capet, as indeed proved the case.

He insisted that his other half-sister Princess Alais, who had been shut up in Winchester Castle throughout most of her childhood and adolescence, should be released from the betrothal to Richard, who had no intention of marrying her or anyone else. To placate his insistent suzerain, Henry promised to marry her off to John instead and swore fealty for the continental possessions to Philip, which he had previously refused to do.

On the intervention of the archbishop of Canterbury and in reward for her cooperation over the issue of Gisors, Eleanor's conditions on her return to England were eased still further. Although she remained in the custody of Glanville's deputy Ralph fitz Stephen, dresses, riding clothes and saddlery were hers for the asking, together with items for the faithful Amaria, now benefiting from her mistress' better fortunes. Easter 1184 was spent at Becket's former palace in Berkhamsted, where Matilda of Saxony came to visit, largely pregnant. From there, the queen moved to Woodstock but was in Winchester for the birth in mid-June of Matilda's son William.[3]

Delighted with the upturn in his fortunes, Richard meanwhile saw his court of familiars swollen daily by those who wanted to curry favour with the prince now destined to be king of England. Disturbed by this sudden popularity and Richard's increasing arrogance, Henry had Prince John come from England, with the idea of making him duke of Aquitaine, thus placing Richard in what had been Young Henry's invidious position of being king without a kingdom. Richard was *not* impressed, even with the promise that John would do homage to him for the duchy. To gain time, he asked for a respite of two or three days and then declared from the safety of Poitiers that he would never part with an inch of his birthright.[4]

At this defiance, Henry provided funds for Geoffrey and John to make war on Richard, thus launching a new round of depredations and death[5] in which Richard was campaigning in Brittany to punish Geoffrey, while he and John were laying waste Poitou in return.[6] In the viscounty of Limoges, Mercadier's mercenaries were on the loose under the pretence of fighting for Richard, while other bands under the son of the count of Toulouse were doing the same ostensibly for the other side. Finally Henry gave in to the protests of the bishops and ordered the three princes to come to London at the end of November.

The Christmas court in Windsor was thus a fraught family reunion, even by Plantagenet standards. Also present were Matilda of Saxony, her husband and children . . . and Eleanor. Resolved not to play Henry's game a second time, she allied herself with Richard in refusing to even consider John being invested as duke of Aquitaine. Playing on the siblings' rivalry, Henry then released the ever-pliable Prince Geoffrey to return to Normandy while keeping John and Richard with him. A change of mind led to Geoffrey being recalled and Richard allowed to return to Poitou after giving patently false promises of good conduct. Rightly fearing his father's change of mind, he took ship before the week was out.

In intervals between warfare and hunting, he was often generous to the poor and particularly so to religious foundations, once declaring in a letter to the abbot of La Sauve Majeure that the abbey was dearer to him than his own eyeballs. This particular progress southwards was several times halted to issue charters granting or confirming privileges – and to establish new towns at St Rémy and elsewhere, to be peopled by offering tax-haven status for merchants and artisans.

Eleanor's youngest son John was now eighteen. Spoiled by his father since the Young King's death, he loved the good life, fine clothes and jewellery – also gambling, with backgammon being a favourite pastime. During Lent 1185 Henry dubbed him a knight and sent him at the head of an army into Ireland after naming him its overlord. Having a whole country to call his own revealed John's true colours: he mocked the unfashionable clothing and long beards of the Irish lords and their halting attempts to speak Norman French. Within an eight-month stay he alienated both them and the Anglo-Norman nobility to the point that Henry replaced him by a viceroy, John de Courcy.

Thanks to the intercession of Matilda and her husband, Eleanor had been living with them at Windsor under conditions that were very comfortable, compared with her years in Old Sarum. Summoned with them in mid-Lent to Rouen by Henry, she had another pleasant surprise on learning that he had solved the problem of Richard's overweening arrogance by sending him an ultimatum to surrender Poitou and Aquitaine immediately to his mother. Should he not comply, Henry threatened to march at the head of an army and reinstall her as duchess by force![7]

His vassals refusing to support him against Henry, Richard rode sullenly to Normandy and declared in front of witnesses that Eleanor was the true mistress of Poitou and Aquitaine. To make the point that he really had become the second young-king-sans-kingdom, Henry had a treaty drawn up confirming Eleanor's plenary powers, on parchment at least.[8] A grandmother of sixty-three, it was natural that she should celebrate this amazing upturn of fortune after eleven years of deprivation by making generous gifts from the proceeds of her own estates to the abbey of Fontevraud and other foundations.

To emphasise that she was acting of her own volition at long last, she announced the gifts to the archbishop of Bordeaux, the bishops and barons and just about everyone else of importance in Aquitaine. Henry seemed to have softened a little since the collapse of the great design, and his health was gradually declining. In November 1185, after acting the peacemaker and brokering a settlement between Philip and the count of Flanders who had been so generous to Young Henry, he was too ill to attend the treaty signing.

Back in England, although Eleanor was now living a fairly normal life, she still had keepers. Henry of Berneval replaced Ralph fitz Stephen as Glanville's eyes and ears, watching her at every turn as she stayed mainly at Winchester, where Princess Alais was still captive. At his next meeting with Philip in Lent of 1186, Henry again promised to marry Alais to Richard or hand back Gisors. If the latter was a conditional promise he had no intention of keeping, the first alternative was out of the question, since Richard had no desire for a wife and it was common knowledge that Alais had been Henry's mistress for years.

Before returning to England on 27 April 1186 Henry neutralised Richard, who continued to style himself duke of Aquitaine[9] in the absence of its duchess, by equipping him with an army of Brabanter mercenaries and sending them to invade the county of Toulouse in alliance with the count of Montpellier and the king of Aragon. The declared aim was to punish Raymond of Toulouse for his support of Young Henry.

Geoffrey was meanwhile playing a different game on the Ile de la Cité. During one of a series of tournaments given by Philip to entertain him, the honoured guest fell in a mêlée. This was not a *joûte à outrance* or fight to the death, but in the confusion he was trampled to death by the horses,[10] despite his armour. Like thousands of unrecorded victims of the sport, he died on 19 August 1186 and was buried with great pomp in the basilica of Notre Dame, Philip having to be restrained from throwing himself into the grave with the coffin.[11]

Eleanor learned of this in Winchester. First the Young King, now Geoffrey. Three of the five sons she had borne to rule an empire were dead. Given Richard's violent way of life, did she already have a premonition about him dying prematurely too?

Philip afterwards demanded as suzerain of the dead prince that Henry send Geoffrey's daughter Eleanor of Brittany to be raised at the French court until she was of an age to be married, so that she would be under his control. When Henry prevaricated, Philip insisted to the point of war. For the first time since falling out with Becket, Henry delegated real authority, dividing his forces into four corps: one commanded by Richard; the second by John; the third by the Count of Aumale; and the fourth by Geoffrey the Bastard.

On 29 March Geoffrey's widow Constance gave birth to her ill-starred son Arthur, whose only good fortune was in her choice of name, which made many superstitious Bretons believe him a reincarnation of the eponymous mythical king. The boy inheriting his dead father's title at birth, Philip as suzerain now sought to bring both him and his sister to Paris with the widowed Constance.

While Henry refused to allow this, he also had no intention of allowing Geoffrey's widow to become one of those powerful mothers who brought their sons up with a view to a great destiny – as the Empress Matilda had brought him up. He therefore exercised his right to dispose of widowed vassals in forcing Constance to marry the young count of Chester, Ranulf de Blundeville, after which Philip's forces marched into Berry, where a new war was only averted by the truce of Châteauroux.

In Paris, seeking the welcome Philip always extended to a disaffected son of Henry, Richard was told – if he did not already know – that his father's talk of marrying Alais to John after making him duke of Aquitaine was a smokescreen. The truth was even worse, Philip said: after twenty-two years of keeping Alais his prisoner and latterly his helpless mistress, Henry intended to marry her himself and make their young bastard son his heir to the throne and all that went with it, to the detriment of the two surviving sons by the marriage to Eleanor.

The plan, if such it was, failed when Alais' child died, but Philip's talk fanned Richard's ever-smouldering animosity towards his father, as his host had intended. In Paris, he was shown every kindness, king and prince spending their days together, sharing their favourite foods at table and drinking from the same goblet, at night sharing a bed. The intensity of their relationship was such that all Henry's bribes failed to persuade Richard to leave Paris.[12] When he eventually did, in his own good time, it was to head straight for Chinon and help himself to considerable funds from the treasury there, which he used to fortify several castles in direct defiance of his father's orders.

Eleanor seems to have spent most of 1187 at Winchester, following from a distance all these manoeuvrings in conditions that were comfortable. With Henry's worsening health, it must have been about then that she realised for the first time that there was a very good chance of her outliving him. Should Richard too die before his father, John was capable of having her locked up for the rest of her life. Therefore it was in her interest to forgive Richard and use what influence she had in his favour.

A new crusade was being preached by Archbishop Joscius of Tyre to recover Jerusalem from the great Saracen general Salah-ed-Din, called Saladin in the West, who had captured the holy city on 2 October 1187. All that remained in Frankish hands was the coastal strip including three vital ports, without which the Latin Kingdom could not survive. A couple of years earlier, Henry had been offered the throne of Jerusalem,[13] but preferred instead to fund the Templars to defend the holy places in his name. In a fit of adolescent enthusiasm, the atheist Prince John took the cross. Although his relative and friend Count Philip of Flanders had gone all the way to Jerusalem to check out the possibilities and returned disillusioned, Richard could not do less. Having taken crusader's vows did not stop him treating rank-and-file captives taken in his campaigns against Toulouse with his usual brutality – until his chaplain Milo came up with the humane solution of pardoning them on condition they swore to accompany him on the coming 'pilgrimage to Jerusalem'.[14]

Dunned to support the new crusade, Henry promised Joscius that he too would take the cross – a bluff which compelled Philip to do the same. Making both monarchs swear to respect each other's status as pilgrims and live in peace until their return from the Holy Land, on 22 January 1188 the archbishop of Tyre pinned a white cloth cross to the cloaks of Henry's retinue, with red ones for Philip and his barons and green ones for the count of Flanders and his men.

All three thereupon declared a new tax to finance the crusade, known as the Saladin tithe: a tenth of all revenues and movable property, with the exception of a knight's horse, armour and weapons, the clergy's books and vestments, and Church treasures. In both Normandy and England protests were raised at this precursor of income tax[15] proclaimed by the bishops, who threatened defaulters with excommunication. Unable to impose it in his domains, Philip was at a financial disadvantage *vis-à-vis* Richard when they did eventually depart on crusade.

In addition, a prolonged Lenten fast was decreed – with no meat to be eaten on Wednesdays, Fridays and Saturdays.[16] Many other details were thrashed out: there were to be no beggars or pardoned criminals on this crusade, but only disciplined fighting men. Fine clothes were banned, as were dice and swearing. Eleanor must have smiled when she learned that there were to be no Amazons this time – nor any other women except 'decent' washerwomen.[17]

While many knights and barons departed early for the Orient, both Henry and Philip could claim a thousand reasons to delay their departure for the Holy Land. From Périgord, Bertran de Born was heard deploring from a distance 'the journey that the kings had forgotten to make'.[18] Few considered it a sin to kill Saracens, but there were some pacifists with the courage to express profound belief in the sanctity of life: a future canon of Lincoln Cathedral, Radulfus Niger held that the terrestrial Jerusalem was a mirage distracting men's minds from the true priority of a spiritual Jerusalem. With extraordinary courage, he raised his lone voice in the wilderness of crusade fever, calling out that it was wrong to kill Saracens because they were human beings, albeit infidels.

After visiting Eleanor briefly in Old Sarum, where she was suffering for her support of Richard, Henry took ship for Barfleur at the head of an army of English and Welsh mercenaries to meet Richard with his Brabanters and Basques converging on Berry to teach the French a lesson. Whatever one side won was soon lost again. At a meeting on 16 August under the ancient elm below Gisors Castle, Richard was sent away by his father when his temper got the better of him. This was not gullible Louis with whom they had to deal: Philip played all the tricks Henry had served on Louis in earlier times, even having the elm cut down at the end of their negotiations to demonstrate that the time for talking was over.[19]

And so it went on: skirmishing, revenge, campaigns, sieges, retractions and lies. At times supporting Henry, Richard on one occasion went so far as to kneel before Philip in his presence and swear allegiance for Normandy, Poitou, Anjou, Maine, Berry, the Limousin and every other land Henry held in fief on French soil.[20] The game was complicated by Geoffrey the Bastard, always faithful to Henry since he had no entitlement except by his hand. But Henry's health and vigour were failing. He was fifty-five, worn out and limping from his leg injury. With failing health went dwindling authority: many barons ignored the summons to the Christmas court of 1188 in Saumur.

During the winter Henry sent Cardinal John of Agnani to exhort Philip to be reasonable or threaten him with excommunication, to which the king of France replied that the dispute was not Church business and asked coldly how much English money the cardinal had smelled.[21] At Easter, when the Lenten truce expired, Henry was too ill at Le Mans to attend a meeting with Philip.[22] His condition worsened. Lesions of the vertebral discs and both internal and external haemorrhoids and their complications were common in men who had spent many hours every day of their adult lives thumping up and down on leather saddles, which is why most of his coevals had retired from warfare. In his case, untreated haemorrhoids worsened into what sounds like an anal fistula, possibly a side-effect of tuberculosis or Crohn's disease, whose patterns of crisis and remission could account for his increasingly frequent and severe spells of ill-health.

Whatever the exact diagnosis, discomfort made it agony to sit on a cushion, let alone mount a horse. Yet his meeting with Philip at the end of May or beginning of June saw him still refusing to back down over Gisors while Philip repeatedly insisted that Alais be married to Richard before he left on crusade and Richard ranted that he would not go to the Holy Land unless John went too, so little did he trust his father not to give everything to the new favourite, once his back was turned.

With Richard's help, and abetted by many of Henry's vassals who thought him near death, Philip reopened hostilities, besieging him at Le Mans. When the defenders fired everything outside the walls to deny food and shelter to the attackers, the blaze got out of hand and ravaged the whole town. Exhausted and ill, Henry waited until the last moment before escaping via the nearest ford, held at great cost in lives by his Welsh mercenaries. Richard caught up with the rearguard, not having had time to don his armour. It was his good fortune to come up against William the Marshal, who disdained to injure him, and had the skill and forethought to drive his lance instead into the prince's horse, which fell and placed Richard out of harm's way as the fight moved on.

Henry's fortunes had never sunk so low. On 3 July Tours fell to the Franks. The following day, Richard refused to believe that his father was unable to leave his bed until Henry arrived for the meeting with Philip suffering from septicaemia and with a high fever. It was so evident that he could neither stand nor sit unaided that Philip spread his own cloak on the ground, but Henry could not dismount. Swaying in the saddle and supported by his companions, he acceded to every demand, agreeing at long last to place Alais in the care of the archbishop of Canterbury or of Rouen pending her marriage and to make good the costs incurred by his victorious adversaries in the recent fighting. In addition, he was to swear allegiance to Philip for all his possessions, pardon all the rebels and depart on crusade by Lent 1190. This last was patently impossible.

The only thing Henry had the strength to refuse was the ritual kiss of peace demanded by Richard, hissing into his ear instead, 'May God let me live to avenge myself on you.'[23]

Succumbing at last to exhaustion and fever, he had to be borne the few miles back to Chinon on a litter, cursing Heaven for having given him such sons and refusing to confess himself despite the pleas of the archbishop of Canterbury and the bishop of Hereford, to whom it was obvious he had not long to live. On the following day, which was 6 July 1189, he finally allowed his bed to be carried into the chapel and there made confession, received absolution and took communion. The final blow for him was to hear his vice-chancellor Roger Malchat or Malcheal read out the list of his vassals who were to be pardoned under the treaty for siding with Philip. The first name read out was that of Prince John.[24] Abandoned by both the princes, Henry was consoled in his last hours only by Geoffrey the Bastard.

In the same ritual of spoliation that had left the corpse of the Conqueror with nothing in which to be buried, the body of the count who had risen to govern an empire was abandoned immediately after death while his servants ransacked the castle for anything of value. Returning to prepare the corpse for burial, they found few suitable clothes, an imitation coronet having to be improvised from the golden tassels of a woman's dress. It was to the nearby abbey of Fontevraud, where he had sought to confine Eleanor fifteen years earlier, that the body was conveyed for the funeral service. The poor from many miles around who were waiting along the route in expectation of the customary last alms were sent away empty-handed because the royal treasury was empty.

The community received Henry's remains with the respect due to a great benefactor, and was shocked that the normally observant Richard paid only a brief visit to make sure his father was dead. Unaware that he would be lying in a coffin in the same abbey church in ten years' time, he stayed kneeling by the bier for a few minutes before heading with no display of grief for Chinon, there to possess himself of whatever remained in the Angevin treasury.

The eulogies concentrated on Henry's achievements as king of England, which were considerable in terms of legislation and stability.

In Eleanor's lands of Poitou and Aquitaine, no one grieved his passing, for he had regarded her duchy as a source of revenue to be milked to the last *denier* and prevented the economy from developing outside the handful of great cities. The epitaph on Henry's tomb at Fontevraud included these lines which seem to hint at the grand design:

> Eight feet of ground is now enough for me
> *whom many kingdoms failed to satisfy.*
> Who reads these lines, let him reflect
> upon the narrowness of death,
> and in my case behold
> the image of our mortal lot.
> This scanty tomb doth now suffice
> for whom the earth was not enough.[25]

Finding the treasury at Chinon exhausted by expenditure on weapons, fortifications and mercenaries' salaries, Richard's solution was to place Etienne de Marsai, Henry's seneschal of Poitou, in a dungeon fettered hand and foot until he consented to hand over out of the fortune made during years of tax-farming, a quarter of the annual revenue of the duchy, amounting to some 30,000 pounds Angevin.[26]

Meeting William the Marshal for the first time since their encounter at the ford, Richard accused the master-at-arms of trying to kill him, and received the reply that the lance could just as easily have been aimed at the rider as the mount, had he chosen to do so. The honest rejoinder, so typical of the man, earned him several commissions in England, not least of which was liberating Eleanor.

As reward for the Marshal's services to Henry and in expectation of similar loyalty in the future, Richard also confirmed his father's promise to William of one of the richest heiresses in England,[27] despite having already bestowed her on Count Baldwin of Béthune, who saw his fortunes diminished in favour of a man more useful to Richard. Aged thirty-five, with his best tournament years behind him, William's high destiny was now assured. A member of the mighty Clare family that was said to be related by blood to everyone who was anyone in England, his bride was sole heir to vast estates on both sides of the Channel, for which reason she had been kept thirteen years a ward of the Crown. William departed for England, well pleased with his reward, and turned out to be as loving a husband as he was a loyal knight.

While requiring loyalty of others, Richard merited once again Betran de Born's nickname for him, Aye-and-Nay. His fellow rebels of yesterday found he had no intention of restoring to them possessions confiscated by his father during the early stages of the recent rebellion despite the specific provisions to this effect in the peace treaty of Villandry. What had been Henry's was now his, and was going to stay so. In their first encounter at Gisors, King Philip found that his formerly intimate friend now refused just as adamantly as his father to hand back the castle in whose shadow they were talking – on the grounds that he would marry Alais after his return from crusade, on which even wives were forbidden, and then be entitled to it as her dowry after all.

At Sées the archbishops of Canterbury and Rouen gave Richard absolution for the mortal sin of bearing arms against his father in defiance of the Peace of God while both of them were bound by their crusaders' oaths. This formality accomplished, he was installed in the presence of 21-year-old Prince John on 20 or 29 July as plenary duke of Normandy. Among his first acts were the confirmation of his younger brother's possessions on both sides of the Channel and the marriage Henry had arranged for him to the count of Gloucester's daughter Hawise or Isabelle, despite Henry I being their common great-grandfather.

After giving up his chancellor's seal, Geoffrey the Bastard was appointed by Richard to the vacant see of York, a measure intended to cool any ambition he might have to wear a crown. Six weeks after Henry's death, Richard was at Barfleur, taking ship to England for the all-important ritual of coronation. The Norman and Angevin kings of England did not immediately succeed, so for him to be recognised as king it was necessary for him to be crowned and seen to wear the crown.

William the Marshal, after stopping only to take a proprietorial look over some of his bride's estates near Dieppe, had found Eleanor at Winchester the previous month, not in prison but already liberated on her own authority, her status having risen overnight on the news of Henry's death from the status of VIP prisoner to that of dowager queen of the dual realm. Although she had not been kept in irons in a dungeon like Etienne de Tours or starved on half rations of bread and water like Robert de Sillé, she had nevertheless been subject throughout to Henry's chief justiciar Ranulf de Glanville as his master's whims relaxed and then reimposed the many restrictions under which she had lived for the last decade and a half. Even during the intervals of house arrest and the two journeys she had made to France, she had been under guard.

She was sixty-seven years old and had spent nearly a quarter of her life a prisoner. Virtually everyone of her generation had died; Bernard of

Clairvaux was not only dead but had been recognised as a saint for over a decade. Most released prisoners or hostages of half her age who have suffered only a few weeks' confinement have one thought only: to go home. Home in her case was a land where people spoke her mother tongue, a land of vines and olives where valiant men composed poetry for fair ladies and she was the virtual queen by birth of a proud and independent people. She had surely merited to live in peace and tranquillity for whatever span was left to her, but Eleanor was an extraordinary person by the standards of any age. She had taken a bet with fate that her will would hold out against all the tricks Henry could play, and she had won out in the end.

But that was not enough for her. She had her sights set far higher than mere retirement and inactivity. Henry had cheated her of the power, the dignity and the privileges that were the prerogative of the queen of England, and she was determined to regain them now.

SIXTEEN

The Lady Eleanor

The readjustment period after long confinement can last years; many ex-prisoners remain institutionalised for life. While Eleanor had not been physically maltreated, nor latterly imprisoned, her mental and physical vigour on release were extraordinary for someone so long deprived of the right to make decisions. She ordered a wardrobe fit for the queen she was, secured the treasury at Winchester and London for Richard so that it could not be used to fund a rebellion against him, and then set off on a regal progress through England such as she had not enjoyed since the early years with Henry, staying in the royal palaces as she wished and with no one daring to lift a hand against her or mouth a word of protest. Her erstwhile jailer, the corrupt but capable Ranulf de Glanville, was still chief justiciar, but answerable now to her.[1]

Having as consort neither sworn a coronation oath nor received pledges of loyalty from Henry's vassals, she turned the ambiguity of her position to advantage. Authority undefined, she travelled from city to city and castle to castle, demanding in the name of 'the Lord Richard and the Lady Eleanor'[2] oaths of fealty from every free man in the realm.

239

A similarly assertive interregnal title had been used by Empress Matilda, who styled herself 'Lady of the English' in 1141 when she confidently expected to be crowned after capturing Stephen.

When there was a charter to be signed, she gave it the force of law with her own seal. At Westminster, with William the Marshal at her side, she had the archbishop of Canterbury witness the oath-taking of the greatest magnates of England. For the first time since the Conquest the succession passed without dispute to the eldest surviving son of a dead king. Many of the lords and their ladies present had been infants at the time of Eleanor's disgrace. Because few people of either sex then lived to her age, people saw in her survival physically and mentally intact the resurrection of a legend. Popular etymology held that her name was a compound of *ali*, the rare and regal sea eagle, and *or*, meaning gold.

It was said that the troubadour Richard the Poitevin had prophesied this upturn in her fortunes: 'the eagle of the broken covenant shall be gladdened by her third nest[l]ing'.[3] Certainly she was at least as much eagle as Henry had been, and there was no doubt she had broken her covenant with Louis. And certainly it was her third child of the marriage with Henry who had raised her to these new heights, no matter what he had done before. Like most medieval 'prophecies', this one was probably the fruit of hindsight, but when it was made is unimportant; that it became legend all over Christendom shows how Eleanor's longevity, formidable will and change of fortunes made her appear more than a mere mortal to her contemporaries. In case anyone was in any doubt about her new powers, she revived the title she had never renounced, styling herself, 'by the Grace of God, Queen of the English'.[4]

Few were the Anglo-Norman barons who resisted her authority, for it was common knowledge that Henry's successor – who since his childhood had made only two brief visits to England, at Easter 1176 and Christmas 1184 – had a passion for warfare on a scale that could only be satisfied against non-Christians and would quit England as soon after his coronation as he had amassed enough money for his postponed crusade. Whom could he trust as regent for an absence of two or three years? Not his power-hungry younger brother or Geoffrey the Bastard. Eleanor was the only person with the experience and authority to do the job who would not try to usurp the throne.

Within forty-eight hours of Richard landing at Portsmouth on 13 August, the 31-year-old warrior-king who had not a word of the language spoken by the majority of his island subjects was reunited with her at Winchester. After having the treasury weighed and counted, he gave orders to pay off Henry's last debt: the 20,000 marks for Philip's costs in the recent war, plus 4,000 marks Richard agreed to add to this sum.[5] Amounting to £16,000, this made a considerable dent in the treasury, estimated at a total of £90,000.[6] On 29 August, despite the opposition of the archbishop of Canterbury to the union on the grounds that bride and groom were related in the third degree of consanguinity, John was married. The archbishop placed the estates of both bride and groom under interdict until Pope Clement III granted a dispensation with the curious condition that the couple should have no intercourse. There was in fact no issue to the marriage.

First seal of Richard

At the same time, to gain the support of the Church, Richard relaxed Henry's requirement that strings of riding and packhorses should be kept in every monastery to service the transportation needs of his unpredictable progresses. To win over the nobility, who had resented Henry's policy – copied from his grandfather Henry I – of diluting their ranks with his *novi homines* or new nobles created by elevating through arranged marriages those who served him well, Richard declared all such unions void – which was a second blow for Etienne de Marsai, whose son was one of the new men.

Taking advantage of the interregnum, the Welsh raided several towns across the border. Like a dog with a rabbit, Richard wanted to race off and subdue them, but Eleanor insisted he be crowned first.[7] On 3 September, five days after John's wedding, the coronation at Westminster Abbey assembled the high clergy and nobility of the realm for a ceremony little changed at the coronation of Queen Elizabeth II almost eight centuries later. Dressed in the height of fashion in silks and furs, Eleanor was installed in state as befitted a dowager queen, with her court of ladies- and maids-in-waiting, and no one doubted that she was the power behind the throne.

Conducted solemnly into the abbey behind a limping William the Marshal bearing the gold sceptre with its golden cross – a falling gangway had injured him while boarding the ship at Dieppe en route to England – Richard prostrated himself before the altar, was raised to his feet and swore the triple oath, to preserve the Peace of God, to fight crime, and to show justice and mercy in his judgements. One of the nineteen archbishops and bishops present then asked the assembled clergy, which included thirteen abbots, and the laity, who included John and ten other earls of the realm plus seventeen barons, if they accepted Richard as ruler. Only after their assent could he be anointed.

Gilbert Foliot having recently died, it was the chronicler Ralph of Diceto, in his capacity as dean of London, who handed to Archbishop Baldwin of Canterbury the oil with which to anoint Richard on hands, breast, shoulders and arms and then the chrism – a doubly sanctified oil used only by bishops – with which his head was anointed as a token of the awful sacrament of kingship.

Richard was girded with a sword, in imitation of the ceremony of dubbing a knight, and then crowned by the archbishop, assisted by two doyens of the nobility. After seating the crown securely – for to lose it would have been an evil omen indeed – the archbishop invested Richard with the ring, the sceptre and the rod. Only now was he officially king of England.

In a general amnesty Henry's exiles were recalled and his hostages released; those he had dispossessed were restored.[8] Many of the heiresses he had been keeping – in some cases for years – to bestow on those who served him well were now given to men who would have every reason to praise Richard's generosity and yet would let him down in his hour of need. Not every woman took her imposed husband without protest. A slightly later example was the widowed Countess Hadwisa, described by one catty chronicler as 'a woman almost a man, lacking only the virile organs',[9] who refused point-blank to marry Guillaume de Fors, one of the commanders of Richard's fleet on the Third Crusade. Only after the Crown had seized her estates in Yorkshire and started selling off everything movable did she give in and marry him.

Anticipating Chapter 39 of Magna Carta, Eleanor released or pardoned in Richard's name many thousands held in prisons or outlawed under the oppressive forest laws, but never judged by due process of law. As Roger of Howden commented, it was proof how well the dowager queen knew from experience the hatefulness of being locked away.[10] And yet in all the pomp and revelry there was no mention on that coronation day of poor Alais, who should have been installed on the throne occupied by Eleanor, but was still languishing in Winchester, and would be for years to come.

The public celebrations cost a fortune, literally. Item: 900 cups. Item: 1,770 pitchers. Item: 5,050 dishes.[11] Richard's banquet at Westminster was strictly an affair for men only – and Christian men at that. At the insistence of Archbishop Baldwin, who argued that their presence would taint the holiness of the sacrament of royalty, the Jews of London were not allowed to mar it by presenting tokens of their respect. Having been introduced into England by the Conqueror, they were under the monarch's direct protection because they fitted nowhere else in the feudal system. When some did appear with presents for the king, they were forcibly ejected from the festivities, news of which generated a rumour that Richard had ordered them killed and their homes ransacked. The resultant violence and plundering spread like wildfire.

To avoid the riots spreading to Normandy and Poitou and driving abroad the ready source of loans and taxes his Jews represented, messengers were dispatched forbidding any such excesses in his French possessions in the name of 'Richard, by the grace of God King of the English, Duke of the Normans and Aquitains, Count of the Poitevins'.[12] In London, orders were given to track down the perpetrators, but only three men were caught: one was hanged because he had stolen from a Christian under cover of the riots, and two others because they had set fires which spread to Christian property.

During the three and a half months he spent in England, most of Richard's energy went into raising money for the crusade. He travelled to Guildford and Arundel in the south, to Salisbury and Marlborough in the west, to Warwick and Geddington in the north and to Bury St Edmunds in East Anglia. While he was there, Henry's go-between Cardinal Agnani arrived at Dover to mediate a monastic dispute at Canterbury. The reins of power firmly in her hands, Eleanor spat a reminder at the importunate prelate that he required a safe-conduct before entering the realm, and ordered him to return whence he had come.[13]

With the proceeds of Henry's Saladin tithe already given to the Templars, every office of the Crown was put up for auction to raise cash. Many manors passed into the hands of the Church by mortgages that could never be redeemed. Faithful administrators found themselves bidding for their own posts. Eleanor could take pleasure in Glanville being dispossessed of the most important secular office in the country and ruined by fines totalling £15,000 of silver.[14] Yet she did not accede to Richard's impulse to have him executed for having been her chief jailer. Glanville's death was not far off in any case. After taking the cross to benefit from the fiscal exemptions available to crusaders, he died outside Acre with Archbishop Baldwin of Canterbury before Richard even arrived there.

Two new justiciars were appointed to take over his duties, both elderly. Bishop Hugh of Durham, who had always kept his distance from Henry and governed much of northern England during his reign, shared office with the old king's closest adviser William de Mandeville, earl of Essex. In naming them, Richard was showing more respect for their integrity than their capacity for the work of governing the realm during his long absence.

Everything was for sale: fiefs, offices, titles. William the Marshal bought the sheriffdom of Gloucestershire for 50 marks. Even exemptions from taking the cross could be purchased, thanks to an indulgence from Pope Clement III that was intended to allow those vital for the running of the country to remain in England without sin. When Hugh of Durham purchased the earldom of Northumberland, Richard quipped merrily that he had made a new earl out of an old bishop.[15] Even the right to fortify castles could be had for money. The *pax Henrici secundi* had been imposed and sustained by a relentless programme of destroying adulterine castles and ruthless control of the barons; during Richard's three-month milking of the island realm the work of decades was undone and the tight rein Henry had used to keep the Anglo-Norman barons in check was slackened to start the process that would end with Magna Carta twenty-six years later.

There is no way of estimating how much money was raised in this way because the greater part went directly to Richard; only if the purchaser of an office could not pay was the debt recorded in the Pipe Rolls. Such was the king's hunger for gold that he offered to sell the entire city of London if he could find a buyer rich enough.[16] The new chancellor, who was also made bishop of Ely, had to pay 3,000 pounds for his seal. William Longchamp was the epitome of the 'new man', raised from obscurity to serve his master unquestioningly. Born in Normandy allegedly the grandson of a serf, he had served as Richard's chancellor in Aquitaine, but knew nothing of England or its language.

However, the measure of their closeness was such that the chancellor's seal went to him despite the bishop of Bath bidding £1,000 more for it. Given three castles and the Tower of London, Longchamp spent the enormous sum of £1,200 on repairing and extending it in one year. The only gift he made to the recently completed cathedral at Ely, obliged to accept him as bishop, were some relics including teeth said to be from the head of St Peter. In the normal way, the prior of the cathedral looked after the running of the establishment, leaving Longchamp free to travel far and wide on the king's business.

Meanwhile, Eleanor was making provisions for the style of life she intended leading as regent for however long the crusade might take. She had recovered her dower property and also had Richard attribute to her the same dower possessions that Henry I and Stephen of Blois had given their wives to cover their outgoings.[17] In addition was the 'queen geld' – the supplementary 10 per cent due to her on all fines paid to the king, although this was sometimes commuted at her discretion.

During the long days and nights with only her maid and her own thoughts for company, she had acquired a worldview that commanded the same resentful respect accorded to such other great women as the Empress Matilda and that other Matilda, wife of William the Conqueror, who had governed Normandy for years to leave her husband free to complete his masterly subjugation of the English. Most importantly, Eleanor was immune to the crusading fever that distorted so many political priorities, having learned at first hand the pointlessness of expending so much wealth and so many lives in pursuit of an unattainable goal. Yet to speak out openly against the call to the cross was impossible; all she could do was counsel Richard to take precautions before leaving his realm.

Among many measures enacted early in his ten-year reign, for which the credit has gone to him by default, yet which owe more to his absence, were the institutions of a single currency and standardised systems of measuring length and weights. The last, known by its Norman-French name 'avoirdupois', continued to be used for everything except precious metals and medicines – measured by the Troy system that had originated in Troyes and apothecaries' weights respectively – until replaced by decimalisation in the latter half of the twentieth century.

If Eleanor showed less concern for the government of England than for the continental possessions, it was because they were vulnerable both from without and within, and especially to the friend of yesterday who was now Richard's principal enemy. The house of Capet had suffered so many wrongs both political and personal at Henry's hands that it was inevitable Philip would seek revenge once released from his crusader's vows. History was to prove her fears justified. The empire built by Henry had reached its apogee; ahead lay a process of attrition and erosion which began with the loss of Normandy a few years after her death and continued for so long that it came to be called the Hundred Years War, ending with the English defeat at the battle on the banks of the Dordogne outside Castillon in July 1473 and the surrender of Bordeaux to the French in October of that year.

Richard had originally made his participation in the crusade conditional on John accompanying him. To this, Eleanor would not agree. Should they both die in Outremer, the consequences for the succession would be unthinkable. Before saying goodbye to England on 11 December, hoping that this would satisfy John's hunger for power and land, Richard bestowed on him a total of six English counties – Cornwall, Devon, Dorset, Somerset, Derbyshire and Nottinghamshire, with a string of honours, towns and fortresses running across the breadth of England.

This made him dangerously rich and constituted a state within the state. More prudent would have been to give him fewer honours and fiefs well separated by lands held by loyal vassals, or alternatively to lock him up for the duration of the crusade. As precedents, there was not only Eleanor's long confinement, but also Henry I's twenty-year incarceration of his elder brother Robert Curthose. However, Richard had so little respect for John that he considered him incapable of mounting a rebellion.

Deciding not to use the safe-conducts from the king of Hungary and the Byzantine Emperor in Constantinople which Henry had procured for the overland route to the Holy Land[18] on which Eleanor had suffered so much during the First Crusade, and refusing to be dependent on the profiteering Pisan and Genoese shipowners for the crossing of the Mediterranean, Richard set sail from Dover on 12 December 1189 with a considerable fleet of his own, assembled by requisitioning every suitable ship from Hull to Portsmouth, plus dozens more from the ports of his French possessions. The accounts kept by Henry of Cornhill, controller of the expedition's budget, reveal that most of the ships cost between £50 and £66, the top price being paid for a vessel the king presented to the Hospitallers. Forty ships were purchased, thirty-three of them from the Cinque Ports, partly in cash and the balance by remitting taxes.

Paymasters gave each ordinary seamen in the crews, numbering from twenty-five for the smaller vessels to over sixty for Richard's flagship *Esnecca*, a wage of two pence per day for one year in advance. The skippers received twice that. The logistics operation was enormous: dismantled siege engines, missiles, arrows, hand weapons, armour, supplies of comparatively long-lasting food such as salted fish and meat, dried beans and cheese all had to be purchased and loaded aboard, including thousands of nails and 10,000 horse shoes of the type with which the heavier European horses were customarily shod and which were not easily obtainable in the Holy Land.[19] All was loaded aboard in a fever of activity.

There was nothing Eleanor could do to restrain Richard with the crusading bit between his teeth. He had dismissed the most efficient administrator in England and was leaving his realm in the care of two old men, neither of whom had experience of the task ahead. He had disrupted the tax machinery by replacing nearly every sheriff with a newcomer who knew nothing of the job. He had weakened the monarchy in a hundred ways and given John such power that he virtually ruled a principality already. Not content with making Geoffrey the Bastard the second most powerful churchman in England, he was taking his hierarchical superior the archbishop of Canterbury on crusade with him.

It was a recipe for disaster. On the very day Richard left England, trouble broke out between Hugh of Durham and William Longchamp, each convinced the other was his subordinate.

Putting in at Calais, the crusader king sent the English fleet onwards to join up with ships lying in ports from Caen to Bayonne while he enjoyed Christmas in Normandy at Bures, so obviously delighted to have left the island that he would visit only once more in his ill-fated reign that rumours circulated among the Anglo-Norman nobility to the effect that he intended giving John England and keeping only the continental possessions for himself.[20] Having already spent 70 per cent of the money raised in England on preparations for the crusade, he turned to fund-raising in the continental possessions and the feudal administration of the dual realm; over two-thirds of all his charters as king are dated within the twelvemonth after his accession.

On 13 January 1190, he agreed with Philip that the truce of Villandry be converted into a peace binding on all their vassals, as was fitting between two monarchs who were fellow-crusaders. A month later even Richard was having second thoughts about the mess in which he had left England. Mandeville having died in December, it was plain that Hugh of Durham could not govern alone, even with Eleanor overseeing him. And although William the Marshal was among those appointed justiciars, being honourably excluded from the preparations for crusade by the two years he had spent in the Holy Land in fulfilment of his deathbed promise to Young Henry, he was convalescing with his bride in Surrey and unable to wield much authority.

In a desperate attempt to undo some of the mischief the sale of offices had caused, Eleanor crossed the Channel to Normandy with Prince John, Geoffrey the Bastard and a squabble of prelates that included both the bishop of Durham and Longchamp. Also with her was Alais, a prisoner of the house of Anjou for twenty-one of her thirty years and now, as a pawn in the power-game that would be played out with Philip after the crusade, to be incarcerated in the grim fortress of Rouen.

To resolve the conflict between Durham and Ely, Richard gave the jurisdiction of England north of the River Humber to Bishop Hugh with Longchamp responsible for the rest, but without specifying exactly what were to be their respective powers. Longchamp could always get what he wanted from Richard; at his request, messengers were dispatched to Rome asking that he be named papal legate, which would automatically make him senior to Bishop Hugh. Backtracking over Prince John and his half-brother Geoffrey, Richard forced them to swear not to return to England without his permission during the next three years. Fearing what John might do in collusion with Philip's vassals if he were penned up in the continental possessions, Eleanor persuaded the king to relax this obligation. Geoffrey the Bastard was, however, to remain in exile – an archbishop of York who was forbidden to set foot in England!

North of the Channel crusading fever was rife, with knights reluctant to go and those without any skill at arms who were sneered at as 'Holy Mary's knights'[21] being sent a distaff as a hint that they should take up women's work instead.[22] A more unpleasant form of the disease was a rash of pogroms in several English towns. At King's Lynn, Norwich and Stamford, a mob of both sexes looted Jewish property, ostensibly to pay for the expenses of men going on crusade. The wealthiest Jew in Britain, Aaron of Lincoln, was on friendly terms with the sheriff of Lincolnshire, who arranged for the community in Lincoln to be given shelter in the castle until the danger was past. But the worst excesses were at York, where the Jews were besieged in the castle and committed a Masada-style mass suicide when it became obvious that they could expect no mercy from their persecutors, and at Bury St Edmunds, where fifty-seven Jews were murdered on Palm Sunday.

Richard was angry that their taxable wealth had been stolen or destroyed. Together with his brother Osbert, newly arrived with a convoy of money from the Exchequer, Longchamp was dispatched to England to pursue the wrongdoers. His other brother Henry had bought the sheriffdom of Herefordshire. At the head of a large force, he travelled north and deposed certain office-holders for failing to stop the riots but could not possibly catch all the rioters, although sixty pairs of iron fetters were purchased for those he imprisoned at Lincoln.[23] Among them was William Longchamp's rival, the bishop of Durham.

Instead of settling these affairs himself, Richard agreed with Philip at Dreux to postpone the departure on crusade until July, so that he could punish some dissident vassals in Aquitaine. With him went his young nephew Henry of Saxony, Matilda's son who was to accompany him on the crusade. To give the lad a foretaste of the sport ahead, they took the castle of Chisi in Gascony, whose seigneur had been indulging in the long-established local practice of robbing and holding to ransom pilgrims and other travellers, and hanged him from his own battlements *pour encourager les autres*.[24] Other preparations, interspersed with hunting in the Talmond, included laying down strict rules for shipboard behaviour on the voyage to the Holy Land and splitting his fleet into five squadrons, of which two were to be commanded by bishops and three by laymen – only one of whom was an experienced mariner.

Judging by the number of charters issued over her own seal in the area, Eleanor spent this time at or near Chinon where her long incarceration had begun.[25] But the relatively minor matters she was settling in those charters did not justify her long absence from England where the new chancellor was exceeding his functions in ways that would make life difficult later on. Appointed as a man who had no friends to favour and therefore everything to gain through assiduously taxing everyone to the hilt, Longchamp epitomised Talleyrand's maxim that performing public office with too much zeal was dangerous. So grasping was he that William of Newburgh described him as having two right hands, while Geraldus Cambrensis painted an even less attractive portrait: swart, malformed, low-browed, small of stature, lame and stammering.[26]

Yet Eleanor stayed in France, intent on something she considered more urgent than putting a power-hungry chancellor in his place. The odds were higher that Richard would die from disease in the Holy Land or on the journey there than in combat, but if he succumbed from whatever cause without an heir, there would be another civil war in England between the supporters of Prince John and those who considered that Geoffrey Plantagenet's three-year-old son Arthur of Brittany had a prior claim as the son of John's older brother. There could even be a tripartite war, for although being an archbishop disqualified Geoffrey the Bastard in theory from succeeding as king the father he had loyally served, he was too old and temperamentally unsuited for preferment in the Church and might well renounce the privileges of clerical office to make a bid for the crown.

Not least of the risks, in Eleanor's view, whether or not a civil war broke out in England, it would be no more than natural for Philip to hasten homewards and invade Normandy and the other continental possessions in defiance of the Peace of God, which protected the possessions of a crusader even after his death.

Concluding Richard's long-postponed marriage to Alais was the easiest solution. She was available and known to be fertile, having borne Henry two children; and she had a strategically valuable dowry. But Richard refused this idea point-blank on the grounds that his pride would not let him stoop to marrying soiled goods – a view with which Eleanor concurred. Despite her own years of confinement, she showed not sympathy but contempt for Alais, even though that unfortunate princess had been brought up with her own children and had had no choice in the matter once Henry decided to indulge his lust. Nor would Richard release Alais to begin her life because that would mean handing back Gisors.

But one way or another, Eleanor decided, it was essential that Richard produce an heir before setting foot on the dangerous soil of the Holy Land.

SEVENTEEN

Richard the Hero

W hile preparations for the crusade went ahead in England and France, Eleanor continued to worry about the succession for both personal and political reasons. As ever, Richard was elusive on the subject and could reasonably claim many more urgent priorities.

The rendezvous with Philip took place ten days late at Vézelay on 1 July. Both kings had already received the symbolic pilgrim's staff and scrip; it was seen as a bad omen when the heavily built king of England leaned playfully on his and snapped it clean in two. Having sworn to be as brothers, neither to return before the other, and to share equally any profit from the joint enterprise, the two monarchs set out on 4 July 1190, travelling together as far as Lyon. The main contingents had already gone ahead. While Philip took the overland route to Genoa, Richard turned south to Marseilles, where his ships would have been waiting, but for contrary winds at the entrance to the Mediterranean.[1] Instead, he hired some Pisan merchant vessels to take his immediate entourage to Genoa, where Philip requested the loan of five English galleys. Richard offered three. Insulted, Philip turned them down. It was the first overt sign of the tension between them that would undermine the whole crusade.

From Genoa, Richard made a leisurely Grand Tour of western Italy, sailing from one port to the next and then travelling by land to where the Pisan ships awaited him for the following stage of the journey. Arriving at the Sicilian port of Messina several days after the French and finding its gates closed to him, he invested the city in a rage, his artificers rehearsing the siege of Acre by assembling a huge siege-tower from the parts stowed in his ships. These enormous structures were given humorously affectionate nicknames by the troops; this one was *Mategriffon*, or 'Greek-killer', because the majority of the inhabitants of Messina were Greek-speaking.

Proclaiming that any soldier who ran away would have a foot amputated and any knight guilty of cowardice would be reduced to the ranks, Richard deliberately let the defenders waste all their ammunition without firing a single shot.[2] From the tower's platform, higher than the city walls, crossbowmen then rained bolts down on the defenders. The battlements thus cleared of defenders, his shock troops lowered the drawbridge and took Messina after only five hours' fighting. The city served as Richard's winter quarters with *Mategriffon* looming over it and a well-used gallows beside it reminding the natives to behave themselves.

On the death the previous November of Joanna's husband William II, the Sicilian nobles had elected his bastard nephew Count Tancred of Lecce as their new ruler to prevent the German Emperor from claiming the throne by virtue of his marriage to William's aunt Constance. Wary of the presence of two crusader armies on his island and rightly fearing Richard's anger at his appropriation of Joanna's dowry to line his own coffers, Tancred was holding Eleanor's second daughter hostage in Palermo at the other end of Sicily.

Richard immediately demanded both his sister's release and the implementation of William II's promise to Henry of precious jewels and ships for use on the crusade.[3] Torn between this and the spectre of Constance reappearing on the island backed by her husband's armies, Tancred chose the lesser evil, restored Joanna to her brother and made good the legacy by a payment of 40,000 ounces of gold, some of which was shared with Philip.

He was looking for a new wife to replace Isabelle of Hainault, who had died in childbirth at the age of twenty,[4] and saw in Joanna a suitable queen for France. A beautiful and spirited woman of twenty-five, polished by her upbringing in Fontevraud and at the court of Poitiers, she was ready for some other great destiny after thirteen years as queen of the cosmopolitan kingdom of Sicily. However, Richard quenched the fires of Philip's fancy with the waters of the Straits of Messina, by seizing the priory of Bagnara on the Calabrian mainland to serve as her palace so there could be no contact between them.[5]

Tancred having sent Joanna's bed with her, Richard now dunned him for the rest of her furniture, including a gilded table twelve feet long, a golden chair and a dinner service of twenty-four gold and silver plates and drinking vessels. Advised by his Muslim counsellors to play upon the mutual jealousy of his two unsought royal guests as Manuel Comnenus had done with the Germans and French in the Second Crusade, Tancred sent valuable gifts to Philip but none to Richard. Instead, he took him on a tour of holy sites near Mount Etna[6] to create an opportunity of showing him letters apparently bearing Philip's seal in which Richard was painted as an untrustworthy cheat, against whom the Sicilians and Franks should unite.

Impetuously accepting the letters as genuine, Richard moderated his demands for Joanna's dowry and signed a treaty acknowledging Tancred as rightful king of Sicily, in which he undertook to defend Sicilian possessions on the mainland against the German Emperor. After declaring Arthur of Brittany his heir, he betrothed him to Tancred's elder daughter[7] and presented his new ally with a sword claimed to be King Arthur's legendary Excalibur. In return, Tancred paid back the last 40,000 bezants of Joanna's dowry and provided nineteen ships.

Dividing her attention between the government of England and the continental possessions and the hunt for a wife for Richard, Eleanor can hardly have been pleased when news of the treaty reached her. While she thought John would make a poor king, for the crown of England to pass to three-year-old Arthur was as good as handing it to Philip on a plate. And once John heard, she knew that his paranoid nature would regard it as carte blanche for treason, since his only reason to behave in Richard's absence was a reasonable expectation of one day succeeding his brother without any struggle.

In Sicily, when Richard confronted Philip with the letters, they were declared forgeries created by Tancred's Muslim counsellors to drive a wedge between two Christian monarchs. That Richard had taken them at their face value was yet another insult to his family, Philip insisted, reciting a long list of other grievances that inevitably included the matter of Alais and the return of Gisors. Having heard rumours of Eleanor sounding out various potential royal brides, he declared that a repudiation of his half-sister after all these years' abuse of her would be an unbearable affront to the house of Capet and earn his undying enmity.[8] Richard retorted that it was contrary to Nature for a man to marry his own father's mistress, who had borne him children.[9] They had come a long way since sharing bed and board in Paris.

Some time in November Count Philip of Flanders, a vassal of Philip who was related to Richard by birth and marriage, brokered a settlement releasing him from his obligation to marry Alais. Under this, she was to be returned to Philip at the end of the crusade with her dowry enhanced by the sum of 10,000 marks which he could use to marry her off to whom he pleased. Philip accepted the settlement as the best he was likely to get, but it was no sudden change of heart on Richard's part that had caused him to yield Gisors. He had heard from Eleanor that she had found him a wife.

Aquitaine had always had close links with its southern neighbour Navarre, whose King Sancho the Wise had a daughter called Berengaria. Flattered at the idea of becoming father-in-law to the king of England, Sancho agreed to the match despite Eleanor refusing to give up any of the English queen's marriage portion, which she intended keeping for herself. Instead, she offered Berengaria the county of Gascony and the Ile d'Oléron, plus several towns on both sides of the Channel.

To finalise the arrangement, Eleanor travelled in person across the Pyrenees to make sure that Berengaria was of such submissive character as to give reasonable hope that Richard might perform his duty of getting her with child. Aged twenty-five, she was no pretty young thing to tease a sex-starved crusader into bed. She was educated, literate, docile and spoke a dialect of Occitan. Most importantly, she was not within the prohibited degrees of consanguinity. As to her looks (see plate 24), all the chroniclers could find in her favour was that she was prudent, gentle and virtuous. Richard was said to have composed a poem in her honour while her father's guest at the court of Navarre in 1177, but that was no more than gallantry.

Given the importance of speed in bringing bride and groom together, it is strange that Eleanor went to Spain instead of sending her bishops to agree the transaction and escort Berengaria to Poitiers. Whatever her reasons for going in person, Berengaria passed her scrutiny and rode back to Poitiers with her future mother-in-law, presumably receiving instruction from Eleanor on the way as to the by no means straightforward wifely duties expected of her.

Money never stayed long in her future husband's treasure chests. Much of the settlement received from Tancred was spent over Christmas in a series of luxurious feasts and magnificent tournaments to persuade the other crusader leaders and their vassals who was the more important of the two monarchs present. But Richard's PR campaign turned sour when a Frankish knight by name of Guillaume des Barres unwisely wounded his vanity in a mêlée and was not forgiven. Because incidents of this kind were bound to occur with so many warriors pumping adrenalin and spoiling for a fight, Philip rightly wanted to leave as soon as possible. Bored by the long wait, some of Eleanor's vassals, including Geoffroi de Rancon, swore to go with him to fight the infidel rather than wait any longer in Sicily with Richard. Others departed without their leaders, who were soon listening to the inevitable tales of their deaths from the climate, food poisoning, disease and internecine conflict.[10]

Eventually trapped by the winter gales, Richard and Philip settled down to sniping at each other while an intermittent stream of clerics and *nuncii* or royal messengers rode and sailed between Sicily and France and England, some of them crossing paths with Eleanor. Putting her sixty-eight years behind her, she was risking the winter weather and the perils of an even longer journey than the recent expedition to Navarre in order to accompany Berengaria across France and through the Alpine passes with the whole length of Italy ahead of her. She knew her son too well to give Richard the chance of not going through with the marriage, were his bride to arrive alone when he had the dual alibi of his crusader's oath of chastity and the papal prohibition on taking women to the Holy Land.

While his mother was exhausting herself on the continent, Prince John was exploiting the universal detestation of Longchamp to travel the length and breadth of the island realm, winning over the Anglo-Norman nobility and the common people, whose language he alone of the royal family could speak fluently. With only a one-in-four chance of a crusader returning from the Holy Land – and Richard was famous for being in the forefront of every fight – making friends with John was three times more likely to pay off than remaining obstinately loyal to a monarch who cared nothing for his English vassals.

Whether by accident or design, at Lodi, south of Milan, Eleanor's path crossed that of the new German Emperor Henry Hohenstaufen on his way to Rome for his imperial coronation. A record of their meeting would be interesting, for Barbarossa's successor was extremely displeased by Richard's recent recognition of Tancred's territorial pretensions in Sicily and southern Italy – and would exact a cruel price for it on Richard's return from the Holy Land. But the meeting passed off with at least the usual courtesies, Eleanor being invited to witness one of the emperor's charters before leaving his court.

From there the simplest route would have been to head for the coast and take ship to Sicily, but Eleanor continued her mission by land, buying safe-conducts as she went, since there had not been time to arrange the journey in advance. Richard currently had some 200 vessels at his disposal, not all of them simultaneously being careened and refitted for the onward voyage. That he did not order one to fetch the dowager queen and the future queen of England, or have his agents on the mainland reserve other shipboard accommodation for them may well have been his last attempt to avoid the marriage in the expectation that he would have left Sicily before Eleanor and Berengaria arrived.

If that was the case, he reckoned without his mother's determination. Pressing on by land until she sent a Sicilian vessel to collect them for the last stage of the long journey, she brought Berengaria across the Straits of Messina on 30 March. It was not a moment too soon, for the French under Philip had finally set sail the previous day. Their departure meant that celebrating the wedding in Sicily would have been more tactful than doing so after arrival in the Holy Land, where it would constitute a flagrant insult to Philip and his half-sister still locked up in Rouen Castle. Yet even the archbishop of Canterbury could not marry a king in Lent, so the wedding was postponed.

It was for Eleanor a brief reunion with her favourite son and Joanna, the daughter she hardly knew.[11] Four extremely busy days after arriving in Sicily, the situation in England caused her to set out on the homeward journey with letters from Richard appointing the Cornish-born Archbishop Walter of Rouen as replacement for the unpopular Longchamp, leaving Berengaria at Bagnara with Joanna as her chaperone. Something of their pointless existence is conveyed in the comment that they were as happy in each other's company as 'two doves in a cage'.[12]

To get around the embargo on women accompanying the crusade by a technicality, they set sail eastbound three days later in advance of the main invasion fleet of 150 sailing ships and 53 galleys. Their vessel was a *dromon* – a fast Byzantine armed merchantmen with fore- and aftercastles, a lateen sail and fifty oars on each side, each rowed by one man. It had ample space for the considerable baggage of the two royal ladies and was escorted by two other vessels.

Leaving Sicily on 10 April, Richard's fleet stopped over in Crete and Rhodes, probably to allow the horses to recover health and strength. Being unable to vomit during storms, many destriers were severely distressed on arrival in the Holy Land, suffering from the diet of dry grain and stale water, and with muscular problems from being cooped up in stalls below decks.[13] Making landfall for the third time at Limassol on Cyprus, where the *dromon* carrying Joanna and Berengaria had been driven by a storm in which two English ships were crippled and pillaged by wreckers, Richard demanded reparation from Isaac Comnenus, the self-appointed Byzantine 'emperor' of the island.

When Comnenus refused, Richard unleashed his army in a blitzkrieg conquest of the island, whose grain harvest would go far to feed the hungry besiegers of Acre, themselves partly besieged by encircling Muslim forces. In a three-week campaign, he added the island to his other possessions. Taken prisoner, Isaac Comnenus' daughter was placed in Joanna's care as a hostage,[14] but it was not until 30 May – eleven months after the joint departure from Vézelay and ten days after Philip's arrival at Acre – that her father surrendered, trusting Richard's promise not to put him in irons. He was instead thrown into a dungeon, fettered with silver chains.

By then Richard was married at last, after putting off this duty of state until only a few months short of his thirty-fourth birthday. With Lent over and no shortage of priests and bishops to perform the ceremony, he could hardly delay any longer. Despite his cruelty and the

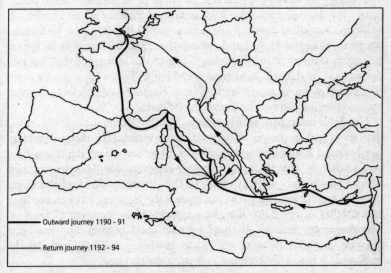

Outward journey 1190 - 91

Return journey 1192 - 94

Richard's route on the Third Crusade

forbidden side of his life, Richard was devout. In order to take communion at the wedding he had to confess and afterwards expiate the sin of sodomy by being publicly flogged in his underwear. Given absolution after the act of contrition, he was united in matrimony to the hapless Navarrese princess who, on having a coronet placed on her head by the bishop of Evreux, became the first and only queen of England who never set foot in the country.

The wedding ceremony took place in the small citadel chapel of St George. The bride's appearance is a mystery, although we know the groom was magnificently attired in a rose-coloured *cotte*, embroidered with silver crescents that glittered in the sunlight, and a scarlet bonnet richly worked with figure animals and birds. His spurs were golden, as was the handle of his sword, and the mounts of his scabbard were silver. The saddle of his sleek Spanish charger also glittered with spangles.[15]

All this splendour and display was, of course, illicit under his crusader's vows. What the bride wore was seemingly of no interest to the celibate chroniclers, for no account survives. Whether or not the eight-year marriage was ever consummated remains as much a mystery as her appearance, for there was no issue. His crusader's vow was not the only obstacle; although Richard had acknowledged paternity of a bastard by a serving girl in his youth, one bastard for a king who died aged forty-one was hardly proof of sexual prowess with women.

Among the wedding guests was the king of Jerusalem – none other than Guy de Lusignan, who had ambushed Eleanor when Patrick of Salisbury was killed twenty years before. Exiled by Henry, he had made his fortune in the Holy Land, where there was always a shortage of European warriors of suitable lineage due to the ravages of the climate, disease and the hazards of intrigue and combat. Following a similar path to that taken by Eleanor's uncle, Prince Raymond of Antioch, he had married Sibylle, sister of the leper King Baldwin.

On Baldwin's death, swiftly followed by that of his six-year-old son – due, some said, to poison – Guy's wife had inherited the throne, making her husband king of Jerusalem. She and her two young daughters had died of disease while living in the siege camp outside Acre, leaving her widower with only a shaky claim to the throne.[16] Guy had therefore come to beg Richard's support not against the Saracen, but because half the nobility of the Latin Kingdom supported his opponent Conrad of Montferrat. Impetuously, Richard espoused the Lusignan cause not only because Guy's family were his vassals but because Philip had already endorsed Conrad of Montferrat's claim to the throne.

Meanwhile, Eleanor was in Rome visiting Celestine III in her capacity as queen-regent of England, and making certain provisions that were to prove timely. It was not the first time they had met. Berengaria or not, she saw no reason to renounce her title, queen of the English, and it was thus she addressed the new pope on Easter Sunday, the day after his election. He was a former friend of Becket and student of Peter Abelard, whom she had known during her years on the Ile de la Cité as Cardinal Giacinto, or Hyacinth.

One of her requests was for the immediate consecration of Geoffrey the Bastard as archbishop of York, to stop him contending for the throne and complicating the Longchamp–Walter–Prince John situation. Her powers of persuasion led Celestine not only to acquiesce but exceptionally also give her Geoffrey's *pallium* – the scarf of lamb's wool that was a bishop's badge of office, and which he usually had to travel to Rome to request in person.

Richard's army anchored off Acre on 8 June. The city had been under siege for two years, for although Saladin was a brilliant general he was unable to stop the constant trickling away of the various Muslim contingents theoretically under his command and never had enough men at his disposal at any one time to mount a relief operation. The French were bearing the brunt of the fighting, along with what was left of the German army that had fought its way through Turkey under Frederik Barbarossa, reduced by many taking the opportunity to return home prematurely after his accidental death by drowning in the icy River Göksu.

Disembarking on 10 June, Richard found Philip ill from dysentery in the siege camp and suffering badly from the summer heat, which rendered even mail armour like an oven, despite the surcoats worn over them as insulation. After three months encamped outside Acre in the heat and stench caused by lack of sanitation, contagious infection and poisoning by unclean food was taking its usual toll of the Frankish besiegers. Some men had already been flogged for resorting to cannibalism.[17] In addition, Philip was depressed by the perpetual bickering of the various European contingents who on occasion cheered a telling blow by the enemy during a sortie, pleased that fellow-Christians of another language or country were in trouble.

Succumbing soon after his arrival to a bad bout of the malaria that had troubled him for years, Richard had himself carried on a litter from point to point, directing operations. With all his years of experience in the arts of war, he had made his preparations well. The latest models of prefabricated English and Poitevin siege-towers and catapults he had brought with him, with their jokey names like *Malvesin* or 'Bad

Neighbour', were added to those already in position around the beleaguered city to ensure its rapid reduction. Far from welcoming this, his allies, who had spent a year and more blockading the city, resented the newcomers, whom they suspected of being likely to claim an inordinate share of the credit for victory. Continuing his policy of undermining Philip, who was paying three gold pieces per man per month to local reinforcements, Richard now poached them by offering four.

In company with Archbishop Walter of Rouen, Eleanor had obtained letters from the Pope demoting Longchamp from the status of prelate. Because of the delays of travel, it was normal to have several sets of letters to fit different circumstances on arrival. She also had letters from Richard to William the Marshal and the other justiciars covering just about every move that Longchamp or Prince John might make. After borrowing 800 marks from the Templars, or moneylenders, she left Rome with Archbishop Walter and journeyed north. Once through the Alps, he headed for England and she returned to Normandy, reaching Rouen on 24 June.

It is impossible to exaggerate the horror behind the sterilised accounts of medieval warfare. Outside the walls of Acre, the besiegers were fighting malaria and dysentery, typhoid fever from contaminated water and tick-borne typhus. Cholera might break out at any moment and rats feeding on the refuse brought the risk of plague. Night and day, the crusaders catapulted into the city missiles of stone and iron and fire, as well as living and dead prisoners and putrid carcasses of animals designed to spread disease among the defenders, who in turn operated counter-batteries of catapults, often returning the same missiles, and raining down on the attackers arrows, stones and fire.

At night the thudding of catapults and rams, the yells of exultation and screams of the wounded, prevented those who were not exhausted from sleeping.[18] The elegant pavilions of the nobles gave some respite from the clouds of flies breeding in the open latrines, and the sand flies and mosquitoes that bit every inch of exposed flesh, but many men slept in the open, even on the ground, despite the risk of scrub typhus.

Saladin sent heralds far and wide announcing the call to lift the siege, but his emirs refused to attack the vastly increased forces of the besiegers.[19] His inability to compel obedience was the crusaders' most potent weapon. On 12 July the garrison, dying of thirst, surrendered in defiance of his orders after a last vain attempt by his nephew to fight a way through with a relief column.

The crusaders' entrance into the city was marred by disputes over booty and fatal outbreaks of violence over rival claims to prestigious locations. Philip's Franks set themselves up in what had formerly been the Templars' quarters, but when Richard's contingent found themselves competing with the Austrians for the royal palace, an incident occurred which was to cost everyone in England dearly. The pennant of Duke Leopold of Austria, floating beside Richard's standard, was torn down and cast by some unnamed Plantagenet knight or man-at-arms into the filth of the moat, used as an open sewer. Given the arrogance of Richard and his followers since their late arrival, the insult was taken as intended.

So bad was the relationship with Philip that, when his son and heir had been ill, Richard reportedly told him as a joke that the child had died.[20] Getting steadily sicker with scurvy from the vitamin-deficient diet, Philip had by now lost his hair and nails,[21] and was so weak that his advisers feared he was dying. From trench mouth or Vincent's disease, he was also losing teeth. Ten days after the fall of Acre, a deputation of Frankish nobles came to Richard, begging him to release their king from the reciprocal oath to return home together. The scornful reply was that it would be a shameful thing to renounce the crusade before the liberation of Jerusalem, but if Philip's life depended on it, he could depart.[22]

With every penny spent, Philip now demanded a half-share in the loot from Cyprus to pay his homeward voyage,[23] to which Richard retorted that he wanted half of Flanders in return, Count Philip having died without heir soon after arriving at Acre.[24] Richard was touching bottom financially and anxiously awaiting the ransom money promised by Saladin for the 3,000 prisoners taken at Acre. On 31 July 1191 Philip set sail from Acre in a small squadron of Genoese galleys, putting in at Tyre before making his way through the pirate-infested Aegean islands via Rhodes and Corfu, where he waited for a safe-conduct from Tancred of Sicily and the German Emperor to pass through their territories.

Back in the Holy Land, Richard was enjoying his now undisputed position as the leader of the crusade, and counting among his forces 10,000 Franks left behind under Hugues de Bourgogne.[25] They proved to be a mixed blessing because they had to be fed and equipped, for which he was relying on the arrival of the 200,000 dinars that had been demanded for the garrison's ransom, of which Philip had renounced his share.

When the ransom was delayed, Richard decided to stop feeding the useless mouths of the surrendered inhabitants of Acre, and personally supervised the slaughter of 2,700 soldiers of the garrison and 300 women and children belonging to them, including infants at the breast.

Roped together in one mass of terrified flesh, they were hacked and stabbed and stoned to death, their bellies slit open in the search for valuables they might have swallowed and the bodies afterwards burned so that the ashes could be sifted for gold or precious stones.[26]

Such massacres were 'justified' militarily on the grounds that news of them would incline the inhabitants of cities similarly besieged in the future to surrender swiftly in the hope of milder treatment. However, even by the standards of medieval warfare and after a century of conflict between European Christians and Muslims in the Middle East, an atrocity on this scale made Richard the bogey man used by Arab mothers for centuries to come to frighten naughty children: 'Be good or *melek Ric* [King Richard] will get you.'

The only real battle of the campaign took place two weeks after leaving Acre. In the forest of Arsouf, south of Jerusalem, massed charges of the heavy Christian cavalry were claimed to have left 7,000 Turks dead on the field of battle, but since Saladin was able to continue harassing the Christian column two days later,[27] this seems an exaggerated body count. Even casualties on a quarter of that scale, together with their injured and dead horses, makes an appalling scene, with wounded Saracens afterwards stripped and killed or left to die in the open. On the winning side, this second victory led to high hopes for the crusade.

In Rome, with the traces of his illness evident on his face and body, Philip was released from his crusader's vow by Pope Celestine.[28] His request to be allowed a dispensation from the Peace in order to seize the opportunity to right the wrongs of the Alais/Vexin/Flanders complex met with no such success, probably because Eleanor on her stopover in Rome had briefed the pope on the Plantagenet reaction to any such move.[29]

Further north, Philip had a meeting with the German Emperor. Henry Hohenstaufen was settling scores with Tancred and ready to listen to all the Franks' tales discrediting the Plantagenet ally of his Sicilian enemies. He was also related to both the insulted duke of Austria and the imprisoned king of Cyprus and his daughter, still held prisoner in Joanna's household. However, the claim that he swore there and then to take personal revenge on Richard, should he pass through any part of the empire on his way home,[30] sounds like a later invention, for there was no particular reason at that moment for Richard to travel across his domains.

In England, William Longchamp had been making enemies at every level. Nobody loved the rapacious chancellor whose exactions drained the country to finance the absent king's distant enterprise, certainly not his fellow bishops, who had only one thought when Archbishop Baldwin of Canterbury died on the crusade. Fearful that Longchamp's intimacy with the king would give him the leverage to have himself installed as primate of all England,[31] they found the moment to strike after Geoffrey the Bastard was consecrated by Archbishop Bartholomew at Tours and invested with the *pallium*.

Not wishing to lose the revenues of the see of York, which had been coming to the Crown as did those of all vacant sees, Longchamp peremptorily ordered the widowed countess of Flanders to prevent Geoffrey reaching England from any of her ports. Diplomatically, she allowed his household, who were under no such embargo, to cross on 13 September and shut her eyes to Geoffrey crossing more quietly the following day. Landing at Dover in mid-morning, he was ordered by the water-guard to report to Longchamp's sister Richeut, wife of the absent castellan, but fled to Canterbury, where Longchamp's men arrested him in St Martin's Priory. Dragged outside with his head banging on the ground, screaming excommunications on those who had laid hands on him,[32] Geoffrey was offered a mount, but refused it as belonging to men he had excommunicated and was forced to walk the twenty miles back to Dover.

His arrest was seen by the bishops as an affront to their collective dignity – an attitude that John was happy to exploit by championing their cause at the Council of Reading. On the strength of the empowerment prudently obtained by Eleanor in Rome, which permitted Archbishop Walter of Rouen to call the chancellor to account if necessary, Longchamp was summoned from Windsor, one day's ride to the east. Learning when halfway there the strength of the forces arrayed against him, he turned tail and took refuge in the Tower of London,[33] for which disobedience he was excommunicated by the archbishop of Rouen. That night the jubilant citizens defied his orders to keep the gates of London closed against his pursuers.

The following morning, several thousand of them gathered in the open ground east of the Tower and called Longchamp to come out and defend himself, which he did astutely and bravely enough, warning them all against John's ambitions and the danger of treason, for which they risked not only temporal justice but also the sanctions of the Church so long as Richard was on crusade. But his arguments were in vain. Two days later, meeting at St Paul's, the Great Council listened to the archbishop of Rouen and William the Marshal read the letters brought back by Eleanor from Messina,[34] after which they banished Longchamp and replaced him as chancellor by Walter of Rouen.

Exceeding their brief, the council gave Prince John the fine-sounding but constitutionally meaningless title 'supreme governor of the realm',[35] which purported to give him precedence over even the chief justiciar. Longchamp's men were summarily dismissed and new castellans, sheriffs and other officials sworn in. Interestingly, in the context of the growth of non-feudal power, the citizens of London exacted from the assembled magnates as the price for their support a recognition of their commune, entitled to elect its mayor, aldermen and other officers.

Holed up in the Tower, Longchamp argued that surrendering his seal and castles would be treason, but gave in after long negotiation. Allowed to keep the castles of Dover, Cambridge and Hereford because they were so far apart as to constitute no threat, he gave his word that he would not leave England without permission, handing over his brothers and chamberlain as sureties. On 12 October he was escorted to the castle at Dover, where his sister had held Geoffrey prisoner.

Lying low there with her for five days, he abandoned his brothers to their fate on emerging the following Thursday disguised as a woman in a long green gown, with the hood pulled over his face. For once, his small and unimposing stature was an asset until, waiting on the foreshore while his servants attempted to hire a boat to take them across the Channel, he was accosted and groped by a curious fisherman. His sex revealed, Longchamp was rescued by his servants, but on being questioned in English by a local woman and being unable to reply, he was attacked by a suspicious crowd and locked up in a cellar.[36]

The universal ridicule earned by his attempted escape was thought punishment enough for the former papal legate who had been so puffed up with pride as to use the royal 'we' on occasion. Before the end of the month, Prince John gave orders that Longchamp should be allowed to leave the country. Spirits rising once across the Channel, the disgraced prelate followed the same path as the Plantagenet princes when they had fallen out with Henry, travelling to Paris, where he was acclaimed with all appropriate ecclesiastical dignity – some said, in return for bribes.[37] Confusingly, he was also confirmed in office by cardinals Jordan and Octavian, in the city on papal.business.[38]

Hearing rumours that they had come to repair the breach between Rouen and Ely, and suspecting anyone who came to her from the direction of Paris, Eleanor declined to receive them when they crossed into her territory at Gisors, ordering the seneschal of Normandy to inform the prelates that they could travel no further without her safe-conduct. Their reply in retreating was to excommunicate the seneschal and his garrison, and place the duchy of Normandy under interdict – without excommunicating its duchess who had neatly avoided putting her name to any specific action for which she could be so punished.

Emboldened by the cardinals' support, Longchamp ignored his own excommunication and excommunicated just about everyone in England who had taken sides openly against him with the exception of Prince John. This incited Geoffrey the Bastard to excommunicate his own suffragan, the bishop of Durham. The archbishop of Rouen escalated matters by placing Longchamp's diocese of Ely under interdict. Even the bishops themselves disagreed about who could excommunicate whom, with results that would have been comic if they were not taken seriously by the mass of the population.

The season of Advent leading to Christmas 1191 was fraught, with entire counties denied the sacrament in the Plantagenet domains on both sides of the Channel. Church bells had been removed and laid on the ground, as were the statues within; weddings could not be celebrated; the dead had to be temporarily buried in fields, awaiting the lifting of the sanctions to be interred in consecrated ground. The man who had caused all this anguish for the common people now attempted to enlist Eleanor in his cause, without success. At Rouen, where she had taken up residence, she avoided meeting Longchamp on the pretext that it was forbidden for a Christian to eat, drink or have any dealings with an excommunicate. At the same time she showed what she personally thought of the widespread abuse of ecclesiastical sanctions by appealing successfully to Celestine to undo all the chaos due to his cardinals' espousal of Longchamp's cause.[39] Visiting the unhappy diocese of Ely a few months later, she took mercy on the population and had the archbishop of Rouen lift the interdict under which they suffered.[40]

To make matters worse, while she was still at Bures holding court for Richard's Norman vassals, Philip returned to Paris on 31 December with the pope's blessing. Holding his court in Fontainebleau, he was hailed a hero of Christendom, much as his father had been after returning from Outremer in 1149. The spin-doctors on the Ile de la Cité acclaimed him as the chief architect of the fall of Acre, whose illness on crusade was due to poison introduced into his food or drink by the enemies whose repeated treachery had eventually forced him to flee the Holy Land.[41] As to who the chief of these enemies might be, there was only one answer. Who would seek to injure a Christian prince dedicated to the salvation of the Holy Sepulchre, if not the family responsible for so many other woes of the Capetian realm?

To reinforce his alibi, Philip went everywhere with a strengthened bodyguard and ordered his vassals to strengthen their fortifications, as though already under threat from Normandy and Anjou. Seeing in this the preparation for a pre-emptive strike, Eleanor in turn ordered similar preparations on her side of the uneasy frontier. On 20 January 1192 Philip met the constable of Normandy near Gisors, showed him the settlement with Richard brokered by the Count of Flanders in Messina, and demanded the return of Alais with her castles.

This being refused despite menaces, he retired with the promise of returning in far greater force, to gain by arms what he could not obtain by negotiation.[42] On other fronts, his return from the Holy Land was enabling him quietly to expand his power base. The succession of Flanders gained him much of Artois, the Amiénois, Vermandois and Beauvais. Having lost most of his father's chief vassals to disease and combat during the crusade, he was determined that their successors would know a strong suzerain from the outset.

About this time Eleanor heard from England that Prince John was planning to stab her in the back, having assembled a small army of mercenaries, with whom to perform knight service as Philip's vassal, invading Normandy alongside the Frankish forces, after which he would marry Alais and be declared duke of Normandy.[43] Refusing to withdraw to her own inherited possessions and lie low while these troubles in the north resolved themselves, Eleanor's instinct was to attack fast. John may have thought that Philip intended establishing him as duke of Normandy and quietly retiring, but she had no illusions that Frankish incursions would stop there; once having transgressed against the Peace of God, Philip would have nothing to lose by moving against the whole Plantagenet Empire, province by province.

Travelling with something like Henry's speed in similar circumstances, she defied the elements in yet another winter crossing of the Channel. Landing at Portsmouth, she ignored Prince John making his preparations in nearby Southampton, rightly reasoning that he was impotent if deprived of the sources of his wealth. Instead, she convened in Windsor, London, Oxford and Winchester a series of meetings of the Great Council.[44] The magnates had been prepared to stand aside from John's manoeuvrings with Philip on condition that their own fiefs in Normandy were not directly threatened. Employing all the tricks of dialectic that she had learned so long ago on the Ile de la Cité and invoking the Peace of God in Richard's protection, Eleanor convinced them that their rightful king was still very much alive and would shortly return from the Holy Land to call them all to account for their actions in his absence.

Talked around by this woman old enough to be their mother – in some cases, their grandmother – the magnates were coerced into threatening John with the confiscation of all the possessions they had allowed him to keep, should he cross the Channel. Sulkily, but without bloodshed, he retired to his castle at Wallingford after dismissing his disappointed mercenaries. Eleanor's political *coup* was a masterly solution to a situation that could have cost thousands of lives, but the respite it bought was short because the game was changed by the reappearance on the board of a piece everyone had thought out of play.

Longchamp crossed to Dover and, from the safety of its castle, declared himself still bishop and chancellor. The magnates now sought to use John's powers as 'supreme governor' to rid themselves of this persistent nuisance. For that, the sulking prince demanded a better price than the £700 in silver which, he said, Longchamp had offered to pay within the week for his support.[45]

In the Holy Land, the majority of the crusaders were dead from one cause or another, with the more prudent survivors heading homeward, their health broken and financially ruined. Enmeshment in the internecine politics of the Latin Kingdom weakened the military effect of those who remained. Both sides in the conflict had their fanatics. The *Sufi* believed that dying in battle with the Christians guaranteed them an immediate place in paradise; what has been called 'the cult of martyrdom' in the Christian military orders likewise encouraged heroic but useless self-sacrifice. By now even the Templars and Hospitallers, whose Orders existed for no other reason than to protect pilgrims and fight the Saracen, were divided on the course to be followed.

The many instances of Richard's personal bravery had become legendary and would eventually win him the posthumous sobriquet 'Lionheart', yet he had failed totally to show the qualities of leadership, decisiveness or persistence in following up temporary gains as Henry would have done. Oblivious of the sufferings of the rank-and-file, he had enjoyed courteous relationships with Saladin and his other noble opponents, sending them jewels, arms, horses and finely bred greyhounds and lyamhounds, trackers kept on a leash and trained to hunt by scent. In return he had been sent fresh fruit and iced sherbets by his gallant enemy during his repeated bouts of malaria. And although he had gained some victories and twice come within sight of Jerusalem's walls, the Third Crusade had failed to recapture the Holy City from the infidel.

The winter was spent uselessly rebuilding the defences of the southern port city of Ashkelon while families and loved ones back home waited and wondered whether they would ever again see the husbands, fathers and brothers who had taken the cross. Raimbaut de Vaqueyras, one of the troubadours who sought refuge in Italy to escape the Albigensian crusade, expressed their anguish:

> *Altas ondas que venez suz la mar*
> *que fai lo vent çay e lay demenar*
> *de mon amic savez novas contar*
> *qui lay passet – no lo vei retornar*
> *E ay, Deu d'Amor !*
> *Ad hora m'dona joy et ad hora dolor!*

[Great waves that come from far, far out to sea / raised up by ocean winds no one knows where / bring me news of my friend, wherever he may be. / He crossed you but has not returned to me. / O, God of Love, why do you / give me joy, and give me such pain too?]

From England came a letter from Longchamp reporting Prince John's conspiracy with Philip to usurp the crown. Yet Richard paid so little attention that Eleanor dispatched John of Alençon, who arrived in the Holy Land in April 1192 with letters from her which Richard could not ignore. In them, she detailed John's plundering of the Exchequer, his exaction of oaths of loyalty to himself from the Anglo-Norman magnates and his plan with Philip's backing to divorce the countess of Gloucester and marry Alais as a prelude to claiming the crown. Echoing Suger imploring Louis to return to his kingdom when his brother Robert of Dreux attempted to usurp him, Eleanor begged her son to abandon whatever project he had in mind and hurry home before it was too late.

But Richard was enjoying his status as the most powerful Christian lord in Outremer. When Guy de Lusignan's many enemies forced him to resign the throne of the Latin Kingdom, he was compensated by Richard with the crown of Cyprus and peopled it as a colony for refugees unwilling to live any longer in the perpetual strife of the Holy Land. Eleanor's grandson by her Capetian daughter Marie of Champagne was dispatched to Tyre to convey to Conrad of Montferrat the news that he was now king of Jerusalem. Before he could be crowned, Conrad was fatally stabbed in the street while returning from dinner with the bishop of Beauvais, leaving the young Count Henry of Champagne as the compromise candidate acceptable to both factions.

Married to Conrad's widow Isabelle within the week – which allowed her scant mourning, even for a widow in the Holy Land – he was installed immediately as monarch of the Latin Kingdom.

Another marriage Richard tried to promote in his efforts to reach a political settlement with Saladin was greeted with less enthusiasm by the nobility of the Latin Kingdom. He offered Joanna as wife to Saladin's brother Al-Adil, known also as Saphadin, the couple then to be installed as king and queen of Jerusalem, with the Latin Kingdom as their dower lands. Carried away by his own enthusiasm, Richard prepared Al-Adil by calling him 'my brother', dubbing him a knight and making arrangements for his baptism. Saladin raised no objection to the mad scheme if it was a way of ridding the country of the Europeans, but the intended bridegroom had no desire to change his faith. The whole plan fell to pieces when Joanna, in one of those outbursts of passionate indignation so rare among feudal noblewomen, refused to marry a Muslim, even should he convert,[46] invoking all the prelates in the Holy Land in her support.[47]

To overcome her defiance, Richard tried to presume upon the pope's authority in the remarriage of widows. When that failed, he promised Saladin that Al-Adil could have his niece Eleanor of Brittany as substitute bride. Geoffrey's daughter was his chattel to dispose of as he wished, but not even Richard can really have believed this a solution; he was casting around in desperation for what looked like a political settlement only because his depleted treasury permitted no other course and he was reluctant to admit total failure.

He had said that victory would be his within twenty days of Christmas 1191. It was not until nine months later that a treaty was signed on 1 September 1192 by Hubert Walter, bishop of Salisbury. Having replaced the dead Archbishop Baldwin of Canterbury as chief chaplain to the army, he had ably but hopelessly pressed the Christian claims in negotiation. The treaty declared Richard and Saladin allies, neither to raise the sword against the other for a period of three years, three months and three days. A condition was that Ashkelon's brand-new walls, in building which Richard had himself worked as a labourer,[48] be razed to the ground. However, the crusaders were permitted to keep the hard-won coastal strip and access to the holy places was guaranteed to pilgrims of all faiths.

Richard's *jonglar* Ambrose went with one party and described to his master the tears with which the Christians gazed upon the alleged sites of the Holy Sepulchre, the hill of Calvary and the tomb of the Virgin, chosen by Constantine's mother Helena when she visited Jerusalem in search of relics during the fourth century. But despite Saladin's gracious offer for Richard to visit Jerusalem as his personal guest, his crusader's oath made it impossible for him to go there other than as liberator of the holy city – a prospect that was now beyond the realms of possibility.

In France, the unrest stirred up by John and Philip had spread as far as Toulouse and caused Bertin, as seneschal of Aquitaine, to invade the county with Eleanor's grandson Otto of Brunswick and Prince Sancho of Navarre, brother of Berengaria. The combined forces captured castles and towns, camping briefly just out of bowshot from the walls of Toulouse before heading north and west to 'pacify' the Auvergne and Angoulême.[49]

Finally, even Richard could not pretend that he was accomplishing anything in Outremer. A week after dispatching Joanna and Berengaria to Sicily, he gave orders at nightfall on 9 October 1192 to weigh anchor in the port of Acre, having insulted so many of his allies that he had to beg an escort of knights from the Master of the Templars in return for the Saladin tithe his Order had received. To travel island-hopping across the pirate-ridden Aegean in a solitary galley was a sorry way to leave the Holy Land for the king who had arrived with 200 vessels under his command.

EIGHTEEN

'Shame on them all!'

As the autumn of 1192 became winter, the trickle of crusaders returning to Normandy became a flood. From them, Eleanor heard tales of Richard's derring-do, his physical strength and peerless bravery in Outremer. But she was not fooled. Contradicting all the boasts of valour and victories was the undeniable failure of this crusade, so like what she had witnessed first-hand fifty years before. The alibis for this sounded to her ears remarkably like those used by the spin-doctors on the Ile de la Cité after Philip's return, except that now it was the underhand tricks of the Franks and Germans and the *poulains* that had prevented the lionhearted king of England and his brave vassals from triumphing over the Saracen.

But where was the King? she asked again and again. The replies were confusing. Richard was known to have left the Holy Land in a fast galley that would have made better time than the pilgrim round ships transporting lesser travellers. After making landfall at Corfu at the end of October, his galley had been seen nearing the friendly Norman harbour of Brindisi.[1] From there, all was mystery.

On land, the homebound crusaders had travelled by whatever means of fortune they could find; commandeering or buying the best horses available, Richard should have made far better time. Yet everywhere Eleanor saw crusaders picking up the pieces of their shattered lives while Joanna's and Berengaria's households waited for him to join them in Rome to share what should have been a triumphal return. Her constitutional status undefined, Eleanor returned to England to keep an eye on bishops Walter of Rouen and Hugh of Durham and the other justiciars. Her Christmas court of 1192 was not a happy one, for John's partisans were not alone in whispering that the king was dead.

There are several partial accounts of Richard's return journey. According to his chaplain Anselm, as reported by Ralph of Coggleshall, they set out for Marseilles with Baldwin of Béthune, his clerk Philip and the Templars. After stopping in Cyprus – a safe enough haven for a few days – Corfu was reached a month after leaving Acre.[2] Across the straits lay Brindisi and the short route home, unfortunately barred by the armies of the German Emperor, alienated both by the Treaty of Messina and by the insult to his vassal Leopold of Austria at Acre.

Richard decided that the best course was to sail around the tip of Italy and land in southern France. Putting in to an Italian harbour that may have been Pisa,[3] he learned that in avoiding one enemy, he was sailing into the trap set by another. Eager to avenge himself on Richard for the humiliation suffered at the hands of Otto of Brunswick, Count Raymond of Toulouse and his allies were defying the Peace of God by setting ambushes all along the French Mediterranean littoral. The alternative of landing on what is now the Costa Brava and heading west to Navarre meant crossing Aragonese territory – a risky business for the son-in-law of Sancho the Wise. Richard therefore back-tracked all the way down the coast of Italy to Corfu, where he hired two Romanian pirate galleys for 200 silver marks to escort him northwards up the Adriatic.[4]

All three vessels were stranded by a storm on the coast of Istria, near modern Trieste – a stretch of territory held by vassals of Leopold of Austria.[5] Disguised as pilgrims, the small party asked the local overlord Count Mainerd for safe-conducts under the Peace of God.[6] This granted, they pressed on with Richard disguised as a rich merchant despite the many Austrian crusaders able to identify him by his height, red hair, warrior's mien and natural arrogance that ill suited the role of a smooth-talking merchant. A Norman from Argentan living in those parts recognised him, but refused to betray the crusader duke of his homeland even for the high reward offered.[7]

Trusting in speed, Richard made a horse-killing ride of over 200 miles in three days, during which he escaped from two ambushes by sacrificing eight Templar knights the first time and six more on the second occasion, before being immobilised by malaria in the village of Ganina near Vienna. Betrayed by the boastfulness of a German-speaking boy he had brought along with him[8] and too weak to mount a horse, he was brought to bay in a sordid tavern, disguised as a scullion. Sick and with only a handful of companions, he still had the Plantagenet swagger and refused to surrender until Duke Leopold of Austria left his Christmas court in Vienna to accept Richard's sword[9] and order him nursed back to health in conditions both fittingly luxurious and extremely well guarded.

Before Twelfth Night Eleanor learned from travellers from Paris of a letter received by King Philip, according to which her son was a prisoner of the very man he had insulted at Acre. Henry Hohenstaufen's letter to Philip ended, 'inasmuch as he is now within our power, and has always done his utmost for your annoyance and disturbance . . . we have thought proper to notify your nobleness . . . knowing that the same is well pleasing to [you]'.[10]

Immediately Eleanor charged the abbots of Boxley in Kent and Robertsbridge in Sussex, to travel to Germany and find out where Richard was being held.[11] On the same mission went Bishop Savaric of Bath, who was related to the emperor.[12] Returning from a trip to Rome, Bishop Hubert Walter, a nephew of the late Ranulf de Glanville, changed course and also headed eastwards.[13] The indefatigable William Longchamp, who claimed to have seen the original letter in Paris, scuttled after them to see what he could find out.

Eleanor was only restrained from taking horse and ship for Germany herself because she did not trust John and Philip once her back was turned. Instead she used diplomatic channels, reminding Celestine III that both Richard and his father had supported him when the Pope was but a cardinal and enlisting the help of princes and prelates in the cause of a crusader protected by the Peace of God. That she had been right not to absent herself in a search that could better be carried out by others was proven when John sneaked across the Channel and demanded fealty of the Norman barons with the backing of Philip, their common overlord, on the grounds that Richard was as good as dead already.[14]

The reply was a resounding vote of no confidence in him at Rouen, where poor Alais was still a prisoner, so he set up court in Alençon until lack of enthusiasm there too compelled him to flee to the safety of Paris. There Philip humoured his pretensions to be duke of Normandy in return for the undertaking to marry Alais after divorcing his wife of three years, Isabelle of Gloucester, on the grounds of their widely known consanguinity.[15]

Seizing the moment, Philip invaded the Vexin, taking Gisors and demanding the surrender of Rouen and the release of his half-sister.[16] Unimpressed by the numbers and equipment of the small Frankish force, the earl of Leicester retorted that he had no orders from King Richard to hand over his hostage, but if the king of the Franks wished to sample Norman hospitality, he only had to cross the drawbridge alone.

With no desire to be taken hostage and traded for Richard, Philip swore to return and exact revenge for the insult[17] before providing funds for John to hire a small army of Flemish mercenaries, with whom to invade England at the end of Lent. Sir John Harington's epigram had yet to be penned: 'Treason doth never prosper: what's the reason? For if it prosper, none dare call it treason.' But the dilemma on both sides of the Channel was an old one. If Richard died in captivity, who would be considered loyal, and who a traitor?

Eleanor reasoned that to imprison John might provoke open conflict with his many partisans and that a better course was to neutralise him by ensuring that crown officers in the channel ports – reinforced by a *fyrd* raised from local men who well remembered the excesses of King Stephen's Flemings in south-east England – arrested any mercenaries who dared set foot ashore and frightened the others away back to Flanders.[18]

Meanwhile, in Germany there was a political tug-of-war over who should have the most ransomable prisoner in the world, Duke Leopold claiming priority both because it was his banner that had been insulted at Acre and he who had taken Richard's sword. As his suzerain, the emperor reminded him that 'duke of Austria' was a courtesy title;[19] for a count to hold a king prisoner was contrary to feudal custom, and therefore Richard must be handed over to him.[20]

Leopold's injured dignity might have inclined him to forego a ransom for the pleasure of letting his unrepentant captive die mysteriously in some unidentified castle, never mind what blast of anathema came from Rome. However, at a meeting in Würzburg during February 1193, they came to terms: against the promise of 20,000 marks from the eventual ransom, Leopold's captive was brought from the castle of Dürnstein, west of Vienna, and transferred into imperial custody at Ratisbon and then Würzburg.

Less than three months after the emperor's letter had been received in Paris – on Palm Sunday, 21 March 1193 – Eleanor's two emissaries tracked Richard down at Ochsenfurt, on his way under escort to the emperor's Easter court at Speyer. Either Longchamp beat them to it, or he arrived soon afterwards.[21] They found him restored to health and in relatively high spirits, having charmed all his guards and their masters with his bluff good humour, his versifying and prowess at all things knightly.

Informed of John's latest treason, Richard again laughed off the idea of his weakling brother usurping the throne with or without Philip's help. He did, however, dispatch Hubert Walter back to England with a letter appointing him archbishop of Canterbury. It was from him that Eleanor learned on 20 April that her beloved son was alive and in good health. In the country there was twofold rejoicing, both that Richard was alive and that Longchamp was not the new primate.

At the time of Archbishop Hubert's departure, the royal prisoner had not been accorded an interview with the emperor, although imperial court gossip was that a sum of 100,000 marks would be asked for his ransom. While Eleanor and the justiciars waited for confirmation of this, they used the news that Richard was alive to defuse the unrest John been stirring up during the period of uncertainty. In this, her constitutionally ambiguous position made her the ideal intermediary; while John might not have consented to surrender his castles to the justiciars, he did agree to hand over to her Windsor Castle, Wallingford and the Peak – on the understanding that they were to be returned to him if Richard were not, for whatever reason, released.

At Speyer the Emperor was more resistant to Poitevin eloquence than Richard's previous captors.[22] Arraigning his hostage before the Easter court, he charged him with a long list of crimes, including the murder of Conrad of Montferrat – a close relative of Duke Leopold. Vastly outnumbered, Richard's entourage included Bishop Savaric of Bath, the abbots of Boxley and Robertsbridge, plus his chaplain and Longchamp. His superior competence in Latin had enabled him on more than one occasion to mock Hubert Walter, who was famous for the grammatical errors he made constantly, sometimes with hilarious results.[23] Confident in his own eloquence, Richard represented himself in Latin as the epitome of knighthood on the greatest of all chivalric enterprises, convincing many of Henry's vassals that he was indeed the incarnation of the knightly ideal.[24]

At the end of his speech, Richard knelt in submission before the Emperor – and burst into tears! It was a gift he had. Bowing to the mood of the assembled nobles, Henry Hohenstaufen lifted his vanquished prisoner to his feet and led him to share the dais. As to the ransom, however, the sum of 100,000 silver marks or £66,000 was confirmed as the price of Richard's freedom. He was to be released when 70,000 marks had been paid, with 200 noble hostages demanded as surety for the balance. This covered retribution for the failure of his brother-in-law Henry the Lion of Saxony to support the imperial design, plus a compensation for the insult suffered by Leopold that would provide a handsome dower on the marriage of his son. The son's bride was a part of the price: she was to be Eleanor's granddaughter Eleanor of Brittany, whom Richard had already offered to Al-Adil in compensation for Joanna's stubborn refusal to marry him.[25]

In addition, the emperor's relative Isaac Comnenus, who was still imprisoned in Cyprus, was to be released. His daughter, held hostage by Joanna and Berengaria in Rome, was to be restored to him. And lastly, 50 galleys and 200 knights were to be furnished for use in the war with Tancred in compensation for the Treaty of Messina having prejudiced the Empress Constance's rights to Sicily.

On Maundy Thursday,[26] the eve of Good Friday, Richard's chaplain left for England with the ransom demand and a letter from him to Eleanor informing her that Longchamp had been the one who stage-managed the all-important interview with the emperor. The amount was there for all to see in ink on parchment: she was required to oversee its collection and to note carefully how much every baron contributed, so that the king would know how much gratitude he owed each one . . . or not. The justiciars were, of course, to give a good example by their own generosity.

Eleanor got to work immediately,[27] appointing five assessors to oversee the ransom collection: Hubert Walter, Bishop Richard of London, the earl of Arundel, the earl of Surrey and Henry fitz Ailwin, the first mayor of London, whose citizens learned they were to contribute at roughly the same rate as barons paying a quarter of their annual rents and revenues and the knighthood, each fee being assessed at twenty shillings.

To amass the ransom from a country impoverished firstly by Henry's Saladin tithe and all the other crusading taxes, required the sanctions of the Church. Formally installed as archbishop of Canterbury on 30 May 1193, Hubert Walter informed the bishops of the realm that they were responsible for collecting the tax from their clergy, those priests who lived on tithes being required to contribute a tenth of their income. Charged with a fourth part of their wealth, the canons of Geoffrey the Bastard's cathedral at York refused to pay, despite every abbey and cathedral having to plunder its treasury for jewels and gold – in return for which promissory notes were given, payable after the king's return. Even the moneyless abbeys of the Gilbertians and St Bernard's Cistercians, who owned no gems or precious metal, were obliged to give a whole year's clip of wool from their flocks.[28]

Having no idea of the real value of money, Richard naturally assumed that whatever sum was demanded for his release would rapidly be paid in the same way that knights defeated in tournaments were ransomed according to their wealth and rank. Since he was the noblest and wealthiest monarch in Christendom, he could hardly expect to be assessed more modestly. It was therefore the duty and privilege of his subjects to pay up.

To prevent his golden tongue gaining even more supporters, the Emperor placed him in close confinement at the grim fortress of Trifels[29] until Longchamp succeeded in obtaining his removal to more relaxed surroundings at Hagenau. He then departed with his master's blessing for England, to assemble the hostages to be held as surety. With spring giving way to summer, Richard was soon again being treated more as guest than prisoner in Hagenau, where the imperial court spent Pentecost. Sharing something of his musical skills, the Emperor even indulged him in some of the rhyming contests at which Richard had excelled in his youth at Eleanor's court in Poitiers.

The constant stream of prelates passing between the Angevin possessions on both sides of the Channel and Richard's various places of detention in Germany, had given him in the eyes of the German nobility more 'the prestige of an imperial statesman . . . than the forlorn dignity of a suppliant'.[30] The emperor's plan to meet Philip in June 1193 was therefore postponed. Incensed by the emperor's failure to consult him since the original letter, Philip wanted a share of the ransom to compensate for the insults he had suffered at Richard's hands. In return, he offered the archbishop of Reims as mediator in the dispute between Henry Hohenstaufen and his disaffected bishops, on condition that Richard stayed right where he was. Meeting Philip at midsummer in Lorraine, the emperor pondered how much an alliance with his neighbour the king of the Franks was worth against the money represented by the ransom.[31]

Confident that he would soon be released, Richard was allowed to write to all and sundry, his captors having no objection if it would speed up the collection of the money. Nor did they prevent the armour Richard had worn in the Holy Land from being taken by Admiral Stephen of Turnham to London for exhibition as an eloquent reproach to his subjects who had not emptied their purses.[32]

Berengaria was a singular omission from her husband's address book, but Eleanor was greeted by the distant prisoner as his 'dear mother' and also formally as 'by the Grace of God, Queen of the English'. He even wrote to the Old Man of the Mountains in faraway Syria, requesting him as chief of the sect of Assassins to confirm that it was his men who had killed Conrad of Montferrat.[33] Predictably, a mysterious reply was received, which Richard waved before the emperor, claiming complete exoneration.

In England, the ransom trickled in; it did not flow. This was partly due to the corruption of the unsupervised collectors working outside the normal Exchequer system, many of whom were afterwards accused of diverting much into their own pockets. As and when each bullion train arrived in London, the gold and silver and precious objects were locked away in St Paul's Cathedral under heavy guard, in sacks sealed with Eleanor's own seal and that of Archbishop Hubert Walter. The first levies having proven largely insufficient, she ordered a second, and then a third, lambasting the tardy and the niggardly. Nor was it any easier to milk the impoverished continental possessions.

An even more unpopular task was the naming of the hostages who would serve as surety until the entire ransom had been paid. Longchamp, more tactful than in the past,[34] had returned from Hagenau not as chancellor and justiciar, but as bishop of Ely – a loyal servant of the Crown, whose duty was to concert with Eleanor the selection of the noble hostages. This was a matter she pushed forward energetically in the hope that it would cause the families of those selected to find some wealth they had omitted to declare, for the greater the amount raised, the fewer the number of hostages to be delivered. Yet she refused to entrust to Longchamp her own grandson William of Winchester, son of Henry the Lion of Saxony. Many other families also refused their sons on the grounds that the bishop of Ely was not a fit person to have the care of boys; they sent their daughters instead.

During all this time Eleanor had to keep her eye on John, who was forbidden to leave England and had all his incoming mail from Paris intercepted. She was also haranguing the pope at a distance for what she considered his lukewarm support. Her secretary, Peter of Blois, now archdeacon of Bath, was famous for his witty puns and epigrams. In accusing Celestine III of keeping the sword of St Peter in its sheath and failing three times to send papal intermediaries, he punned that the legates had been leashed and not loosed upon the emperor: in succinct Latin, they had been *potius ligati quam legati*.

Complaining that, if her son had been rich, they would have come running to be rewarded by generosity, Eleanor signed herself not

'Queen by the Grace of God' but 'Queen of the English by God's anger'.[35] As duchess of Aquitaine, she was also not above including a thinly veiled hint that the Cathar heresy so widespread in the south of France would be allowed to flourish there unchecked if the papacy did not earn her gratitude.[36]

Double standards indeed for Eleanor, who had herself turned away cardinals Agnani, Jordan and Octavian when it suited her. And what more could the pope do? He had excommunicated Duke Leopold for laying hands on a crusader and threatened Philip with excommunication under the Peace of God if he took advantage of Richard's captivity. He had even waved the threat of interdict over England, should the ransom not be forthcoming. With vast Church possessions at risk in Germany and Henry Hohenstaufen having large forces still in Italy, he could not force the emperor to do anything.

In Midsummer 1193 Richard was moved yet again – this time to Worms on the Rhine, where his charm earned him the liberty to order his falconer and favourite birds sent out from England, with a consignment of clothes and utensils for his personal use. At a five-day plenary court, the emperor weighed all the possibilities in the light of Philip's representations and confirmed that the royal prisoner would be released against sureties when two-thirds of the ransom had been brought to Germany at his risk in transit. The bad news was that the amount was to be increased by 50 per cent – the extra 50,000 marks being in lieu of Richard's direct help in the campaign against his ally Tancred. The number of hostages was increased accordingly.

Henry Hohenstaufen seems to have been in two minds about Richard's claim that he had persuaded the German bishops to end their long dispute, but the change of episcopal policy was due to Celestine's urgings on his behalf. In addition, Richard was responsible for a reconciliation between the houses of Hohenstaufen and Saxony, with Henry the Lion being offered the emperor's cousin Constance as bride for his son, a nephew of the royal captive.

It was probably at Worms that Richard composed a *sirventès* addressed to his half-sister Marie de Champagne sometime towards the end of 1193 expressing his impatience with the pace at which his subjects were getting the money together.

> Ja nuls hom pres non dira sa razon
> adrechament, si com hom dolens non
> mas per confort deu hom faire canson

Pro n'ay d'amis, mas paure son li don
Ancta lur es, si per ma resenzon
soi sai dos yvers pres.

[No prisoner can put his case for long / without self-pity making it sound wrong / but still for comfort he can pen a song. / My many friends offer little, I hear. / Shame on them all if they leave me here / unransomed for a second long year.]

The emperor having addressed a letter to the magnates of England on 20 December confirming that he had set 17 January as the day for the release of his 'dear friend Richard',[37] the dear friend summoned the archbishop of Rouen and Eleanor to join him at Speyer for Christmas with all the money so far collected, so he could be sure both it and the hostages would all be handed over by the due date. Before leaving England with an impressive retinue and large escort, Eleanor appointed Archbishop Hubert Walter chief justiciar on Richard's instructions, which made him the indisputable ruler of the country in her absence or until the king should return.

On 6 January 1194 they arrived in Cologne. On 17 January at Speyer she was informed that her son's release was to be delayed after all, an alternative offer having been received from Paris. Philip was bidding 50,000 marks and John 30,000 marks if Richard were kept prisoner until Michaelmas – by which time they hoped to have possessed themselves of the continental Plantagenet assets. Alternatively, they offered monthly instalments of £1000 so long as Richard was held captive. On learning of this, the Great Council deprived John of all his possessions, in addition to which he and his chief partisans were excommunicated. Under Hubert Walter's guidance the council also denounced Longchamp to the pope in a letter heavy with all their seals, which was to be shown first to Richard in Germany so that he would know what they thought of his ex-chancellor.

At Mainz on 2 February 1194, Eleanor's joy at seeing her son for the first time in three and a half years was tempered by an unpleasant surprise on learning that Philip had raised the French offer to 100,000 marks, with another 50,000 from John – a sum equivalent to the whole ransom from England – if Richard were handed over to them or held in Germany for another year.[38]

Seeking a counter-counter-offer, the Emperor showed the letters to her and Richard. Whatever the barons and bishops of England thought of Longchamp, he still enjoyed the king's favour and was one of the spokesmen who addressed the imperial court in Eleanor's presence that day, pointing out that Philip and John had no chance of amassing the colossal sums, totalling many times the annual taxation income of the whole of France, even if they did manage to conquer and plunder Normandy and the other Angevin continental possessions.

The political complication for Henry Hohenstaufen was that, if he allowed Richard to walk free he would lose the French support in the dispute with his bishops at a time when the English were hardly going to love him. He therefore demanded that Richard admit he held England as a vassal of the emperor.[39] The king's advisers were horrified, but what did it matter to Eleanor if he thus changed allegiance from Capet to Hohenstaufen? As to an annual tribute demanded, what was a promise of that worth to a son of Henry of Anjou?

On 4 February, Richard was at last released after swearing fealty to the emperor and declaring with his customary eloquence that he held his possessions on both sides of the Channel as a vassal of the Emperor, to whom he would pay a yearly fee of £5,000. Doffing his bonnet, he placed it in the emperor's hands, signifying that he renounced his vassalage to the house of Capet. One last requirement was that the archbishop of Rouen, who had played a leading part in the negotiations, should be left behind as a hostage.

Learning that his enemy was free, Philip managed to get a message to Prince John in England, warning him that 'the devil was loose'. In terror, John fled the country and took refuge in Paris.[40] Given the unrest he had fomented in England during the crusade and the long captivity, it was Richard's nature to hurry home and punish those who had committed treason. Only Eleanor's influence can have persuaded him to the roundabout but statesmanlike route they followed, spending a weekend with the bishop of Cologne, staying with the duke of Louvain in his castle at Antwerp, and stopping at Brussels and many other places to make and confirm alliances that might one day be useful on this, the eastern flank of Philip's realm.

At Antwerp, the faithful Stephen of Turnham welcomed Eleanor and his king aboard the *Trenchemer*, from which they trans-shipped to a larger vessel at the mouth of the Schelde for the night and back to the faster *Trenchemer* for the Channel crossing next day. Fearing the patrols which Philip was suspected of having set to intercept them,[41] they weighed anchor in the evening, landing at Sandwich 'at the ninth hour of the day' on 12 March.[42] Six weeks after leaving Speyer, they rode from there to give thanks at Becket's tomb in Canterbury Cathedral and spent the night in Rochester Castle.

This may have been Eleanor's way of giving the citizens of London time to deck with banners and bunting the city that had contributed a sizeable share of the ransom. To the ringing of all the bells in London, Richard was led in procession to St Paul's, now empty of its treasures. Agents of the emperor come to oversee payment of the balance outstanding had expected to find a country on its knees after all the exactions.[43] Hardship there was in the country, but the pace of business in London made them comment that the ransom had been set far too low.

Richard's gratitude to his jubilant subjects was limited to a stay of a few hours only. On 18 March he was at Bury St Edmunds – giving thanks at the shrine of one of his favourite saints, the eponymous martyred king of East Anglia – before heading north to Nottingham, where a small-scale but bitter civil war had just ended. Eleanor travelled with him all the way because he knew nothing of English or Anglo-Norman customs and sensitivities and she did not want the arrogance that had caused all his problems in Outremer to alienate his vassals who had still to make good their pledges for the unpaid part of the ransom.

After the Great Council meeting that dispossessed John, Archbishop Hubert Walter had departed at the head of an army equipped to reduce his castles with copious supplies of arrows, armour, shields, pitch and sulphur for Greek fire, plus mangonels to hurl it. Marlborough surrendered in a few days, Lancaster too. John's castellan at St Michael's Mount in Cornwall dropped dead from a heart attack when he heard Richard was back in England.[44] But John's castle at Tickhill was still holding out. The garrison offered to surrender if he would guarantee their lives. The king refused, but Bishop Hugh of Durham, commanding the loyalist besiegers, took it upon himself to agree terms.

Nottingham itself held out until Richard arrived there on 25 March. The defenders did not believe who he was until he donned his armour and led the assault, taking the outerworks and many prisoners, whom he hanged on a gallows erected in full view of the castle. Hubert Walter arrived with reinforcements for the besiegers' ranks. Two days later, Hugh of Durham arrived with the prisoners he had taken at Tickhill. Within twenty-four hours, Nottingham too had surrendered and the rebellion was over.

A Great Council was summoned there, in the heart of the territory that had been loyal to John. While its members were assembling, Richard amused himself for a few days at one of Henry's old haunts, Clipstone on the fringes of Sherwood Forest, where the hunting of stag and boar so pleased him that he compared it favourably with his own

Talmont. This was the stuff of the triumphal return at the end of every Robin Hood film, although whether a meeting in some greenwood glade between a loyal outlaw and the returned crusader king – as described in the fourteenth-century *Ballad of Robin Hood* – actually took place, is anyone's guess.

On Wednesday 30 March, in the hastily repaired great hall of Nottingham Castle, 72-year-old Eleanor in all her majesty as dowager queen surveyed the assembled earls of the realm and the bishops and archbishops doing obeisance to her son, whose return she had done more than anyone else to secure. But the moment of national elation and thanksgiving for the king's salvation was brief. He was angry with his English subjects, who had paid the lion's share of the ransom too slowly, as though the fifteen months' imprisonment was their fault. He wanted not their acclamations, but more money to hire mercenaries and buy equipment to repulse Philip's advances in Normandy, where he had already taken several castles and appeared before the walls of Rouen.[45]

All the offices and privileges bought five years earlier now had to be bought anew. To the few protesters, he replied that while he and his heroic crusaders had faced death, all the stay-at-homes had been growing fat on the profits of war.

Those survivors *par excellence*, the three Longchamp brothers, were again in the ascendant. Henry, imprisoned after William's flight to France from Dover Castle, bought the office of sheriff of Worcestershire, while Osbert was named sheriff of Norfolk and Suffolk. The hated bishop of Ely offered 1,500 marks down and 500 marks annually per county to be named sheriff of Yorkshire, Lincolnshire and Northamptonshire, but was outbid for Yorkshire by Geoffrey the Bastard, who offered 3,000 marks for that county alone to ensure that William Longchamp had no authority in his see. Even Prince John's unhappy wife, Isabelle or Hawise of Gloucester, had to pay £200 to keep her dowry lands and marriage portion.

Teams of clerks were kept busy day and night noting all this down. On the third day, Richard moved on to the question of taxation. Demands for the arrears in payment of ransom contributions were sent out. In addition, he announced his requirement that every knight in the realm should perform one-third of his knight service by crossing to Normandy with him.[46] This would have produced a total force of around 2,000 knights, but the demand was more probably intended to raise the scutage paid in lieu, so that he could hire mercenaries. Here he was on thin ice for, as Bishop Hugh of Lincoln asserted in 1197, knight service was owed to the king by his English vassals for war in England, not abroad.

To squeeze the last drops of wealth out of a country exhausted by the ransom, Richard named Longchamp chancellor once more, for who knew more than he about milking England down to its last penny? In addition to new taxes, the pre-Conquest land-tax last levied in 1162 was reintroduced. Known as Danegeld, its rate was set at two shillings for every hide of cultivated land recorded in the Domesday Book, with none of the traditional exemption for Church lands. The poor monasteries that had no precious objects to sell were ordered to surrender their wool-clip for the second year running in settlement of their assessments. The Pipe Rolls show the cost of hauling wool from the Cistercian foundations in Yorkshire to Holme in Norfolk and hiring ships to transport it to Germany.[47] Among the many individual victims was William the Marshal, called on to pay four shillings for his wife's estates in Sussex.[48]

The last subject on the agenda was Richard's oath of fealty to the emperor and his undertaking to pay an annual fee to Henry Hohenstaufen. To the barons of the realm this was a shameful thing,[49] to offset which it was decided that the king should be recrowned at Winchester. It was almost forty years since Henry had last held a ceremonial crown-wearing; no one could remember the ritual. So messengers sped off to Canterbury to consult the records of the ceremonial used when Stephen of Blois had been recrowned at Canterbury in 1141 to reaffirm his sovereignty after release from imprisonment by Empress Matilda.[50]

Resenting the delay this meant in his departure for Normandy, Richard agreed reluctantly. Knowing how quickly matters of state wearied him, Eleanor stayed close, witnessing on 8 April his charter setting out the honours due to King William of Scotland when called to the English court. A week later she was still at his side when he dined at Winchester Castle on Saturday 16 April. The following day, which was either just before or just after her seventy-third birthday, she sat in state on the gospel side of the cathedral on a specially built dais surrounded by her court of young ladies – the noble heiresses waiting to be bestowed as rewards upon those who had served the Crown well in the recent troubled times.[51]

Poor unwanted Berengaria was conveniently out of the way in Poitiers. Alais was a prisoner in Rouen. It was Eleanor in all her regal glory who was the only queen in England that morning when her son processed with Longchamp on his right side from nearby St Swithin's Priory and up the aisle beneath a canopy borne by a count and three earls, one of whom was his bastard half-brother William Longsword of Salisbury, to the altar where Archbishop Hubert Walter was waiting.

Business after the ceremony included setting the ransoms for the noble prisoners taken at Tickhill and Nottingham and dispatching 10,000 marks to Germany to ransom Archbishop Walter of Rouen. Hoping to make the collection of his prisoners' ransoms quicker than his had been, Richard authorised a considerable expenditure on fetters and chains to make sure the conditions in which they were kept were less comfortable than his in Germany.

Second seal of Richard

His habitual impatience was not helped by more bad news from France. On 24 April, less than six weeks after the landing at Sandwich, he and Eleanor arrived at Portsmouth. In the East Richard had been impressed by the manoeuvrability of galleys, far less dependent on the wind than traditional English ships, and determined to build a fleet of them, with which to control the Channel. Portsmouth, surrounded by a wall, was to be his admiralty, shipyard and homeport where the newly constructed galleys would safely berth in a fortified harbour. With his customary enthusiasm for everything martial, he threw himself into this new enterprise, but also found time to go hunting, interrupting his sport when riots broke out between his Welsh and Flemish mercenaries, turning the half-built streets of Portsmouth into a battleground.

No sooner was everything ready than the weather changed. Chafing at the bit, Richard ignored the advice of his captains and ordered men and horses to embark on Monday 2 May. After a day and a night being driven everywhere but towards France, with the horses cooped up in their stalls suffering more and more, he abandoned the attempt and returned to land, to everyone's great relief. The prolonged stay cost over £100 in lodgings. It was not until 12 May that the fleet of 100 vessels great and small carrying the levied English knights and the mercenary force could weigh anchor and set sail for the port of Barfleur.[52]

Richard's second visit to England as king had lasted – although far longer than he wished – a bare two months. Neither he nor Eleanor would ever set eyes on the island realm again.

NINETEEN

Cruel News from Châlus

Eleanor's reappearance from across the sea at Richard's side had for their continental vassals all the characteristics of a dual return from the dead. If his mother seemed almost supernatural by virtue of her great age and extraordinary vitality, there was no doubt that the king in his prime was flesh and blood – the greatest warrior in Christendom, so far as his loyal subjects were concerned.

The squire of William the Marshal reported how at the news of his coming, church bells rang out everywhere and the common people expressed their joy in hymns and dances[1] while the turncoats among the marcher lords prepared to change sides yet again as Eleanor and he progressed in state from Barfleur to Caen and Bayeux.

Their third or fourth night after disembarking was spent in the house at Lisieux of Archdeacon John of Alençon – the trusted messenger who brought to Richard in the Holy Land Eleanor's appeal that finally set him on the homeward path. Here they received a visitor under cover of darkness. Deprived of Philip's subsidies, dispossessed of his own castles and revenues by the Great Council, John Lackland now merited the sobriquet Lack-all. Fearing Richard's anger and hoping that she would mediate for him, he sought an interview with Eleanor first.[2]

Richard had been trying to persuade his troops to ride through the night to relieve the siege of Verneuil. He assured John of Alençon he held no animosity for his brother. So apt to use floods of tears on occasion himself, he was often moved by the penitential weeping of others. And so it proved this time. Echoing Henry's words when the princes repented of their treason, he pardoned John and blamed instead the evil advisers who had led his 'little brother' astray.[3]

John was twenty-six at the time. Sitting down to a freshly cooked salmon Richard had been given for his own dinner, he must have been immensely relieved at this reception. To prove on whose side he now was, he was given a retinue of knights and men-at-arms with whom to relieve the garrison of Evreux by cutting Philip's lines of communication and forcing him to withdraw.[4]

In dealing with the Frankish incursions, Richard was at his best: his genius for assessing military priorities and driving horses and machines to destruction and men to their limits of endurance had his excommunicated enemy on the run within days. Archbishop Walter of Rouen joined him in Normandy with William Longchamp, leaving England in the capable hands of Archbishop Hubert Walter of Canterbury, who as chief justiciar ruled the kingdom wisely and well for the rest of Richard's reign, being made a cardinal the following March.

Before long Philip was backtracking in panic,[5] abandoning equipment and supplies in the knowledge that his betrayal of Richard while imprisoned in Germany meant that he could expect, if taken prisoner, no feudal kiss of peace. After redressing the situation temporarily in Normandy, Richard swung south towards the Loire Valley to recover the castles handed over by John and those of Châteaudun and Loches, which he himself had yielded and now recovered with the aid of a mixed force of Flemings and Navarrese mercenaries led by Berengaria's brother Sancho, including probably a corps of the Genoese crossbowmen, in whom Richard placed great faith. Other specialists included 150 artillerymen with trebuchets and other missile launchers to batter the château of Taillebourg into submission, razing it so thoroughly to the ground shortly after Geoffroi de Rancon's death that no trace of the twelfth-century building remains.

Time and again Philip fled at Richard's approach, abandoning near Vendôme not only his siege-engines but also his chapel fittings, the treasury and the precious chancery documents listing Richard's vassals who had sworn direct allegiance to the Frankish Crown during the exile.[6] While William the Marshal kept these safe, Richard pressed onwards with his Flemish mercenary commander Mercadier, at one point after the battle of Fréteval in July 1194 coming within minutes of capturing Philip and his personal escort. Informed by a lone Fleming met by the roadside that his prey was far ahead, Richard galloped straight past the humble country church in which his enemy was hiding. He was well into Frankish-held territory when his horse foundered and Mercadier had to find him a remount on which to rejoin his own forces.[7]

Moving south, Richard tore into Aquitaine where the internecine feuding had flourished unchecked during his four-year absence. Here he was on home ground: the fortresses provisioned and manned against him were as familiar to his military mind as a sibling's face, every weakness known in advance. Throughout July he and Mercadier's men ravaged the countryside yet again. After taking the count of Angoulême's fortress-city in a single evening, he wrote to Archbishop Hubert Walter that they had captured 40,000 men-at-arms and 300 ransomable knights.[8] The numbers were probably exaggerated, but Richard's swift decisions, martial prowess and personal courage succeeded within three months in restoring his continental possessions from the Channel to the Pyrenees to something like peace[9] and in expunging the disgrace of his imprisonment.

One of the many promises on which he reneged was the undertaking in the Treaty of Worms to hand over to Duke Leopold within seven months of his liberation the daughter of Isaac Comnenus. With Leopold now threatening to execute his sureties in retaliation for this, Baldwin of Béthune – one of the small band that had been captured with Richard in Austria – was chosen by the other, more recent, hostages to travel to England and fetch the girl. However, hearing on the return journey that Leopold had died, he turned back with his charge and returned her to England.[10] The ransom never was paid in its entirety, the German Emperor waiving the last 17,000 marks as a contribution to Richard's war against their common enemy, Philip.[11]

Eleanor's court at Poitiers had never recovered from Henry's purge of 1174, and she had not the energy to bring back to life the great audience hall beside the Maubergeonne Tower where Berengaria held her lonely and inconsequential court when not in her dower lands further north in Maine.[12] The haven to which Eleanor retired in order to distance herself from the turmoil of the world was the monastery/convent to which Henry had sought to consign her. As Fat Louis had installed his chancery and war office in St Denis, so she set her modest staff up in Fontevraud, midway between the Channel coast and the Pyrenees. On her way to Mass each morning, she walked over the permanent inhabitants of the abbey church and past Henry's tomb with its effigy showing his restless hands stilled at last and quietly holding the sceptre of state (plate 29).

Fontevraud's several thousand religious and lay inhabitants included an upper stratum of noble ladies whose husbands had tired of them or found a more advantageous match, plus those who had chosen to put the Peace of God between themselves and a society that used their bodies, titles and possessions as the disposable filling in the sandwiches of treaties and alliances. To this elegant society Eleanor came as a natural queen regardless of the worldly titles she claimed.

During the Norman campaign of 1194, Richard suffered several setbacks. Attempting to relieve the siege of Aumale, he narrowly escaped capture by Guillaume des Barres, his enemy from the winter on Sicily. The Frankish knight abandoned three other captives in the attempt, thereby losing their ransoms. Another of Philip's men, Alain de Dinan, did unhorse Richard, who managed to remount in the skirmish and make good his escape. At Gaillon on the Seine, which he was besieging in order to get money for the construction of a new castle to replace Gisors, now in Philip's hands, he was wounded in the knee by a crossbow bolt fired by Cadoc, Philip's mercenary castellan. His stricken horse falling on top of him, Richard's injuries took a month to heal.

Such was the devastation from fire and sword that the Church once again called for a halt to the violence, resulting in a truce signed by Richard and Philip on 23 July. A month later, by a letter dated 22 August, Richard made tournaments legal at five named places in England,[13] ignoring the possibility this presented for an assembly of several hundred or more knights, fully armed and accoutred, being used to mask a nascent rebellion. His excuse to the Church was that tournaments prepared knights for what they would experience when he led them back to the Holy Land. Few English knights had responded to his call to take the cross; uppermost in his mind was the income he could expect from sales of licences to promote tournaments and the fees due from every participant, ranging from 20 marks for an earl down to 2 marks for a landless knight.[14]

While he held his Christmas court in Rouen, Eleanor remained at Fontevraud, where a stream of clerical and lay visitors brought her news from all over Europe. Toulouse had been re-attached to Aquitaine fortuitously by Count Raymond falling out with Louis. When he died in the first days of the new year, his son Young Raymond had everything to gain by changing allegiance. Since neither of her husbands had solved the long-term problem of the breakaway county by force of arms, Eleanor began exploring a different solution.

About the same time, while hunting in Normandy, Richard was advised by a hermit who recognised him in the forest to remember the destruction of Sodom and give up his forbidden pleasures before the hand of God fell on him.[15] At Easter 1195 he fell seriously ill and took this as a warning to moderate his lifestyle. While most of his energy still went into warfare, something of the Plantagenet wildness had gone out of him. Although still as avid for taxes as ever, he also performed good works like feeding the poor from his own pocket at times of famine and making good to religious communities the debts owing for their treasures taken to pay his ransom.[16]

Inevitably, the truce was infringed – this time by Philip, who broke through to within 12 miles of Rouen. Alais was hurried away to Caen and moved from one fortress to another as the tide of battle ebbed and flowed. She was now thirty-four, an age by which most women of the time were dead. With her life's clock stopped on the day she had been handed over to Henry by Louis Capet as a girl of ten, she had never known liberty and was a stranger to her own family.

Under the Treaty of Louviers in January 1196, Philip gave back all the territory gained from Richard in return for the Norman Vexin.[17] With Alais' dowry castles he also recovered his half-sister and married her off to Guillaume de Ponthieu, whose domains divided Normandy from the territory of Richard's ally Baldwin of Flanders. So Alais disappeared from history, after spending a lifetime captive in the gilded cage of a family that despised her as she was used and abused in turn by Henry, Eleanor and Richard.

Confirming the clause in the Treaty of Messina that had caused so much trouble, Richard again named Arthur his heir, but when he ordered Constance of Brittany to bring her son to Rouen, she was imprisoned by the husband Henry had imposed on her, Earl Ranulf of Chester. Hastening to his nephew's rescue, Richard found that he had been spirited away to Paris and was being brought up in Philip's household with Crown Prince Louis. For John, this was good news: it seemed that he must by default now be recognised as heir to the whole Plantagenet Empire. He kept a low profile none the less – as well he might, having had his estates restored to him the previous year on condition of good behaviour.

Like the Empress Matilda, 31-year-old Joanna had kept her title as queen of Sicily on being widowed. Killing two birds with one stone, Eleanor now dangled before Young Raymond of Toulouse the idea of rejecting his second wife Bourguigne de Lusignan to become the husband of a titular queen. The match would restore Joanna's wealth, ruined by Richard spending all her dowry on crusade, and it would also wean Raymond away from the temptation of pledging fealty to Philip, whose cousin he was. The only complication was that Raymond was still excommunicate for the repudiation of his first wife and would incur the censure of the Church in sending away his second spouse, but there was always a complaisant churchman to sort out that kind of problem.

The marriage duly took place in Rouen during October 1196,[18] witnessed by Berengaria, who otherwise lived quietly in her dower lands. So important in Eleanor's eyes was the clause in the marriage contract providing for Joanna's offspring to inherit the county of Toulouse that Joanna had no more say in the matter than when Henry dispatched her as a girl to Sicily. But what was love, except a game of *What If?* played by poets and virgins? Even that great romantic Bernat de Ventadorn, who had sworn to be true to his regal mistress until death, had written before he died,

> *Estat ai com om esperdutz*
> *per amor un long estatge*
> *mas era'm reconogutz*
> *qu'ieu avia faih folatge.*

[I was a man by love destroyed. / It ruled my mind for far too long. / But now at last I've understood / that I have lived my life all wrong.]

Another arranged marriage that year ensured Richard the gratitude of his bastard half-brother William Longsword, awarded the daughter of the count of Salisbury.[19] A hint of satisfaction can be read on the eroded features of Longsword's effigy in Salisbury Cathedral, despite that year going on record as one of famine and disease so rampant in England that corpses of the rural poor were shovelled into mass graves because there was no time to bury them individually.

So widespread was the misery and suffering north of the Channel that a social reformer by name of William fitz Osbern travelled to Normandy to lay before Richard the plight of the urban poor who were bearing an unfair share of the crippling burden of taxes. An educated man and ex-crusader, he pleaded his case so well that the king let him go, but once back in England he suffered the fate of those too good for their time. Archbishop Hubert Walter as chief justiciar ordered his arrest one day when fitz Osbern's self-appointed bodyguard was absent. Claiming sanctuary in Bow Church, the would-be reformer was forced out when it was set on fire at the archbishop's orders. Dragged bloodily through the streets of London behind a team of horses, he was hanged at Tyburn with nine companions, his followers digging out so much ground beneath the gallows for souvenirs that they had to be kept at bay by armed soldiers.

Richard had decided to replace Gisors as a barrier to any Frankish move on Rouen by building an impregnable castle on a spur of rock at Les Andelys dominating the Seine Valley. Castle-building rarely took place on virgin land; it displaced existing population and disrupted the economic life of the area, such as food production and markets. Quarries had to be opened up, masons and other skilled labour brought in, local labourers impressed, the new chapel might disturb existing parish demarcations, vineyards and fields were ruined and forests cleared – as at Bures where Henry's rebuilding had required the felling of 1,000 mature oaks.

At Les Andelys an entire town was being constructed by the riverside to support the castle. The chosen site lay in the domains of the archbishop of Rouen, who refused his consent on the grounds that he was not being compensated for the loss of revenues to the see, and placed Normandy under interdict in retaliation for Richard's high-handedness. Appealing to the pope over the prelate's head, Richard ordered William Longchamp to lead an embassy to Rome, well provided with money for bribes. In order to avoid Frankish territory, the embassy travelled south into Poitou, where Longchamp fell ill and died in Poitiers early in February 1197, unmourned by anyone in England except his immediate family and his close friend, Richard's chaplain Milo.[20] Another death that year was of Marguerite the Young Queen, who died on pilgrimage to the Holy Land, at Acre.

The humiliation of the confinement in Germany had played a part in Richard's personality change. It was there that he learned to moderate the arrogance that had made him so many enemies before and during the crusade and there too that he first became Good King Richard,[21] winning the hearts of most of the Emperor's vassals who met him – which was why they approached him to resolve the knotty problem of succession when Henry Hohenstaufen died suddenly in Messina on 28 September 1197 after releasing Richard from the oath of fealty given under duress at Mainz.

Of the two contenders for the imperial throne, the infant son of Constance of Sicily was unacceptable to the German electors by virtue of his minority and although Philip of Swabia, the late emperor's brother, had much support in the south he was not well thought of in the north or by the bishops of the empire. In this dilemma the hero of Christendom seemed an ideal compromise candidate to many of the northern barons and bishops of the empire, who had come to know him personally.[22] His father must have turned in his grave when Richard failed to leap at their invitation, which would have enabled him to close a vice around Philip by constructing the greatest empire since Rome, comprising England, Wales, Ireland, all France and the German Empire north and south of the Alps.

Richard lacked the strategic vision, but looking after his friends was another matter. As he had used his influence in the Holy Land in favour of his nephew Henry of Champagne, so he now proposed Matilda's son Otto of Brunswick in opposition to the election of Philip of Schwabia. Otto had served Richard loyally after remaining in France when his father returned to Germany. He had even been named count of Poitou – a post for which his youth and haughty disregard for local customs and laws made him a disastrous appointment, despite Eleanor's tutelage.[23]

That apart, he was now a knight of proven valour, schooled in the arts of warfare by his famous uncle, and well thought of by the Church, to capitalise on which Richard borrowed 2,125 marks from a Lombard banker to grease palms that could be influential on Otto's behalf at the papal court.[24] He also outfitted his nephew in considerable splendour for his return to Saxony. Endowed with a liberal supply of money for bribes and presents to the German electors, Otto departed with Richard's blessing en route to Liège. Unwelcome there, he continued with the archbishop of Cologne to that city before leading the archbishop's knights at the assault of Aachen, which surrendered on 10 July. Within twenty-four hours he was married to the infant daughter of the duke of Lorraine, whose head was too small and whose neck too weak to wear a crown at the coronation next day.[25]

To Philip the Otto–Richard alliance was a new menace. In addition, the Church had forgiven neither his invasion of a crusader's lands nor his violent rejection of his Danish wife Ingeborg immediately after the wedding night on 14 August 1193. Contemporaries hypothesised that he had discovered she was not a virgin, or that she was sexually deformed or had bad breath. Unable to plead consanguinity in this case, he eventually adopted the humiliating argument that she had unmanned him, since admitting impotence enabled him to argue non-consummation. Whatever the truth, she remained confined in the convent of Soissons so that he could live in sin on the Ile de la Cité with his German mistress Agnès de Méranie and their children.[26]

With the whole world and Heaven too against him, there seemed nothing to lose by invading Normandy at its weakest point, adjacent to the lands of Ponthieu, united to his cause by poor Alais' body. Before he was driven back by Richard with help from Mercadier and William the Marshal, Philip had taken several castles and refused to give them up. Once again he was within minutes of capture when a bridge collapsed under the weight of too many men and horses fleeing from their pursuers close behind, and dumped him in a river, drowning twenty of the armoured knights riding with him.[27]

Richard had taken a calculated chance in leaving his main force far behind. The confusion of the skirmish at the bridge is evident from these lines in the 'life' of William the Marshal:

And in that place we unhorsed Mathieu de Montmorency and Alain de Ronci and Fulk de Gilerval with a single lance and kept them captive. Of the Frankish force there were captured at least one hundred knights. We send you the names of the more important, and you shall have the names of others when we know them, for Mercadier took about thirty whom we have not seen.[28]

Three knights unhorsed with one lance; the Marshal was not boasting. It is interesting also to note that the Flemings under Mercadier kept their own captives for ransom in addition to their pay.

From Rome at Christmas 1197 came Cardinal Peter of Capua on a peace mission. William the Marshal's squire described him as having been to a school where he had learned to prove black was white,[29] but not all the dialectic in the world could have reconciled Richard with the suzerain who had betrayed him during the exile. Nor was he amused when the cardinal argued that under canon law a bishop could not be imprisoned, and therefore he should release the battling bishop of Beauvais, who had been unlucky enough to be captured by Mercadier in May 1197 and was held in the tower of Caen.

For the mercenaries who took him prisoner, the bishop represented a source of ransom, but although offered 10,000 silver marks, Richard refused to accept it. The reason was not that the prisoner was Philip's uncle, but that he was one of the many in the Frankish host with whom Richard had fallen out personally in the Holy Land. A war of words had ensued between them, with each blistering *sirventès* from Richard answered by an equally well-composed poem from the bishop.

To the idea that he should release so arrogant a cleric, he furiously compared the inaction of the Church on his behalf when a prisoner in

Germany to its lively interest in the bishop's problems.[30] His ears ringing with a furious reminder that the prisoner had not been arrested as a bishop but captured in battle as an armed knight, unidentifiable with his visor closed,[31] the cardinal was dismissed with a warning never to return.

On a visit to Caen, Eleanor tried to solve the impasse diplomatically by asking to have the captive brought before her during one of Richard's many absences on campaign. The guards did not dare refuse. On the way, the primate, fettered hand and foot, managed to break away from them and hurl himself at the door of a church. The door being locked, he clung to the ring handle of the latch desperately invoking the Peace of God at the top of his voice. Eleanor's plan came to nothing with Richard's refusal to recognise the Bishop's right to sanctuary, after which he was transferred to even stricter confinement in Chinon.

A huge comet was sighted in July 1198 and, like all natural phenomena of this nature, considered an evil omen, although it is hard to imagine what could have been feared as worse than the famine and the ceaseless laying waste of vast tracts of land as first Philip's and then Richard's forces advanced and retreated. At long last, during a meeting in January 1199 conducted between Richard shouting his terms from a boat in mid-river and Philip on horseback on the bank, a five-year truce was agreed, motivated on both sides not so much by the approach of Lent as financial exhaustion. Neither monarch could have known that before the expiration of the five years, Normandy would be lost to the English Crown. The captains and the kings departed, the mercenaries too: returning to Flanders, Mercadier and his men found a bonus by plundering the merchants at the great fair of Abbeville.

After Richard's departure from the talks with Peter of Capua, his representatives had recourse to the traditional method of bridging rifts between royal houses, and cast around for a daughter of the house of Anjou who could be married to Philip's son Prince Louis. However, before anything could come of this, tragedy stalked Eleanor yet again.

Despite twice capturing the Capetian treasury, Richard had spent every penny on paying his mercenaries, strengthening old fortresses and constructing new ones, of which his pride was the *bellum castrum de rupe* or Château Gaillard – the 'Mighty Castle' at Les Andelys, supposedly impregnable due to all the latest ideas in castle-building that he had picked up on his travels, including rock-cut ditches and concentric walls and flanking towers with carefully worked-out fields of fire.[32] The cost rocketed to 11,500 pounds Angevin over two years, more than any other castle had ever cost.

Despite scutages raised in England during three years in succession from 1194, compared with seven in the thirty-five years of Henry's reign, Richard was always bemoaning the lot of a sovereign whose vassals did not hear his summons when his purse was empty. The country was suffering famine and epidemics of unidentified plague, during which unrest had broken out in a quickly suppressed popular rebellion in London. In a *sirventès* addressed to the count of Auvergne, who was once again exploring the possibilities of direct allegiance to Philip, Richard included these reproachful lines:

> Vos me laïstes aidier
> per treive de guierdon
> e car saviès qu'a Chinon
> non a argent ni denier.

[You no longer support me / since my pay ceased to flow. / My treasury's empty / as you very well know.]

It seemed like an answer to Richard's prayers when he heard of a hoard of Roman gold unearthed on the land of Count Aymar of Limoges shortly before Easter 1199,[33] the pride of which was a plaque depicting a king or chieftain seated at table surrounded by courtiers or members of his family. To his demand that the trove be handed over to him, Count Aymar offered to go halves – a reply that incensed Richard, coming as it did from a vassal who had been attempting to undo the knots of his allegiance by going over to Philip, and should have been all too eager to ingratiate himself.

The gold had been taken for safekeeping to the castle of Châlus, held by two sergeants-at-arms. Being low-born, their names were never certain, but were probably Pierre Brun and Pierre Basile. With them was a makeshift garrison totalling thirty-eight men, women and children.[34]

An alternative explanation of the siege is that Richard had set his sights on capturing the largest gold mine in France, not far from Châlus. Whichever is true, he defied the Lenten truce by sending Mercadier to besiege the castles of Nontron and Piégut, while he headed for Châlus with about one hundred men. At their approach on 25 March, the defenders were desperate because he had already announced that he would give no quarter.

It says much for the construction of the castle that the paltry force of defenders held out for three days. What happened after its fall is a good example of the level of violence and bloodshed in the routine siege of a relatively unimportant castle. On the evening of 26 March, Richard was checking the progress of the conscripted local peasants labouring for his sappers undermining the wall. Its entrance shielded by wattle fences from the hail of missiles, they had dug a huge cavern in the hillside. The roof was propped up with tree trunks copiously packed with pig carcasses smeared with pitch and other combustible material which, when fired, would consume the props and bring the wall down, making a breach through which the attackers could swarm.

Richard was wearing a helmet but no armour and carrying a buckler to fend off stray missiles fired from the arrow slits high up in the walls of the keep. Their own supplies of arrows long since exhausted, the garrison was reduced to scrambling about at risk to life and limb, picking up missiles that had been fired at them and failed to break or deform on landing. Pierre Basile had spent the day dodging the incoming fire under the shelter of a huge frying pan from the castle kitchen used as a shield and was now at the arrow slit still visible in the wall of the keep, hoping for a target of opportunity before the light went (plate 21).

There are two versions of what happened next. In the first, distracted for a moment, Richard let his shield drop at the very second a reused arrow from his own armoury flew through the air to pierce his shoulder. Giving no sign to the mercenaries around him of the pain he was suffering, he mounted his horse and rode back to the house commandeered for his use.

The more credible version is that the missile was a reused crossbow quarrel. Robin Hood and William Tell apart, the longbow as a military weapon was used less for marksmanship than to provide a massive barrage of missiles falling from the sky into which enemy troops had to advance through a dangerous confusion of terrified and injured horses.

The accurate range of a crossbow was greater and the speed of the quarrel faster than an arrow, which is why the weapon had been outlawed by the Lateran Council of 1139 as being unchivalrous. Ironically, Richard was one of the kings whose troops had used this weapon in defiance of the ban both in Cyprus and the Holy Land. He was also credited by Guillaume le Breton with introducing the weapon into France.[35]

Caught literally off guard, he was hit by the quarrel where the neck joined the left shoulder.[36] While it would have been difficult to conceal an arrow nearly three feet long sticking out of his neck, a far shorter quarrel could have been hidden in the poor light in order not to depress the mercenaries' morale. He had many times been wounded, and this was not the first crossbow bolt to pierce his skin. After riding back to his quarters, he was laid on a couch, where Mercadier's medic attempted to pull out the missile in the flickering light of torches. The wooden shaft broke off, as it was designed to do, revealing the mark of the Angevin armoury at Chinon but leaving the metal head still in the wound. In his clumsy efforts to remove this, the medic cut deeper and deeper into the shoulder muscles.[37]

Bandaged and plastered and fortified with alcohol, the only analgesic available, Richard carried on directing the siege next day, but infection had entered his tissues, whether on the quarrel or the hands and knife of the medic. By the morning of 28 March the stench of gas gangrene and steadily increasing pain told him that an agonising death lay ahead. In his years of campaigning he had personally seen thousands of men, women and children dying at his command or in his cause. He therefore had no illusions what was happening and sent a sealed letter to Eleanor in Fontevraud, instructing her to come to Châlus with all possible speed.

She in turn dispatched the Abbess Matilda of Bohemia, who was the most discreet of messengers, to tell Berengaria to come from Maine. That errand discharged, she was to try to find John, whose precise whereabouts in the north were unknown. Eleanor's choice of a nun for the second part of this errand hints that she suspected John of being in an area where an Angevin knight, or even a cleric from Fontevraud, might not be welcome.

Setting out herself with the abbot of Turpenay and a small escort, she covered the distance of more than one hundred miles that separated Fontevraud from Châlus by travelling day and night.[38] Despite her speed, the stink of the gases formed by bacteria in the wound and the discoloration of the necrosed tissue told her that her son was beyond any help save spiritual consolation from his chaplain and crusading comrade, Pierre Milo.[39]

However, Eleanor had come not to nurse, nor to give way to her feelings, but to safeguard the succession and discreetly unburden Richard of his last wishes. Who was present, apart from herself, remains a mystery. If a testament was dictated to Milo or the Abbot, it was never to see the light of day although Otto was said to have been generously remembered, as were Richard's favourite religious foundations like La Sauve Majeure, east of Bordeaux. As to the succession, there is no record of the clause in the Treaty of Messina appointing Arthur ever being rescinded; had Richard changed his mind and named John, Eleanor would have acted differently in the immediate future.

Putting his spiritual affairs in order, the dying king was up against the awkward fact that his last confession was before the wedding to Berengaria seven years before. This was later camouflaged by the chroniclers pretending that the soul of the great hero of Christendom had been labouring under an unchristian hatred for Philip, which he had not been prepared to renounce.[40] The more likely reason not to have confessed was the refusal of a genuinely pious believer to pretend contrition for his homosexuality so that he could take the sacrament after absolution. Only on his deathbed could he sincerely say that he would not commit the sin again.

As one of the final acts before meeting his Maker, he had the now victorious mercenaries, who had slaughtered all the other defenders, haul Pierre Basile before him in chains, and pardoned the sergeant-at-arms as being the instrument of God's displeasure at his defiance of the Lenten truce.[41] Despite the royal pardon and the gift of a pouch of gold coins from Richard, Basile was later flayed alive by the mercenaries and hanged from the battlements.[42]

Disposing of the parts of his own body, Richard commended his heart to Rouen, where Young Henry lay among the former dukes of Normandy, and his body to Fontevraud, there to be buried at the feet of his father in atonement for a son's betrayal. To England, he gave not a thought. About 7 p.m. on 6 April, eleven days after he was wounded, and after receiving absolution and communion from Milo the Chaplain, Eleanor's favourite son died in agony at the age of forty-two.

What happened to the treasure of Châlus, the greed for which had caused Richard's death, is unknown. Was the flaying alive of Pierre Basile an act of vengeance for daring to kill a king or a torture to make him betray the whereabouts of the treasure? Since it was never heard of again, the likelihood is that either it never existed or was hacked up and shared out among the mercenaries, later being melted down.

Fortz chausa es, wrote Gaucelm Faidit: it is a awful thing . . .

> . . . *car cel q'era de valor caps e paire*
> *lo rics valens Richartz, reis dels Engles*
> *es mortz. Ai Dieus, cals perd'e cals dan es!*
> *Cant estrains motz e cant greus ad ausir.*
> *Ben a dur còr totz hom qu'o pot sofrir.*

[. . . for the very father-figure of valour, / brave Richard, King of the English, is dead. / God knows, 'tis a terrible thing to be said. / Only the hardest-hearted man can hear / such cruel news without shedding a tear.]

Despite her grief, Eleanor could not permit herself the luxury of mourning. There was no time for that. Torn between the total unsuitability of both Arthur and John as successors to all Richard's titles, she rode back to Fontevraud at the slower pace of a funeral cortège, using the time to try to find a way of ensuring that the empire she and Henry had built should not crumble to dust one short decade after his death.

TWENTY

A Choice of Evils

With Berengaria never having been crowned in England, but only by the bishop of Evreux in Limassol – and being in any case unable to face down such a powerful mother-in-law – it was Eleanor, who had clung at such cost to her titles, who was the unquestioned queen of the English, duchess of Normandy and duchess of Aquitaine. For the second time, a king's death had left her the only crowned figure of regal authority in England and the continental possessions.

When the cortège reached Fontevraud, churchmen high and low were already there, including the persistent Peter of Capua presenting condolences on behalf of the Pope. Berengaria was present to mourn officially the husband she had never known, and whom she was to survive by a celibate widowhood of thirty-one years devoted to good works, including the foundation of the Cistercian Convent of L'Epau near Le Mans, where her effigy can still be seen in the chapter house (plate 24). With her came Matilda of La Perche, daughter of Matilda of Saxony, to press the case of a third contender for the succession. Her brother was Richard's favourite nephew, Otto of Brunswick.

Eleanor's dilemma had included him. Of the three, he was the nearest to Richard, and for a while he had been duke of Aquitaine in name at least. But he knew nothing of England, and that was the key to it all. John knew both the country and the language, but . . . Still, she wavered.

The eulogies spoke of the dead king as indeed the father-figure of valour, although many remembered him as an irresponsible monarch, whose arrogance and passion for war had twice impoverished his subjects. The Lionheart sobriquet came much later, deriving from the reverse of his seal, which showed him mounted in full armour and brandishing his sword with a shield that differed from Henry's in being not blank but bearing a *lion passant* from 1195 onwards. During the last year of his life this begat two others, to become the three golden *lions passants* still a feature of the English royal standard.

In Normandy on 7 April William the Marshal received a letter dictated by Richard after his injury, appointing him keeper of the castle of Rouen and guardian of its treasure. Staying at the priory of Notre Dame du Pré across the river was Archbishop Hubert Walter. Guessing that the wound was serious, they discussed the succession, William supporting John and the Archbishop Arthur.[1] On 10 April a second messenger arrived with news of the king's death four days earlier.

Hugh, the much-travelled bishop of Lincoln, met the Abbess Matilda on the road and was taken into her confidence,[2] which caused him to hurry southward to officiate at the funeral in Fontevraud. There he took precedence over the bishops of Agen, Poitiers, Angers and a host of lesser clergy swarming to the royal funeral like bees to honey. Among the mourners were the seneschals who had served Eleanor and Richard and now waited anxiously to know who was their new master.[3] Arthur, John or Otto?

The news of his brother's death reached John dallying in treason yet again. Disenchanted with he considered Richard's meanness in paring his allowances to the bone, he had been attempting to form a new power block by exploiting the mistrust of Constance of Brittany and the Breton lords for Richard, Philip and anyone else who was not a Breton. Hastily disentangling himself from these now potentially dangerous friends, John hastened south. His first port of call was not Fontevraud but the nearby Angevin treasure castle at Chinon, whose treasury was empty. There he met Bishop Hugh of Lincoln returning from the funeral, and attempted to enlist the venerable churchman– diplomat's support in his cause as Richard's successor.[4]

The original courageous purpose of Hugh's journey to Anjou had been to protest over the punitive taxation in England, despite his own clergy and those at Angers, where he had been staying, urging him never to confront Richard about money. Such was the lawlessness of the country that his treasury and horses had been stolen en route, but still he had pressed on with his mission. Although he had enjoyed a relationship of mutual respect with Henry, Hugh disapproved of all the princes born to what he considered Eleanor's adulterous and consanguineous second marriage – and specifically of John, who was so scarred by his childhood experience as an oblate that he had no time for religion.

Despite John's promise of bribes, Bishop Hugh consented only to return to Fontevraud with him and see how matters lay. There, despite the gratitude he owed to Abbess Matilda – presumably left far behind on the road from Brittany – for the delicate errand she had performed so discreetly, John flouted her wishes by hammering on the abbey door and demanding to be shown his brother's tomb,[5] until restrained by Bishop Hugh, who diplomatically obtained permission for him to enter.

In Paris Philip proclaimed as suzerain of the continental possessions that Arthur, being the son of an older brother, took precedence over Richard's younger brother John. Emboldened by this, Constance used Arthur's name to appoint Guillaume des Roches the new seneschal of Anjou, in opposition to John's candidate Amaury de Thouars.

On Easter Sunday, 18 April, Bishop Hugh preached in the abbey church at Fontevraud a homily none too subtle on the duties of kingship. It was quite normal for the congregation to fidget and chatter among themselves, for except at the three great feasts of Easter, Whitsun and Christmas they did not take communion, but only witnessed the service. John's behaviour, however, exceeded the normal bounds. Growing bored, he twice yelled at Bishop Hugh to cut the sermon short, and was taken aback the third time when ordered to leave the sanctuary.[6] It was not an auspicious beginning for a prince who needed all the support he could get, especially from the Church.

He also needed Eleanor, as dowager queen and witness to Richard's last wishes, to rebut Philip's announcement that Arthur was the legitimate successor. But Eleanor had withdrawn from the world, to hide her grief. With all his shortcomings and vices, Richard alone of her sons had been of the same ilk as William IX and Prince Raymond of Antioch – a fitting poet–count of Poitou and warrior–duke of

Aquitaine, for whose sake she had thought worthwhile all her efforts to keep her heritage intact.

On 21 April, three days after John's angry exchanges with Bishop Hugh, she disciplined herself to resume her feudal duties, affixing her seal to a charter confirming the gift to the abbey of Turpenay of a vivary or fish-farm at Langeais in consideration for its abbot's help in the arrangements after Richard's death. John was one of the witnesses, but is described only as her 'very dear son' and 'Count of Mortain'.[7] The other significance of the charter is the question it raises: for what was the Abbot being rewarded at this fraught time? Had he been present when Richard dictated a will that Eleanor suppressed, naming Arthur of Brittany or Otto of Brunswick to succeed him? Was the gift a reward for silence? Three months later, on 21 July, Richard's confidant Milo the Chaplain was also rewarded by gifts to his abbey of Le Pin. Was this for long and faithful service, or something else?

Shortly after Easter, news reached Eleanor at Fontevraud that a consortium of Breton barons with Arthur and his mother Constance had been joined by many barons and knights from Maine and Anjou under Guillaume des Roches, whom she had last seen at the funeral. Marching against Angers, only a day's ride from Fontevraud, they took it without opposition.[8] Le Mans and several other cities went over to them, Count Aymar of Limoges exacting revenge for the fateful siege of Châlus by lining up also on Arthur's side.

The news forced Eleanor reluctantly to give her backing to John, who hurried north to be invested on 25 April by Archbishop Walter of Rouen with the ceremonial sword and golden crown of the dukes of Normandy. Even at this solemn moment, John could not control his disrespect for the Church, joking with his cronies during the service and dropping the ceremonial sword. Crowned duke of Normandy – a vital step towards the throne of England – he sent the ever-loyal William the Marshal and Archbishop Hubert Walter across the Channel with orders to see every royal castle prepared for civil war.[9] They were also to extract from all free men an oath of fealty to John as duke of Normandy and son of King Henry. He would not be king of England until crowned there.

Many of the Anglo-Norman magnates gathered in council at Nottingham could find little good in him, except that he knew the country and spoke the language which Richard had not learned and even Henry had never properly mastered, using an interpreter for any important conversation. Their final decision was to accept him, but on conditions that laid the foundation for Magna Carta sixteen years later. In Normandy, so little confidence had they in their new duke's ability to keep the duchy independent of Philip that many barons and knights claimed the protection of the Peace of God by going on pilgrimage or answering the call of the Fourth Crusade to the Holy Land until the political–military situation had stabilised.[10]

Normandy and England went together, as they had done for 133 years. As far as the other possessions of Henry's empire were concerned, Eleanor was not prepared to give John Poitou and Aquitaine. Luckily she had at her side Mercadier, who had served both Henry and Richard and was now her man so long as she could pay him. Ordering his mercenaries back with all speed from the Limousin, he led them against the coalition forces, presenting the rare phenomenon of two *ad hoc* armies confronting each other, each with a woman at its head. Constance's forces fell back on Le Mans, leaving Angers to be sacked by Eleanor's men under Mercadier, whose reward was to hold its principal citizens for ransom.

Meanwhile, John as duke of Normandy was leading a force of Normans into Maine. In retaking Le Mans, fire and sword were again the order of the day, but Constance had slipped away with Arthur to Tours, where Philip again took charge of the boy as an important piece to be saved for later in the game. The immediate danger over, Eleanor wheeled south to make a regal progress through her own domains of Poitou and Aquitaine, accompanied by an impressive retinue of bishops and barons.

In the midst of this turmoil ex-Queen Joanna caught up with her in Niort, bearing a tale of betrayal and attempted murder. Loyally suppressing a revolt by some of Count Raymond's vassals while he was campaigning elsewhere, she had narrowly missed death when her own knights changed allegiance and set fire to her tent. Whether she had been wounded in the attack, or burned, is unclear, but she was pregnant and too deeply shocked to keep up with her mother's exhausting

Seal of John

itinerary further than La Rochelle,[11] from where Eleanor dispatched her to Fontevraud, to be cared for by the nuns while she continued her grand tour.[12]

She was not seeking to solicit her vassals' loyalty to John, who was to them a distant figure who had spent much of his life on the wrong side of the Channel and had neither Richard's valour nor his poetic prowess to commend him. Instead, she reintroduced herself to her vassals – most of whom had not been born when she inherited the duchy in 1137 – as mother of one legendary dead hero and granddaughter of the great crusading troubadour-duke William IX. It is an illustration of her attitude to John that she did not think it worthwhile to attend his coronation at Westminster on 27 May, at which he buckled the belt of earldom on William Marshal in the expectation of long and loyal service – an expectation that was not disappointed.

Taking advantage of his absence from France, Eleanor made overtures to Philip, whom she met at Tours in mid-June, swearing fealty to him for Poitou and Aquitaine and receiving in return the kiss of peace. Satisfied that her inheritance was now safe from John, she continued dispensing gifts and confirming privileges on an exhaustive tour that lasted until mid-July, gathering support for herself not only from her barons but also from the burgeoning communities of merchants and free artisans in the cities, four of which received from her their freedoms: La Rochelle, Poitiers, Saintes and Oléron, where she put her seal to what is considered the first code of maritime law in France.

At St Jean d'Angély she authorised the foundation of a commune, compensating the abbey out of her own pocket for the taxes it would thereby lose. In Bordeaux, however, she found it difficult to balance the appeal of the burgesses for their freedom against the authority of the Archbishop, the chapter and religious foundations both inside and outside the walls. Here she was up against those very freedoms and privileges that had been the price demanded by Geoffroi de Lauroux for negotiating her marriage to Louis sixty-two years before.

Her compromise was to grant to the citizens exemption from taxes and feudal duties without going so far as to authorise them to form a commune electing its own mayor and officers. In compensation, she did, however, grant them a mint in the city.[13] Elsewhere, too, the Church, with which so many of her predecessors had been at odds, was generously treated, as at Richard's favourite abbey of La Sauve Majeure. Its founder Geraldus having recently been declared a saint by Innocent

III, Eleanor confirmed the charters given to the foundation by Louis and Henry and Richard and Otto, extending the annual fair to two weeks' duration.[14]

Having quietened internal dissent with these tactics, she turned her attention to the strategy for safeguarding the integrity of the duchy, which was once again threatening to fragment into two separate entities, north and south of the Garonne. Philip having accepted Arthur's homage for the three Angevin counties, she had no wish to give John any rights over Aquitaine in case he lost Normandy or died without issue, in which case Arthur would succeed by default. She therefore made a convoluted but feudally sound arrangement.

Maintaining that Richard's dukedom had been for his lifetime only and was not therefore part of his inheritable estate, she reasserted plenary powers for herself on the grounds that she had never actually renounced her titles as countess of Poitou and duchess of Aquitaine even during the fifteen agonising years when Henry used every trick to force her to do so. She then ceded the county and duchy to John on condition that he swear fealty to her and renounce all his rights for the duration of her lifetime or until such earlier time as might suit her. Her price was that he confirm all her prerogatives as queen of England, which kept her still the richest woman in the world.

She was at Rouen with John towards the end of June when Joanna caught up with her again, pleading poverty because she received no allowance from her husband.[15] Arguing that her own wealth was already committed, Eleanor persuaded John to grant his sister an annual pension of 100 marks.[16] At the time he was being dunned for repayment of the money Richard had borrowed from the Lombard bankers to buy Otto's election as emperor, but had so little reserves that he solved the problem by granting total exemption from customs duties to a merchant of Moissac, who then discharged the debt to the Lombards. John also gave Joanna a lump sum of 3,000 marks.

In September, the sick and pregnant ex-queen of Sicily was still in Rouen, her condition preventing a return to Fontevraud. Feeling near death, she dictated a testament leaving the major part of the 3,000 marks to be disposed of by Eleanor in charitable works for the religious and the poor, with explicit mention of a legacy towards the costs of a new kitchen for the convent at Fontevraud, in consideration for which she wanted to be buried there as a nun.

Advanced pregnancy being normally an insuperable barrier to becoming a bride of Christ, Eleanor sent for Abbess Matilda to solve the problem. At the same time, fearing the worst, she summoned Hubert Walter who diplomatically regretted that, although archbishop of Canterbury, he had no powers to admit the dying ex-queen to the Order, as this was the prerogative of the Abbess. To calm Joanna's desperate pleas, Eleanor pressured him to call a council of clerics including some nuns from Fontevraud, who agreed that the wishes of the ex-queen of Sicily were so extraordinary that they must be divinely inspired. With this alibi, he admitted her to the Order shortly before she died[17] and was delivered by Caesarean section of a son, who survived just long enough to be baptised Richard after his dead uncle.

In the space of five months in her seventy-eighth summer Eleanor had lost a son and a daughter before her very eyes. With Marie de Champagne having also died during the siege of Châlus, only of the ten children borne to Louis and Henry only Eleanor of Castile and John survived. Escorted by John, the grieving dowager queen accompanied the funeral cortège towards Fontevraud, after prising out of him a modest pension for Joanna's two maids-in-waiting, left penniless by the demise of their mistress.[18]

It was somewhere near the pillaged city of Le Mans that they met Guillaume des Roches, whom John enticed into changing sides again[19] by confirming him as seneschal, to the detriment of Count Amaury of Thouars, who then declared for Philip and helped Richard's old enemy Guillaume des Barres to spirit Constance and Arthur away to the safety of Paris.[20]

The new king of England had intended spending Christmas 1199 north of the Channel, not having been back there in the six months since the coronation, but decided to hold his Christmas court at Bures instead. Early in January between Les Andelys and Gaillon he met Philip, who had been rendered somewhat more amenable to relinquishing Arthur's claim to Maine and Anjou because of the setbacks suffered by Constance's forces there after their initial successes. He now offered to allow John to swear fealty for Normandy, Anjou, Maine and Brittany, with Arthur in turn to do homage to John for Brittany. The price for this recognition of John's succession was his confirmation of Richard's cession of the Norman Vexin plus the county of Evreux plus a relief for his lands or *rechatum* payment of 20,000 English marks.[21] The money having to be raised by a special *carucage* tax in England earned the new king a second unfortunate nickname: Softsword.

The other item on the agenda was the marriage of Philip's son Prince

Louis to Eleanor's granddaughter Princess Urraca of Castile, whose dowry was to be provided out of Capetian territory taken by Richard. This was Eleanor's way of reuniting her blood with that of the Capetians after two generations' interval, for the match had been first mooted when she travelled to Tours and swore fealty to Philip in mid-June.

With John in England trying to collect 20,000 marks from a land stripped bare by Richard's voracity, Eleanor took the long road south from Poitiers to Castile with a retinue that included the archbishop of Bordeaux. Even in a heated motor vehicle this can be a tough journey in winter. That she felt it necessary to go in person despite her approaching seventy-eighth birthday indicates how crucial she felt the choice of bride to be. Before the end of the first day's ride, not far from the site of the ambush in which Patrick of Salisbury had died and William the Marshal nearly lost his life, she fell into another ambush. The Lusignans were intent on revenge for her engineering the repudiation of their relative Bourguigne by Raymond of Toulouse and demanded in return for Eleanor's liberty the county of La Perche, sold by them to Henry years before.[22] Pragmatic as ever, Eleanor yielded what Hugues de Lusignan demanded and hurried on her way, following the old pilgrim roads to Spain and defying the winter conditions in the Pyrenean passes.

She was received at Alfonso VIII's court in Palencia with all the courtesies appropriate to the doyenne of European royalty. In the civilised luxury of a Christian palace enhanced by all the comforts and knowledge of its Muslim neighbours, she had time to regain her strength and get to know her grandchildren because there was no point in hurrying back for a wedding that could not take place before the end of Lent. Why then had she been in such a hurry to get there? Three of Eleanor of Castile's daughters were of 'marriageable' age. Berengaria, the eldest, was already betrothed to the heir of the neighbouring kingdom of Leon, and thus not available. Meeting their intimidating grandmother for the first time in the presence of Philip's emissaries,[23] the other two adolescent princesses may not have known that they were *both* being assessed.

Comparing the girls with her instinct for people honed by the events of an extraordinary life, Eleanor decided that fourteen-year-old Urraca was a less good choice than her younger sister Blanca. Had she perhaps a *frisson* on first seeing this girl of twelve who so closely resembled herself at that age, with her broad features and fearless gaze, her long brown hair and her cool classical beauty – and who had also grown up and been educated in a court where troubadours were welcomed and honoured as they had been at Poitiers so long before? Something of the sort occurred, for there was no doubt in Eleanor's mind. On the pretext that Urraca's name would sound outlandish to Frankish ears, whereas Blanca translated easily as Blanche, the choice was formalised and the rejected elder princess engaged instead to the heir to the throne of Portugal.[24]

The return journey across the Pyrenees by the pass of Roncevaux, where the Augustinian abbey alone offered sparse accommodation for the night, lasted well into Lent against the stream of pilgrims taking advantage of the warmer weather to set out for Santiago de Compostela. Stopping to celebrate Easter in Bordeaux, Eleanor was greeted by Mercadier, who had not accompanied her all the way to Spain because he was acting as constable of Aquitaine, but was going to escort her and Blanca north. On 9 April, taken unawares in what may have been a drunken street-fight, he was fatally stabbed by a mercenary from another band led by one Brandin,[25] whom some believed to be in the pay of John. Whether his killing was premeditated or spontaneous, it came as a severe blow to Eleanor, who now had no one on whom she could rely or keep order in her name.

She summoned up the strength to accompany Blanca to Fontevraud, where she stayed to recover from the journey from Castile, Blanca under her Gallicised name of Blanche being escorted by the archbishop of Bordeaux and the bishops of Saintes and Poitiers to Richard's 'impregnable' Château Gaillard in Normandy. There she was the guest of her uncle John until the marriage could be celebrated by the archbishop at the small church of Port-Mort in Norman territory on the right bank of the Seine a few miles south of Château Gaillard. The ceremony had to be performed on Norman soil because Philip's territory still lay under interdict and he was unable to attend, being excommunicate. John too was absent, having constituted himself a hostage on Frankish soil so long as Arthur was in Normandy.

Constance of Brittany was another notable absentee, having been diagnosed as suffering from leprosy. Her son was now fourteen, the same age as the groom. After witnessing his Castilian cousin's marriage Arthur did homage to John for Brittany with Philip's consent,[26] after which he accompanied the young couple to the palace on the Ile de la Cité where Eleanor had first arrived with Louis, aged fifteen. There, no church bells rang out to welcome them, for under interdict every bell was lowered to the ground.

Blanche was to justify Eleanor's choice by becoming one of France's greatest queens, who in 1230 checked the attempt by her cousin, England's Henry III, to regain the French territories lost by their uncle John so early in his reign. She even came within an ace of commanding her own invasion fleet from Boulogne, and remained the lifelong counsellor of her son Louis IX, canonised as Saint Louis – making Eleanor the only woman ever to number two royal saints among her great-grandsons, the other being San Fernando of Spain.

TWENTY-ONE

To a Death in the Morning

When escorting Blanche to Rouen for the wedding, the archbishop of Bordeaux had been charged by Eleanor with another duty: the undoing of John's consanguineous marriage of convenience to Isabelle of Gloucester, which was never going to provide an heir for the throne of England. Shortly afterwards, the pliable bishops of Avranches, Bayeux and Lisieux cut the knot between the king and his estranged wife[1] which left him free to seek another spouse while at the same time keeping his hands on her dowry. Visiting Eleanor at Fontevraud, where another spell of illness had immobilised her, he found that she had her eye on another Iberian princess as a suitable bride for him. As a result, in July 1200 an embassy was dispatched to the court of Portugal.[2]

Making a cautious progress through Poitou, a county where he was not universally welcome, John was busy settling the usual feudal trivia: confirming Richard's gift of the manor of Vieux-Sauloy to Eleanor's cook Adam for an annual rent of one pound of pepper and other arrangements for her butler and maid-in-waiting, which imply that this time she really was retiring from the world.

Even he must have been surprised when two of his Saxon nephews tracked him down and informed him that his nephew Otto had not renounced the dukedom of Aquitaine or the estates bestowed on him by Richard and expected to receive the benefits therefrom. They also demanded on Otto's behalf one-half of his late uncle's treasury and his jewels, claiming that this had been Richard's dying wish at Châlus. Was this what the abbot of Turpenay had been silent about? Or had Milo the Chaplain, who certainly knew Otto personally, taken it upon himself to inform the real beneficiaries of an oral testament subsequently concealed by Eleanor? Whatever the truth of that, John's reply was to send the two young Saxons away empty-handed after citing his agreement with Philip not to give any assistance to Otto, who was at war with Philip of Schwabia, then an ally of Paris.

Uneasy among the Occitan-speaking nobility of Poitou, John was greatly relieved that the Lusignan family was friendly after the recovery of the county of La Marche as the price of Eleanor's release. Accepting their offer to mediate between him and the disaffected counts of Limoges and Angoulême, John enjoyed the lavish Poitevin hospitality of the family until his lust was aroused by the fresh young beauty of a girl living in the household. Isabella, the fourteen-year-old betrothed of his host Hugues IX, was the daughter of count Aymer of Angoulême.[3] For once the loins and the brain were sending the same message, for her marriage to Hugues would unite two powerful and ambitious neighbouring families controlling another wedge of territory that could split the Angevin lands, this time by separating Poitou from Gascony, which is why it had been both Henry's and Richard's policy to play on the natural enmity of the two clans.

Discreetly sounding out her father, John found him delighted by the idea of his daughter sitting on the throne of England. He advised, however, that this would mean war with the Lusignans when they found out. John accepted the risk and the count devised an excuse to summon Isabella home. Sending Hugues de Lusignan and his equally proud and violent brother elsewhere on the business of their estates in Normandy and England, John took a circuitous route via Bordeaux and Agen back to Angoulême with Archbishop Hélie of Bordeaux in tow.[4]

Informed on 24 August by the archbishop of the changed plans for the morrow, on which she had been due to wed Hugues, Isabella was married to John in Angoulême Cathedral next day.[5] There is no sign that the bridegroom did any work during the next forty-eight hours except for signing one charter, but some event obliged him to cut the honeymoon short, for he then hastened to put the stout walls of

Chinon between his bride and her disappointed suitor – to the embarrassment of his emissaries returning from Portugal with an agreement for the marriage to the Portuguese princess.

Eleanor had not attended the wedding. Possibly she was too weak to undertake the three-day journey. She may have taken pleasure in seeing the Lusignans repaid in their own coin, for she endowed John's young bride with the cities of Niort and Saintes. Yet this gift compared poorly with her generosity to Berengaria of Navarre, which could be because she knew that John was stirring up a hornets' nest. Once again the celibate chroniclers had a field day, imputing the entire business to Isabella for rousing the king's lust, Matthew Paris referring to her as 'an animal'.

To compensate Hugues de Lusignan, John gave him as wife one of his wards, a cousin of Isabella's named Matilda. While accepting this offer, Hugues IX and his brother were biding their time for revenge. From Chinon, the honeymooners made a leisurely progress through Normandy, crossing to Portsmouth in October. After Isabella's acceptance by the Great Council, John was recrowned and she was crowned in Westminster Abbey on 8 October at a ceremony for which no expense was stinted. Afterwards they went on a protracted tour of England to impress on his subjects that he was not a foreigner like Richard, who came to the country merely to milk it of taxes. At the Christmas court held at Guildford there were many who were taken in by John's charm, his ability to speak English and his beautiful young wife.

Although Bishop Hugh of Lincoln had allegedly died muttering what sounded like a prophecy that the son of Louis would avenge his father's memory against the children of the faithless wife who had left him, John had acted as a pall-bearer at the bishop's funeral without a care in the world. At first, it seemed Hugh's predictions had been wrong. The New Year of 1201 seemed to usher in a new age of peace between the Capetian and Plantagenet dynasties. At Easter in Canterbury John and Isabella revived the custom of crown-wearing, which Henry had put in abeyance.[6]

This was the calm before the storm.

Eleanor had been ill again, but seemed at last to have found a champion to replace Mercadier in the person of her cousin Amaury de Thouars, whom she attempted to reconcile with John by writing that he alone of all their Poitevin vassals had done her no wrong. Amaury urged him to deal swiftly with the complications caused by his marriage to Isabella of Angoulême. Instead, John ordered the constable of Normandy to seize Driencourt, one of the Lusignan castles in the duchy, and gave him orders to harry the family at every turn and despoil them of all their possessions.

On 14 May John and Isabella left England, but his ship had to put into the Isle of Wight while hers continued to Normandy. Staying at Château Gaillard shortly afterwards,[7] they were invited to Paris and spent four weeks in June and July at the palace on the Ile de la Cité as guests of Philip,[8] who politely moved out to Fontainebleau for the duration of their stay, to avoid embarrassing them by his excommunicate status. Paradoxically it was on this occasion that both monarchs pledged 2½ per cent of all their revenues for the year to the relief of the Holy Land.[9] It was true that the Lusignans had appealed to their mutual overlord over John's kidnapping of Isabella, but Philip was biding his time and stipulated only that the matter should be placed before a council of the magnates of France at some unspecified future date.

Shortly afterwards at Chinon, John and Isabella were joined by Berengaria, to whom he had refused so far to pay any of the money from her dower estates, having tried to persuade her to come to England earlier in the year to settle the issue. She had wisely preferred to stay in France, hoping that the backing of the archbishop of Bordeaux at Chinon and the proximity of Eleanor, who had arranged her marriage in the first place, would win her suit. She was proven right when John settled on her an annual pension of 1,000 silver marks and the possession of Bayeux and two castles in Anjou.[10] The generosity was not for love of his widowed sister-in-law, but as a preliminary to an alliance with her brother Sancho VII of Navarre, who had upset the Church by campaigning in North Africa in the service of the Almohads, during which time he had lost the provinces of Alava and Guipúzcoa to Castile.

Alliances were changing in the north of France too. On the death of Constance of Brittany at the end of August, Arthur aligned himself openly with Philip, of whom he was still a ward. John's heavy-handedness with the Lusignans was playing into his enemies' hands: Aymar of Limoges and Raymond of Toulouse took the Lusignan side. Autumn came, and John made the surprising decision to challenge Hugues le Brun and his family to trial by combat, in which each side would be represented by champions. The reply from the other side was another appeal to Philip, who summoned John to appear before a council. Throughout the winter, John prevaricated.

If Eleanor thought she would end her days in peace, she was wrong; one of her bitterest moments was yet to come. She spent Christmas at

Fontevraud, far from John's and Isabella's court at Caen, while Philip held in check the Lusignans, Toulouse, Limoges and Arthur. In March 1202, his patience paid off. His mistress Agnès de Méranie having died while John and Isabella were in Paris, Rome legitimised his bastards by her and lifted his excommunication.[11] At the end of Lent, on 28 April he summoned John to Paris, this time not as a friend but as a vassal who had failed to do homage for Normandy after Richard's death, and for the injury he had done Hugues de Lusignan. To John's reply that no king could be treated in this way, Philip retorted quite properly that he had not been summoned as king of England, but as duke of Normandy and count of Anjou, in which capacities he owed a vassal's obedience.

Invoking the custom that dukes of Normandy had no obligation to treat with their suzerain anywhere except on the borders of the duchy, John agreed to a meeting there but never arrived at the rendezvous. Having taken his measure during their connivance at the time of Richard's captivity and during the month John and Isabella spent on the Ile de la Cité, Philip knew Henry's youngest son was not of the stuff that had made his father ruler of an empire; nor was he a master of the arts of war like Richard. Testing the ground as he went, Philip invaded Normandy to within a short ride of Rouen itself and celebrated his victorious advance by knighting Arthur, accepting his homage as duke of Brittany and count of Maine and Anjou – and betrothing him to his newly legitimised daughter, the Princess Marie.

All this rather went to Arthur's head. In the heat of the moment, that immature prince set out with only 200 knights to Tours,[12] hoping there to link up with reinforcements from Brittany. The Lusignans arrived with the news that Eleanor had left Fontevraud, heading south for the security of her palace inside Poitiers' city walls, but had to take refuge when two-thirds of the way there in the border town of Mirebeau. Ignoring the fail-safe compact she had made with John, Arthur considered that her forced consent would enable him to add 'count of Poitou and duke of Aquitaine' to the string of titles conferred by Philip. The Frankish knights with him counselled caution, but the Lusignans wanted to get their hands on Eleanor so that they could hold her hostage. Without her long experience of politics and warfare, they argued, John would be swiftly driven from French soil.

With their help, Arthur broke into the walled town of Mirebeau, where Eleanor retreated to the citadel with a handful of knights and men-at-arms. When Arthur came to its gate to parley, he seemed to find nothing wrong in besieging his own grandmother, at one point offering to let her proceed in peace, providing she recognised his 'right' to Aquitaine. In despair that a descendant of hers had sunk so low, Eleanor dragged out the negotiations, playing for time in the expectation of help from Chinon and/or from John, to whom she had dispatched messengers.

He was recruiting new forces 100 miles away near Le Mans to make up for the feeble support he had received from England. For once he acted with a speed and effectiveness that would not have disgraced Henry or Richard in the same situation. Riding day and night, he covered the 80 miles in two days, to arrive at Mirebeau before dawn on 1 August[13] at the head of a band of mercenaries from Chinon, together with Guillaume de Braose, Guillaume des Roches and others who, well knowing John's vicious streak, had made it a condition of their support that he should not condemn to death any of Arthur's supporters captured in the town, to many of whom they were related.

Arthur's men had meanwhile forced the citizens to wall up the damaged gates of the town to prevent any surprise sortie by Eleanor's party, leaving only one gate through which men and supplies were brought in. In the belief that a relieving force could not arrive for days, it had been left open and unguarded all night. Through it, the mercenaries from Chinon stole silently into Mirebeau and began killing in the half-light of dawn. The sleeping Bretons and Franks and the Lusignan men were cut down half-awake. Guy de Lusignan, interrupted halfway through the breakfast of roast pigeon he was sharing with Arthur, was among those who managed to mount and head for the gate, only to have his horse killed under him in the street and be taken prisoner. In the close-quarter fighting, John severed the sword hand of a knight confronting him.[14] Arthur and Eleanor of Brittany were taken prisoner by Guillaume de Braose, who would pay dearly for his knowledge of what ensued.

After releasing his mother from the citadel and promising that Arthur would come to no harm, John ignored feudal practice by insisting that all the prisoners be handed over to him against an undertaking to share the ransoms with those who had taken them. He then ordered 250 captured knights to be chained to farm carts regardless of their status and driven through the countryside facing rearwards all the way to his castles in Normandy, where they were hidden away and moved from time to time so that would-be rescuers could not know who was held in which fortress.

Isabella's former intended, Hugues le Brun, was incarcerated in fetters at Caen, and Arthur held similarly in irons at Falaise Castle, 15 miles away, which had been emptied of every other prisoner. His sister Eleanor was among those shipped to England. Her exact whereabouts a mystery for years to contemporaries, she was held prisoner at Bristol Castle for four decades until dying there.

Many of the men transported with her were blinded, castrated or otherwise mutilated or starved to death in flagrant breach of John's undertakings before the assault. His thirst for revenge alienated many who had helped him take Mirebeau and were related to the maltreated prisoners. In despair of getting John to abide by the rules they had agreed before the raid, Guillaume des Roches and Amaury de Thouars changed sides yet again and swore allegiance to Philip for the duration of Arthur's imprisonment, subsequently capturing Angers in his name.

Eleanor, meanwhile, had returned to Fontevraud and, feeling her strength going at last, sought the protection of the Peace of God by taking the veil. However, the military advantage after Mirebeau went unexploited by John, who had no evident strategy in mind even after Philip, looting and setting fire to Tours, withdrew his forces. The Lusignans were ransomed after swearing fealty to John and surrendering what remained of their castles on their territory, but broke their word immediately.[15]

John and Isabella spent a leisurely Christmas at Caen, he apparently so obsessed with his young wife that he did not rise before midday. In England his agents were raising taxes high and low; the *Liberate* Roll recorded writs authorising payments from the Exchequer that amounted to the staggering sum of £14,733 6s 8d sent to Normandy between 17 October 1202 and 8 October 1203.[16] The confusion of the royal finances may be guessed at from the *rotulus redemptionis* record that some of the Norman barons had not yet fully paid their share of Richard's ransom.[17]

John could never control the temptation to borrow from whatever source presented itself. Once at Cognac, his treasury being exhausted, he was forced to borrow 100 marks from local merchants in order to replace the sick and exhausted mounts of his household so they could continue on their way.[18] The payment of Richard's ransom had been facilitated by the professional services of the main moneychanger in Rouen, Val Richer, who had also played a part in financing Château Gaillard. He now fed John's hunger for money, available at a price from a banking network that stretched from Rouen to Genoa and Cologne. Another Rouenais who lent money was Laurent du Donjon, who shrewdly secured his repayment from the English, not the Norman, Exchequer. And there were always of course the Jews, whose high rate of defaults in payment by their royal clients must have been offset by reinsurance in order for them to stay in business.

The result of all this borrowing and unproductive royal spending was inflation. In a decade, livestock prices had doubled and those of grain almost tripled,[19] exaggerating the food shortages. Scutages were levied annually from 1201 to 1206.[20] Although all this money flowing in from England helped to pay garrisons of the marcher castles, John made little other preparation for the next onslaught apart from constantly declaring that when he was ready he would retake in one blow everything Philip had conquered so far.

His most important prisoner, Arthur, was clearly guilty of treason, but Henry had pardoned his three elder sons after the rebellion of 1173–4 and John had himself been pardoned by Richard for conniving with Philip to keep him in prison more or less indefinitely. The 'reasonable' solution would have been that of Henry I, who had kept his better-entitled elder brother Robert Curthose prisoner for twenty years. But John was paranoid. In January 1203 he interviewed his nephew at Falaise, when Arthur refused to back down even after six months' solitary confinement in chains, insisting instead – if one believes the accounts – that John renounce in his favour all the territories which he should have inherited on his uncle Richard's death.

While Arthur may have had the courage to refuse homage to his uncle, it is unlikely that he would, after so long a period of sensory deprivation chained in an unlit dungeon on a near-starvation diet of bread and water, have invented such a dangerous claim. Had he too somehow learned of an oral testament by Richard while dying at Châlus, giving him some legal title to what he was demanding?

It would seem that John thought so, for shortly afterwards he decided to make Arthur irrevocably unfit to rule Brittany or anywhere else. It provides a little perspective that in the same month he wrote to his chamberlain Hubert de Burgh, ordering him to exchange a prisoner in his charge for an engineer named Ferrand, captured by Philip. Observing the *lex talionis* or law of retaliation, he instructed Hugh that 'if Ferrand be delivered whole, let Peter be delivered whole also. But if Ferrand be lacking in any limb, Peter must first be deprived of the same limb and then delivered in exchange.'[21] It was a violent age: husbands beat wives, parents beat children, monks beat each other to improve their souls, courts of justice ordered flogging, mutilation, death[22] and ordeal by hot iron and water.

John ordered Arthur to be blinded and castrated. Of the three men-at-arms detailed for the job, only one agreed to go through with it and so botched the start of his grisly task that Hubert de Burgh countermanded the king's orders and later defended his action by claiming that if he had carried them out the king himself would have been riven by remorse.

Meanwhile, Isabella was besieged at Chinon by Amaury de Thouars. From Le Mans John sent a mercenary force under Pierre de Préaux, which relieved the siege and escorted the queen of England back to John. Relief at her deliverance had not softened her husband's heart. Not even the Channel could protect John's other captives from his malevolence. Twenty-four of them were murdered or starved to death at Corfe Castle in Dorset on his orders. After spreading rumours that Arthur had died of a mysterious illness and having his clothes distributed to the poor as a way of sounding out public reaction, John had him secretly removed to Rouen where his new custodian Robert de Vieux Point was given the castles of Appleby and Brough in faraway Westmorland as reward for his silence.

On 2 April, the Wednesday before Easter, John was staying at the fortified manor house of Molineux a few miles downriver from Rouen when Guillaume de Braose, whose captive Arthur technically was, declared that his own affairs obliged him to resign from John's service. In front of witnesses, including three justiciars, he added that the young count of Brittany had been in good health when handed over to the king's custody and that he washed his hands of any further responsibility for him.[23] The following night, John is alleged to have taken his nephew out of the citadel of Rouen by a postern gate with a few accomplices. Forced into a small boat, Arthur was stabbed to death either by his own uncle or an accomplice and the body thrown, weighted, into the middle of the Seine.[24] Whatever the precise truth, the story comes close because he was never seen again.

There are two records that differ little in essentials. The *Philippide*, an account of Philip's reign written by his chaplain Guillaume le Breton, might well have been black propaganda to besmirch the name of an enemy, but the annals of the abbey of Margam in Wales were almost certainly based on information from Guillaume de Braose,[25] who held estates near there among many others with which he was richly rewarded by his unstable king until suddenly divested of them in 1208 after his wife Matilda indiscreetly referred in public to John's role in the murder. Seizing their estates, John attempted to silence the whole family. With his wife and sons – one of whom had been made bishop of Hereford by the king – Guillaume fled to Ireland and took refuge with relatives. John sent a large force after them, capturing Matilda and one son, who were both starved to death in one of his prisons.

Within a fortnight of the fateful Thursday evening in April 1203

Eleanor received a messenger at Fontevraud bearing an oral message too confidential to be put in writing. With it came a cryptic letter from Guillaume de Braose attesting to the truth of what the messenger, Brother John of Valerant, had to impart.[26]

With the furious Bretons encroaching from the West and the lords of Maine going over to Philip, Normandy was cut off from Anjou. Guillaume des Roches captured Saumur on 23 April 1203 for Philip and the castle of Beaufort only a few miles from Fontevraud.[27] John's most respected emissaries, including the archbishop of Canterbury and William the Marshal, were unable to negotiate any terms from Philip. Eleanor's wisdom in denying Aquitaine to John for her lifetime was now evident: technically, the duchy was not yet his. With Chinon still holding out against him, Philip swung away to the north.

Throughout the spring and summer the tide of war swung steadily in his favour as one after another of John's vassals deserted him. Where was he? they asked time and again. The answer was a mystery, for the king had become so paranoid that he travelled at night, telling no one his destination and moving his treasury, his hostages and his chancery so often that even his own clerks could not find out where he had gone. By August, he had lost the eastern third of Normandy, including Vaudreuil, 12 miles from Rouen, protected now only by Château Gaillard, under siege by Philip. Stung at last into action, John attempted to relieve the fortress by river but failed with heavy casualties because someone miscalculated the tides.

To add to its other miseries, Normandy lay under interdict, the conduct of the mercenary troops on whom he was now totally dependent having alienated the bishops. William the Marshal's biographer blamed this on John's inability to control the troops of his mercenary commander Louvrecaire, who 'maltreated the people and pillaged them as though he were in an enemy's country'.[28] By December John held only Rouen and Château Gaillard, with the counties of Mortain and Cotentin and a stretch of the coast.

By now all his Norman vassals wished the conflict over. Towards the end of the month, their disaffection was fuelled by rumours that he had left Rouen and crossed the Channel with William the Marshal, saying that he was going to seek aid and counsel from the English barons but leaving the garrisons in Rouen and Château Gaillard to fend for themselves. That he had gone was true, although whether he had intended to return with money and men for the defence of Normandy remains a mystery. In any event, few Anglo-Norman barons were prepared to supply men for the war; those who had more to lose south of the Channel declared for Philip. Nor could John continue to pay the mercenaries, for his coffers were empty.[29] Although he continued to delude himself that all he had lost would be regained by one masterstroke,[30] his Christmas court at Canterbury was a sad affair.

In Fontevraud and Poitiers Eleanor was still attended by her small household of faithful relatives and followers who had been with her for years. Seemingly, she wished to play no further part in the affairs of the world, but the world would not leave her alone. Early in March 1204 she received news of the fall of Richard's 'impregnable' Château Gaillard at the end of a five-month siege. During the winter the local villagers had been rounded up and driven into it by the besiegers, but then expelled as useless mouths by the defenders, who included many of their own relatives. Trapped between the lines, where one woman gave birth in the open air, they were driven to eat grass and roots to calm the pangs of hunger, starving to death in the winter cold until Philip at last took pity on the survivors and let them through the lines.

Château Gaillard's loss signalled more clearly than any other event the end of Normandy as a fief of the English Crown. At this stage, not even Bertran de Born could pretend war glorious or that the desolation was other than total. He wrote:

> Reisme son, mas res no ges
> e comtat, mas no coms ni bar.
> Las marchas son, mas nolh marques
> e'l ric chastel e'lh bels estar
> mas li chastela non i so. . . .

[No king to call the kingdom his, / the county is no baron's land / and marches now are *sans* marquis. / Fine houses and great castles stand / but their castellans are all long gone. . . .]

Three and a half weeks later Eleanor closed her eyes for the last time, on 31 March. At dawn next day not all the chambermaids in France could awaken the April Queen. Whether this was in the palace at Poitiers or in Fontevraud is a matter on which the chroniclers differ, but all agree that she was dressed in nun's robes at her request and laid to rest in the crypt of the abbey church[31] between Henry and Richard, not far from Joanna's grave. The tombs were desecrated during the Revolution, and subsequently restored in the abbey church with their effigies, but empty. Moved again during archaeological excavations in the 1990s, they are a target for tourists' cameras as the sunlight, filtered by the stained-glass window of Richard's shield, shafts through the dust of ages (Plate 27).

It is the nature of eulogies to proclaim only the good things of a life spent, but Eleanor's in the necrology of Fontevraud is an understatement: 'She improved on her high birth by the honesty of her life, the purity of her morals, the flower of her virtues and by her life without reproach she surpassed almost all the queens of this world.'[32]

As to honesty, she was true to Aquitaine all her life and stood regardless of the price to herself between the duchy and Louis and Henry, its overlords by marriage to her – and continued to protect it from John and Philip to her dying day.

The tribute to her morals is a subtle reminder not to credit the slanders so typical of her time, by which her many enemies sought to diminish her. Women of her class knew that indulging their emotions other than in fantasy unfitted them for the high destiny to which they had been raised since infancy. That is why they needed the courts of love and why the compositions of *trobairitz* and *trobador* still have the power to move the hearer. As to a life without reproach, Eleanor was guilty of many acts morally reprehensible to modern minds, but within a few weeks of her death Rouen had fallen, and with it the last hope of John regaining Normandy. Since Poitou had passed to John on Eleanor's death, Philip sent Guillaume des Roches to conquer it in his name. Only the ungovernable province of Gascony would remain a fief of the English Crown for another two and a half centuries.

It is conventional for biographers to claim that theirs is the definitive work on the subject, yet the closer one gets to Eleanor of Aquitaine, the more certain it is that she was a far more extraordinary person than the chroniclers even hint at. The richest woman in her own right ever? Yes, she was. One of Europe's most courageous and powerful queens? Indubitably. The first 'grandmother of Europe'? The title does not do justice to a queen whose grandchildren and great-grandchildren sat on thrones from Ireland to the Holy Land.

But Eleanor was more than all that. She was a woman frequently obliged by birth and circumstance to act the traditional male role in government, diplomacy and war – and to stay clear-headed and decisive when inwardly riven by grief.

There is a terrible poignancy in the two carved heads on the wall of the nuns' kitchen at Fontevraud, whose construction was paid for by her and Joanna (plates 1, 5, 28). Still stylish with her turban headdress, still of commanding presence yet with wrinkled brow and face marked by eight decades, the aged duchess–queen gazes with inner regret for her own lost youth and sacrificed dreams at the girl she was in the full flush of youthful beauty.

That is what it looks like at first sight, but then one recalls that the woman who fought Henry's will for fifteen years of captivity never weakened herself with vain regret or self-pity. It is more likely that the anonymous sculptor has captured the old queen at the very moment she was bidding farewell close to that very spot to Princess Blanca, on her way to wed Prince Louis at Port-Mort.

Chisel has conspired with stone to convey the anguish of all the noble and royal girls dispatched to foreign lands to bear children in loveless marriages – for Eleanor knew exactly the loneliness, the pain and the hostility to which she was condemning this granddaughter of twelve so like herself at the same age in looks, intellect and spirit. If there was one thing worse than being such a pawn, perhaps it was to be a mother or grandmother trapped in a system which gave her no alternative to sending her own girls to the fate she knew all too well.

APPENDIX A

The Search for Eleanor's Face

One of the frustrations for an author researching a character born early in the twelfth century lies in the hunt for a true likeness. The later medieval passion for portraiture had not begun, and that less reliable source, the beautifully illuminated capital letter in hand-copied manuscripts, was in abeyance as a result of Cistercians like Abbé Bernard of Clairvaux, who thought that to use more than one colour in a capital distracted the eye from the text and therefore the mind from God.

Although no documentary confirmation exists, the statues of the royal couple in the south-west portal at Chartres (plates 3 and 6) have for many reasons always been accepted as portraits of Eleanor in her early twenties, together with Young Louis before the Second Crusade. The high skill of the sculptor inclined researchers to consider these accurate portraits.

From that age until her effigy at Fontevraud there was only one other accredited and photographed representation of Eleanor: an ambiguous double portrait possibly of her and Henry in the reconstructed Romanesque cloister of New York.

Luckily, in Aquitaine there was a tradition of sculpting commemorative heads at each succession. Used on capitals or set into church walls, they were a way of reminding the common people who were their new masters. The three heads in Bordeaux Cathedral (plates 2, 8, 9) are examples of this, but are darkened by time and unlit, of less than life size and have been reset long ago into the wall of the nave about nine metres high. To complicate photography even more, a hugely hideous wooden pulpit makes a frontal view impossible. By using a 102 zoom lens and a very powerful flash, it was something of a triumph for me to see them at last for the first time, thanks to some Adobe software. At last I could see what bride, groom and Geoffroi de Lauroux looked like on the day of Eleanor's wedding to Louis. And if the sculpture is not of the best quality, it still conveys the beauty, the spirit and lively intelligence of Eleanor.

In 1964 two amateur historians working in the ruined rock-cut chapel of St Radegonde on the Falcon Rock above Chinon town removed a flake of limewash to discover a finger painted directly on the rock. The finger led to a hand which became a sad-faced woman on horseback with four other riders and parts of their mounts in a fresco measuring 1.15 2 2.65 metres (plate 16). The fresco, of superior quality but fading from exposure and partly destroyed by moisture seeping through the rock in places, was dated to the later twelfth century and the richly dressed and crowned figures identified as red-bearded Henry of Anjou and Eleanor, with Joanna, Richard and Geoffrey.

Since the scene depicted is just after the failed rebellion of 1173–4, the captive queen was fifty-two at the time. While not exactly a portrait, her bold chin, hair colour and lack of wimple concord with the other known likenesses and verbal descriptions.

On the evening after photographing the fresco, I was staying nearby in the old leper hospital of the abbey of Fontevraud – the Hostellerie St Lazare. As a guest, I was able to stroll through the abbey gardens alone after they had been closed to the public for the night, hunting for I didn't know what. It was very frustrating to be in a place that Eleanor had visited many times and where she spent the last years of her life: you feel near to something, but there is nothing to see except the effigy in the abbey church.

I had visited the abbey before, but never late in the evening. It was the angle of the setting sun that drew my eye to one of the ornamental corbels just below the roof of the nuns' kitchens, the construction of which was financed by Eleanor and Joanna (plate 28). By searching for the images of Eleanor's time in hundreds of twelfth-century buildings on both sides of the Channel, I had learned to decode some of the messages that sculptors leave in their work. Most corbels are in-your-face; the obscene and erotic ones would lose their impact otherwise. Yet this finely carved old woman's head with the stylish turban headdress (plate 5) was unusual in its twisted posture, the head gazing with palpable feeling at . . . A cloud passed across the sun and like a spotlight a single shaft illuminated a beautiful and very familiar young girl's head further round the curved wall (plate 1). This had to be another angle of the face I knew so well at Chartres. . . .

It was a moment that would excite any biographer who had been hunting years for likenesses of such an elusive subject. The first corbel had to be of Eleanor aged seventy-eight when she retired to Fontevraud; the other must either be herself when young and beautiful or Blanca of Castile, her granddaughter who so closely resembled her as a girl – which in a sense was the same thing.

One learns in pursuing the long trail of research to beware the danger of believing what is convenient. Fortunately, my friend Norman Douglas Hutchinson has spent many years studying faces professionally as a portraitist whose sitters include two queens – Elizabeth II of Britain and the late Queen Mother. The different angles at which I had been obliged to take the various photographs at Bordeaux, Chartres, Fontevraud and Chinon gave him less problem than I had thought, because he was looking for the concordances of eyes, brow ridges, nose and mouth – which still betray the subject whether painted by Modigliani or drawn by a media cartoonist.

One incongruent detail was the smallness of the mouth in the head at Bordeaux Cathedral. Possibly, Norman thought, it was fashionable at the time for girls to have small mouths, so the unknown Bordelais sculptor had cheated a little to flatter his young Duchess. The effigy is stylised and the fresco is, like most frescoes of the period, a painting with a message and not intended as a portrait. In all other respects, he was satisfied that we were almost certainly looking at the same person as she aged through more than six decades and great suffering.

APPENDIX B

Eleanor's Poetry and Song

The compositions written and performed at Eleanor's courts in London, Angers and Poitiers were far from being all love songs. The 1,100 texts in medieval Occitan still extant, attributed to 450 poets, are the legacy of a cultural explosion that influenced all subsequent European lyrical poetry and might well have stimulated the Renaissance three centuries earlier than was to be the case, had not Simon de Montfort's genocidal Albigensian Crusade effectively stamped out the fires of the southern civilisation shortly after Eleanor's death.

The forms of the verses are as varied as the subjects. *L'amor de lonh*, or love from afar, is the yearning for a lady whose charms are withheld or distant, and becomes her would-be lover's overlord by unattainability. In mystical love she is the Virgin Mary, whose praises were sung by the monk Marcabru. *La canso* is a love song, generally of five or six short verses and a refrain. *L'alba* is a song in which a watcher warns the lady that dawn approaches and she must leave her lover or risk discovery by an informer who will tell her husband.

Of other popular themes, the *pastorela* tells of a pretty shepherdess being surprised by a knight, who pays her court; sometimes she yields, but she can refuse and call the other shepherdesses to her aid. *La balada* is a song to dance to, *la romança* an account of an amorous adventure, *la tenson* or *joc partit* a philosophical dialogue. *Lo sirventès* is a satire on human nature, religion or politics.

L'ensenhament is literally a lesson in verse on morals or behaviour, for the troubadours were preaching a whole philosophy, vaunting the qualities of *leialtat* or loyalty and *drechura*, which is sincerity – and *pretz*, meaning a proper self-esteem. *Valor* is a sense of values, *melhorament* self-improvement, and *jòi* not just a transient emotion but the sense of moral well-being that comes from leading an honourable life. Perhaps strangest of all for feudal times was the ideal of *paratge*, meaning equality – not of wealth or power, but of personal dignity.

If yearning for the beloved and the pain of separation are themes common to *trobador* and *trobairitz*, some themes are peculiar to the female view. In the masculine *planh*, the poet laments the death of a hero such as Richard Coeur de Lion or William IX; the poetess laments her unheroic beloved who has died. Among other typical themes were prayers for the Virgin's intercession, like this one by the *trobairitz* Na Bieiris de Romans. *Na Maria, prètz e fina valors* is a profane rewrite of the *Hail Mary*, recently approved by Urban IV:

Per ço vos prèc, si'us platz, que fin amors . . . e gauziment e dous umilitatz . . .

[I beg you, please, confer on me / a pure love and joy and sweet humility . . .]

Another poetess, Na Castelosa of Auvergne, expressed the anguish of being abandoned by her lover:

> *Mout avètz fach long estatge*
> *Amics, pòis de mi'us partitz*
> *et es mi greu e salvatge*
> *car me juretz e'm plevitz*
> *que als jorns de vòstra vida*
> *non ascetz domna mas me. . . .*

[You've let a long time pass, my friend / since the sad day you left me / and yet you swore until life's end / to have no other lady. . . .]

The troubadour's romantic compositions are masculine and self-centred; the pain that hurts is always his, but the *trobairitz* relates to other women in her situation, as in this anonymous warning 'not to make the same mistakes I did':

> *Domna qui amic non a,*
> *ben si gart que mais non n'aia*
> *qu'amors ponh òi e demà*
> *ni tan ni quan non s'apaia*
> *senes còlp fai mòrt e plaia*
> *tal no'n garia per nul mètge que ja n'aia*

[The lady who has no lover, / let her never take one either, / for Love hurts today and tomorrow / and leaves you with naught but sorrow / and the wound that does not kill / but leaves you grieving still.]

Troubadours and *trobairitz* both gave advice, but usually the men were positive, while often the ladies, like this anonymous Catalan poetess, were saying *don't*.

> No'l prenatz lo fals jurat,
> que pèc es mal ensanhat, Jana delgada.
> No jaga ab vos el lit,
> mes vos i valrà l'amic, Jana delgada.

[Don't marry this cheat, sweet Jeanne / for he is stupid and unlettered. / Don't take him to your bed, sweet Jeanne. / Your boyfriend would be far better.]

And a young *trobairitz* could ask an older woman for advice:

> Na Carenza ab bèl còrs avenenz
> donatz conselh a nos doas serors
> e car saubetz mielhz triar la melhors
> consilhatz mi segon vostr'escienz. . . .
> Penrai marit a vòstra conoissença
> O'starai mi pulcela?

[O fair and gracious Lady Carenz, / please advise us two sisters what is best. / You know better than us what stands the test / from your own long and rich experience. . . . / Shall I find me a husband, would you say / or stay single? Which is the way?]

The *trobairitz* Contesa Beatrix de Dia wrote of the heartache when betrayed by her lover:

> En grand pena lo còr me dol
> per un cavalièr qu'ai perdut.
> En tot temps aquò siá sauput
> que l'ai contentat mòrt e fol.
> Ara per el soi traïda.

Tant amor es pas pro amor
quand l'ai contentat nuèit e jorn
Al lèit e tota vestida.

[Let this be known by one and all: / my heart is rent with pain, you see / for the lover who has left me / though I pleasured him body and soul. / Betrayed by him, I'm sore distressed. / I need his love, but he's gone away / though I pleasured him night and day / both in bed and when fully dressed.]

But the saddest of all *trobairitz* poetry is the *canso de mau maridada*:

Si anc fui bèlha ni prezada
ar sui d'aut en bas tornada
qu'a un vilan sui donada
tot per sa gran manentia. . . .

[Though once for beauty I was renowned / now the whole world's turned upside-down. / Just because he's rich and powerful / they've given me to a man who's evil. . . .]

Although love was an important theme of both male and female troubadours, the word *amor* means far more than just carnal desire, while *fin amar* is pure and perfect love in what came to be the courtly sense. In Occitan, love is the motor of all things, so much so that a common way of saying 'because' is *per amor de*.

Some academics have traced the inspiration of the troubadours to Ovid's *Art of Love*, but the thrice-married Roman poet was compiling a male hunter's manual of tricks to snare the female prey, whereas troubadours depicted women as desirable equals or unattainable superiors lording it over men they enslaved. A more likely inspiration lies in the erotic and romantic poetry of Moorish Spain.

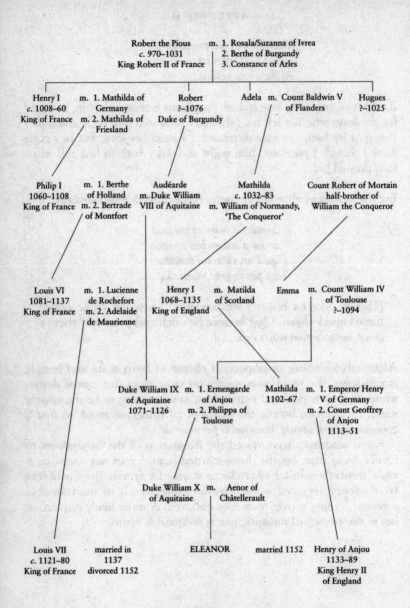

Eleanor's relatedness to Young Louis and Henry of Anjou

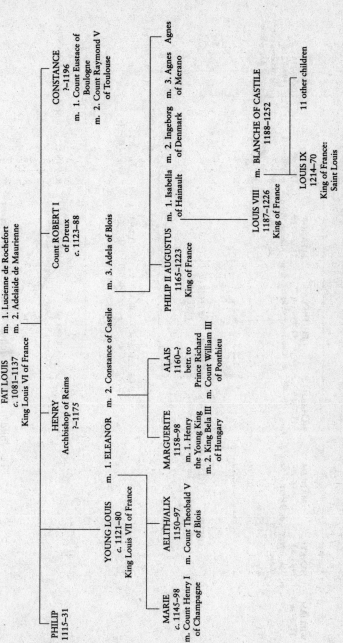

Eleanor and the House of Capet, including her marriage to Young Louis and that of her Castilian granddaughter Blanca/Blanche to Prince Louis, later Louis VIII of France

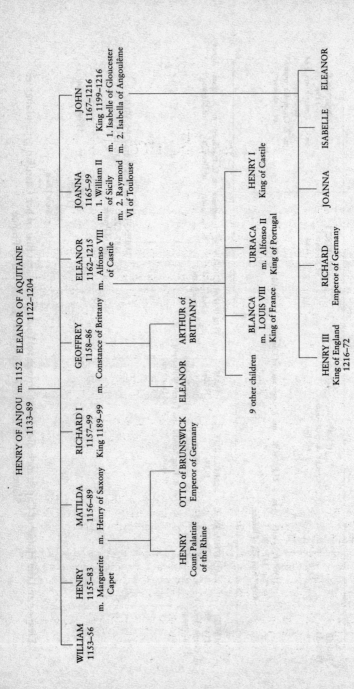

The children and grandchildren of Eleanor and Henry

Notes and Sources

1. All translations are by the author, unless otherwise indicated.
2. The Occitan texts quoted in the original come from many sources and do not conform to any standard orthography.
3. Names of principal characters are in their modern English forms. Since chroniclers and historians refer to twelfth-century figures in Latin, French and English forms and with many variations of spelling, familiar names have been retained; others have been simplified to avoid confusion, e.g. Rotrou of Warwick, Archbishop of Rouen is called 'Rotrou of Rouen'.

Sources:

PL   J.P. Migne, *Patrologiae Latinae* (221 vols), Paris, 1844–64
RHF   *Recueil des Historiens des Gaules et de la France*, ed. L. Delisle (24 vols), Paris, 1869–80
Richard   A. Richard, *Histoire des Comtes de Poitou*, Paris, Picard, 1903, vol. II

Chapter 1: The Aquitaine Succession

1. He is also referred to as William VIII, being the eighth Count of Poitou to bear the name, but to avoid confusion is here treated as the tenth Duke William of Aquitaine; for the same reason his father the troubadour duke is called William IX.
2. A tomb discovered at Padrón in Galicia in 813 was declared that of Saint James or Sant'Iago in Spanish. Compostela is a corruption of the Latin *campus stellae*; an angel was said to have revealed the whereabouts of the tomb in a field to which believers were led by a star.
3. RHF, vol. XII, p. 435.
4. Fragment of a prayer by the early twelfth-century Gascon troubadour Cercamon, a contemporary of both William IX and William X.
5. Richard, p. 56.
6. He was also King Henry I of England.

7. C. Radcliffe, *Medicine and Society in Later Medieval England*, Thrupp, Sutton, 1997, p. 151.
8. A. Molinier, *Vie de Louis le Gros par Suger, suivie de l'histoire du roi Louis VII*, Paris, 1887, p. 128.
9. Richard, p. 58: '*Ludovicus filius noster iam in regem sublimatus*'.
10. Ibid.
11. Molinier, *Suger*, p. 128.
12. Ibid.
13. RHF, vol. XII, p. 435.
14. The dates of the expedition to Bordeaux are disputed. Those given here fit all the known facts and are computed on the rate of advance for a mixed force of cavalry and infantry, plus baggage train. See Richard, p. 61.
15. A. Hyland, *The Horse in the Middle Ages*, Thrupp, Sutton, 1999, p. xi.
16. The elevated western façade, in which counterbalanced bells are hung, is a feature of Romanesque churches in the south-west.
17. There being no accents in French at the time, the name was also written Alienor (with a terminal 'd' when declined in Latin), and Aanor and Leonora or even Elinor, the variant Shakespeare used.
18. *L'Histoire de Guillaume le Maréchal*, ed. P Meyer, vol. 3, Paris, 1901, p. 28.
19. In French, *Ne quittez pas un fil avant la fin d'avril*.
20. In Occitan, *A l'entrada del temps clar*.
21. Molinier, *Suger*, p. 128.
22. Ibid., pp. 58–9.
23. L.M. Paterson, *The World of the Troubadours*, Cambridge, Cambridge University Press, 1993, pp. 103–4.
24. C. Higounet and A. Higounet-Nadal, *Grand Cartulaire de la Sauve Majeure*, Etudes et Documents d'Aquitaine series, University of Bordeaux III, 1996, ref. 1280, '*quo defunto ilustri aquitannorum duce et comite pictavis guillelmo per filiam ipsiu alienordi nobis sorte matrimonii cedit*'.
25. Using ferries across the Gironde at Blaye or the Garonne and Dordogne further south, plus the Charente at Taillebourg.
26. *Chronique de Touraine*, ed. A. Salmon, Tours, 1894, p. 134.
27. *Ordericus Vitalis, The Ecclesiastical History of England and Normandy*, ed. T. Forester (4 vols), London, 1853, vol. IV, p. 182.

Chapter 2: Mistress of Paris, Aged Fifteen

1. R. Bartlett, *England under the Norman and Angevin Kings*, Oxford, Oxford University Press, 2000, p. 537.
2. Like others housing a black virgin, the cathedral is oriented south-west to north-east, so it is really the south-western portal.
3. '*in sordibus generamur, in tenebris confovemur, in doloribis parturimur*'. From *Feria IV hebdomadae sanctae sermo 6*, in *Sancti Bernardi opera*, ed. Leclercq, Rome, Talbot & Rochais, 1957.
4. John VIII, Epist. XXXVI (28 Oct. 876) in PL, vol. 126, p. 690.

5. C. Higounet, J. Gardelles and J. Lafaurie, *Bordeaux pendant le Moyen Age*, Bordeaux, Delmas, 1963, p. 169.

6. *Vitis vinifera* is not native to France, but was introduced by Roman merchants seeking a cheaper and better-tasting alternative to expensive imported Provençal and Italian wines with the flavour of retsina, due to the pine resin used to waterproof the terracotta amphorae in which they were shipped. First attempts to cultivate Italian varieties of grapevine failed for reasons of soil chemistry. It was not until vine roots were brought from Epirus (Turkey) and planted in their own soil in trenches hacked out of the bedrock near St Emilion that the most important industry of the south-west began.

7. *Mer* here meaning a tidal river.

8. Molinier, *Suger*, p. 150.

9. Bernard of Clairvaux, *Epistolae*, in PL, vol. CLXXII, p. 286.

10. Ibid., pp. 257–9.

11. Stephen of Paris, quoted in A. Kelly, *Eleanor of Aquitaine and the Three Kings*, Cambridge, MA, Harvard, 1950, p. 13.

12. Hence the expression 'a good trencherman' from *tranche*, a slice of bread.

13. B.S. James, *The Letters of St Bernard of Clairvaux*, Thrupp, Sutton, 1998, Letter 80.

14. His later rebuilding of Lanfranc's Canterbury Cathedral resulted in the choir there being a twin of the choir in St Etienne.

15. The term was first used by Raphael and other Renaissance artists, scornful of work they considered on a level with the barbarian Gothic tribes that had destroyed the Roman Empire and its classical culture in the fifth century AD. In the eighteenth century, examples were made of Notre Dame and many other churches, whose original medieval stained glass was destroyed *en masse* and the painted walls, columns and statues scrubbed bare.

16. Derived from *paradis* because the elaborately carved western walls and doors of churches telling biblical stories for the illiterate were used as a backdrop to represent paradise in the three-day mystery plays during the Age of Faith.

Chapter 3: The Scandalous Pagan Queen

1. Grammar, rhetoric and dialectic.

2. Arithmetic, music, geometry and astronomy.

3. James, *Letters of St Bernard*, Letter 317 and note.

4. Ibid, Letter 80.

5. In Latin, *Sic et Non*.

6. John of Salisbury, *Epistolae*, in PL, vol. CIC, p. 113.

7. Since replaced by the Gothic cathedral on the same spot.

8. *Love Lyrics from the Carmina Burana*, ed. and trans. P.G. Walsh, Chapel Hill, NC and London, University of North Carolina, 1993, p. 73.

9. James, *Letters of Saint Bernard*, note to Letter 209.

10. Molinier, *Suger*, p. 151.

11. Richard, p. 67.
12. PL, vol. CLXXVIII, p. 185.
13. James, *Letters of St Bernard*, note to Letter 235.
14. Ibid., Letter 239.
15. See, for example, G.R. Evans, *Bernard of Clairvaux*, Oxford, Oxford University Press, 2000, p. 69: *ecce pax non promissa sed missa, non dilata sed data, non prophetata sed praesentata*.
16. James, *Letters of St Bernard*, Letter 92.
17. Ibid., Letter 326.
18. Bernard of Clairvaux, *Vita Prima*, in PL, vol. CLXXXV, p. 327.
19. W. Vandereycken and R. van Dath, *From Fasting Saints to Anorexic Girls*, London, Athlone Press, 1996, p. 15.
20. M. Furlong, *Visions and Longings*, London, Mowbray, 1996, p. 65.
21. The canons of Bordeaux rejecting the Benedictine Rule he sought to impose on them, Geoffroi placed the cathedral of St André under interdict, its altars overthrown, the Host removed and the doors locked. He was not to return to Bordeaux for five years.
22. In Latin, *cum assensu reginae Alienordis ducissae Aquitanorum*.

Chapter 4: 'I married a monk'

1. *Ilm aljebr wa'lmuqabalah*, literally 'the putting together of parts', was a term also used for mending broken bones.
2. In Latin, *pax ecclesiae*, promulgated in AD 990 at Charroux, Narbonne and Le Puy.
3. M. Bull, *Knightly Piety and the Response to the First Crusade*, Oxford, Clarendon Press, 1993, p. 57.
4. Ibid., p. 55.
5. In Latin, *treuga* or *treva dei*, first codified in 1027 at the Synod of Elne, near Perpignan.
6. A. Hyland, *The Medieval Warhorse*, Thrupp, Sutton, 1994, p. 59.
7. *Ex chronico Mauriniacensi*, in RHF, vol. X, p. 87.
8. Vermandois as a vassal needed to ask permission to marry. Aelith, being unmarried, was Louis' ward to give to whom he pleased.
9. G.R. Evans, *Bernard of Clairvaux*, Oxford, Oxford University Press, 2000, p. 15.
10. James, *Letters of St Bernard*, Letters 294–8.
11. Richard, p. 106.
12. James, *Letters of St Bernard*, Letter 296.
13. E. Panofsky, *Abbot Suger on the Abbey Church of St Denis*, Princeton, NJ, Princeton University Press, 1946, p. 115.
14. F. Heer, *The Medieval World*, London, Weidenfeld & Nicolson, 1962, p. 330.
15. Panofsky, *Abbot Suger*, pp. 64–7.
16. In Latin, *Hoc vas sponsa dedit Aanor regi Ludovico, Mitadolus avo, mihi Rex, santisque Sugerius*.

17. The broad porch spanning the width of the building at its western end where the unbaptised, the lepers and sinners whose penance had not been discharged were allowed to listen to the services taking place within.

18. *William of Newburgh Historia Rerum Anglicanum*, ed. R. Howlett, RS 82, vol. I, p. 93.

19. Salerno had in the eleventh century a famous teacher of midwifery called Tortola de Ruggiero. Her revolutionary book, *De passionibus mulierum curandorum ante, in et post partum* – The Care of Women before, during and after giving Birth – recommended cleanliness, avoidance of noise, stress and worry, and the use of opiates to relieve pain.

Chapter 5: Crusading Fever Sweeps Europe

1. At the time the word 'crusade' was not used; crusaders thought of themselves as being pilgrims on the journey to Jerusalem, or to the Holy Sepulchre.

2. A. Maalouf, *The Crusades through Arab Eyes*, London, Al-Saqi Books, 1984, p. 134.

3. *Historia rerum in partibus transmarinis gestarum, or William of Tyre A History of Deeds done beyond the Sea*, ed. and trans. E.A. Babcock and A.C. Krey, 2 vols, New York, Columbia University Press, 1943.

4. Maalouf, *Through Arab Eyes*, p. 135.

5. Abu el-Farraj, quoted in ibid., p. 136.

6. *William of Tyre History*, vol. 2, p. 77.

7. Ibid.

8. Maalouf, *Through Arab Eyes*, p. 137.

9. *Vita Sugerii* in RHF, vol. XII, p. 108.

10. Literally, 'ox ford'.

11. Bull, *Knightly Piety and the Response to the First Crusade*, p. 5.

12. *Historia rerum anglicanum*.

13. Evans, *Bernard of Clairvaux*, p. 12.

14. 'Chaplain' is a translation of *capellanus*, from *capella* meaning 'chapel'. The first illiterate Carolingian king, Pépin the Short, entrusted the writing and checking of written documents to his clerics whose original position of trust had been to look after the court's most precious relic: the cappa or torn cloak of the martyred St Martin of Tours.

15. James, *Letters of St Bernard*, p. 323.

16. Ibid., p. 393.

17. Bernard, *Epistolae*, p. 566.

18. Hyland, *Warhorse*, p. 65.

19. Ibid.

20. *Odo de Deuil De Ludovici VII francorum regis profectione in oriente*, ed. H. Waquet, Paris, Paul Geuthner, 1949, p. 10.

21. Ibid., pp. 30–2.

22. Ibid., p. 26: *stilum vertamus*.

23. J. Michaud, *Bibliothèque des Croisades* (4 vols), Paris, 1829, vol. III, pp. 402–4.

Chapter 6: Luxury in Contantinople, Massacre on Mount Cadmos

1. *Odo*, pp. 34–5.
2. Ibid., pp. 36–7.
3. Kamal ad-Din, the chronicler of Aleppo, quoted in Maalouf, *Through Arab Eyes*, p. 145.
4. This is exactly what happened when, on 13 April 1204, the Fourth Crusade sacked the Christian capital on the Bosporus in a four-day orgy of killing and destruction – and thus ended the thousand-year role of Byzantium as the bulwark of Europe against Asiatic inroads.
5. The modern name 'Istanbul' is merely a corruption of the Greek words *stin poli*, meaning 'into the city'.
6. *Odo*, pp. 44–5.
7. Ibid.
8. RHF, vol. XVI, p. 11.
9. Smaller-scale Turkish or Arabic baths.
10. Robert of Clari, in *Three Old French Chronicles*, ed. E.N. Stone, Seattle, University of Washington 1939, p. 139.
11. *Odo*, pp. 54–5.
12. *William of Tyre History*, vol. 2, p. 168.
13. Ibid., pp. 169–76.
14. Guillaume de Nangis, *Chronique*, in Guizot, *Collection des Mémoires relatifs à l'Histoire de France*, 32 vols, Paris, 1823–36, vol. XIII, p. 31.

Chapter 7: Accusation in Antioch, Joy in Jerusalem, Defeat at Damascus

1. First recorded in Europe in 1187.
2. Heer, *Medieval World*, p. 100.
3. *Odo*, pp. 79–80.
4. *William of Tyre History*, vol. 2, p. 179.
5. Ibid., p. 80.
6. Ibid., p. 179.
7. Ibid., p. 180.
8. Heer, *Medieval World*, p. 111.
9. Jacques de Vitry, in Michaud, *Bibliothèque*, vol. I, pp. 175–7.
10. Ibid.
11. John of Salisbury, *Historiae Pontificalis Quae Supersunt*, p. 53.
12. *Gesta Louis VII*, in Michaud, *Bibliothèque*, vol. I, p. 255.
13. Howlett, *William of Newburgh Historia*, vol. I, p. 32.
14. Bernard of Clairvaux, *Epistolae*, in PL, vol. CLXXXII, p. 394.
15. Suger, *Epistolae*, in RHF, vol. XV, p. 509.
16. *William of Tyre History*, vol. 2, pp. 180–1.

17. John of Salisbury, *Historiae Pontificalis Quae Supersunt*, ed. R.L. Poole, Oxford, Clarendon Press, 1927, p. 53.
18. Gervase of Canterbury, *Opera Historica*, ed. W. Stubbs (2 vols), vol. I, p. 149.
19. *William of Tyre History*, vol. 2, p. 182.
20. 'Te peto, te colo / te flagro, te volo / canto, saluto', quoted in Kelly, *Eleanor*, p. 64.
21. J. Prawer, *The History of the Jews in the Latin Kingdom of Jerusalem*, Oxford, Clarendon Press, 1988, p. 48.
22. After Suger's death on 13 January 1151, he was elected Abbot of St Denis, only to be accused of malpractice and homicide until Bernard of Clairvaux came to his defence.
23. *William of Tyre History*, vol. 2, p. 184.
24. Maalouf, *Through Arab Eyes*, p. 147.
25. A corruption of *beau sang*, or Christ's Blood.
26. Ibn Al-Qalansis, quoted in Maalouf, *Through Arab Eyes*, p. 148.
27. *William of Tyre History*, vol. 2, pp. 187–94.
28. Maalouf, *Through Arab Eyes*, p. 150.
29. Suger, *Epistolae*, in RHF, vol. XV, p. 509.
30. Higounet, Gardelles and Lafaurie, *Bordeaux pendant le Moyen Age*, p. 153.
31. Ibid., p. 155.
32. *William of Tyre History*, vol. 2, p. 150.

Chapter 8: Eleanor's Greatest Gamble

1. Kelly, *Eleanor*, p. 69.
2. Modern Frascati.
3. John of Salisbury, *Historiae Pontificalis Quae Supersunt*, pp. 51–3.
4. In Latin, 'Regi invicto ab Oriente reduci frementes Laetitiae cives 1149' and 'Turki ad ripas Meandri caesis fugatis'. See F.A. Gervaise, *Histoire de Suger*, vol. III, Nevers, 1721, p. 349.
5. Otto of Friesing, in Michaud, *Bibliothèque*, vol. II, p. 538.
6. *Bernard le Trésorier, Continuation de . . . Guillaume de Tyr*, in Guizot, *Collection des Mémoires*, vol. XIX, p. 568.
7. Heer, *Medieval World*, p. 128.
8. Robert of Torigni, *Chronicle*, ed. R. Howlett, Rolls Series No. 82, vol. 4, p. 162.
9. J. Chartrou, *L'Anjou de 1109 à 1151, Foulque de Jerusalem et Geoffroi Plantagenet*, Paris, 1928, p. 66.
10. Howlett, *William of Newburgh Historia*, vol. I, p. 70.
11. Bernard of Clairvaux, *Epistolae*, p. 575.
12. Giraldus, *De Principiis*, ed. G.F. Warner, Rolls Series No. 21, vol. VIII, p. 309.
13. Howlett, *Robert of Torigni Chronicle*, p. 162.
14. E.R. Labande, *Pour une image véridique d'Aliénor d'Aquitaine*, in *Bulletin de la Société des Antiquaires de l'Ouest*, 4th series, 1952, vol. 2, p. 198.

15. Howlett, *Robert of Torigni Chronicle*, p. 162.
16. Ibid., p. 163.
17. *Chronique de Touraine*, ed. A. Salmon, Tours, 1894, p. 135.
18. *Historia Gloriosi Regis Ludovici VII*, in RHF, vol. XII, p. 127.
19. *'elle trompait le roi en pleine cour'*.
20. Richard, p. 108.
21. Ibid.
22. *'elle était de celles-là qui aiment à être battues'*. Richard, p. 110.
23. Howlett, *William of Newburgh Historia*, vol. I, p. 93.

Chapter 9: A Son at Last

1. Howlett, *Robert of Torigni Chronicle*, p. 165.
2. Bartlett, *Norman and Angevin Kings*, p. 140.
3. Ibid.
4. *De Nugis Curialum*.
5. Walter Map, *De Nugis Curialium*, ed. F. Tupper and M.B. Ogle, London, Chatto & Windus, 1924, pp. 2–4.
6. *Letters of Arnulf of Lisieux*, ed. F. Barlow, Camden Society Third Series, 1939, No. 10, p. 14.
7. Tupper and Ogle, *Map*, pp. 71, 298, 302–3.
8. Richard, p. 113.
9. Ibid., p. 114.
10. Ibid., p. 113.
11. Tupper and Ogle, *Map*, p. 278.
12. Richard, p. 115.
13. The Occitan word *trobador*, pronounced 'troubadour', comes from the same root as modern French *trouver*, and means a person who invents or finds something.
14. Referring to the beloved by masculine pronouns was a troubadour device emphasising the vassalage of the lover. Similarly, medieval Arabic poets addressed their ladies as *sayiddi*, or 'lord' – P. Dronke, *Medieval Latin and the Rise of the European Love Lyric*, Oxford, Clarendon Press, 1968, p. 16.
15. Richard, p. 115.
16. Ibid., p. 116.
17. Ibid.
18. Dom J. Vaissete, *Abrégé de l'histoire générale de Languedoc* (5 vols), Paris, 1799, vol. III, p. 87.
19. Kelly, *Eleanor*, p. 87.
20. Literally, 'the monastery to the west'.
21. *Roman de Brut*.
22. The original meaning of 'minstrel' was simply 'servant' from Low Latin *ministerialis*.
23. J. Southworth, *Fools and Jesters at the English Court*, Thrupp, Sutton, 1998, pp. 35–47.

Chapter 10: Court Life with Henry

1. Modern usage still reflects the eleventh- and twelfth-century class divide, with Anglo-Saxon words such as 'sheep', 'calf', 'cow' and 'swine' for the animals herded by the native peasantry but French equivalents like 'mutton', 'veal', 'beef', 'pork' and 'bacon' for the meat that ended up on the tables of their Norman overlords.
2. A. Mortimer, *Angevin England*, Oxford, Blackwell, 1994, p. 215: '*un faux français sai d'Angleterre*'.
3. In Henry I's charter founding Reading Priory, he declared having endowed it 'for the salvation of my soul and that of King William my father and King William my brother and William my son and Queen Matilda my mother and Queen Matilda my wife'. His daughter was also called Matilda. Similarly, when Empress Matilda died in 1167, her epitaph at the abbey of Bec in Normandy mentioned that she was 'daughter, wife and mother of Henry'.
4. Bartlett, *Norman and Angevin Kings*, p. 670.
5. Ibid., p. 212.
6. Ibid., p. 162.
7. Ramsay, Amt and Green, quoted in Bartlett, *Norman and Angevin Kings*, pp. 173–4.
8. Stubbs, *Gervase Opera Historica*, vol. I, p. 160.
9. *John of Salisbury Life of Becket*, ed. J.C. Robertson, Rolls Series No. 67, vol. II, p. 302.
10. If eight pence in the pound was his rate of interest, at 240d = £1 it must have been the monthly and not the annual rate, for borrowing was an expensive luxury at the time, to cover the high percentage of loans never repaid.
11. William fitz Stephen, *Life of Becket*, ed. J.C. Robertson, Rolls Series No. 67, vol. III, p. 17.
12. Ibid., p. 19.
13. Stubbs, *Gervase Opera Historica*, vol. I, p. 161.
14. Kelly, *Eleanor*, p. 97.
15. Howlett, *William of Newburgh Historia*, p. 103.
16. *Constitutio domus regis*, quoted in Bartlett, *Norman and Angevin Kings*, p. 131.
17. H. Hall, *Court Life under the Plantagenets*, London, Swan, Sonnenschein & Co., 1899, p. 244.
18. B. Hindle, *Medieval Roads*, Princes Risborough, 1989, p. 30.
19. Peter of Blois, *Epistolae*, in PL, vol. CCVII, p. 47.
20. William fitz Stephen, *Life of Becket*, vol. III, pp. 12, 22.
21. Richard, p. 121.
22. Now displayed in the British Museum.
23. J.C. Parsons, *Medieval Queenship*, Thrupp, Sutton, 1994, p. 71.
24. G Sivéry, *Blanche de Castille*, Paris, Fayard, 1990, p. 23.
25. Richard, p. 122.
26. Cirot de la Ville, *Histoire de l'Abbaye de la Sauve Majeure*, Paris and Bordeaux, 1844, p. 177.

27. Ibid.
28. Ibid.
29. Labande, *Image véridique*, p. 201.
30. Richard, p. 122.
31. Ibid., p. 123.
32. The author of *Sermo Lupi ad Anglos*, who was credited with converting King Canute to Christianity.
33 '*le nombre effrayant de princesses*', in RHF, vol. XVI, p. 1.
34. William fitz Stephen, *Life of Becket*, p. 29.
35. Kelly, *Eleanor*, p. 107.
36. Richard, p. 124.
37. Howlett, *Robert of Torigni Chronicle*, p. 197.
38. Ibid., p. 198.
39. Richard, p. 127.

Chapter 11: King, Queen, Bishop

1. Kelly, *Eleanor*, p. 109.
2. Richard, p. 127.
3. Labande, *Image véridique*, p. 201.
4. Richard, p. 128. Also, Berengaria was a fairly common name in southern France and Spain; this was not the princess Richard was to marry on the Third Crusade and make her the most frustrated queen in England's history.
5. William fitz Stephen, *Life of Becket*, pp. 53–4.
6. Richard, p. 129.
7. Howlett, *Robert of Torigni Chronicle*, p. 201.
8. Kelly, *Eleanor*, p. 110.
9. Meaning 'snake', it was a poetic name for a Viking longship.
10. Richard, p. 132.
11. Stubbs, *Gervase Opera Historica*, vol. I, pp. 167–8.
12. *Ralph of Diceto Opera Historica*, ed. W. Stubbs (2 vols), Rolls Series No. 68, vol. I, p. 303.
13. Roger of Howden, *Chronica*, ed. W. Stubbs (4 vols), Rolls Series No. 51, vol. I, p. 208.
14. Howlett, *William of Newburgh Historia*, vol. I, p. 159.
15. Labande, *Image véridique*, p. 202.
16. Kelly, *Eleanor*, p. 115.
17. Robertson, *John of Salisbury Life of Becket*, p. 305.
18. Herbert Bosham, *Life of Becket*, ed. J.C. Robertson, Rolls Series No. 67, vol. III, pp. 187–8.
19. Ibid., p. 185.
20. Kelly, *Eleanor*, p. 116.
21. Herbert Bosham, *Life of Becket*, ed. J.C. Robertson, Rolls Series No. 67, vol. III, p. 208.
22. Ibid., p. 250.

23. Kelly, *Eleanor*, p. 114.
24. Stubbs, *Ralph of Diceto Opera Historica*, vol. 1, p. 329.
25. Stubbs, *Roger of Howden Chronica*, vol. I, p. 224.
26. William fitz Stephen, *Life of Becket*, p. 50.
27. Herbert Bosham, *Life of Becket*, ed. J.C. Robertson, Rolls Series No. 67, vol. III, p. 298.
28. Ibid.
29. *Edward Grim Life of Becket*, ed. J.C. Robertson, Rolls Series No. 67, vol. II, p. 395.
30. Howlett, *Robert of Torigni Chronicle*, p. 333.
31. Herbert Bosham, *Life of Becket*, ed. J.C. Robertson, Rolls Series No. 67, vol. III, p. 233.
32. Howlett, *William of Newburgh Historia*, vol. I, p. 142.
33. *Chronicle of Melrose*, ed. A.O. and M. Anderson, London, Perry Lund Humphries & Co., 1936, p. 79.
34. Warner, *Giraldus De Principiis*, p. 165.
35. *Ralph Niger Chronica*, ed. R. Anstruther, Caxton Society 1851, p. 168.
36. Benedict of Peterborough, *Gesta Regis Henrici Secundi*, ed. W. Stubbs, Rolls Series No. 49, vol. II, p. 231.
37. *Ranulf Higden Polychronicon*, ed. J.R. Lumby, Rolls Series No. 41, vol. VIII, p. 54.

Chapter 12: Rift and Separation

1. Richard, p. 140.
2. R.W. Eyton, *Court, Household and Itinerary of Henry II*, London, 1878, p. 112.
3. William of Malmesbury, *De Regum Gestis Anglorum*, ed. W. Stubbs, Rolls Series No. 90, vol. 2, p. 494.
4. M.W. Labarge, *Women in Medieval Life*, London, Hamish Hamilton, 1986, p. 25.
5. Bartlett, *Norman and Angevin Kings*, p. 6.
6. Warner, *Giraldus De Principiis*, p. 157.
7. Richard, p. 147.
8. Stubbs, *Ralph of Diceto Opera Historica*, vol. 1, p. 303.
9. Hyland, *Horse in the Middle Ages*, p. 99.
10. Benedict of Peterborough, *Gesta Regis Henrici Secundi*, ed. W. Stubbs, Rolls Series No. 49, vol. 1, p. 226.
11. Hyland, *Horse in the Middle Ages*, p. 100.
12. Stubbs, *Gervase Opera Historica*, vol. I, p. 226.
13. Howlett, *William of Newburgh Historia*, vol. 1, p. 234.
14. Stevenson, *Ralph of Coggeshall*, p. 97.
15. In Latin, *causa conjugii ab amore non est excusatio recta*.

Chapter 13: Rebellion and Betrayal

1. W. Urry, *Thomas Becket: His Last Days*, Thrupp, Sutton, 1999, p. 116.
2. Ibid., p. 18.
3. RHF, vol. XIII, pp. 131–2.
4. Richard, p. 150.
5. Ibid.
6. Ibid., p. 151: *comes pictavensorum et dux aquitannorum*.
7. Ibid.
8. Stubbs, *Roger of Howden Chronica*, vol. II, p. 34.
9. Richard, p. 154.
10. Ibid., p. 163.
11. Ibid., p. 155.
12. RHF, vol. XIII, p. 143.
13. Bartlett, *Norman and Angevin Kings*, p. 257.
14. Urry, *Becket*, p. 116.
15. Ibid.
16. Ibid., pp. 48–9.
17. Ranulf de Broc travelled with them, but was not present at the murder.
18. J. Attali, *Les Juifs, le Monde et l'Argent*, Paris, Fayard, 2002, p. 197.
19. RHF, vol. XIII, p. 148.
20. Richard, p. 164.
21. Ibid., p. 165.
22. Ibid., p. 161.
23. Stubbs, *Ralph of Diceto Opera Historica*, vol. I, p. 371.
24. Richard, p. 166.
25. Stubbs, *Roger of Howden Chronica*, vol. II, pp. 40–6.
26. Howlett, *William of Newburgh Historia*, vol. I, p. 170.
27. In Occitan, *Oc e No*.
28. Jordan Fantosme quoted in Bartlett, *Norman and Angevin Kings*, p. 255.
29. Richard, p. 173.
30. For Latin text of letter in full, see RHF, vol. XVI, pp. 629–30.
31. RHF, vol. XIII, p. 158.
32. RHF, vol. XII, p. 420.
33. RHF, vol. XIII, p. 158.
34. Stubbs, *Roger of Howden Chronica*, vol. II, p. 61.
35. RHF, vol. XIII, pp. 158–9.
36. Ibid., p. 443.
37. Warner, *Giraldus De Principiis*, p. 164.
38. Stubbs, *Gervase Opera Historica*, vol. I, p. 248.
39. Howlett, *William of Newburgh Historia*, vol. I, pp. 194–5.
40. Stubbs, *Roger of Howden Chronica*, vol. II, p. 63.
41. Richard, p. 179.
42. Ibid., p. 180.
43. Stubbs, *Ralph of Diceto Opera Historica*, vol. I, p. 394.
44. Ibid., p. 179.

Chapter 14: From Palace to Prison

1. Stubbs, *Gervase Opera Historica*, vol. I, pp. 256–7.
2. Warner, *Giraldus De Principiis*, p. 306.
3. Richard, p. 205.
4. Stubbs, *Gervase Opera Historica*, vol. I, p. 256.
5. *Gesta Henrici Secundi*, vol. I, p. 114.
6. Stubbs, *Ralph of Diceto Opera Historica*, vol. I, p. 428.
7. Stubbs, *Roger of Howden Chronica*, vol. II, p. 94.
8. *Gesta Henrici Secundi*, vol. I, pp. 122–3.
9. Stubbs, *Roger of Howden Chronica*, vol. II, p. 143.
10. *Gesta Henrici Secundi*, vol. I, p. 242.
11. Stubbs, *Ralph of Diceto Opera Historica*, vol. II, p. 7.
12. J. Bradbury, *Philip Augustus*, Harlow, Longman, 1998, pp. 52–3.
13. Richard, p. 206.
14. RHF, vol. XVII, p. 450.
15. *L'Histoire de Guillaume le Maréchal*, ed. P. Meyer, 3 vols, Paris, Geuthner, 1891–1901, vol. III, pp. 70–4.
16. Stubbs, *Gervase Opera Historica*, vol. I, p. 303.
17. Warner, *Giraldus De Principiis*, p. 302.
18. Richard, p. 211.
19. Kelly, *Eleanor*, p. 214.
20. RHF, vol. XVIII, p. 213.
21. Tupper and Ogle, *Map*, p. 180.
22. Richard, p. 214.
23. Stubbs, *Roger of Howden Chronica*, vol. II, p. 278.
24. RHF, vol. XVIII, p. 214.
25. Richard, p. 219.
26. Howlett, *Robert of Torigni Chronicle*, p. 306.
27. Meyer, *Guillaume*, vol. III, p. 81.
28. Richard, p. 220.
29. Meyer, *Guillaume*, vol. III, p. 84.
30. Richard, pp. 223–4.
31. *Sappi ch'i son Bertram dal Bornio, quelli / che diedi al re giovane i ma' conforti. / Io feci il padre e'l figlio in sé ribelli . . .*

Chapter 15: A Prisoner of Moment

1. Richard, p. 227.
2. That is, from *rex francorum* to *rex franciae*.
3. Richard, p. 228.
4. *Gesta Henrici Secundi*, vol. I, p. 311.
5. RHF, vol. XVII, pp. 457–60.
6. Richard, p. 229.
7. Ibid., p. 233.
8. Ibid., p. 234.

9. Ibid., p. 236.
10. *Gesta Henrici Secundi*, vol. I, p. 296.
11. Stubbs, *Ralph of Diceto Opera Historica*, vol. II, p. 41.
12. Richard, p. 239.
13. Stubbs, *Ralph of Diceto Opera Historica*, vol. II, p. 33.
14. Richard, p. 243.
15. Stubbs, *Gervase Opera Historica*, vol. I, p. 42.
16. *Gesta Henrici Secundi*, vol. II, p. 19.
17. Stubbs, *Roger of Howden Chronica*, vol. II, p. 335.
18. In Occitan, *el pasatge qu'an si mes en obli.*
19. Stubbs, *Roger of Howden Chronica*, vol. II, p. 47.
20. *Gesta Henrici Secundi*, vol. II, p. 50.
21. Stubbs, *Roger of Howden Chronica*, vol. II, p. 363 '*sterlingos regis Angliae olfecerat*'.
22. Meyer, *Guillaume*, vol. III, p. 99.
23. Warner, *Giraldus De Principiis*, p. 296.
24. Meyer, *Guillaume*, vol. III, p. 114.
25. Stubbs, *Ralph of Diceto Opera Historica*, vol. II, p. 65.
26. RHF, vol. XVII, p. 490.
27. Meyer, *Guillaume*, vol. III, pp. 118–19.

Chapter 16: The Lady Eleanor

1. H.G. Richardson, 'The Letters and Charters of Eleanor of Aquitaine', *English Historical Review*, LXXIV, p. 200.
2. Stubbs, *Gesta Regis Henrici Secundi*, vol. II, p. 75.
3. In Latin, *aquila rupti foederis tertia nidificatione gaudebit.*
4. In Latin, *gratia dei regina angliorum.*
5. Pipe Roll I Richard I, p. 5.
6. Stubbs, *Roger of Howden Chronica*, vol. III, p. 8.
7. Stubbs, *Gervase Opera Historica*, vol. I, p. 457.
8. Stubbs, *Roger of Howden Chronica*, vol. III, p. 6.
9. Stubbs, *Ralph of Diceto Opera Historica*, vol. II, p. 51.
10. Stubbs, *Roger of Howden Chronica*, vol. III, p. 4.
11. Pipe Roll I Richard I, pp. 21, 30, 216.
12. In Latin, *gratia dei rex Angliorum dux Normannorum et Aquitanorum, comes Pictavorum.*
13. Stubbs, *Ralph of Diceto Opera Historica*, vol. II, p. 72.
14. Gesta Hen II, p. 71.
15. Ibid., p. 87.
16. Howlett, *William of Newburgh Historia*, vol. I, pp. 304–6.
17. Stubbs, *Roger of Howden Chronica*, vol. III, p. 27.
18. Stubbs, *Ralph of Diceto Opera Historica*, vol. II, p. 51.
19. Pipe Roll II Richard I, pp. 53, 104, 112–13.
20. Howlett, *William of Newburgh Historia*, vol. I, p. 306.
21. P. Coss, *The Knight in Medieval England*, Thrupp, Sutton, 1993, p. 44.

22. Bartlett, *Norman and Angevin Kings*, p. 369.
23. Pipe Roll II Richard I, p. 3.
24. RHF, vol. XVII, p. 419.
25. Richard, p. 268.
26. Giraldus, *De Vita Galfedi*, ed. J.S. Brewer, Rolls Series No. 21, vol. IV, p. 420.

Chapter 17: Richard the Hero

1. Stubbs, *Gesta Henrici Secundi*, vol. II, p. 114.
2. P. Warner, *Sieges of the Middle Ages*, London, Penguin, 1968, p. 120.
3. Stubbs, *Ralph of Diceto Opera Historica*, vol. II, p. 85.
4. Ibid., p. 77.
5. Stubbs, *Gesta Henrici Secundi*, vol. II, p. 126.
6. Ibid., p. 158.
7. Ibid., p. 133.
8. Stubbs, *Roger of Howden Chronica*, vol. III, p. 99.
9. Warner, *Giraldus De Principiis*, p. 282.
10. *Itinerarium peregrinorum et gesta regis Ricardii*, ed. W. Stubbs, Rolls Series No. 38, vol. I, p. 171.
11. E.R. Labande, 'Les Filles d'Aliénor d'Aquitaine – Etude Comparative', in *Cahiers de Civilisation Médiévale*, XXIX, 1986, p. 109.
12. *Pierre de Langtoft Chronicle*, ed. W. Stubbs, Rolls Series No. 47, vol. II, p. 49.
13. Hyland, *Medieval Warhorse*, p. 146.
14. Stubbs, *Roger of Howden Chronica*, vol. III, p. 111.
15. Stubbs, *Itinerarium*, p. 197.
16. Kelly, *Eleanor*, p. 269.
17. Bradbury, *Philip Augustus*, p. 89.
18. Stubbs, *Itinerarium*, p. 254.
19. Maalouf, *Through Arab Eyes*, p. 210.
20. S. Runciman, *A History of the Crusades*, vol. III, Cambridge, Cambridge University Press, 1954, p. 53.
21. Guillaume le Breton, *Philippide*, in Guizot, *Collection des Mémoires*, vol. XII, p. 108.
22. Stubbs, *Roger of Howden Chronica*, vol. III, pp. 123–4.
23. Howlett, *William of Newburgh Historia*, vol. I, p. 354.
24. Stubbs, *Gesta Henrici Secundi*, vol. II, p. 171.
25. Richard, p. 214.
26. Maalouf, *Through Arab Eyes*, p. 211.
27. J. Gillingham in *Anglo Norman Warfare*, Woodbridge, Boydell, 1994, p. 196.
28. Howlett, *William of Newburgh Historia*, vol. I, p. 358.
29. Kelly, *Eleanor*, p. 275.
30. Stubbs, *Roger of Howden Chronica*, vol. III, p. 167.
31. W. Stubbs, *Historical Introduction to the Rolls Series*, London, 1902, p. 227.

32. Giraldus, *Vita Galfedi*, pp. 382, 387–93.
33. Stubbs, *Roger of Howden Chronica*, vol. III, p. 144.
34. Stubbs, *Gesta Henrici Secundi*, vol. II, p. 212.
35. In Latin, *summus rector totius regni*.
36. Giraldus, *Vita Galfedi*, pp. 410–11.
37. Stubbs, *Gesta Henrici Secundi*, vol. II, p. 221.
38. Stubbs, *Ralph of Diceto Opera Historica*, vol. I, p. 419.
39. Ibid., p. 420.
40. Ibid., pp. 431–2.
41. *William of Newburgh Historia*, vol. I, pp. 266–7.
42. Kelly, *Eleanor*, p. 297.
43. Stubbs, *Gesta Henrici Secundi*, vol. II, p. 236.
44. Ibid.
45. Stubbs, *Ralph of Diceto Opera Historica*, vol. I, p. 434.
46. *Bohaddin Suite de la Troisième Croisade*, ed. M. Reinaud, in Michaud, *Bibliothèque*, vol. IV, pp. 334–8.
47. Kelly, *Eleanor*, p. 278.
48. Stubbs, *Gesta Henrici Secundi*, vol. II, p. 192.
49. Richard, p. 280.

Chapter 18: 'Shame on them all!'

1. Stubbs, *Roger of Howden Chronica*, vol. III, p. 194.
2. Stubbs, *Ralph of Diceto Opera Historica*, vol. II, p. 106.
3. Stubbs, *Gesta Henrici Secundi*, vol. II, p. 221.
4. Stubbs, *Roger of Howden Chronica*, vol. III, p. 185.
5. Howlett, *William of Newburgh Historia*, vol. I, p. 382.
6. Ralph of Coggeshall, *Chronicon Anglicanum*, ed. J. Stevenson, Rolls Series No. 66, p. 54.
7. Ibid., p. 55.
8. Stubbs, *Roger of Howden Chronica*, vol. III, p. 186.
9. Stevenson, *Ralph of Coggeshall*, p. 56.
10. Stubbs, *Roger of Howden Chronica*, vol. III, p. 195.
11. Ibid., p. 198.
12. Ibid., p. 196.
13. Howlett, *William of Newburgh Historia*, vol. I, p. 388.
14. Stubbs, *Roger of Howden Chronica*, vol. III, p. 204.
15. Stubbs, *Gervase Opera Historica*, vol. I, pp. 514–15.
16. Stubbs, *Gesta Henrici Secundi*, vol. II, p. 236.
17. Stubbs, *Roger of Howden Chronica*, vol. III, p. 207.
18. Stubbs, *Gervase Opera Historica*, vol. I, pp. 514–15.
19. Richard, p. 281.
20. Howlett, *William of Newburgh Historia*, vol. I, pp. 286–7.
21. Stubbs, *Roger of Howden Chronica*, vol. III, p. 198.
22. Ibid., p. 199.
23. Bartlett, *Norman and Angevin Kings*, p. 485.

24. Howlett, *William of Newburgh Historia*, vol. I, p. 388.
25. Stubbs, *Roger of Howden Chronica*, vol. II, pp. 215–16.
26. Derived from the Latin anthem sung on this day: *mandatum novum do vobis* – 'A new commandment I give to you', from the text of John 13:34.
27. Stubbs, *Roger of Howden Chronica*, vol. III, p. 210.
28. Stubbs, *Ralph of Diceto Opera Historica*, vol. II, p. 110.
29. Ibid., pp. 106–7.
30. M. Powicke, *The Loss of Normandy*, Manchester, Sandpiper/Manchester University Press, 1999, p. 93.
31. Kelly, *Eleanor*, p. 307.
32. Stubbs, *Roger of Howden Chronica*, vol. II, p. 288.
33. Stubbs, *Ralph of Diceto Opera Historica*, vol. II, p. 127.
34. Kelly, *Eleanor*, p. 310.
35. In Latin, *regina in ira dei*.
36. Richard, p. 283.
37. Stubbs, *Roger of Howden Chronica*, vol. II, p. 227.
38. Howlett, *William of Newburgh Historia*, vol. I, p. 402.
39. Stubbs, *Roger of Howden Chronica*, vol. II, p. 202.
40. Meyer, *Guillaume*, vol. III, p. 134.
41. Howlett, *William of Newburgh Historia*, vol. I, p. 404.
42. Stubbs, *Roger of Howden Chronica*, vol. III, p. 235.
43. Stubbs, *Ralph of Diceto Opera Historica*, vol. II, p. 114.
44. Stubbs, *Roger of Howden Chronica*, vol. III, p. 238.
45. Ibid., pp. 239–41.
46. Ibid., p. 242.
47. PR 5 Richard I, pp. 44, 69.
48. PR 7 Richard I, pp. 261–2.
49. Henry's homage to Louis and Philip being in respect of the continental possessions only.
50. J.H. Round, *Geoffrey de Mandeville*, London, 1892, p. 138.
51. Stubbs, *Roger of Howden Chronica*, vol. III, p. 248.
52. Ibid., p. 251.

Chapter 19: Cruel News from Châlus

1. Meyer, *Guillaume*, vol. III, p. 137.
2. Stubbs, *Roger of Howden Chronica*, vol. III, p. 134.
3. Meyer, *Guillaume*, vol. III, p. 137.
4. Gillingham in *Anglo Norman Warfare*, p. 204.
5. Stubbs, *Ralph of Diceto Opera Historica*, vol. II, p. 117.
6. Richard, p. 293.
7. Powicke, *Loss of Normandy*, p. 102.
8. Stubbs, *Roger of Howden Chronica*, vol. III, p. 257.
9. Stubbs, *Ralph of Diceto Opera Historica*, vol. II, p. 119.
10. RHF, vol. XVII, p. 575.
11. Richard, p. 295.

12. *Giraldus Cambrensis De Rebus a Se Gestis*, ed. H.E. Butler, London, 1937, p. 153.
13. Stubbs, *Ralph of Diceto Opera Historica*, vol. II, p. 120.
14. Bartlett, *Norman and Angevin Kings*, p. 206.
15. RHF, vol. XVII, pp. 573–4.
16. Stubbs, *Roger of Howden Chronica*, vol. III, p. 290.
17. Ibid., vol. IV, p. 3.
18. J. Vaissete, *Abrégé de l'Histoire générale de Languedoc*, 5 vols, Paris, 1799, vol. III, pp. 219–40.
19. Richard, p. 299.
20. Ibid., p. 305.
21. Stubbs, *Gesta Henrici Secundi*, vol. II, p. 146.
22. Stubbs, *Roger of Howden Chronica*, vol. IV, p. 37.
23. Richard, p. 313.
24. Ibid.
25. *Flores Historiarum*, ed. H.R. Luard (3 vols), Rolls Series No. 95, vol. II, p. 117.
26. Kelly, *Eleanor*, p. 337.
27. Stubbs, *Roger of Howden Chronica*, vol. IV, p. 56.
28. Powicke, *Loss of Normandy*, p. 122.
29. Meyer, *Guillaume*, vol. III, p. 152.
30. Ibid., p. 156.
31. Meyer, *Guillaume*, vol. II, pp. 52–3.
32. Powicke, *Loss of Normandy*, pp. 168, 281.
33. Stevenson, *Ralph of Coggeshall*, p. 94.
34. Richard, p. 324.
35. J. Bradbury, *The Medieval Archer*, Woodbridge, Boydell, 2002, p. 77.
36. Ibid.
37. Stubbs, *Roger of Howden Chronica*, vol. IV, p. 81.
38. Stevenson, *Ralph of Coggeshall*, p. 96.
39. Ibid., p. 98.
40. Ibid., p. 96.
41. Stubbs, *Roger of Howden Chronica*, vol. IV, p. 83.
42. Ibid., p. 84.

Chapter 20: A Choice of Evils

1. Meyer, *Guillaume*, vol. III, pp. 159–60.
2. *Magna Vita Sancti Hugonis Episcopi Lincolniensis*, ed. J.F. Dimock, Rolls Series No. 37, pp. 282–3.
3. Richard, pp. 332–3.
4. Dimock, *Magna Vita Sancti Hugonis*, pp. 286–7.
5. Ibid., p. 288.
6. Ibid., pp. 290–3.
7. Richard, p. 333.
8. RHF, vol. XVIII, p. 325.

9. Stubbs, *Roger of Howden Chronica*, vol. IV, p. 88.
10. Powicke, *Loss of Normandy*, p. 128.
11. Richard, p. 341.
12. Ibid., p. 335.
13. Ibid., pp. 345–6.
14. Cirot de la Ville, *Histoire de . . . la Grande Sauve*, Bordeaux, 1845, vol. II, p. 84.
15. Vaissete, *Abrégé*, vol. III, p. 246.
16. Richard, p. 357.
17. Stubbs, *Roger of Howden Chronica*, vol. IV, p. 96.
18. Richard, p. 361.
19. *Roger of Wendover Flores Historiarum*, ed. H.G. Hewlett, Rolls Series No. 84, vol. I, p. 289.
20. Stubbs, *Roger of Howden Chronica*, vol. IV, pp. 87, 97.
21. Often rendered as 30,000 marks, perhaps because the Annals of Margam say £20,000, but Powicke says both copies of the treaty give 20,000 marks.
22. Richard, p. 335.
23. P. Niño, *Sumario de los Reyes de España*, Madrid, 1782, vol. III, p. 36.
24. Kelly, *Eleanor*, p. 359.
25. Stubbs, *Roger of Howden Chronica*, vol. IV, p. 114.
26. Ibid., p. 115.

Chapter 21: To a Death in the Morning

1. H.G. Richardson, 'The Marriage and Coronation of Isabella of Angoulême', *EHR* 61, 1946, pp. 289–314.
2. Stubbs, *Ralph of Diceto Opera Historica*, vol. II, p. 170.
3. Stubbs, *Roger of Howden Chronica*, vol. IV, p. 119.
4. Richard, pp. 340–78.
5. Meyer, *Guillaume*, vol. III, p. 162.
6. Stubbs, *Ralph of Diceto Opera Historica*, vol. II, p. 172.
7. Stubbs, *Roger of Howden Chronica*, vol. IV, pp. 89, 97.
8. Ibid., p. 164.
9. A. Delaborde, *Bibliothèque de l'Ecole des Chartes*, pp. 306–13.
10. Richard, p. 390.
11. Guillaume le Breton, *Vie de Philippe-Auguste*, in Guizot, *Collection des Memoires*, vol. XI, p. 221.
12. Guillaume le Breton, *Philippide*, vol. XII, p. 159.
13. Ibid., p. 162.
14. Richard, p. 407.
15. Stevenson, *Ralph of Coggeshall*, p. 139.
16. Powicke, *Loss of Normandy*, p. 160.
17. Ibid., p. 233.
18. Richard, p. 376.
19. R. Mortimer, *Angevin England*, Oxford, Blackwell, 1996, p. 154.

20. Ibid., p. 46.
21. In Latin, *eodem modo demembratus*. See Rotuli Normanniae in turri londinensi asservati, ed. Hardy, T.D., London, Record Commission 1835, p. 25.
22. Mortimer, *Angevin England*, p. 22.
23. Guillaume le Breton, *Philippide*, p. 170.
24. RHF, vol. XVII, pp. 682–3.
25. Powicke, *Loss of Normandy*, p. 468.
26. Richard, pp. 424–5.
27. Kelly, *Eleanor*, p. 381.
28. Meyer, *Guillaume*, vol. III, p. 171.
29. Ibid., pp. 172, 174–5.
30. Roger of Wendover, vol. 1, p. 317.
31. Peter of Blois, *Opera Omnia*, in Migne, vol. CCVII, pp. 431–4.
32. Richard, p. 438.

Further Reading

Rather than giving an exhaustive list of works only available in libraries closed to the general public, it seems more helpful to provide a short list of current books which will be of interest to those seeking more information on the period of Eleanor's life.

Bartlett, R., *England under the Norman and Angevin Kings*, Oxford, Oxford University Press, 2000

Cherchi, P., *Andreas and the Ambiguity of Courtly Love*, London, University of Toronto, 1994

Coss, P., *The Knight in Medieval England 1000–1400*, Stroud, Sutton, 1993

——, *The Lady in Medieval England 1000–1500*, Stroud, Sutton, 1998

Dronke, P., *Medieval Latin and the Rise of European Love Lyric*, Oxford, Oxford University Press, 1968

Evans, G.R., *Bernard of Clairvaux*, Oxford, Oxford University Press, 2000

Furlong, M., *Visions and Longings: Medieval Women Mystics*, London, Mowbray, 1996

Hyland, A., *The Horse in the Middle Ages*, Stroud, Sutton, 1999

James, B.S. (ed.), *The Letters of St Bernard of Clairvaux*, Stroud, Sutton, 1998

Labarge, M.W., *Women in Medieval Life*, London, Hamish Hamilton, 1986

Le Patourel, J., *The Norman Empire*, Oxford, Oxford University Press, 1976

Maalouf, A., *The Crusades through Arab Eyes*, London, Al-Saqi, 1984

Mortimer, R., *Angevin England*, Oxford, Blackwell, 1996

Parsons, J.C. (ed.), *Medieval Queenship*, Stroud, Sutton, 1994

Paterson, L.M., *The World of the Troubadours*, Cambridge, Cambridge University Press, 1993

Petzold, A., *Romanesque Art*, London, Weidenfeld & Nicolson, 1955

Powicke, M., *The Loss of Normandy* (second edition), Manchester, Sandpiper/ Manchester University Press, 1999

Purdon, L.O. and Vitto, C.L. (eds), *The Rusted Hauberk*, Gainesville, University Press of Florida, 1994

Southworth, J., *Fools and Jesters at the English Court*, Stroud, Sutton, 1998

Urry, W., *Thomas Becket, His Last Days*, Stroud, Sutton, 1999

Index

(Note: Page numbers in italics refer to illustrations)